TYPOGRAPHY

Mimesis, Philosophy, Politics

MERIDIAN

Crossing Aesthetics

Werner Hamacher
& David E. Wellbery
Editors

Edited by
Christopher Fynsk
With an Introduction by
Jacques Derrida

Stanford
University
Press

Stanford
California
1998

TYPOGRAPHY

Mimesis, Philosophy, Politics

Philippe Lacoue-Labarthe

Stanford University Press
Stanford, California

© 1989 by the President and Fellows of
Harvard College

Reprinted by Stanford University Press in 1998
by arrangement with Harvard University Press

CIP data are at the end of the book

In memory of Eugenio U. Donato, 1937-1983

Editor's Preface

Eugenio Donato left no projected table of contents for the collection or collections of essays by Philippe Lacoue-Labarthe that he hoped to publish in translation. In Lacoue-Labarthe's own recollection, it is clear that Donato originally planned to make "Typography" the centerpiece of a first volume, and considered joining to it "The Echo of the Subject" and Lacoue-Labarthe's essays on Hölderlin and Diderot. Since Donato also commissioned a number of other translations of essays by Lacoue-Labarthe, it is possible that his final project would have taken a different form altogether.[1] But I have followed the initial plans in establishing the present volume (adding only "Transcendence Ends in Politics") because they have struck me as following most appropriately from the guiding principle that "Typography" should provide the basis for an initial presentation in English of Lacoue-Labarthe's work.

"Typography" was by no means Lacoue-Labarthe's first significant philosophical publication. It was preceded by "La Fable," "Le Détour," "Nietzsche apocryphe," and "L'Oblitération" (essays collected in *Le sujet de la philosophie*),[2] as well as by the book on Lacan written with Jean-Luc Nancy, *Le titre de la lettre*.[3] But as Lacoue-Labarthe explains in his "Avertissement" to *Le sujet de la philosophie* (subtitled *Typographies I* and anticipating in this way *Typographies II*, which was published in

---

1. The remaining translations will appear in a volume to be published by the University of Minnesota Press.

2. *Le sujet de la philosophie* (Paris: Aubier-Flammarion, 1979).

3. *Le titre de la lettre* (Paris: Galilée, 1973).

1986 with the principal title *L'imitation des modernes*),[4] "Typography" gathers and reformulates the questions broached in the previous essays—questions turning essentially upon the problem of the relation between philosophy and literature as it appears in and between the texts of Nietzsche and Heidegger. By recasting this topic in terms of the question of mimesis, and by tracing through the texts of Plato and Heidegger a properly philosophical effort to contain its destabilizing effects, "Typography" defines a problematic that has organized and guided virtually all of Lacoue-Labarthe's work since the time of its publication. Or more precisely, it opens the site that Lacoue-Labarthe's writing continually retraverses in an ever-widening trajectory that moves not only through the philosophical tradition whose "mimetology" Lacoue-Labarthe seeks to delimit, but also through the domains of politics, literature, theater, music, and painting.

It would not be inappropriate, I believe, to say that Lacoue-Labarthe has been elaborating since "Typography" a *thought* of mimesis; for his questioning moves at the level of, and from out of, Heidegger's effort to delimit the metaphysics of representation (which has programmed the translation of mimesis as "imitation") and Heidegger's meditation on such guiding words for Western thought as *physis, techne,* and *aletheia.* It would also not be inappropriate (though one would have to take the measure of Lacoue-Labarthe's own wariness in relation to this term) to speak of a "thesis" (or theses) on mimesis: in the pages that follow, Lacoue-Labarthe attempts to elaborate its abyssal "logic" and to define how this logic is at work in any structure of (self-)representation or identification—be it in philosophy, literature, art, or politics. And as the question of mimesis leads Lacoue-Labarthe to the limits of each of these domains as they have been circumscribed in the Western tradition, and thus to their point of articulation (again abyssal), it lends his thought an astonishing scope and force—a *general* critical power.

But it is also a thought that "knows" itself to be at grips with something exceeding any conceptual grasp, and that constantly gives itself up, in writing, to the experience[5] or trial of its own finitude. It is a thought that is *preoccupied* with its own "desistance" and that draws

4. *L'imitation des modernes* (Paris: Galilée, 1986).
5. I draw here upon the title of Lacoue-Labarthe's book on Celan, *La poésie comme expérience* (Paris: Christian Bourgois, 1986).

from this passion, or this obsession, the energy of its extraordinary rigor and persistence. I defer here to Jacques Derrida's introduction, and will not try to develop further the dimensions of Lacoue-Labarthe's properly tragic gesture of thought. But I would emphasize with Derrida that the coherence of Lacoue-Labarthe's work is not that of a "system" in the traditional sense of the term, and that if Lacoue-Labarthe elaborates a thesis concerning an irreducible instability in any positing of identity, he is also constantly aware that this thesis must fold upon itself at some point in its exposition. Lacoue-Labarthe is seeking the *limits* of the philosophical as such, and this leads him to a practice of reading and writing that is powerfully coherent, but that does not have as its end the production of an oeuvre that is architectonic in nature. His work is thus characterized by an irreducible multiplicity to which the essays that follow bear witness, even while they suggest something of the coherence that derives from Lacoue-Labarthe's persistent effort to follow the *fil conducteur* of the question of mimesis.

As the reader will observe—and most immediately in comparing the two essays on Hölderlin contained in this volume—the "multiplicity" to which I refer inheres in the very style of Lacoue-Labarthe's writing. In order to respect this dimension of Lacoue-Labarthe's work, and to bring forth the extreme attention he gives to the problem of philosophical exposition (his own first of all), I have sought to bring to each of the translations a single notion of fidelity and to assure a continuity in their *manner* of translation, even while respecting as much as possible the individual contributions of each translator. I want to thank each of the translators for their patience with my efforts in this properly impossible task. Particular thanks go to Peter Caws for permission to use his translation of "Transcendence Ends in Politics" and for his approval of my additions and minor changes. I also want to thank Jan McVicker for her invaluable assistance in tracking down a large quantity of bibliographic information, Kimball Lockhart for his very generous critical reading of my translation of Jacques Derrida's introduction, and Maria Ascher for her unusually deft editing. Finally, I want to express my gratitude to Linda Brooks for inviting me to undertake this project.

The English language is not always receptive to the kind of work Lacoue-Labarthe undertakes in relation to his own language. He is a *syntaxier* in the tradition inaugurated by Mallarmé, and French syntax allows movements that are simply not reproducible in English. But my hope is that the occasional *forcing* in lexical choice and in some of the sentence constructions proposed in the following pages will point in the direction of what these translations have inevitably failed to capture of the rhythms and the unfailing precision that characterize Lacoue-Labarthe's writing. I would even hope that it will serve as an echo of the singular strangeness that inhabits his texts and constitutes their signature.

Contents

Introduction: Desistance

by Jacques Derrida

Parentheses

(Parenthetically I wonder: How are they going to translate *désister*? They'll have to consider the place this word occupies in Philippe Lacoue-Labarthe's work. It seems discreet, and yet so many paths cross there! Then they'll have to manage, in another, non-Latin language, the relations between an entire family of words. Words that in our tradition bear a strong philosophical tenor. Verbs such as *exister, subsister, consister, persister, insister, résister, assister*—and undoubtedly others I'm forgetting; then too, nouns without corresponding verbs: *substance, consistance, constance, instance, instant, distance.*

Désister, which is much rarer, announces perhaps something other than an additional term in this series. Perhaps it doesn't mark anything negative. Perhaps the *dé* does not determine the *ister*, or rather, as we will see, the *ester*. Perhaps the *dé* dislodges it radically, in an uprooting that would gradually dislocate the whole series, which seemed merely to be modifying a common stem and assigning complementary attributes to it. A powerful meditation on the root, on the a-radicality of *ist, est, ister, ester:* here is what we might follow, among other paths, across Lacoue-Labarthe's texts. Lacoue-Labarthe, for his part, occasionally employs the verb *désister*, or the noun *désistement*. For reasons that I will have to explain, I propose *désistance*, which for the moment is not French.

Désistance is the ineluctable.

There are, to begin with, at least two experiences of the ineluctable. I might say offhand, to formalize things a little: two *typical* experiences.

The first type: this has to happen—*il faut que cela arrive* (How are they going to translate *il faut*? Has to, is to, ought to, must, should?)—this cannot and must not be eluded. This has to begin sometime, someday, in accordance with the necessity of what will have been announced in the future tense. I, the one who says it, precede and anticipate in this way the advent of what happens to *me,* which comes upon me or to which I come. I am then like the (free) subject or the (aleatory) accident of the ineluctable. The latter does not constitute me. I am constituted without it.

Second type: what announces itself as ineluctable seems in some way to have already happened, to have happened before happening, to be always in a past, in advance of the event. Something began before me, the one who undergoes the experience. I'm late. If I insist upon remaining the subject of this experience, it would have to be as a pre-scribed, pre-inscribed subject, marked in advance by the imprint of the ineluctable that constitutes this subject without belonging to it, and that this subject cannot appropriate even if the imprint appears to be properly its own. We can begin to see here the outlines of what we will be analyzing a little further on: a certain constitutive *desistance* of the subject. A (de)constitution rather than a destitution. But how could a desistance be constitutive or essential? It puts off (from itself) any constitution and any essence. The imprint of the ineluctable is not one imprint among others. It does not entail a multiplicity of characters, determinations, or predicates—including the ineluctable, among others. No, the imprint, the *typos,* of this pre-inscription is the ineluctable itself. Ineluctability is pre-impression, and this marks the desistance of the subject. I am not simply the subject or the supporting basis of the imprint or of "my" impressions. But this does not imply that the ineluctable might be conceived of as a genetic program or a historical predestination; rather, the latter are supplemental and late determinations of it. Let us not be too quick to draw a conclusion from this preliminary exercise. Its purpose, in parentheses, is only to strike the keynote for what follows and to lay out the terms of the ineluctable.

Why begin this way? For at least two reasons. First of all, Lacoue-Labarthe's work, his oeuvre, resembles, for me, the very *trial* of the ineluctable: insistent, patient, thinking—the experience of a very *singular* thought of the ineluctable. The word "singularity" might lead us to think of novelty. And in fact the reader will have to recognize something quite evident: a very new configuration, following unprecedented schemas, joins here the question of Being and that of the subject in its philosophical, political, ethical, poetic, literary, theatrical, and musical dimensions, in the reasons and the madness of its autobiography. A different thought of mimesis and of the *typos* gives access *today* to these figures and to this configuration. But the idea of novelty still remains too bound to that of a periodization, or, in the best of cases, to an epochal structure of the Heideggerian type. And as we will see, certain questions addressed to Heidegger, notably on the subject of the subject, on *Gestell* and on mimesis, would seem to prompt some reservations in relation to a history of Being and its epochs. As for the word "configuration," it already presupposes too much in the way of *consistency,* stability, and identifiable collectedness in the *figure*—two of the richest problematics in this book—for us to rely upon it. A new configuration—yes, very new; but this novelty disturbs the very possibility of the *configurable.* And the word applies neither to a period, nor to an epoch, even less to a fashion. Perhaps not even to a history. To what, then? We'll have to be patient; I'll try to explain why. One must learn to read Lacoue-Labarthe, to listen to him, and to do so at his rhythm (learn to follow his rhythm and what he means by "rhythm")— that of his voice, I would almost say his breath, the *phrase* which is not even interrupted when it multiplies caesuras, asides, parenthetical remarks, cautions, signs of prudence and circumspection, hesitations, warnings, parentheses, quotation marks, italics—dashes above all—or all of these at once (for example, he writes "I" and "me" in quotation marks, not even excepting his own name at the end of "Typography," at the moment when he exposes himself the most on the subject of the subject and exposition—or presentation [*Darstellung*]). One must learn the necessity of a scansion that comes to fold and unfold a thought. This is nothing other than the necessity of a rhythm—rhythm itself.

I had a second reason for beginning this way, in parentheses: I was unable, for my part, to avoid trying to follow the thread of a word, *désistement,* which I believe to be untranslatable—this, at the very moment of introducing a translation. And I could not avoid asking myself why I did it. Is it a law? These words never manage to avoid me. I jump right in, and I would be hard put to choose between two hypotheses: choice or compulsion. This introduction will serve to remove the alternative. It will tie a thought of untranslatable idiom to the "logic" of a double constraint (double bind, double obligation: one must—one must not—avoid; one must avoid avoiding, but one cannot avoid avoiding and one must not do so).[1]

I haven't really begun this introduction, but here it is in parentheses already well along—ineluctably. In certain languages—ours—a few

---

1. Derrida will work throughout this text with the term *éviter.* In order to keep this motif in view, I have translated the word in almost every case as "avoid"—at the cost of occasionally losing the more passive connotations of "evade" and the sense of destiny in "the inevitable."—C.F.

words articulate a syntactic formation that lends itself to redoubling the movement of negation: *ne pas ne pas* ("not not"), not do something that already consists in not doing—not avoiding or not eluding. The ineluctable thus belongs to this family, as does the unavoidable. One designates in this manner what cannot or must not be eluded, or avoided. The undeniable appears to be part of the same series, but it says something more, or less. It names negation or de-negation, even super-negation [*sur-négation*], the supplemental *ne pas* one finds at work in the other terms of the group. This supplementary redoubling of negation is not necessarily reducible to the work of dialectic or to an unconscious denegation. Lacoue-Labarthe will help us, perhaps, in stepping back from a Hegelian, Marxist, or Freudian interpretation of such a possibility. And *désistement* might be one of its names.

In the prehistory of this introduction—to carry on with my story— I was troubled even before beginning: How are they going to translate the word *désistement,* its discreet and at the same time insistent recurrence in Lacoue-Labarthe's work? How have they already translated it? I don't want to know yet; it's better that I not know. I write this even as Chris Fynsk, in Strasbourg, puts the final touches on the translation, now finished. But I haven't read it. One can imagine a few solutions. The verb exists in English: "to desist." The codes of jurisprudence generally predominate here, as in French. But the term does not allow a reflexive construction, which is always obligatory in French: *se désister,* to renounce a suit or some legal action, a responsibility. What is more, in English it always designates, it seems to me, a temporal interruption (to cease, to stop, to leave off). Hence a certain divergence and very different syntactic possibilities. It is true that the word "desistance," at least if one domesticated it in French, naturalized it, repatriated it to the point that it lost its common meaning of "cessation," would be closer to what Lacoue-Labarthe seems to want to mark with *désistement.* But the difficulty, precisely, lies elsewhere, and this is why the word *désistance,* in French, a word that Lacoue-Labarthe never uses and that moreover does not yet exist, could prove useful. On the condition that it not be simply transcribed in English, without further precautions, as "desistance"![2] This does not simplify the task, I admit— but is that the point? Lacoue-Labarthe's own use of *désistement* already

---

2. Double bind. The word, taken back from English ("repatriated"), is not to be translated as itself ("transcribed," J.D. says—but how can one signal the difference?). As translator, I see no solution other than *standing down*—and will trust that this is also heard in each occurrence of this word still in translation.—C.F.

marks a departure from the French idiom: the word can barely be translated in current French. *Désistement*—henceforth I will speak of the "desistance" of the subject—does not carry the *juridical* sense that initially imposes itself in normal usage, even though one can decipher in it a certain relation to the law. Nor does it let itself be determined reflexively (as in *se désister*—the only accepted form in "normal" French). But if the "desistance" of the subject does not first signify a "*self*-desistance," we should not come to some conclusion thereby about the passivity of this subject. Or about its activity. Desistance is better for marking the middle voice. Before any decision, before any desition (as one might also say in English to designate a cessation of being), the subject is desisted without being passive; it desists without desisting itself, even before being the subject of a reflection, a decision, an action, or a passion. Should one then say that subjectivity *consists* in such a desistance? No, that's just the point—what is involved here is the impossibility of *consisting,* a singular impossibility: something entirely different from a lack of consistency. Something more in the way of a "(de)constitution."[3] We shall try to analyze it, but let us already recognize the following: the great task of the translator—his madness, his agony, the aporias he confronts—proceeds always from some initial strangeness, from the gap already opened in the idiom of the original text.

Indeed (to further tangle the threads of this prehistory), I almost began this introduction precisely with the problem of translation. But did I avoid doing so? Have I not already done it? Lacoue-Labarthe's work might also be read as a thought constantly at grips with the most serious thing at stake in translation, as a thought that is prey to transla-

3. For example, in a passage that we will be citing and reading again, Lacoue-Labarthe says: "For this reason, I have already proposed to speak of (de)constitution [in *Le sujet de la philosophie*]. But this is makeshift. What should be noted here, with and against Lacan, and going back from Lacan to Reik, is that there is a constant though muffled breakdown of the imaginary, of the resources of the imaginary. The imaginary destroys at least as much as it helps to construct. This explains, perhaps, why the subject in the mirror is first of all a subject in 'desistance' (and why, for example, it will never recover from the mortal insufficiency to which, according to Lacan, its prematuration has condemned it) . . . The figure is never *one* . . . [There is] no essence of the imaginary. What Reik invites us to think, in other words, is that the subject 'desists' because it must always confront *at least* two figures (or one figure that is *at least* double) . . . this destabilizing division of the figural (which muddles, certainly, the distinction between the imaginary and the symbolic, and broaches at the same time the negativity or absolute alterity of the 'real')" ("The Echo of the Subject," pp. 174–175; see also p. 141, and, for example, "Typography," p. 116).

tion, a thought *of* translation; an experience of thought for which translation would not be a problem among others, an object, something that would satisfy an obligation, or what a conscience or a conscientious subject would face up to—but rather the experience of thought itself, its most essential and most risky passage, in those places where the experience of thought is also a poetic experience. Privileged examples: *Gestell,* mimesis, *rhuthmos,* and so many other words—in truth, other phrases—that take these words into their web. And then there are the translations Lacoue-Labarthe published elsewhere (signs of which appear in this book) that bear witness to the same experience: his translation of the translation of Sophocles by Hölderlin (a madness upon madness), and his translation of Celan, an incomparable poet-translator one never reads alone—I mean without taking into account the genealogy of so many other poets. For however impressive the coherence of the texts gathered in this collection might be, it should not allow us to forget the extensive and highly differentiated range of fields traversed by so many of Lacoue-Labarthe's other texts (written sometimes in other modes, both poetic and philosophic), which the English-speaking reader will find available, I hope, before too long. This coherence does not take the form of what in philosophy is called a system—for essential and explicit reasons that all lead back to desistance, and to the disarticulation or the dehiscence that it inscribes in every totality. The insistent, even persistent return of this motif traces out merely the silhouette of a unity, and more of a rhythm than an organic configuration.

So I have just reread these texts. A joy to rediscover, to discover in another manner, the force and the exigent character, the uncompromising vigilance, of a faithful thought. *Justly* faithful, and precisely to the ineluctable. It is as though this thought of desistance never desisted. For almost twenty years now, this thought remains for me—if I may be allowed to say this, and the American reader ought to know it—a strange measure, the precise inordinacy, so to speak, of what will inevitably have to be thought tomorrow: its resource, its task, its fortune. In saying this, I am not in any way yielding to the conventions of the introduction, or to an evaluation it cannot not prescribe. No doubt because he was sensitive to what I have shared with Lacoue-Labarthe and to what he has given me, our friend Eugenio Donato, who originally had the idea of putting together this collection, had wanted me to write its introduction. What I share with Lacoue-Labarthe, we also both share, though differently, with Jean-Luc Nancy. But I hasten immediately to reiterate that despite so many common paths and so much work done in common, between the two of them and between the three of us, the work of each remains, in its singular proximity, absolutely different; and this, despite its fatal impurity, is the secret of the idiom. The secret: that is to say, first of all, the *separation,* the nonrelation, the interruption. The most urgent thing—I'll try to work on this—would be to break with the family atmosphere, to avoid genealogical temptations, projections, assimilations, or identifications. And, as we will see, it is not because they are impossible that the temptation should be any more avoidable. Assimilation or identificatory projection: these are what Lacoue-Labarthe constantly puts us on guard against. He uncovers their fatal character, the *political* trap they hold, even in Heidegger's "unacknowledged" and "fundamental" mimetology,[4] in an interpretation of originary mimesis as imitation. Whether one accepts or refuses imitation, then, the result remains the same: a failure to recognize originary mimesis as desistance. A first point of reference for taking a still preliminary measure of the path followed: once the consequences of the Heideggerian *Destruktion* or the Nietzschean demolition have been followed out as far as possible (and not without laying bare the irreducibility of the one to the other), once the irrecusable necessity of these moments has been assumed, the way in which they are *impossible to get around* (*incontournable* is Lacoue-Labarthe's word,[5] and along with *l'irrécusable,* let us add it to the series of super-negations), the stubborn permanence in these two thoughts of a still Platonic *apprehension* of mimesis will be brought forward, an onto-mimetology. An equivocal and troubling repetition. Lacoue-

---

4. "Heidegger's constant refusal . . . to take seriously the concept of *mimesis* . . . It seems to me more and more difficult not to see a fundamental *mimetology* at work in Heidegger's thought" ("Transcendence Ends in Politics," p. 297). "An unacknowledged mimetology seems to overdetermine the thought of Heidegger politically" (ibid., p. 300).

5. "A thought can be less than infallible and remain, as we say, 'impossible to get around' [*incontournable*]" (p. 269). In this essay, which can also be read as a very necessary meditation on *ananke* (*Notwendigkeit*) as it is interpreted in Heidegger's "Rectoral Address," we may follow the thread of the ineluctable and the distribution of its terms: "avoided," "unavoidable," "not disavow," "incontestable" (p. 268), "irreparable," "unpardonable," "inevitable," "unrenounceable," "impossible to circumvent," "difficult to avoid" (p. 269), "not forbid," "not disavow," "inevitable" (p. 271), "unyielding" (appearing in the Address and cited on p. 277), "undeniable," "unbreachable" ("cannot be broken into"), "impossible to counter" (p. 287), "inescapable " (in the passage cited from the Address, p. 292).

Labarthe does not oppose it and does not criticize it; he is not even sure that he is deconstructing it, or that "deconstruct" is the best word for describing what he does with it by reinscribing it in another structure: *abîme, Unheimlichkeit, double bind, hyperbology.* He opens upon an entirely different thought of mimesis, of *typos* and of *rhuthmos,* a thought which, while borne by the impetus of Nietzschean-Heideggerian deconstruction, nevertheless impresses upon it, as we will see, a supplementary torsion, reorganizes the entire landscape and brings out, or brings into play, new questions: on another dimension of the subject, of politics, of literary or theatrical fiction, of poetic experience, of auto- or hetero-biography.

Imprint and caesura, the sharp-edged signature of this work interrupts the most powerful of filiations. Ineluctably, at the most necessary moment: when that tradition can no longer think or secure what it repeats as its own traditionality (exemplarity, identification, imitation, repetition). The signature interrupts, or rather marks with an incision, the fold along which metaphysical onto-mimetology is destined to divide or desist, the onto-mimetology that runs from Plato to Aristotle, from Hegel to Heidegger, but also the one that continues in a more surreptitious manner in Nietzsche, Freud, and Lacan. The idiom of this signature (but let us not forget, there is also a desistance of the idiom) remains atypical in relation to what is identified, too quickly and too often, above all in the United States, with the name "poststructuralism." And its caesura is all the more marked and marking in that this signature avoids avoidance or denegation; it never flees confrontation (*Auseinandersetzung*—translated in French as *explication*) and the most redoubtable proximity to thoughts that it overtaxes with constantly renewed questions. Exemplary probity, both prudent and adventurous—a superior probity which, without giving way to a dogmatic moralism, submits the ethical demand to the trial of thought.

Hence, of course, the need for these multiple distinctions, which should be enumerated and respected: this belongs neither to metaphysical onto-theology, nor to onto-mimetology (a concept forged by Lacoue-Labarthe and which no longer corresponds to an epochal or historial unity of a Heideggerian type, since the delimitation of onto-theology in the history of Being still belongs to the (non-)ensemble of onto-mimetology); and while not *stricto sensu* Nietzschean or Heideggerian, it is to no greater extent Marxist, Freudian, Lacanian, poststructuralist, or post-modern. And yet, despite these dissociations, these distances taken which are neither critiques nor oppositions, one never has the feeling of isolation or insularity. Another figure suggests itself to me, but it is only a figure: that of a besieged force. Besieged because it exposes itself on all sides, even to the question: What is obsessionality?[6] What is obsessionality when an ineluctable double bind makes it so that one cannot close a line, or a parenthesis, except by opening another on another front? And what would the question "What is . . . ?" with its epochs (and the suspension of an *epoche* is also a setting in parentheses, or even, as we will see shortly, a setting in parentheses of the thesis or the thetic in general), have to do, or not have to do, with madness? The besieged force remains impregnable because it has no figurable site, a single site, a single figure; it has no proper identity, properly proper. Unstable and destabilizing, it presses and harries out of its desistance all the others in turn, without letting down, without granting them the least respite. Hence the "style," the ethos, the "character" (and here I refer to the problematic that begins and complicates itself as it unfolds in Chapter 2, in the section titled "The Novel Is a Mirror"), the rhythm of the warnings. Lacoue-Labarthe multiplies parentheses in order to caution us at every instant against omissions, avoidances, simplifications: from all sides, overdetermination can return to suprise us, one might miss a twist or a fold, traps are everywhere, the double bind leaves no way out, nor does the hyperbologic—one has to know this in order to begin to think. And the warning is not finally meant to protect anyone. It stands watch so that one will not fail to expose oneself: don't forget that you are exposed, that you must expose yourself on this side and then again on the other—don't avoid exposition, which in any case won't miss you, or me.

This presupposes at some moment a contract, a moment of alliance,

6. The question of obsession, of the obsessing, of the obsessional returns quite regularly in all of these texts and at the heart of the problematic of mimesis, *typos,* and *Gestell.* It is even the question of the "style of questioning" (see, for example, "The Echo of the Subject," p. 191). And it is the question of writing itself, beginning with the writing signed by Lacoue-Labarthe, who, in any case, never misses any of this. The end of "L'Oblitération": "One can always ascribe writing, particularly when it is precautious, to a conjuring mania, or to the repetition compulsion. But perhaps it is strictly impossible to write anything other than this: 'What obliges me to write, I imagine, is the fear of going mad.'" It is a line from Bataille, and Lacoue-Labarthe adds that it is just as valid for "Nietzsche" as it is for "Heidegger" (*Le sujet de la philosophie* [Paris: Aubier-Flammarion, 1979], p. 176). For example. Or: "[What vacillates is] the most basic narcissistic assurance (the obsessional 'I am not dead,' or 'I will survive')" (p. 195). Obsessionality, here, is no longer a clinical category.

fidelity. One must read, and to do this one must come to terms, negotiate, compromise. Fidelity to what, finally, or to whom? Well, perhaps to the very thing that you, who besiege me with such necessity, who are already there before me, did not avoid, or could not not avoid (does this come down to the same thing?), and that therefore takes the form of the ineluctable. This form is terrifying, for it lends itself to all figures, all schemas—it is unstable and amorphous. A singular fidelity to what finally no longer even demands fidelity. But would there ever be a fidelity without the faith called for by such dissymmetry?

It would have been best not to multiply the preliminary, preambulatory precautions for this introduction and jump immediately outside the parentheses. But how? The temptation was also there to begin, by way of exergue, with yet another long parenthesis on the subject of a very brief parenthesis I would have cited, only seven words. I would have masked a proper noun, thus pretending to replace the most irreplaceable, a proper noun, by another: figure, fiction, simulacrum of synonymy. In "Typography" (p. 62 below), one encounters the following, in parentheses: "(in any case, Heidegger never avoids anything)."

Oh, really? How so? Is such a thing possible?

On first reflection, my impulse is to respond: It's difficult to know whether this is true of Heidegger or of anyone; but if it were true of someone, it would be true of he who dared write, "Heidegger never avoids anything"! Unless this is the one thing he should have avoided saying or thinking. For after all, how can one dare write such a thing? By what right? And is there any sense in advancing such a proposition about someone, anyone? What is the meaning of this provocation?

Let's not rush. In one sense, indeed, it is possible not to avoid anything: never pass by a question, a possibility, a truth, and a truth about truth, a necessity. Never miss a twist or a fold. But one can also, in a second sense, not avoid anything, even the worst: mistakes, weaknesses, misapprehensions, inhibitions, omissions, compromises—also avoidances and denegations. Compulsively. As is said in common French: never miss a one [*ne pas en manquer une*]. When Lacoue-Labarthe says of Heidegger that "he never avoids anything," he clearly means this in the first sense: the good sense of the expression. Heidegger stands up to things, never avoids anything: this is why there is no "getting around him." And yet, Lacoue-Labarthe's abyssal irony inscribes this incredible parenthesis in an analysis devoted entirely to describing the way in which Heidegger passes by, circumvents (more or less) deliberately, the very thing that he, Lacoue-Labarthe, wants not to avoid. For he is concerned with "tracking down" (*dépister* is his word) the tortuous strategy Heidegger employs to avoid what he does not avoid, to avoid without avoiding. Heidegger's denegation? Lacoue-Labarthe's denegation regarding Heidegger's denegation which he would like to pick up in the text [*relever*] and yet at the same time (double bind) not sublate? If not, then what does "avoid" mean? And what about "denegation"? Especially when it is a matter, as we will verify in a moment, of a "vast movement" by Heidegger, his "maneuver" (I cite Lacoue-Labarthe), in a thought concerned with thinking, over and above the meaning of an onto-theology without which the very concept of denegation could not have been formed, the *unthought* itself. Concerned with thinking not just this or that unthought, but the structure, the possibility, and the necessity of the unthought in general, its quasi-negativity (the *un*-thought is un-*thought*, he reminds us), which, whatever Heidegger says, I'm not sure gathers each time in the unity of a single site, as if there were only *one* unthought in which each great thought—and herein would lie its very greatness—would find its secret law. But I will return to this shortly.

What are we to understand by "avoid" or "deny" when this unthought of unthinking itself [*l'impenser*], that of Heidegger, involves motifs such as writing, poetic or fictional *Darstellung,* the subject of enunciation, the madness or politics of this subject, the unity of the text, and so on—various signifying terms without which philosophy and psychoanalysis, logic and pragmatics, would have difficulty defining these figures that are calmly named "avoiding," "denying," "eluding," etc.? These common determinations can no longer suffice, and it is here, at this limit, that Lacoue-Labarthe's gesture seems to operate a far-reaching strategic displacement. For one of the most daring and unprecedented analyses in "Typography," the very one in which it is indicated that "in any case, Heidegger never avoids anything," multiplies around these questions a series of troubling diagnoses on the matter of a Heideggerian "maneuver." For the moment, I find no word more appropriate than "diagnosis," though I mean it in the sense of Nietzschean genealogy, whatever reservations one should hold, with Lacoue-Labarthe, on the latter. These diagnoses are all the more grave in that they neither accuse nor criticize anyone: they merely indicate a certain fatality that one will never escape simply by de-limiting it. And these diagnoses are all the more interesting, in each of their formulations, in that they concern movements by which Heidegger will have appeared to avoid this or that (we will see why in a moment), and open, in their very act of delimitation, the space of Lacoue-Labarthe's singular problematic, truly without precedent. What are these formulations? Let me first cite them, as such—indeed, in their simple *form*—before coming, outside parentheses, to the thing itself. First of all, Lacoue-Labarthe tells us, Heidegger "'eliminates' ['*évacue*'] (or *sublimes*)." Note, as always, the signs of prudence, the vigilant circumspection, the insurance taken against all the risks to which he does not fail to expose himself at every instant: quotation marks around "eliminates," as if to withdraw immediately an unsatisfactory word (Heidegger never eliminates anything—no more than does Lacoue-Labarthe); then *sublimes* is in italics. And in parentheses. For the word might seem to be borrowed from a foreign and very problematic context (the Freudian aporetics of sublimation). But a necessary point of passage is held open by the word itself, which leads back to the question of the sublime, present elsewhere in the confrontation with Heidegger and with regard to a certain unpresentability of the entirely other. Heidegger, then, "'eliminates'" or "*sublimes*" *three* questions that, according to Lacoue-Labarthe, are moreover the *same*. On this unity or this unicity, I will myself have a question, but this too will be for later. One single question, then, one question in three, the same question "always in view and always thrust aside" (p. 62) in such a way that Heidegger "could fail to attend to it, simply pass right by it—or even pretend to not "pay attention to it."

It would therefore not be impossible to pretend to not pay attention. More precisely: to do so in a thoughtful reading or a meditation, for in "everyday life" we know that nothing is easier. As always, Lacoue-Labarthe gives generous credit to the thought he examines, or "tracks down." He credits it with the greatest strength, the greatest cunning, the most lucid *knowledge*—one which can never be taken unawares by the questions one might put to it.

> It is no doubt possible to *track down* in the whole of the procedure Heidegger follows when dealing with *Zarathustra,* and already in the very positing of the question that governs it ("*Who* is Nietzsche's Zarathustra?"), a kind of vast movement turning around a question that Heidegger *well knows* cannot be avoided or eluded (in any case, Heidegger never avoids anything), but which he judges must be "cut off from its support," and taken from behind, in order to *neutralize its power*. ("Typography," p. 62; my emphasis—*J.D.*)

One can therefore neutralize *power* and thus avoid in a certain way what one cannot avoid *seeing* or *knowing*. A whole strategy, a whole war in relation to this power can therefore be employed, can deploy its "maneuvers" or manipulations. The essential question here bears less upon the fact of the maneuver than upon the course chosen: "But why does Heidegger's maneuver here go by way of *Gestalt*? Why does it even go beyond *Gestalt* in search of *Ge-stell*? Once again, what happens with (the word) *Ge-stell*?" ("Typography," p. 62).

Here we are, then—here is the content, if one may say so, of the question: *Ge-stell*, or the word "Ge-stell," for the division between the word and the thing is difficult to make, for essential reasons. What is at stake in the thing is also a language's affair. But this "content," as we will see, retains in fact a necessary relation to what one commonly calls "form": *Gestalt*, presentation (*Darstellung*), exposition, fiction, everything involved with *Darstellung* in the network of significations with the stem *-stellen,* an entire hive that it disorganizes perhaps by putting it to work, perhaps also because it does not belong to it quite as simply as it might appear to. Heidegger, in any case, is said to have avoided it, knowing full well [*pertinemment*]⁷ that he was thus circumventing, at least provisionally, the ineluctable.

But further on, the tracking, the following of traces, becomes more relentless. Hemmed in, Heidegger "cannot avoid falling." Can that be said? It's true—this is a man who never avoids anything. To follow the trail, this is also *nachstellen,* and in "Typography" Lacoue-Labarthe proposes a translation: "to track or be after; to avenge." Where is it that Heidegger cannot avoid falling? It is still a matter of *Darstellung* and of the Platonic paradigm of the mirror. This latter,

> is therefore—in fact—a paradigm of *Darstellung*. But it is fixed, a trick paradigm—a trap consisting of an artfully camouflaged hole into which Heidegger, in a certain way, cannot avoid falling. And it is a mimetic fall—if there ever was one—since he falls for the trap while trying to outdo Plato. This can be "seen." I ("I") mean that all of this is perfectly legible: there are signs, and the "accident" does not occur without leaving traces. (p. 89)

You saw them—no, you *read* the quotation marks, the quotation marks in parentheses. This accident was not an accident—the fall was inevitable; but we are no longer dealing here with the subject (I) of a

7. This is what we need to know. What does it mean to know? And what would the super-negation of the ineluctable have to do with the knowledge of knowledge? For, ten pages earlier, Lacoue-Labarthe asked—already on the subject of Heidegger, and already in parentheses: "(does one ever know what he knows . . .)" (p. 53). So we must also place quotation marks around this knowledge. "The Echo of the Subject": "But why does Reik, who 'knows,' want to know nothing about it?" (p. 197).

perception or of a science, of a seeing or a knowing. What happened to Heidegger, or with him, under his name, is grave in another sense, and his nonavoidance no longer answers to these categories. A moment ago, we were told that Heidegger never avoids anything. Almost thirty pages later, we hear that "he could not avoid falling" into a carefully camouflaged "hole." If this ineluctable no longer answers to the categories of seeing and knowing, to the logic or psychoanalysis of denegation, one may have an inkling of the singular nature of what is at stake when Lacoue-Labarthe gets into the traces left by this fatal accident (which one might almost call necessary or essential). The deciphering, whose stages I cannot try to reconstitute here, answers to no established discipline: neither to seeing nor to knowing, neither to hermeneutics nor to psychoanalysis. Nor do I think one can speak here of a philosophical method or of a philosophical reading.

Is it absolutely necessary to give it a name? Lacoue-Labarthe seems to describe a strategy: "turning movement," "cut off from behind," "take from behind," "maneuver." But also the failure, the expiration, the fall, the great lapse of a thought. What must Lacoue-Labarthe's strategy be, this strategy without hostilities for tracking down traces, upsetting or catching Heidegger's grand maneuver by surprise—itself not a simple maneuver among others (military, methodical, scientific, logical, psychoanalytic, hermeneutic, philosophical)? In fact, it is a maneuver involved with the most constraining Platonic tradition, and finally with the entire onto-theology that follows from it, up to the very concepts of onto-theology, the history of metaphysics, even *Ge-stell*—and within these latter, the determination, thought to be derived and secondary, of the subject or of subjectity (*Subjectität*).

These are, in short, some of the questions I asked myself when I came up against this short parenthesis ("(in any case, Heidegger never avoids anything)")—the only phrase, undoubtedly, against which I could not help reacting initially in protest. This is why, spontaneously, I almost began that way. Resistance—for this was a resistance on my part—often indicates the sensitive point in a reading, the point of incomprehension that organizes it. "How can he write this?" I asked myself. And of anyone? How could someone, a finite thinker, and a thinker of finitude, never avoid anything, even while knowing, "full well," what he avoids when he avoids? Above all, when this thinker of finitude takes seriously the necessity of the unthought, to the point of recognizing in it the essential condition, almost the source of thought—something entirely different from a lack: "What is unthought in a thinker's thought is not a lack inherent in his thought. What is *un*-thought is such in each case only as the un-*thought*," Heidegger says (note 22, p. 61), and Lacoue-Labarthe reminds us.

When Paul de Man dared say that Rousseau's text bore no "blind spot," I felt the same impatience. Impatience is never justified. It should incite one to take one's time and to submit oneself to what is not self-evident—without avoiding it. Hence I offer, if I may, a first piece of advice, at the point of closing this long parenthesis: work at reading and rereading these difficult texts (with their incidental phrases, quotation marks, and parentheses), themselves and those they examine; work at going along with their strategy, made up of audacity, cunning, and prudence, and with the intractable necessity that constrains them, with their rhythm, above all, their breath—ample periods and the deep respiration of thought. Their time is that of a long-distance run during which you follow someone who continually addresses you; he turns to you, describes the ups and downs of terrain he knows well, interrupts himself and then starts right in again, warns you of the risks involved, of pitfalls and traps waiting ahead, jumps you'll have to take, of the stretch you can't see yet, of the necessity of a detour and of marking a different pace, inventing another stride in order to cross the finish line or open a new path. If sometimes you have the feeling that you are dealing with a thinker who is panting or harried, don't kid yourself: you are reading someone who on the contrary is tracking—*polemos* without polemics—the most powerful thoughts of our tradition. I close the parenthesis. Is this possible?)

Ge-stell

So I will begin, here, with this example. Because it announces Lacoue-Labarthe's *manner* and *maneuver,* the hand or the rhythm of his surgery. And because I cannot do more in an introduction. Accepting the risks of this limitation, and hoping above all that the reader will turn to Lacoue-Labarthe himself, I will stick to three examples, each time following a single thread: desistance. Each of the examples will bear the signature of a foreign word, foreign first of all to the language to which it seems to belong. It will correspond to a kind of madness in translation, as in the tradition: obsession and schiz, siege and caesura, double bind, fatality and impossibility of reappropriation, hyperbology, ineluctable dis-identification. I will take another risk by applying to myself another rule of limitation: to lead only into those places where

Lacoue-Labarthe sharpens his thought of desistance by testing it against those thoughts that are both the most foreign and the closest, thus the most resistant (for example, the thoughts of Nietzsche, Heidegger, Freud, Lacan).

Beyond anthropological pathos and that of so-called positive forms of knowledge, Lacoue-Labarthe has always accorded to madness the dignity of a major question for thought. Without "demagoguery" and without "psychagogy."[8] Before asking whether insanity must be excluded or mastered—that is to say, domesticated—by philosophy, one must try to think its obsession with madness: a certain way in which philosophy is regularly visited, haunted, inhabited by madness. There is a domesticity of "philosophical madness." At its beginning and at its end, "Typography" opens upon this predestination of philosophy to madness. The examples (they are only examples) are Rousseau (his ". . . and this is how we become mad," from the preface to *La nouvelle Héloïse*), Nietzsche ("The Significance of Madness in the History of Morality," in *Daybreak*), but also Kant, Comte, and Hegel. Among all the paths available in these extraordinary and profuse analyses, I should isolate the thread that links madness to a new "question of the subject." Lacoue-Labarthe takes it up, taking up again even the title, and sends it off again in an unprecedented manner. He has been doing this now for almost fifteen years,[9] with discretion, patience, and rigor, in a kind of

8. "We have some reason to be suspicious of all the 'demagogic,' 'psychagogic' phraseology with which one claims today—without, it is true, too great a risk—to speak in the name of madness" ("Typography," p. 46).

9. At least since "L'Oblitération" (1973, subsequently included in *Le sujet de la philosophie*), which already ties the question of madness to that of the subject. The word "desistance" is not yet present there as such; rather, we find "(de)constitution of the subject" (pp. 138, 157, and *passim*). The verb "to desert" [*déserter*] is perhaps the term that best announces the *désister* of which I will be speaking, for example in this passage which establishes in a remarkable fashion the axioms, so to speak, of this problematic: "What interests us here, as one will have suspected, is neither the subject nor the author [a question and a precaution taken up again in Chapter 5, p. 251—*J.D.*]. Nor is it the 'other,' whatever one places under the term, of the subject or the author. It would be rather (to limit ourselves provisionally to the sole question of the subject) what is *also* at play in the subject, while being absolutely irreducible to some subjectivity (that is to say, to any objectivity whatsoever); what, in the subject, 'deserts' (has always already deserted) the subject *itself,* and which, prior to any "self-possession' (and following another mode than that of dispossession), is the dissolution, the defeat of the subject in the subject or *as* the subject: the (de)constitution of the subject, or the 'loss' of the subject—if it were possible, that is, to conceive of the loss of what one has never had, a kind of 'originary' and 'constitutive' loss (of 'self')." (*Le sujet de la philosophie,* p. 151).

solitude, and without engaging in the "return to the subject" which has recently been animating Parisian conversations, and which (and this is in *the best of cases,* no doubt the least dogmatic and the most refined) certain authors believe they find in Foucault's very last works. Nevertheless, *in every case,* a rigorous reading of Heidegger, an effective working-across his text on the subject of subjectity, has been carefully omitted.[10]

Lacoue-Labarthe does something entirely different. He does not propose to restore, rehabilitate, or reinstall "the subject"; rather, he proposes to think its desistance by taking into account *both* a deconstruction of a Heideggerian type *and* that about which he thinks Heidegger maintained a silence.

What "silence"? The word appears at least twice. What it designates is not without some relation to the ineluctable. Even if he "never avoids anything," Heidegger remains silent on something about *Darstellung* that is not easily domesticated, ordered, classed in the great family of

---

The placing in parentheses of the "de" in "(de)constitution" signifies that one must not hear it (any more than in the case of "desistance") as a negativity affecting an originary and positive constitution. The italicizing of the *as* signifies that the "subject," as such, (de)constitutes itself in this movement of *desistance* and *is nothing other than* the formation of this movement. For this reason it also signifies that the subject cannot be simply omitted or dissolved, or passed over in silence in the name of a deconstruction of subjectity—of the epoch of subjectity (*Subjectität*) in the sense defined by Heidegger. Hence, at this point already, the distance taken in regard to the latter; and this is what immediately follows after the passage that I have just cited. Lacoue-Labarthe calls into question, already, a certain Heideggerian "sublimation": "Now this is precisely what Heidegger's text touches upon—but only to take it up again immediately (or even in advance), to sublate it (which is also to say sublimate it) in and as thought. What 'this' is is 'madness,' and 'madness' such as it declares itself, or rather does not declare itself, in *Ecce Homo*." (*Le sujet de la philosophie,* pp. 151–152.)

10. Heidegger was almost never named by Foucault, who in any case never confronted him and, if one may say so, never explained himself on his relation to him. This is also true of Deleuze. This did not prevent Foucault from declaring in his very last interview: "My entire philosophical development [*devenir*] was determined by my reading of Heidegger." Nor did it prevent Deleuze, in the very last pages of his book on Foucault, from speaking of a "necessary confrontation of Foucault with Heidegger." (Gilles Deleuze, *Foucault* [Paris: Minuit, 1986], p. 115.) How, then, is one to interpret, retrospectively, this twenty-five-year silence? I must be brief. If, in attending to this silence, one thinks at the same time of those who like Lacoue-Labarthe have constantly taken into account, in its most difficult, hazardous, indeed "necessary" dimensions, the said "confrontation" with Heidegger, one obtains—allow me to say nothing on the subject here—a kind of film of the French philosophical scene in this quarter-century. To be deciphered: again the avoiding of the unavoidable.

Ge-stell (*bestellen, vorstellen, herstellen, nachstellen*). It introduces a disorder to which Heidegger does not attend, or, as is said somewhere, to
which he pretends not to pay attention. Heidegger's "silence" on the
subject of *Darstellung* can be deciphered in two ways: either he neglects the fact that *Darstellung* belongs to *Ge-stell,* and thus neglects
everything that it would oblige him to take into account (Lacoue-
Labarthe recalls all of this); or else he inscribes *Darstellung* in a homogeneous series and thus reduces it to being merely a mode among
others. In his delimitation of an "onto-typology," Heidegger remains
"elliptical" (this word also appears twice—pp. 56, 59) in regard to the
relation between, on the one hand, work and suffering (a propos of
Jünger's *Der Arbeiter: Über den Schmerz*), and, on the other, representation by figure (*gestalthafte Darstellung*). And in his "relatively elliptical treatment of Jünger's relation to Hegel," Heidegger also observes
a "certain silence"[11] on the relation between the metaphysics of *Gestalt,*
or the representation of Being as figure, and *Darstellung,* namely, "literary presentation." And what holds for Jünger would hold also for
those other "writers," Nietzsche and Rilke. Ellipsis and silence signal a
"loss"[12] that is something other than the "disappearance of a word"
and that concerns the derivation *stellen-darstellen.* In examining "what
happens" with "(the word) *Ge-stell*" and the impossibility of its translation, Lacoue-Labarthe defines the site of a new "question of the subject." Here is its "content"—it is the passage I cited a moment ago for
its "form":

11. "Typography," p. 59. See also p. 62: "From *Ge-stell,* among other things, not
only *Gestalt* but *Darstellung* itself ((re)presentation, exposition, *mise-en-scène,* etc.) can
be derived. Or, more precisely, *Gestalt* and *Darstellung* can be derived together from *Ge-
stell,* among other things, even though Heidegger *never,* unless I am mistaken, *explicitly
marks this relationship* [emphasis added—*J.D.*], and to see it, we must link together and
at the same time make 'homogeneous' several relatively independent texts. Even
though, in fact, everything happens here as if the commonality of origin, the *homogeneity* of *Gestalt* and *Darstellung*—symptomatically left unmentioned, I must insist, when
it was a question of folding Jünger back upon Hegel—were, in one way or another,
something very troublesome. Because, in effect, Mimesis is at play here."
12. Lacoue-Labarthe writes in "Typography": "One *inevitably* [emphasis added—
J.D.] runs the risk of getting lost somewhere—or of losing all continuity of derivation.
For example, *between* two or three texts, in the area of (the question of) *Darstellung;*
or, to be more precise and to keep hold of the thread that we have already begun to
follow, in the area where (the question of) *Darstellung* is, in effect, connected with
Mimesis. In the beginning, however, everything goes rather well" ("Typography,"
pp. 64–65). A long and tight analysis of numerous texts (I can only invite the reader to
follow it) then demonstrates the process and the effects of this "loss of *Darstellung,*"

I ("I") will not return here to the way in which Heidegger, in a single move, "eliminates" (or *sublimes)*, for the sake of a primary *destination* of the unthought [*l'impensé(e)*] in Nietzsche (i.e., in "Nietzsche"), at one and the same time the question of the "poetic" or "fictional" ("literary") character of *Zarathustra,* the question of a certain dispersion or breaking up of the Nietzschean "text" (more difficult to get around, however, than "the absence of the work"—a capital work—wherein the un-*thought* it-self *would organize itself* with the essential "articulation" of a few fundamental words), and, finally, the question of Nietzsche's "madness." Elsewhere, it seemed to me possible to show—but to be honest, it was a bit obvious—that these three questions are really only one, or more exactly, that they all gravitate around a single, central question, at the same time always in view and always thrust aside (constantly proposed, moreover, in terms unacceptable to *thought:* metaphysically marked, and therefore constantly condemned—without "appeal"), and this is the question of the *subject.* The question of the "subject of enunciation," let us say, or of "writing"—nothing, in any case, that might be simply, that is, immediately, assimilated or *identified* with the subject of the "metaphysics of subjectivity," under any form whatsoever. ("Typography," pp. 61–62)

"Typography," and what is now coming together under this title,[13] take their force in large measure from the impressive articulation in "a single central question" of this question of the subject, which Lacoue-Labarthe removes from the Heideggerian deconstruction—that is to say, from the delimitation of an onto-typo-logy or a metaphysics of subjectivity. He removes it by showing how Heidegger removes himself from it; and, most important, he leads back into its unicity, which is also a center of gravity, a great number of questions. Among them, "a certain breaking apart of the 'text'"—the Nietzschean one in this case, but with regard to which I wonder (actually this is only a certain uneasiness) whether Lacoue-Labarthe does not himself risk a reduction. He does this with the best justification in the world, since this

---

which "can scarcely be a simple matter" (p. 72) and be limited to "the disappearance of a *word*" (p. 73), even though there is the case of a text where Heidegger drops the word immediately after having cited it in the coupling "*Her-* and *Darstellen*" (p. 73). That *Darstellung* should be "lost" does not mean that some thing should have been lost—the term designates rather a certain inattention to the abyssal structure that can always divide it and fictionalize it. The question then becomes: "How, then, is *Darstellung* lost? And what is the consequence of this loss for the interpretation of mimesis?" (p. 73). Cf. also p. 79: "the loss of *Darstellung.*"

13. Derrida refers here to the subtitles of *Le sujet de la philosophie* and *L'imitation des modernes: Typographies I* and *Typographies II.*—C.F.

re-elaborative gathering is the best possible strategic lever for a deconstructive reading of Heidegger—but it is not without confirming
in passing the fundamental axiom according to which the un-*thought*
of a thought is always single, always unique,[14] constituting in a certain
way the very site out of which a thought gives—or gives itself—to
think. Lacoue-Labarthe proceeds as though the way in which Heidegger defines the un-*thought* of Nietzsche, or the un-*thought* in general,
implied in its turn only a sole and unique un-*thought:* that around
which or out of which the Heideggerian thought would organize itself. But is this not to repeat, in relation to Heidegger, what Lacoue-
Labarthe himself accused Heidegger of, namely privileging a "primary
destination of the un-thought"—that of Nietzsche for Heidegger, that
of Heidegger for Lacoue-Labarthe? What if Heidegger's unthought
(for example) was not one, but plural? What if his *un*thought was believing in the unicity or the unity of the un*thought*? I won't make a
critique out of my uneasiness, because I do not believe that this gesture
of gathering is avoidable. It is always productive, and philosophically
necessary. But I will continue to wonder whether the very "logic" of
desistance, as we will continue to follow it, should not lead to some

14. One might reread the passage from *Was heisst denken?* that Lacoue-Labarthe
himself cites at the moment he comes to pose a second question concerning translation
(p. 60). The first concerned the untranslatable *Ge-stell;* here it is less a matter of knowing what it *means* than "how it functions" and "what purpose it serves." The other concerns the Heideggerian project of "translating" *Zarathustra* and submitting it to an
"allegorical" treatment. This time, translation involves, beyond "expression" or "poetic
ornament," an "unthought." Heidegger: "To acknowledge and respect [the language of
thinkers] consists in letting every thinker's thought come to us as something *in each case
unique,* never to be repeated, inexhaustible—and being shaken to the depths by what is
unthought in his thought. What is unthought in a thinker's thought is not a lack inherent in his thought. What is *un*-thought is such in each case only as the un-*thought*"
(cited in "Typography," note 22, p. 60). (I have emphasized "in each case unique,"
which is here the indispensable correlate of the very thinking of thought. Where unicity
is lacking, thought itself, as also the un-*thought* of thought, will not come about. This is
what Lacoue-Labarthe respects perhaps a bit more than I do: this unicity, and the affinity between this unicity and thought itself. On this point, my little respect, or what
torments my respect, can signify two things: either that I do not know (how to recognize) what thought is authentically and am not sufficiently concerned about it, *or else*
that I do not exclude the possibility of some residue of an *un*-thought in this Heideggerian determination of the un-*thought,* which still holds too much to the unique *site* of
gathering. What if one called thought (but perhaps another name would be needed) the
dislocation, even the desistance, of this unicity or this unity, of this *site* of gathering?
For one might show that this question leads back constantly through Heidegger's notion of the topology of Being and everything it gathers under the words *Ort* and *Erör-
terung:* that is to say, precisely, gathering.)

irreducible dispersion of this "unique central question," as question of the subject—to its dis-identification, in some sense, its dis-installation. And I will continue to ask whether the "subject" in question, even if it exceeds the limits of the "metaphysics of subjectity" or onto-typology, does not continue to reflect, or to collect in its gathering force, in the unicity of its question, something of the Heideggerian unthought. In short, I will be asking whether it is not necessary to separate the two questions brought together here: that of the "subject of enunciation" and that of "writing." But no doubt Lacoue-Labarthe does so, and this is even what he calls *typography,* beyond the formulation and the strategic moment I have just isolated somewhat artificially.

The strategy of "Typography" is of a subtlety I could not hope to account for here. At the risk of magnifying in an exaggerated fashion its basic traits, I will read in it first a kind of general destabilization or disinstallation. General, first of all, because they are redoubled. This redoubling has to do with the essence, without essence, of mimesis, with the fact that it *is* not, that it does not exist, but *desists,* and that this involves nothing negative. To think it, one must not install oneself (upside down) in Plato's mimetology as it is finally confirmed by Heidegger. One must not *rehabilitate,* seek to claim, or save a mimesis defined as a "declination," "instability," accidental "disinstallation," or "fall" that has happened to truth—to that *aletheia* interpreted by Heidegger in his reading of the tenth book of the *Republic* in a curious fashion as *Unverstelltheit:* installation, non-disinstallation, stele. If an abyssal redoubling must be thought as destabilizing truth or the stele from its origin, as one might say, one must still not give in to the almost irresistible temptation to generalize the mimesis condemned by Plato or to rehabilitate it in conferring upon it the noble status of an originary mimesis.[15] The line to be crossed, for such a temptation, seems so subtle that no one—I would say not even Lacoue-Labarthe—can constantly mind it. The difference can be marked simply with visible or invisible quotation marks around the word "originary." And when one wants to underscore the notion that mimesis does not have the (destitute) status of a fall or an accidental derivation, one is indeed tempted to call it,

15. Lacoue-Labarthe will be more and more precise, in subsequent texts, about the paradoxical—hyperbological—constraints that "mimetological overdetermination" exerts upon thought and discourse. He will even term the "thought of a mimesis without models or an 'originary mimesis'" the "'negative metaphysics' of the moderns." In this same text, he announces his reservations concerning a rehabilitation and a generalization of mimesis, be they modern or post-modern. See *L'imitation des modernes* (Paris: Galilée, 1986), pp. 278, 281, 283 in particular.

"against" Plato, "originary," "'originary'"—while making it clear that the quality of being originary is incompatible with that of mimesis, and so on.

The fold or abyssal redoubling of which we are trying to speak does not, therefore, come to destabilize a truth that would already be (*serait déjà;* or *esterait,* as one sometimes renders it in French). Desistance is first of all that of truth. This latter never resembles itself. Hence its resemblance to mimesis. But how is it possible to resemble mimesis without already being contaminated by it? And how can one think this original contamination in a non-negative and non-originary fashion, in order to keep from letting one's statements be dictated by the dominant mimetologism? Etcetera. Truth, then, never resembles itself. It withdraws, masks itself, and never ceases, says Lacoue-Labarthe, who this time uses the reflexive construction, to desist [*se désister*] (p. 118).

Before we focus on this result, let us note what in the lexicon justifies the privilege given to this word, *désister;* and above all what it is that, in relating it to the quasi-radical *ist,* or rather *stare,* in French *ester,* uproots it, removes desist, desistance, from the series of "stances" to which they seem to belong (subsistence, substance, resistance, constancy, consistency, insistence, instance, assistance, persistence, existence, etc.). As it is put to work by Lacoue-Labarthe, "desistance" is not a modification, above all not a negative one, of *ester.* The *dé* would super-mark precisely this: its non-belonging to the family of *ester.* I have already suggested this, and I return to the point now in order to complicate a bit more what will be at stake in the translation. One should know that *ester* is not only a kind of root. The word exists in French, even if it is rare. It has a meaning that is above all juridical, like *se désister,* and signifies "to present oneself," to appear [*apparaître, comparaître*] in a court of justice. *Ester en jugement* (to appear in court, to plead), *ester en justice* (to go to law), is to present oneself before the law as plaintiff or defendant. Now, it happens that as a result of this semantics of presentation or appearance, this act of presence, if you will, it has sometimes been thought that one might translate *Wesen,* as it is used in a Heideggerian sense (normally translated in English as "essence"), by *ester* or *estance.*[16] Let me then risk this suggestion: if *beyond* its place in a juridical code, and *in* the way it is put to work "typographically," *désistance* does not modify *estance,* and does not belong

16. See in particular Gilbert Kahn's translation of *Einführung in die Metaphysik* entitled *Introduction à la métaphysique* (Paris: Gallimard, 1967). Here is an excerpt from the

to it as one of its determinations, but rather marks a rupture, a departure, or a heterogeneity with respect to *estance* or *Wesen;* if it says neither absence nor disorder or inessentiality, neither *Abwesen* nor *Unwesen,* nor even some *Entwesen* (this latter removed from its trivial connotation); then it would be quite difficult to retranslate it into the code, the problematic, or even the question of the meaning or truth of Being—or, if you prefer, into "Heidegger's" language. This does not mean that nothing more would pass, or happen, between the two languages; but the passage would be offered by another abyss, the one of which Heidegger speaks and *also* another. I don't know whether Lacoue-Labarthe will accept my hypothesis, or even whether it will interest him. Perhaps he will refuse it straight off; perhaps on the contrary it will appear to him to go without saying—he who once wrote: "I have a lot of trouble not seeing in Heidegger's "Being," if it is still Being and if it is Heidegger's Being, the same thing as (if not the very possibility of) Levinas's "otherwise than Being."[17] Perhaps. Perhaps (and here is the opening I'm working at, perhaps in vain) desistance, as I read it in Lacoue-Labarthe, calls for an "otherwise than Being" (otherwise than *ester*), still an other, and which would be neither "Heideggerian" nor "Levinasian" (these qualifications impose on us a stupid economy), without ceasing to open, between these two thoughts, so close to one another and so heterogeneous, the way of passage for a thinking translation.

Estance, the meaning "estance," would thus find itself destabilized in itself, without this appearing as a negativity. De-sistance, that of truth first of all, would condition all the positions and all the stances that it nevertheless ruins, in effect, and sets spinning from within. A question of translation, again, and a passage between the Greek (*aletheia,* translated or interpreted by Heidegger as *Unverstelltheit*), the German (*Gestell* and the words formed with *stellen,* whose resources are laid out in the section titled "The Stele"), and the Latin (*sto, stare,* and so on). We should pause for some time around this point of passage, the privilege of which, for those of us who write more in Latin, is found described

---

index of German terms: "*Wesen:* essence, estance, lorsque ce sens est surtout verbal et, par là, exclut toute référence à la quiddité. *Wesen:* ester, se réaliser historialement comme essence, sans donc que celle-ci soit donnée hors du temps comme modèle pour cette réalisation; *wesensmässig:* selon son estance; . . . *anwesen:* adester; *An-wesen:* adestance; *Anwesenheit:* présence: *Ab-wesen:* ab-sence; *ab-wesend:* ab-sent. *Unwesen:* inessentialité, désordre" (p. 225).

17. *L'imitation des modernes,* p. 271.

in a note.[18] Lacoue-Labarthe does not seek in this note (nor will I) to dissimulate the abyss opened beneath what is here named a *Witz*. Abyss, hiatus, or chaos:

> Heidegger in fact plays constantly on the drawing together (if not the pure and simple "assimilation") of *stehen* and *stellen*, even while maintaining a certain difference between them. It is as if he identified the *stal* of *stellein* (which means to equip, but also, in the middle voice, to send word, to send for) with the *sta* of *stele*, column or stele (cf. *istemi*, or, in Latin, *sto*, *stare*)—thus proceeding (as is so often the case in Heidegger) finally more by philological *Witz* than by any true etymologism . . . even though in a text very close to the one that concerns us primarily here . . . Heidegger notes, in passing, that the Greek word *thesis* (which derives from the—simple—Indo-European root *dhe*) can in German be translated at the same time by *Setzung*, *Stellung*, and *Lage*.

Desistance perhaps brings into the light of day, gives birth to, the insanity or unreason, the *anoia* against which Platonic onto-ideology, or even Heidegger's interpretation of it (pp. 101ff.), is established, installed, stabilized. But just as it is not reducible to a negative mode of the stance, it is not to be confused with madness—though in doubling or disinstalling everything that secures reason, it can resemble insanity. Madness against madness. The double bind oscillates between two madnesses, for there can also be a madness of reason, of the defensive stiffening in *assistance*, imitation, identification. Double bind between the double bind and its other. I jump here, by ellipsis, in the direction of Hölderlin and "The Caesura of the Speculative," but I will come back to this point:

> [For now] the historical scheme and the mimetology it presupposes begin slowly, vertiginously, to vacillate, to distort, and to hollow out in an abyssal manner. And if you also consider that the structure of supplementation, defining in sum the mimetic relation in general, the relation between art and nature, is in Hölderlin's eyes fundamentally a structure of *assistance* [emphasis added], that it is necessary if man is to be prevented from [*pour éviter que l'homme*] "taking flame in contact with the element," then you will not only understand what the stakes were for him in Greek art (it was a matter, finally, of dealing with a "madness" brought about by excessive imitation of the divine and speculation), but you also will understand why in the modern epoch—even though this epoch *reverses, in principle* [emphasis added], the Greek relation be-

18. See note 31, pp. 66–67.

tween art and nature—one must indeed repeat what is most Greek in the Greeks. Begin the Greeks again. That is to say, no longer be Greek at all.[19]

Desistance: mimesis or its double. Desistance, *that is to say*, and *in other words*, what it doubles and engulfs, *aletheia*. Immediately, the new "question of the subject" calls for another experience of truth. Another engagement of Heideggerian deconstruction: one that involves *playing* (mimesis plays, there is some play in it, it allows some play and forces one to play), playing (at) the return of a truth determined as *homoiosis*, adequation, similitude, or resemblance, but that is also removed, through this return that is played at and played out, from the Heideggerian interpretation (accuracy, exactitude, e-vidence) which finds itself destabilized in its turn. Destabilized not only through a movement of destabilization, but through this movement of desistance that dislodges it from any relation to a possible stance.

It will indeed be necessary to take a detour and a return path—or, rather, to follow the trajectory of a *supplementary loop*. Both *inside and outside* the path of epochality. I would be tempted to call such a loop a ring, or even a band. A certain *circulation*, as we will see, takes on the value of a prescription: (double) obligation, injunction, bond [*alliance*].

Mimesis

A *critical* question—the question of criticism, in other words, of *decision:* one cannot avoid missing mimesis as soon as one identifies it and wants to decide on its truth value. One would not find it if one had not already missed it in looking for it; that is, if one did not have faith in its identity, its existence, or its consistency. This is what Plato, Heidegger, and Girard do in very different, but finally analogous ways. In the extraordinary bidding scene that he stages between them, Lacoue-Labarthe sends off the latter two, so to speak, back to back, though not without playing (to keep to this code of games and strategies) one against the other. Girard would like to "appropriate" or "identify" mimesis. Thus, he fails to seize it; or rather, "infallibly," says Lacoue-Labarthe—the ineluctable as always—he betrays its essence precisely by conferring upon it an essence or a property, a truth to be revealed. Here the ineluctable comes down to missing the lack, or—still more

19. See "The Caesura of the Speculative," p. 222. See also what immediately follows this passage on the subject of the double bind and Hölderlin's *withdrawal* or "madness."

paradoxical—missing this lack whose structure, finally, is not negative: it is to appropriate or decide upon a proper being where there is only the im-proper or the non-proper. The latter remains all the more ungraspable in that it is not negative; it defies all those dialectics which, literally, it lets loose, liberates, induces. Such is, without being (so), mimesis as desistance.

> [The act of differentiating, appropriating, identifying, *verifying* mimesis] would without fail betray the essence or property of mimesis, if there were an essence of mimesis or if what is "proper" to mimesis did not lie precisely in the fact that mimesis has no "proper" to it, ever (so that mimesis does not consist in the improper, either, or in who knows what "negative" essence, but *ek-sists,* or better yet, "de-sists" in this appropriation of everything supposedly proper that necessarily jeopardizes property "itself"). Which would betray its essence, in other words, if the "essence" of mimesis were not precisely absolute vicariousness, carried to the limit (but inexhaustible), endless and groundless—something like an infinity of substitution and *circulation* (already we must again think of Nietzsche): the very lapse "itself" of essence. ("Typography," p. 116)

We are far from any mimetologism, from the interpretation of mimesis as imitation, or even as representation, though the re- of re-petition, at the origin of all re-presentation, has to do with desistance (p. 112). Desistance of the "same," therefore, and of the "essence"; like "proper," one can do no more than write these words in quotation marks, insofar as one must leave them in their own language.

From the passage I have just cited, let us retain for a moment the word *circulation.* It is italicized; and it will lead us toward this feigned but necessary rehabilitation of truth as *homoiosis* which no longer belongs to Heidegger's epochal interpretation. If Girard, referring mimesis to the subject of desire, interprets it as assimilation, indifferent reciprocity, and thus finally as a general instability or disinstallation, he nevertheless guards the hope of a *revelation* of mimesis. Lacoue-Labarthe seems first of all to set Heidegger against this—not the interpreter of the *Republic* for whom mimesis is also disinstallation as fall, decline, diminution of truth (of truth as *Unverstelltheit*), but the one for whom the aletheic withdrawal remains inadequate—"inadequation" itself—to any opposition of the adequate and the inadequate, of presence and absence, and thus to any revelation (for example, religious or anthropological). I cite the word "inadequation" because it bears the entire burden of this movement. This inadequation does not belong to the couple "adequate/inadequate" of truth as *homoiosis,* as it is delimited by Heidegger and situated in a manner that makes it decid-. able. Nevertheless, it is necessary that this lexicon, this simulacrum or this fiction, reassume its "right" (precisely that of mimesis) in disturb-ing the order of a history of truth as Heidegger recounts it to us. The desistance or de-stabilization of *aletheia,* within it (by or as mimesis), reintroduces an inadequation or an instability belonging to *homoiosis,* which resembles what it nevertheless displaces. Hence the vertigo, the unease, the *Unheimlichkeit.* Mimesis "precedes" truth in a certain sense; by destabilizing it in advance, it introduces a desire for *homoiosis* and makes it possible, perhaps, to account for it, as for everything that might be its effect, up to and including what is called the subject. All of this

> is not unrelated, strange as it may seem, to that determination of truth that Heidegger always endeavored to consider as secondary and derived (the determination of truth as *homoiosis,* as adequation, similitude, or re-semblance), but that would in its turn be *displaced,* in any case removed from the horizon of accuracy and of exactitude (of e-vidence), never being rigorously where one expects to see it or precisely what one wants to know. In other words, an unstable *homoiosis* that *circulates* endlessly between inadequate resemblance and resembling inadequation, con-founding memory as well as sight, upsetting the play of *aletheia* and in-deed carrying its breakdown right up to the very means of signifying its difference—so inapprehensible (imperceptible) is the agitation that this unstable *homoiosis* imparts to the Same. ("Typography," p. 121)

Along with the Same, there is the economy, the law of the *oikos* that finds itself radically destabilized by the desistance of mimesis: "any his-toric or historial economy," any guarantee of critical, theoretical, or hermeneutic reappropriation. One can say that it unsettles, finally, all discourse, be it that of a certain deconstruction, to the extent that the discourses of Girard or Heidegger could be said to belong, however "unequally" (p. 123), to deconstruction. Lacoue-Labarthe calls for a "(de)construction" "more positive than critical, something, as it were, *not very negative.* Credit should be given, in other words, to the philo-sophical even in its very lapsing, in its exposure and failure, in the de-fault of its so-called (or rather self-proclaimed) infallibility. Indeed, one should *sustain* to the end the philosophical *thesis* itself, the thesis ac-cording to which—always—truth and knowledge *are needed* [and thus lacking: *il faut* la vérité et le savoir]" (p. 123).[20]

20. Let me refer here to note 29, p. 41, concerning the word "(de)construction."

What has just happened? One deconstruction comes out of the other. By re-accentuating, *remarking* the truth of adequation, by holding it no longer simply for a secondary, inscribable, classified, decidable determination, Lacoue-Labarthe dislocates the epochal history scanned by the Heideggerian deconstruction. Not that he rehabilitates, as it stands, the truth of adequation or *homoiosis*. On the contrary, he makes an abyss appear in it, a disturbing and destabilizing power that it draws from a pre-originary mimesis. This "truth" is now no longer simply derived from an other, more original truth. Haunted by mimesis, it now plays a much more determinant role than the one to which Heidegger seemed to confine it. Hence the sort of loop or supplementary torsion, that *ring* or link which is both one more and one less in the epochal chain. This more-and-less dissimulates itself, but its effect is not simply local. It disorganizes the essential schemata—I would not venture to say the axiomatic or regulative principle—of the Heideggerian deconstruction. Thus, in a certain manner, the deconstruction signed by Lacoue-Labarthe, if the word "deconstruction" still fits, would no longer bear any filiation to that of Heidegger. Not only does it no longer resemble it, if only thereby in its style, but it ceases to pursue, develop, continue, prolong it. It interrupts it. It no longer resembles it? Certainly it does, but it merely resembles it. In truth, it interrupts it. And so far as truth is concerned, the resemblance remains troubling. Obviously, one must think together the two propositions which I have advanced here and which describe another double bind, one that might be uncovered in Lacoue-Labarthe's very writing: (1) he cannot and should not be read without Heidegger, since he never writes without pursuing an interminable reading of Heidegger; (2) and yet, what he does remains entirely different.

But aside from the double bind that holds him, by this supplementary link, to the "uncircumventable" necessity of the Heideggerian questions, another consequence imprints itself upon all of these texts. What consequence? Beyond the fundamental ontology that ordered and unified all fields and that Heidegger himself suspended at a given moment, beyond the power of gathering that continued to exert itself over an epochal history of Being, a diversity is liberated that can no longer be called a multiplicity of regions or ontological fields. This diversity now offers itself to Lacoue-Labarthe's typography, a typography that is no longer fundamental: philosophy, theater, poetics, painting, music, "auto-biography," politics. These are no longer regionally constituted domains, and one can no longer speak glibly of the essence of the poetic, of the political, the theatrical, and so on. There is no longer a central question that always stays the same.

For example: as it will later develop, particularly in "Transcendence Ends in Politics" (chapter 6), "Poétique et politique," "Histoire et *mi-mèsis*," "L'Antagonisme,"[21] and almost everywhere in *Typography I* and *II,* the political dimension of this link appears clearly. Between, on the one hand, a thought of mimesis that dislocates the Heideggerian deconstruction or disturbs the possibility of the epochal delimitations it sets to work (for example, the space of an onto-typology) and, on the other hand, the strictly, literally political interpretation of the Nietzschean or Heideggerian *text* (in the latter case, I mean by "text" Heidegger's acts-and-works), one can recognize at every step the differentiated coherence. I can't demonstrate it here. But if the genre of the introduction—why deny it?—calls for peremptory evaluations, then let us say that on these grave and formidable problems, I know no judgment more sure than Lacoue-Labarthe's, none more rigorous and prudent, more attentive both to the inconspicuous fold and to the vast sweep, the measureless breadth of what one cannot even easily continue to call a scene, a sequence, a period, or a history—a terrifying deportation, in any case, whose inordinacy still seems to defy even the hope of a judgment and a justice. And yet there is the instance, the exigency of the *il faut* I have just cited; there is philosophy and its law. This thought of de-sistance is one of the most demanding thoughts of *responsibility.* The fact that the traditional categories of responsibility no longer suffice places irresponsibility rather on the side of these categories.

How can one assume a responsibility in desistance, the responsibility *of* desistance itself? One can vary or deconstruct all the predicates of responsibility in general, yet one cannot completely reduce the *delay:* an event, a law, a call, an other are *already* there; others are there—for whom and before whom one must answer. However "free" it is supposed to be, the *response* inaugurates nothing if it does not come *after.* Prescription, typography, *ethos,* ethics, character, delay.

The (de)constitutive disappropriation of the subject, that destabilization to which Mimesis *submits* it from the "beginning"—this is what gives desistance the phenomenal form of "delay." In "Typography" the word appears twice: "delay in coming to speak," "belated-

---

21. These last three essays appear in *L'imitation des modernes. —C.F.*

ness [*retard*] (impossible to overcome) with respect to its [the child's]
'own' birth"[22]—that kind of pre-maturation which philosophical anti-
mimesis has always wanted to efface. But *Bildung* and *paideia* could
finally only confirm, by this "supplemental birth," the irreducibility of
a typo-graphical structure, of a "character" (*ethos* or *typos*) already in
subjection. One might invoke here the subject's preinscription in a
symbolic order that always precedes it. But the desistance of which
Lacoue-Labarthe speaks disturbs even the order with and in which
Lacan defines this situation: a logic of opposition and of splitting, an
identification of the Other, in short the very thing that mimesis—as
close as can be to resemblance—ruins, destabilizes, (de)constructs:

> Traversed from the very beginning by a multiple and anonymous dis-
> course (by the discourse of the other*s* and not necessarily by that of *an*
> Other), the "subject" is not so much (de)constituted in a cleavage or a
> simple *Spaltung*—that is, in a *Spaltung* articulated simply in terms of the
> opposition between the negative and presence (between absence and
> position, or even between death and identity)—as it is splintered or dis-
> persed according to the disquieting instability of the improper. Whence
> the obsession with appropriation that dominates through and through
> the entire analysis of mimesis, of mimetism, and that works to create—
> well before a concern is shown for the problematic of the lie—its full
> economic (and consequently political) bearing. ("Typography," p. 128)

22. "Typography," p. 127. A bit further on, the inevitable is precisely *delay*. See on
this point the entire paragraph that explains how "theorization, for the one who writes,
is not only inevitable, but absolutely *necessary*," and why there is always a "mirror in a
text," "the only conceivable means of overcoming the inevitable delay of the 'subject' in
relation to 'itself' and of stemming at least to some extent that inexorable lapse or failing in which something is stated, written, etc." (p. 138). Once again, the subject as thus
written (in quotation marks) is not the one Heidegger deconstructs. It is perhaps even
the one against whose desistance Heideggerian deconstruction protects itself (and seeks
relief [*assistance*]). This "subject" does not identify itself. Either with the other or with
itself. Of course, it seems to *do* nothing else, and in effect it does nothing other than
identify itself. But this very fact, the *effect* of subjectivity, bears witness to the contrary.
It proves and undergoes the contrary. If the subject identifies itself, it is because it can
never be identical, never identify itself—with itself or with the other. The condition of
possibility of identification is nothing other than its impossibility, both of them ineluctable. Like mimesis. The subject, which is thus de-subjectivized, would not have to
identify itself were it not for the desistance that makes absolute identification absolutely
impossible for it.

Delay and "prematuration," which go together—the belatedness in regard to the
subject's "own" birth—inscribe the subject in an experience of "abortion" of which I
will have to speak again.

All of the traits isolated here seem pertinent, and we are given, it seems to me, the rule governing their selection, both for Platonic discourse (one may consult the analysis that immediately follows this passage in "Typography") and for Lacanian discourse, including its "concern . . . shown for the problematic of the lie" (p. 129). And who will think that Platonism is out of date when we see Lacan denouncing in mimesis—in other words, in de-sistance—madness, feminization, hysteria?[23]

Rhuthmos

In the beginning, rhythm, says von Bühlow. Another way of marking the fact that there is no simple beginning; no rhythm without repetition, spacing, caesura, the "repeated difference-from-itself of the Same," says Lacoue-Labarthe[24]—and thus repercussion, resonance, echo, reverberation. We are constituted by this rhythm, in other words *(de-)constituted* by the marks of this "caesuraed" stamp, by this rhythmo-typy which is nothing other than the divided idiom in us of desistance. A rhythm collects us and divides us in the prescription of a character. There is no subject without the signature of this rhythm, in us and before us, before any image, any discourse, before music itself. "Rhythm would also be the condition of possibility for the subject," as Lacoue-Labarthe says in "The Echo of the Subject" (p. 195). We are "rhythmed" (pp. 202 and 206) in such a way that rhythm no longer comes to us as a predicate. The "character" it imprints or prescribes is not the attribute of the being we are, not an attribute of our existence. No, before the stance of our being-present, before its consistency, its existence, and its essence, there is rhythmic desistance.

To treat rhythm is thus not to add a chapter to the new typography of the subject. It is to think desistance as it is *written*. "Before" any specular reflexivity, before any autographical "image" and even any autographical (autobiographical or autothanatographical) "discourse." Nevertheless, the question of the *autos* and its self-relation as rhythm, traversing all of Lacoue-Labarthe's work, finds its most impressive un-

23. I refer here to the entire passage surrounding this proposition: "the 'subject' *desists* in this, and doubly so when it is a question of man (of the male)" ("Typography," p. 129).

24. See "The Echo of the Subject," p. 196. At the heart of a thought of rhythm, and as rhythm itself, "One differing in itself" (*En diapheron heauto*). Lacoue-Labarthe often cites Heraclitus, and Hölderlin citing Heraclitus.

folding in "The Echo of the Subject." Point of departure: the relation between autobiography and music, a reminder concerning "desistance" [*désistement*] and above all the necessity for deconstruction of taking on "the site of greatest resistance." Which are the proper nouns that most properly indicate this site? Heidegger, of course, and Lacoue-Labarthe makes this clear immediately. But it will be necessary to add Freud and Lacan, for the debate will finally be more strenuous and more specific with regard to them. Reik too, though the case seems still more complicated, as we will see, in this extraordinary dramaturgy where no secure place is ever won. An implacable fidelity, an exemplary probity pushes Lacoue-Labarthe to respect every fold, every overdeter-mination of the scene, *recalling one to another, both for and against*. A Lacanian quadrangulation against the Oedipal theory and thus against Freud; a thematics of voice and rhythm in Reik against specular or op-tical theoreticism, or even Freud's verbocentrism—which is again found in Lacan, whose division between the imaginary and the symbolic this thematics blurs. And finally Reik's relapse and his "theoretical failure," his subjection to Freud and the triumph of the Oedipal structure, etc.

Why does the motif of rhythm, when articulated in this manner with that of typographical inscription, possess such effective deconstruc-tive power?

Because it ties together several possibilities. It makes it possible to open a new problematic of the subject (of its "character," of what pre-scribes it or preinscribes it, also divides it according to the cut and the repetition of a desistance) by turning the Heideggerian deconstruction away from a metaphysics of subjectity—that is to say, by removing the subject from its determination by the notions of the self, conscious-ness, representation, and optical or discursive objectivity, and by thus assuming in it a psychoanalytic dimension. But simultaneously, the motif of rhythm makes it possible to deconstruct, in a certain philoso-phy of psychoanalysis, *both* the hegemony of the visual, of the image or of the specular, *and* the hegemony of discursivity—for example, that of the verbal text in music. These two hegemonies have never been in-compatible; on the contrary, they are coordinated in the history of metaphysics, which still commands these psychoanalytic theories, from Freud to Lacan. Rhythm—the spaced repetition of a percussion, the inscriptive force of a spacing—belongs neither to the visible nor to the audible, neither to "spectacular" figuration nor to the verbal represen-tation of music, even if it structures them *insensibly*. The structuration that a moment ago I called rhythmotypical or typorhythmic must remain outside the order of the sensible. It belongs to no sense. This is also why, despite appearances, "The Echo of the Subject" is less concerned with music than with rhythm in music or in dance. But to speak of the nonsensible character of rhythm is not to declare it intelligible. Cadence and caesura, rhythmotypy opens the possibility of an intelligible sense or meaning; it does not belong to it. (Nietzsche, in passing, *laterally:* "to mistake the rhythm of a sentence is to mistake the very meaning of the sentence" [p. 161].) I say *laterally* because this thought of rhythm has always *haunted* our tradition, without ever reaching the center of its concerns. And "The Echo of the Subject" is also a text on the haunting return of music, musical obsession, or rather the reverberation, the return of rhythm. This is a very ancient war. It is "normal" that rhythm be repressed, if one may say so, and even by the *theories* of repression. The pressure it exerts, and the pressure exerted upon it, form a compression, a *compulsion,* one could say, which is marked or scanned regularly by traces: all of them signaling that rhythmotypical compulsion constitutes (we should translate: de-constitutes), desists the "subject" in the knot that lies at its core, in its "soul," in its ineluctable destiny—any name you wish for the dis-location of this destinal site. An ineluctable laterality, then, on the margins of a philosophy entirely preoccupied with avoiding rhythm: Hölderlin ("All is rhythm [*Rhythmus*], the entire destiny of man is a single celestial rhythm, just as the work of art is one unique rhythm" [p. 139]), Mallarmé ("because every soul is a rhythmic knot" [p. 140]). On the margins of philosophy, before it: I'm thinking of work now well known, in particular that of Benveniste, on the use of the word *rhuthmos* (by Leucippus, for example) to designate a graphic configuration. Heidegger, indeed, recalled that Georgiades had translated *rhuthmos* by *Gepräge* (imprint, seal, type, character). This is no doubt true, but it did not prevent him from bringing the problematic of the *typos* back to the onto-typology of which I spoke earlier, and that of the subject back to his determination of the epoch of subjectity: a double reason, at a different degree of generality, for reading in "The Echo of the Subject" a new inflection in the displacement of the Heideggerian deconstruction—another knot in the supplemental loop I defined a few moments ago. But Heidegger is not at center stage in this scene, whose turbulence is, properly speaking, unimaginable (for it is also a matter of what goes beyond the image, the imaginary, the spectacular, and the specular—or renders it indeterminable). Were it not for this unimaginable, I would say of "The Echo of the Subject" that it can be read as a resonating *theater,* a series of dramatic reversals, a great tragic mythology sweeping along with it philosophers, musicians, and psychoanalysts in a constant multiplication of filiations, denials of filiation or paternity, dramas of specularity, mimetic rivalries, linked knots of double binds, transgressions and re-Oedipalizations of the law, detriangulations and retriangulations: Mahler, von Bühlow and Beethoven, Reik, Abraham, and Freud. But also Heidegger and Lacan, Rousseau, Hegel, Nietzsche, and Girard. And Groddeck and Thomas Mann and Leucippus. And Wallace Stevens. I'm undoubtedly leaving out more than one. And Lacoue-Labarthe. For let us never forget: what he says of the double bind—of which he speaks more and more in his texts and which happens to be named here at the very moment when it is a matter of a subject "who 'desists' because it must always confront at least two figures (or one figure that is *at least* double)" (p. 175) and when, in passing, he is destabilizing the Lacanian distinction between the imaginary and the symbolic—what Lacoue-Labarthe undergoes, in saying this, of the double bind, is the experience of the ineluctable. It is an experience which there can be no question of my (("I")—Lacoue-Labarthe) escaping. I write myself in writing about how things are written in this autobiographical, allo- and thanatographical theater. If I posited or proposed anything at all in this writing, it would not be merely a theory, or even a practice of the double bind according to the measure of an immense tradition—a tradition marked in its rhythm, continued and interrupted, by what all these proper nouns appear to sign. I present myself, or rather *write myself,* sign my own desistance, the impossible itself, as an experience of the double bind, the poetic experience of the double bind. Double constraint, double law, knot and caesura of a divided law, the law of the double. The knot and the caesura, the obligation and the break—that's rhythm. And is rhythm not the double law—and vice versa? The task would be to think this. And the supplementary ring of *this* deconstruction would be nothing other, would have no other modality than this double constraint that no dialectic could ever overcome.

Unless—unless the double bind as such is still too linked to opposition, contradiction, dialectic; unless it still belongs to *that kind* of undecidable that derives from calculation and from a nervous dialectical contraction. In which case, it would be necessary to think an other undecidable, to interrupt *this* double bind with a gap or a hiatus—and recognize in an arrhythmic caesura the respiration of rhythm. This necessity is still awaiting us.

But as you can see, an introductory essay cannot answer to the measure of a text like this. I am leaving the substance of things, the *background* of the scene, to subsequent readings and meticulous rereadings. As I committed myself to do, I am following only the threads of the debate Lacoue-Labarthe openly conducts with those who represent the strategic site of greatest resistance. As concerns Heidegger, we have begun to measure its dimensions. There remain Freud, Lacan, and Reik.

Freud: he admits to not having "experience" with music and musicians. When he privileges the text to the detriment of music, he prudently limits the scope of his assertions to those individuals who are not "really musicians." Even if it is formulated with some uneasiness, this limitation was frequently emphasized by Reik. It confirms the general organization of the theory, a certain logocentric theoreticism. Freud orders all interpretation around the articulation of discourse and figuration (*Darstellbarkeit,* figurability), a semiotics of verbal signifiers and visual forms.

Lacan: the least one can say is that he does not break with this theoretical structure. Lacoue-Labarthe does not propose a "critique" of his text. As always, he proceeds "with and against Lacan" (p. 174). This was already the case in *Le titre de la lettre* (written in collaboration with Nancy). But he demonstrates that what appears *theoretically* accurate and even insuperable is a certain theoreticism. The latter is inscribed in that ontology of the figure (a figural and fictional ontology) that Lacoue-Labarthe is constantly concerned with delimiting, and that submits the Lacanian recasting of Freud to the look, to the theoretical, to the specular, and to the speculative. And therefore to an onto-mimetological interpretation of mimesis. The demonstration bears principally upon the conditions under which the Oedipal triangle is open to the mythic quartet or to the "quaternary system," not to mention the theory of fictional figurality in "The Mirror Stage." The theory of narcissism (and the notion of an "imaginary death")

> "[brings] back into vigor the eidetic transcendence of Platonism whose logic Heidegger brought forth, . . . [and the mediation of this "fourth element," the imaginary death, would be constitutive] of the "giving of meaning" itself, or of what establishes, in its unverifiable truth, as Lacan said, "the measure of man." . . . In which case, and this is indeed what

Lacan stated in conclusion, the theory of narcissism is nothing other than the truth of the *Phenomenology of Mind*. ("The Echo of the Subject," pp. 171–172)

But if this quaternity remains "very Hegelian, perfectly dialectical," the entire discourse on the splitting, the alienation, the *Spaltung* of the subject remains a dialectical ontology of the lack and of negativity, a logic of opposition: the very logic, one will remember, that a thought of mimesis comes to double, disturb, and destabilize. The "loss of the subject," in the Lacanian sense, its very ek-sistence, has as its paradoxical effect a suturing, or let us say rather, an obliterating, of desistance. Here again, the experience of desistance is prey to the double bind:

> Thus, because it takes into account this discord that no speculation can dialectize because it is inscribed in the specular relation itself, it is very likely that we are dealing here with a *loss of the subject,* undermining in advance any constitution, any functional assumption, and any possibility of appropriation or reappropriation. This loss of the subject is imperceptible, however, and not because it is equivalent to a secret failing or hidden lack, but because it is strictly indissociable from, and doubles, the process of constitution or appropriation. For this reason, I have already proposed [in "L'Oblitération"] to speak of (de)constitution. But this is makeshift. What should be noted here, with and against Lacan, and going back from Lacan to Reik, is that there is a constant though muffled breakdown of the imaginary, of the resources of the imaginary. The imaginary destroys at least as much as it helps to construct. More precisely, it continually alters what it constructs. This explains, perhaps, why the subject in the mirror is first of all a subject in "desistance" (and why, for example, it will never recover from the mortal insufficiency to which, according to Lacan, its prematuration has condemned it). It explains also the delay, the inhibition, the *après-coup* effects, the deterioration—in short, everything belonging to the deadly repetition at work in more than just so-called obsessional neurosis. We are dealing here not with a pure rupture of the economic in general, but with the slow erosion of appropriation . . . The dialectic of recognition itself does not perhaps function so well, not only because every subject is on its way to death, or even because it is irremediably separated from itself (as "subject"), but simply because it comes to itself only in losing itself.
>
> The "theoretical" consequence (though at the limit of the theorizable): the figure is never *one*. Not only is it the Other, but there is no unity or stability of the figural; the imago has no fixity or proper being. There is no "proper image" with which to identify totally, no essence of the imaginary. ("The Echo of the Subject," pp. 174–175)

I want to interrupt this citation for a moment in order to emphasize the coherence of these words in their political dimension, even if the latter is less marked in "The Echo of the Subject" than, for example, in more recent texts devoted to Nietzsche or Heidegger. Less marked does not mean absent: when the stakes identified are none other than the psychoanalytic institution or identification in general, they are obviously, and immediately, political: "why would the problem of identification not be, in general, the essential problem of the political?" This is the conclusion of "Transcendence Ends in Politics" (p. 300), and the analysis leading up to it follows paths analogous to the one I have been tracing: ek-sistence (not desistance) defined by Heidegger in a still onto-typological fashion in the "Rectoral Address," an "unavowed mimetology" that would be "overdetermining politically Heidegger's thought," a certain double bind in national identification (imitation and refusal of imitation), etc. It is still a matter of an interpretation of mimesis, and of a desistance prey to the double bind inasmuch as there is no "essence of the imaginary." Lacoue-Labarthe continues immediately in "The Echo of the Subject":

> What Reik invites us to think, in other words, is that the subject "desists" because it must always confront *at least* two figures (or one figure that is *at least* double), and that its only chance of "grasping itself" lies in introducing itself and oscillating *between* figure and figure (between the artist and the scientist, between Mahler and Abraham, between Freud and Freud). And this perhaps accounts for the logic of the double bind, the "double constraint" . . . Everything seems to point to the fact that this destabilizing division of the figural (which muddles, certainly, the distinction between the imaginary and the symbolic, and broaches at the same time the negativity or absolute alterity of the "real") is precisely what is involved in the "musical obsession," connecting it, as a result, with the autobiographical compulsion itself.

Here is "what Reik invites us to think" [*ce qu'engage à penser Reik*]. Beyond Freud, already beyond Lacan, but with them, and falling back regularly under the law they represent, submitting to it anew each time he threatens to transgress it. He falls back and submits. The words "failure" and "submission" recur on almost every page of this magnificent text.[25] For what Reik invites us to think is what Lacoue-Labarthe

---

25. My emphasis: "the book [Reik's *The Haunting Melody*] is a '*theoretical failure*'" (p. 148). "It is as if Reik blurred all the divisions (often strict) to which Freud *submits*, and got stuck in that sort of hole or gap between the 'symbolic,' if you will, and the

thinks and what Reik could deliver only by not knowing how to deliver himself from it. Not that it is a matter here of a simple liberating transgression—and the conclusion of "The Echo of the Subject," once the thought has been delivered, has nothing triumphant about it. In truth, it does not conclude, except by a "perhaps": "Perhaps it is impossible to get beyond the closure of narcissism, even by shaking its specular

---

imaginary, which is not necessarily occupied by something like the 'real,' even if it be consigned to impossibility. This, of course, will not be without its consequences—even if the *theoretical failure* is certain" (p. 153).

We will see that the subject Reik ends by *submitting* to that to which Freud *submits* and to which Lacan *submits* (this is what "will not be without its consequences")—an ineluctable chain of the same submission, the same failure. A singular "rivalry" in mourning (p. 157). "[Everything] that can and should hold our attention in Reik, everything in his work that makes it more than a simple repetition of Freud—that is to say, its *'theoretical failure'* . . . Reik's *theoretical failure,* or rather, working through him, *the general failure of the theoretical*" (p. 163). The latter consists in reflecting Freud in the repetition of the Goethean motif of "repeated reflection" (*wiederholte Spiegelung*), a specular reduction of the catacoustic. "He was seeking, in short, to define a kind of 'musical' essence of the subject. Nevertheless, he was not unaware of the fact that to *submit* to the theoretical was to lose all chance of reaching his goal. This is why the theoretical 'failure' is also a 'success' and the *inhibition* will never be truly lifted" (p. 167). "The double *inhibition* at work here: both theoretical, by *submission,* and also literary, artistic" (p. 173). "We must start again, here, from Reik's theoretical failure, or rather from his theoretical *quagmire,* since 'inhibition' certainly has something to do with it. Why does he get bogged down?" (p. 176). "This is not only why his theory of autobiography is *abortive,* but also why the autobiography itself cannot be written" (p. 179). I emphasized *abort* because this word says something more in regard to the event of a singular failure: a birth, rather than an origin, takes place without taking place, a nameable subject will have been carried which is stillborn or "comes to itself only to lose itself." All of this is also carried in the "Maternal Closure" upon which the final pages open. But I also emphasized this word because it belongs to the title of a book announced by Lacoue-Labarthe (*L'avortement de la littérature*). I would have emphasized for the same reasons the word *exemplarity,* another announced title, another major motif of this thought. I extend my index (an introductory essay is a somewhat garrulous index when it is not an irremediable betrayal): "We are on the verge of the *second theoretical floundering* . . . The narrative recounting this second failure warrants our pausing for a moment" (p. 180).

What the term "floundering" [*enlisement*—also translated above as "quagmire"] adds to the term "failure" and then to "abortion" is perhaps the image of a slow sinking into a terrain whose limits are not distinct, whose sites cannot be set off against one another, whose ground is not solid. This has to do with the structure of a limit without opposition. And the slowness has to do with repetition, with the compulsion to repeat: one does not advance, one advances in place, one repeats the failure—the inhibition, rather than paralyzing, obliges one to make the same gesture, and each movement causes one to sink further. Things do not happen just once, in running up against a model" (p. 205). That is to say, the optical, theatrical, theoretical, and Oedipal model that forces Reik's relapse and the repeated failure, the "theoretical failure" which is nothing other than the failure in theory, and because of theory—the failure to theorize this very thing which as experienced in thought cannot be theorized, and which is rhythm, even more than music. This latter experience does not go beyond theory in the direction of some occult region where affect would have to be put before knowledge. On the contrary, it makes it possible to think the law of the theoretical—as such. Lacoue-Labarthe analyzes patiently, with a kind of rigorous compassion, the return of this law in Reik's text, in its theoretic-autoanalytic adventure. He recognizes in it all its daring moves, the "suspicions"[26] about Freud, the intimations of what he "invites us to think" without thinking it himself—namely the closure in which remains, and will remain, a psychoanalysis still too

---

limit, as the simple word "failure" might lead us to think. And above all, what produces and aggravates the floundering, namely this situation in which the effort to get out by lifting oneself up only mires one further, is that the repetition grows heavier, takes on the autobiographic or autoanalytic *narrative*, as lucid as it is impotent, of the floundering itself. Reik is the first to recount, in repeating it, the "initial and repeated *mistake*": "The failure of my attempt did not teach me a lesson in this direction" (p. 180). "I must admit to myself that I have failed again because I have been too ambitious" (p. 189). Lacoue-Labarthe: "It is, in fact, to *submit* purely and simply to the Freudian programming. Nonetheless, it is not quite so simple either (p. 181). And here, formalized in the most economical fashion possible, the scene of a *resistance to desistance, the scene of assistance:* "But it happens that in Reik's own text—on one occasion—these *three questions* are *assembled together* [how about that—there it is again]. Perhaps without his knowing it (though I'm not so sure), and in any case without result. As though it were already *too late,* and as though the *theoretical submission to Freud* prevented Reik from *letting go* to the point of renouncing the renunciation—a renunciation which, despite everything, determines his fragile narcissistic *recovery* [*(re)-saisie*] in the demand for paternal *assistance* (whereby theory, here Oedipus, triumphs twice over)" (p. 190). And the "too late" is still resonating.

26. The word "suspicion" itself, a "suspicion . . . hastily covered over," bears more strictly on the possibility of thinking rhythm *itself,* "before" music, almost without it. The word returns several times (pp. 203–204) in one of the striking passages on the shofar, whose three groups of notes, as Reik specifies, "[are] distinguished only by a change of rhythm" (p. 204). The shofar, Reik had remarked, is not a musical instrument; the sound it produces "is more like the bellowing of a bull than music" (p. 204), and the Jewish tradition does not attribute the invention of music to a gift from God.

But beyond the word, Reik suspects Freud—this time accusing rather than expressing an intimation—of having insisted "one-sidedly [on] the determining role of the text" (p. 182) and of having in general "neglected" the factor of the musical expression of a certain emotion in the tune" (p. 186).

Greek, in any case too Platonic (onto-typological, onto-eidetic, mimetological, etc.),[27] and into which he falls back, submitting himself to it.
He subjects himself. The movement by which he institutes himself as a
subject, in the course of an analytic autobiography "haunted" by the
return of music and rhythm, is also the movement by which he *subjects
himself* to the law represented by Freud. He subjects himself out of defense, inhibition,[28] resistance before the very thing that engages his
thinking and in which he engages our thought: a certain desistance of
the subject in the experience of the double bind and its rhythmic
(de)constitution. He cannot not avoid the unavoidable. He resists desistance, consolidates his subjecity in this subjection, this very failure,
in this renunciation, of which, as several signs manifest clearly, he was
well aware. One might say that in surrendering to this resistance, he
had to abdicate before the responsibility of thinking, of thinking that
with which he engages our thought. He, Reik, desisted before the task
that seemed incumbent upon him: to think ineluctable desistance. This
is not a moral offense, of course, but how is it possible? Read "The
Echo of the Subject." In a labyrinth which I will not try to reconstitute, and which no commentary could "double" (for its course is
unique, and all along it a logic of resonance substitutes itself for that of
the mirror: Echo undoes Narcissus, transforming in this way the whole
space of this logic, its whole temporality), I will propose merely a supplementary thread. Not in order to dramatize a reading that has strictly
no need of it, or in order to play at Ariadne. But in order to approach
somewhat the signature of Lacoue-Labarthe when he says "I" (in
quotation marks, here and there throughout his work), when he speaks
of madness, of style, of autobiography or allobiography, of death or of
music, of Reik—or of an other, for he who is named Reik in this text is

27. This would be the place for a patient examination: too Greek or too "Platonic"?
Can one connect what in a pre-"Platonic" or pre-"philosophical" Greece would not yet
be onto-typological or mimetological with the Judaic vein toward which the experience
of the shofar points? One should follow, in Lacoue-Labarthe's work, and more precisely
in this context, at the very heart of psychoanalysis, the debate between the Greek, the
German, and the Jew. It resonates everywhere. Can one say of the Jew or the German
what is said of the Greek in "Hölderlin and the Greeks": *"The Greeks' proper is inimitable
because it never took place"* (p. 246)?
28. The resistance to desistance takes the form of inhibition—its general form,
which no longer represents a clinical category or the definition of a "pathological"
symptom. Inhibition is *unavoidable.* In general. No rhythm without it. One can say the
same of the double bind. See on this point the pages already cited, in particular pp. 167
and 173.

also anyone who has linked, at the edge of madness (what is that exactly, the edge—the *bord?*), the autobiographical adventure, and his
doubles, and the other, and death, to the musical obsession (Rousseau,
Nietzsche), to the concern with rhythm (Hölderlin, Mallarmé, Nietzsche again). Reik, and all of them—these are Lacoue-Labarthe, you'll
say, rushing to identify the identifications; and if that's the case, I wish
you luck if some day you hope to call a halt to it in this genealogical
chain. But no, Lacoue-Labarthe could not *read* Reik as he did except
insofar as he broke the identification, or knew how to follow him while
always removing the barriers to which the other's resistance was cling-
ing. And each time he removes one of these limits, he explains its
source and its mechanism, and then its ineluctable return. In this
gesture, and by this rhythm—you'll be able to verify this—Lacoue-
Labarthe is at every instant as close and as far from Reik as he could
possibly be. And he tells you everything you need in order to think the
law of this paradox.

He even has a name for the law of the paradox: it is the *hyperbologic.*[29]

29. This *hyperbologic* is expressly defined in "Diderot: Paradox and Mimesis" (for example, p. 260) and in "The Caesura of the Speculative" (for example, p. 233). It programs the inevitable effects of a "logic" of mimesis. In this precise context, where the
question concerns the actor, this hyperbologic regularly converts the gift of everything
into the gift of nothing, and this latter into the gift of the thing itself. "The gift of
impropriety"—in other words, the "gift of mimesis"—is the "gift of general appropriation and of presentation" (p. 260). But this is not, as we see, a "context" or an "example" among others. It is a matter of appropriation and (de-)propriation in general.
The play of the *de-*, on which I have been working since the beginning of this essay,
might well belong to this hyperbologic. Without being negative, or being subject to a
dialectic, it both organizes and disorganizes what it appears to determine; it belongs to
and yet escapes the order of its own series. What I said in starting out about desistance
would hold equally well for the hyperbologic of *disinstallation* ("Typography," pp. 120
and 133), *(de)constitution* ("*L'Oblitération*," "Typography," pp. 259 and 260; "The
Echo of the Subject," p. 174), *disarticulation* ("The Caesura of the Speculative,"
p. 234; "Hölderlin and the Greeks," p. 245), *disappropriation* [*(dé)propriation*] ("Typography," pp. 133 and 135; "Diderot: Paradox and Mimesis," p. 265; "The Caesura of the
Speculative," p. 231; "Hölderlin and the Greeks," p. 245), and *deconstruction* ("Typography," pp. 65 and 123; "The Echo of the Subject," p. 141; "The Caesura of the Speculative," pp. 212, 234). Taking into account the supplementary ring of which I have
spoken, the meaning of "deconstruct"—a word which Lacoue-Labarthe says elsewhere
he does not consider "in the least 'worn out'" (*L'imitation des modernes*, p. 282)—bears
sometimes the sense of a task, sometimes that of an event, of what occurs in any case in
a "practical" situation, for example of Hölderlin (cf. "The Caesura of the Speculative,"
p. 221). I have remarked that Lacoue-Labarthe sometimes writes "*(de)construction*"
("Typography," p. 123).

At this moment, when I have to cut things short, too late or too early, I'll take up only one example: the *caesura*. There is no rhythm without caesura. And yet, as Hölderlin reminds us, the caesura "itself" must be "antirhythmic" (p. 234), even arrythmic. This interruption does not have the dialectical cadence of a relation between rhythm and non-rhythm, the continuous and the discontinuous, etc. It interrupts alternation, "the constraint of *opposition* in general" (p. 212), dialectic and the speculative, even the double bind (pp. 236ff.) when it retains an oppositional form. It is ineluctable—and it does not spare avoidance:

> It prevents [*éviter*] (a protective gesture, which does not necessarily mean a "ritualistic" one) the racing oscillation, *panic,* and an orientation toward this or that pole. It represents the active neutrality of the interval between [*entre-deux*]. This is undoubtedly why it is not by chance that the caesura is, on each occasion, the empty moment—the absence of "moment"—of Tiresias's intervention: that is to say, of the intrusion of the prophetic word. ("The Caesura of the Speculative," p. 235)

When in Sophoclean tragedy it marks the withdrawal of the divine and the turning back of man toward the earth, the caesura, gap or hiatus, plays at and undoes mourning. A *Trauerspiel* plays at mourning. It doubles the *work* of mourning: the speculative, dialectic, opposition, identification, nostalgic interiorization, even the double bind of imitation. But it doesn't avoid it.

Gap or hiatus: the open mouth. To give and receive. The caesura sometimes takes your breath away. When luck is with it, it's to let you speak.

Jacques Derrida

I

Typography

Almost everywhere it was madness which prepared the way for the new idea, which broke the spell of a venerated usage and superstition. Do you understand why it had to be madness which did this? Something in voice and bearing as uncanny and incalculable as the demonic moods of the weather and the sea and therefore worthy of a similar awe and observation? Something that bore so visibly the sign of total unfreedom as the convulsions and froth of the epileptic, which seemed to mark the madman as the mask and speaking-trumpet of a divinity? Something that awoke in the bearer of a new idea himself reverence for and dread of himself and no longer pangs of conscience and drove him to become the prophet and martyr of his idea?—while it is constantly suggested to us today that, instead of a grain of salt, a grain of the spice of madness is joined to genius, all earlier people found it much more likely that wherever there is madness there is also a grain of genius and wisdom—something "divine," as one whispered to oneself. Or rather: as one said aloud forcefully enough. "It is through madness that the greatest good things have come to Greece," Plato said, in concert with all ancient mankind.

Have you not observed that imitations, if continued from youth far into life, settle down into habits and second nature in the body, the speech, and the thought?

Yes, indeed, said he.

We will not then allow our charges, whom we expect to prove good men, being men, to play the parts of women and imitate a woman young or old wrangling with her husband, defying heaven, loudly boasting, fortunate in her own conceit, or involved in misfortune and possessed by grief and lamentation—still less a woman that is sick, in love, or in labor.

Most certainly not, he replied.

Nor may they imitate slaves, female and male, doing the offices of slaves.

No, not that either.

Nor yet, as it seems, bad men who are cowards and who do the opposite of the things we just now spoke of, reviling and lampooning one another, speaking foul words in their cups or when sober and in other ways sinning against themselves and others in word and deed after the fashion of such men. And I take it they must not form the habit of likening themselves to madmen either in words nor yet in deeds. For while knowledge they must have both of mad and bad men and women, they must do and imitate nothing of this kind.

Most true, he said.

Well, then, neighing horses and lowing bulls, and the noise of rivers and the roar of the sea and the thunder and everything of that kind—will they imitate these?

Nay, they have been forbidden, he said, to be mad or to liken themselves to madmen.

Let us go a step further: all superior men who were irresistibly drawn to throw off the yoke of any kind of morality and to frame new laws had, *if they were not actually mad,* no alternative but to make themselves or pretend to be mad . . . "How can one make oneself mad when one is not mad and does not dare to appear so?"—almost all the significant men of ancient civilisation have pursued this train of thought . . . Who would venture to take a look into the wilderness of the bitterest and most superfluous agonies of soul, in which probably the most fruitful men of all times have languished! To listen to the sighs of these solitary and agitated minds: "Ah, give me madness, you heavenly powers! Madness, that I may at last believe in myself! Give deliriums and convulsions, sudden lights and darkness, terrify me with frost and fire such as no mortal has ever felt, with deafening din and prowling figures, make me howl and whine and crawl like a beast: so that I may only come to believe in myself! I am consumed by doubt, I have killed the law, the law anguishes me as a corpse does a living man: if I am not *more* than the law I am the vilest of all men. The new spirit which is in me, whence is it if it is not from you? Prove to me that I am yours; madness alone can prove it."

Nietzsche, *Daybreak,* and Plato, *Republic**

In the long run, the question posed here is that of "philosophical madness."

What can be said, *for example,* about Rousseau's madness—or Nietzsche's? Indeed, what about Hegel (who "believed he was going mad") or even Kant? Or Comte? Or probably others still, even if they have not passed as mad, or if it is not entirely customary for us to consider them fully as "philosophers"?

* *Epigraph:* The first and third sections are from Friedrich Nietzsche, *Daybreak,* no. 14 ("The Significance of Madness in the History of Morality"), trans. R. J. Hollingdale (Cambridge: Cambridge University Press, 1982), pp. 14–16. The second section is from Plato's *Republic* (III, 395d–396b), trans. Paul Shorey, in *The Collected Dialogues,* ed. Edith Hamilton and Huntington Cairns (Princeton: Princeton University Press, 1961). All subsequent citations of Plato in this essay are from this volume.

To begin to formulate our question, then, provisionally, and still from a distance, we ask: What can be said about madness when it touches (on) philosophy? When it seizes a philosopher or when a philosopher lets himself be taken by it, when he lets himself succumb to it, fall into it—*go under?* Is this an "accident" or the effect of a necessity, of a "destiny"? Is it to be understood "empirically" (in whatever form: psychological, historical, sociological, and so on) or must one go in search of its cause—that is to say, its *reason*—within philosophy itself? And in either case, what is involved? The same thing, the same *concept* of madness? Is it possible to decide?

Is it possible, *for example,* that there is some philosophical predestination to madness, some philosophical predetermination of madness, evidence of which might be found in the fact that it should be more toward its end (or what it thinks as such) that philosophy, pushed to its limit, exhausted, unsettled, exasperated, was forced to undergo such a trial? And what would be the value of this kind of hypothesis? What would it involve, above all, in relation to philosophy?

These are classic questions, now classical—accepted. Which does not mean that they are for this reason pertinent. Far from it. But it is nevertheless indispensable that we hold on to them—that we not rush to overturn them and imagine that, by simply deciding to, one can change questions. In fact, there is even some likelihood, some chance, that the "thing itself" depends on it. Perhaps, after all, madness itself springs from certain questions, and even—why not?—from some of *these* questions (from the presupposed, *for example,* of some of these questions).

This is the reason for our asking, in short (indeed, it is hard to see how we could do anything else): how can we read, *for example,* how can we place or situate, how can we "recognize" (we are not saying "interpret") the opening lines of Rousseau's *Confessions* ("I fashion an enterprise which has no previous example . . .") or *Dialogues?* Or Kant's last texts? Or Schopenhauer—and not only the "last" Schopenhauer? Or Nietzsche's writings—*all* of Nietzsche's writings from the year 1888?

What should we do, *for example,* with *Ecce Homo?* or even with just *Ecce Homo*'s prologue?

And with this, *for example,* within the prologue?

Seeing that before long I must confront humanity with the most difficult demand ever made of it, it seems indispensable to me to say *who I am.* Really, one should know it, for I have not left myself "without testimony." But the disproportion between the greatness of my task and the *smallness* of my contemporaries has found expression in the fact that one has neither heard nor even seen me. I live on my own credit; it is perhaps a mere prejudice that I live . . . Under these circumstances I have a duty against which my habits, even more the pride of my instincts, revolt at bottom—namely, to say: *Hear me! For I am such and such a person. Above all, do not mistake me for someone else! . . .*

I am, for example, by no means a bogey, or a moralistic monster—I am actually the very opposite of the type of man who so far has been revered as virtuous. Between ourselves, it seems to me that precisely this is part of my pride. I am a disciple of the philosopher Dionysus; I should prefer to be even a satyr to being a saint . . .

Among my writings my *Zarathustra* stands to my mind by itself. With that I have given mankind the greatest present that has ever been made to it so far. This book, with a voice bridging centuries, is not only the highest book there is, the book that is truly characterized by the air of the heights—the whole fact of man lies *beneath* it at a tremendous distance—it is also the *deepest,* born out of the innermost wealth of truth . . . Here no "prophet" is speaking, none of those gruesome hybrids of sickness and will to power whom people call founders of religions. Above all, one must *hear* aright the tone that comes from this mouth . . . Such things reach only the most select. It is a privilege without equal to be a listener here. Nobody is free to have ears for Zarathustra . . . Not only does he speak differently, he also *is* different . . .

Now I go alone, my disciples. You, too, go now, alone. Thus I want it . . .

One repays a teacher badly if one always remains nothing but a pupil. And why do you not want to pluck at my wreath?

You revere me; but what if your reverence *tumbles* one day? Beware lest a statue slay you! . . .

Now I bid you lose me and find yourselves; and only *when you have all denied me* will I return to you.[1]

What should we do with this?

What are we to make of it if we refuse to think—of course—that there could be only pure incoherence or insanity in these lines, but also when we have some reason to be suspicious of all the "demagogic," if not "psychagogic," phraseology with which one claims today—without, it is true, too great a risk—to speak in the name of madness? What are we to make of it if, *for example,* (fascinated) fear and incomprehension are indissociably at play there?

1. Friedrich Nietzsche, *Ecco Homo,* in *Basic Writings of Nietzsche,* trans. Walter Kaufmann (New York: Random House, 1968), pp. 673–676.

We are proposing a *task* that is obviously immense—even should we attempt, no doubt in vain, to reduce it to a "reading" of Nietzsche—and, in all likelihood, inexhaustible. We will be content, therefore, to explore the terrain. Not in order to mark it out, to circumscribe or describe it, to survey it, or to go around it in advance—in the now dominant style of the proprietor (whose desire to "construct," as we know, can hardly be dissimulated); for there is nothing "here" that can be delimited or can serve as ground(s)—*a fortiori* that one could appropriate. Instead, we will explore the terrain merely to go into it a bit, to clear approaches, to begin, at most, to break a path: to see what it leads to, what happens (where we find ourselves, if we find where we're going . . .). An essay, let's say. And without deceiving ourselves too much, without forgetting that we will certainly have to begin again, in a different way, (at least) another time, by other means, following different approaches, and so on—it should become evident that this goes without saying.

Onto-typo-logy

Wanting to be what we are not, we come
to believe ourselves something other
than what we are, and this is how we
become mad.

—Rousseau, Preface to *La nouvelle
Héloïse*

This is why I ("I") will start from a precise point.

And perhaps since we have just had a sample of it, a certain "doubling" of Nietzsche.

That is, in order to limit the field of investigation (and in order not to have to go back too far), I will start from a certain relationship, woven explicitly, in *Ecce Homo,* by the author of the text (he who says "I," signs with his name, presents and exposes *himself,* recounts his life and work, retraces his origins, claims his absolute *originality,* complains of not being recognized for what he is, judges himself incommensurable with anyone else, and so on) with "Zarathustra"—the text so entitled, of course, but also "Zarathustra himself, as type" (if not simply *Zarathustra himself*)—whose "story," he (the author) makes it his duty to "tell" (the genesis, therefore, *and* the construction, *and* the encounter), whom he is bent on distinguishing from any other figure we might think of as analogous (here again, it should not be a matter of

"confusion"), whom he constantly cites in support of his "own" statements, or behind whom he constantly takes cover (whom he constantly
enlists, if you will, as his spokesman), until it finally comes out—"Have
I been understood?"—that, in "what precedes" (and this could finally
designate the entire book, all its teaching), the author, himself, has not
said "a word" that he had not already said "five years ago through the
mouth of Zarathustra."

On this strange relationship, much more complex than it might appear, and than it appears in *Ecce Homo*—much more complex, too,
than certain earlier texts allowed us to foresee: such "youthful" sketches
as *Euphorion* (or even *Empedocles*), or the prologue-epilogue of *The
Wanderer and his Shadow*—on this (more or less) false "identification,"
constantly played at (simulated) and dis-played [*dé-jouée*], on the way
in which Nietzsche "himself" posits this relationship (the way he explains himself and does not explain himself, it has been said, only half
justifies it), on what this relationship entails, moreover, on the eve of
the "breakdown," in the way of "delirium" and of an unsettling "exaltation"—on all of this, the commentaries are innumerable. That is to say,
too numerous.

I will therefore restrict myself, to sharpen my focus still further, to
considering only one of them—one that, to be honest, is not quite a
"commentary." In fact, it is a matter of a "simple" ("double") remark
that Erwin Rohde made upon receiving the first part of *Zarathustra,* a
remark that, although made "five years" prior to the time of *Ecce Homo*'s
composition (the letter, since it is one, is dated December 22, 1883), is
not, for this reason, any less "penetrating." It must be said that friendship, a mixture of complicity and rivalry, plays its part here. This must
be said because everything, in these questions, is *biographical.*

Here is what Rohde says. It consists of two very brief statements:
"The Persian sage is no doubt yourself . . . Plato created his Socrates
and you your Zarathustra." The whole interest of this remark obviously lies in its "philological" character. But, as always happens with
the obvious, this will take some time to demonstrate . . .

That Rohde should have recognized Nietzsche's "identification"
with Zarathustra, that he should thus have "unmasked" Zarathustra
(or "Nietzsche") in passing, is, after all, scarcely surprising. By this, I
mean that it was neither very difficult, nor very risky, nor, under this
form at least, of very great reach. But that he should have then in turn
identified this "identification," and related it back to the Platonic *model*—
this is much more surprising. In principle, Nietzsche should have been

expecting it. We can at least suspect that he was neither altogether in-nocent nor altogether ignorant in the matter.² Moreover, it is probable that Rohde himself knew, in one way or another, that he had a chance of hitting upon something. As proof, we have the response that Nie-tzsche made two months later, that is to say, the silence or "denega-tion" that he opposed to Rohde—who in this instance was styled a *homo literatus:* "My Zarathustra is finished in its three acts. It is a sort of abyss of the future—something to make one shudder, especially the joy in it—Everything in it is my own, without model, comparison, or precursor [*Es ist alles drin mein Eigen, ohne Vorbild, Vergleich, Vorgänger*]; a person who has once lived in it will return to the world with a differ-ent face."³

2. Compare, for example, in addition to the courses devoted to Plato, the lectures of 1874–1876 on the history of Greek literature, where Nietzsche, ranking highest the "great art" of "the writer Plato" (reversing, in this way, some of his previous proposi-tions, such as those of the *Birth of Tragedy*), also explicitly mentions the existence of a type of dialogue—in the tradition of *sokratoi logoi* inaugurated, according to Aristotle, by Plato—called *magikos*. The form, he observes, is one that Aristotle himself, among others, supposedly engaged in (this is in fact what Diogenes Laertes tells us) and in which it was customary to represent Socrates meeting with an Oriental "magi," princi-pally Zoroaster. Allow me to refer here to my own "La Dissimulation" (in *Nietzsche aujourd'hui,* vol. 2 [Paris: Union Générale d'Editions, 1973], pp. 9–36).

3. Letter of February 22, 1884. It is certainly not insignificant that this letter begins by turning round the motif of solitude and that of lost friendship: "In reading your last letter, . . . it was as if you pressed my hand and looked at me sadly—sadly, as if you wanted to say: 'How is it possible that we have so little in common and live as in differ-ent worlds! And yet once—.' And that is how it is, friend, with all the people I love: everything is *over,* it is the past, forbearance; we still meet, we talk, so as not to be silent; we still exchange letters, so as not to be silent. But the look in the eyes tells the truth: and this look tells me (I hear it often enough!), 'Friend, Nietzsche, you are completely alone now!'"

Similarly, it is not insignificant that again in the same letter, after having rejected the idea of a resemblance or a kinship between Zarathustra and anyone whomsoever (if not with himself—and, as we know, he will *also* speak of Zarathustra, or of *Zarathustra,* as his "child"), Nietzsche immediately moves to an apology for his own style that pre-figures, almost literally, his "last declarations," especially those of *Ecco Homo:* "But I must not speak of this. From you, however, as a *homo literatus,* I will not keep back a confession—it is my theory that with this *Zarathustra* I have brought the German lan-guage to a state of perfection. After *Luther* and Goethe, a third step had to be taken—look and see, old chum of mine, if vigor, flexibility, and euphony have ever consorted so well in our language. Read Goethe after reading a page of my book—and you will feel that that "undulatory" quality peculiar to Goethe as a draftsman was not foreign to the shaper of language also. My line is superior to his in strength and manliness, without becoming, as Luther's did, loutish. My style is a dance, a play of symmetries—and in a

The odds are that Rohde didn't recognize this "different face." Just as it is likely that he didn't understand the first thing about either this "abyss" or this terrifying "joy." In general, these are the kinds of things of which one "understands" nothing—for want, perhaps, of having *heard* them [*entendu*]. But, for the moment at least, the essential does not lie here. Better to stay with Rohde and, let us say, his "intuition" (if not his suspicion) concerning "Zarathustra."

Of what interest is it exactly?

Or, if you prefer, what exactly is a "philological" interest?

It is first of all—and no doubt essentially—a *philosophical* interest.

By reintroducing Plato—and Socrates—where most of the time they are not expected, Rohde's remark, however "formal" it may be, clearly touches "Nietzsche's thought" at its very center, or at least what passes for it. In any case, it appears to entail, at least if we draw out all its consequences, enough to challenge the account sanctioned by Nietzsche himself of his relation to Platonism and, consequently, to philosophy as a whole: that is, the well-known version of Nietzsche's *inversion* of Platonism, of the *Umdrehung des Platonismus*. It is true that in these matters things can never be pinned down so simply; and the weapon here is double-edged. For inasmuch as a reversal (as Heidegger exhaustively repeated) is inevitably inscribed and always remains caught within the very thing of which it is the reversal, bringing it back again, it is also clear, if we do in fact draw out all the consequences, that such a challenge is nothing other, when all is said and done, than a kind of confirmation. The reversal, as we also know, folds and closes upon itself indefinitely. Failing any "accident," it is an endless *circulation*—a movement, moreover, wherein (and according to which) the eternal return, under any of its "aspects" whatsoever, is always strictly *implicated*.

But is this so certain? Or so clear?

For this is just the point: that between Zarathustra and Socrates (or Nietzsche and Plato) there should be, there could be, this disconcerting (if not truly concerted) *analogy* that Rohde uncovers and Nietzsche denies—this is something that Heidegger, first of all, should recognize

---

leap it passes beyond them and mocks them. This enters the very vowels. Forgive me! I shall take care not to confess this to anyone else, but you did once (I think you are alone in this) express delight in my language. In any case I have remained a poet, in the most radical sense of the word—although I have tyrannized myself a great deal with the antithesis of poetry.—Ah, friend, what a crazy, silent life I live! So alone, alone! So 'child'-less." Excerpts from *Selected Letters of Friedrich Nietzsche,* trans. Christopher Middleton (Chicago: University of Chicago Press, 1969), pp. 219–221.

without difficulty, he who carried the interpretation of the Nietzschean reversal as far as possible and who so rigorously delimited its place, function, and consequences within (the history of) metaphysics itself. Everything considered, it is even incontestable that the existence of this analogy should reinforce such an interpretation. And all the more so— in relation to what concerns me here at least—in that if Heidegger, despite his very great mistrust of the way in which the concept of madness has been used (or can be used) in relation to Nietzsche, *assigns* the so-called "madness of Nietzsche" somewhere, it is indeed in linking it plainly, *essentially,* to the *Umdrehung,* to the reversal of Platonism, at least insofar as this reversal ends and completes itself by "twisting" (*Herausdrehung*) free from Platonism.[4]

But this is not the case: the possibility of this analogy clearly does not interest Heidegger. We can never, unless I am mistaken, find the least allusion, even the least bit direct or "positive," to a hypothesis of this kind. What we find instead (and supposing we had reasons to look for it), would resemble more, though always in an implicit way, a deliberate refusal to consider it.

Which is what happens at least twice.

It happens a first time when Heidegger attempts to characterize the type of figure (*Gestalt*) that Zarathustra represents—and if there is a search for an "antecedent," it is Parmenides (and not Plato) who is summoned:

> Who is Nietzsche's Zarathustra? The question now is: who is this teacher [*dieser Lehrer*]? [Heidegger here takes Zarathustra as the spokesman (*Fürsprecher*) for Dionysus and the *Lehrer* of the Eternal Return and of the Overman.] Who is this figure [*Gestalt*] who appears within metaphysics at its stage of completion? Nowhere else in the history of Western metaphysics is the essential figure of its respective thinkers actually poeticized [*gedichtet*] in this way, or, more precisely and literally, thought out: fictionally thought out [*er-dacht*]; nowhere else, except at the beginning of Western thought in Parmenides, and there only in veiled contours.[5]

4. Compare *Nietzsche,* vol. 1: *The Will to Power as Art,* trans. David Farrell Krell (New York: Harper and Row, 1979), p. 202: "During the time the overturning of Platonism became for Nietzsche a twisting free of it, madness befell him. Heretofore no one at all has recognized this reversal as Nietzsche's final step; neither has anyone perceived that the step is clearly taken only in his final creative year (1888)."

5. Heidegger, "Who Is Nietzsche's Zarathustra?" trans. Bernard Magnus, in *The New Nietzsche: Contemporary Styles of Interpretation* (New York: Dell, 1977), p. 77. *Er-*

It happens a second time, even more indirectly (and perhaps, here, one must push things a bit), when Heidegger attempts to *distinguish* Socrates within the succession of Western thinkers. The text has been pretty much worked over in the light of other themes. Moreover, it is written entirely in reference to a note of Nietzsche's, itself well known (although enigmatic), and offers essentially—though this is against Nietzsche—a commentary upon it (but we know that it is necessary to interpret Nietzsche, as one would any great thinker, "against himself").[6]

Heidegger speaks here of the withdrawal, of the turning aside of "what gives us to think":

> Whenever man is properly drawing that way [in the direction of the withdrawal], he is thinking—even though he may still be far away from what withdraws, even though the withdrawal may remain as veiled as ever. All through his life and right up to his death, Socrates did nothing else than place himself in this draft, this current, and maintain himself in it. This is why he is the purest thinker of the West. This is why he wrote nothing. For anyone who begins to write out of thoughtfulness must inevitably be like those people who run to seek refuge from any draft too strong for them. An as yet unwritten history still keeps the secret why all great Western thinkers after Socrates, with all their greatness, had to be such fugitives. Thinking entered into literature . . .[7]

From one text to the next, at least in regard to the question raised here (I am only rereading them in fact within this perspective), the lesson, as always, is perfectly clear. For if Zarathustra is a *figure,* in the strongest sense (and we will see in a moment that for Heidegger it is a historical necessity that commits metaphysics, in the process of completing itself, since Hegel, to (re)presenting itself (*sich darstellen*) in figures, as well as to representing (*vorstellen*) transcendence, from the perspective of the "subjective" determination of Being, as the form, figure, imprint, type of a *humanity*: Nietzsche's Zarathustra, Jünger's Worker, even Rilke's Angel)[8]—it is also true that such "figuration" is

---

denken is here translated as "fictionally thought out" (more literally, "fictioned in thought": *fictionner par la pensée*) not only to suggest the most banal meaning of the word in German (to image, to invent, to fabricate, etc.) but also in order to respect a certain proximity of this word to (or a certain distancing from) *Er-dichten* (not *Dichten*)—in short—to the *act of fictioning* [*fictionner*] that will appear further on.

6. *Nietzsche,* vol. 1, p. 24.

7. Heidegger, *What Is Called Thinking?* trans. J. Glenn Gray (New York: Harper and Row, 1968), p. 17.

8. Should we add Freud's Oedipus and Marx's Proletarian? This is a question that one can always cast out, when the occasion arises, in order to see where it will finish, if it

programmed from the most distant sources of metaphysics (in this instance, since Parmenides, but we will understand soon enough, even if this causes some difficulties, that Plato, in a certain way, is not without some responsibility here)—and in the same way, on the contrary, Socrates, insofar as he is free of precisely any compromise with writing and literature, *is not a figure,* and consequently could not ever be confused, *as such,* with, for example, the (re)presentation that Plato has given him: that is, could never be identified with (or as) a construction, indeed, as Rohde suggests, a "creation," of Plato. If Heidegger refuses to consider even the least analogy between Zarathustra and Socrates, or the least literary rivalry between Nietzsche and Plato, it is finally, even though Plato should already belong to the space of literature, for the simple reason that from the point of view (if it is one) of the history of Being, there is no common measure between Socrates *himself* and the rest (including Plato's Socrates).

Which does not mean that a common measure would not exist in general between the Greeks and the Moderns. On the contrary. In whatever way the exact moment of thought's "entry" into literature might be determined (does it begin with Parmenides or with Plato?), the *Er-denken* of the last figure of metaphysics is not unrelated to that of its initial figure, and Nietzsche will never have done anything more, practically, than "unveil" a project hidden in Parmenides. In any case, we are fully aware that if there are marked periods, epochs, even turning points in the history of metaphysics, there is in reality—and for the reason, no doubt, that there is no history but that of the Same—only one *same* history (of metaphysics): this, the historial, presupposing the radical *heterogeneity* of Being within its *own* (un)veiling to be the Same (not the identical), is strictly *homogeneous.*

Under these conditions, then, why not recognize, or why refuse to recognize, the hypothesis of a relation between Nietzsche and Plato of the kind suggested by Rohde? What is it that here *restrains* Heidegger? Or even, possibly (does one ever know what he knows . . .), what is it

---

ever will. As concerns the Heideggerian problematic of the *Gestalt,* the essential references are, in addition to the commentary of Hegel's Introduction to the *Phenomenology of Spirit* (*Hegel's Concept of Experience,* trans. Kenley Dove [New York: Harper and Row, 1970]): the commentary on Rilke in "What Are Poets For?" in *Poetry, Language, Thought,* trans. Albert Hofstadter (New York: Harper and Row, 1971), pp. 89–142; the discussion with Jünger in *The Question of Being,* trans. William Kluback and Jean T. Wilde (New York: Twayne, 1958); and, of course, the lecture "The Question of Technology," in *"The Question Concerning Technology" and Other Essays,* trans. William Lovitt (New York: Harper and Row, 1977), pp. 3–35. I will return to this question shortly.

that alarms him? What could there be in such a relation that would render it questionable or superficial with respect to the depth and the level of seriousness at which the problematic of the figure is to be reached?

Heidegger's refusal, if there is one, is all the more surprising here because whenever the question of the *figure* arises, it is indeed Plato—that is, the Platonic determination of Being—that is called into question. Whether directly, as in the epistolary dialogue with Jünger, or indirectly (and assuming that the essence of "European nihilism" is already known), as in the commemoration of Rilke. Why Plato? For this reason, above all: that the *Gestalt*—the advent of the figure as the proper site for the unfolding of the most modern metaphysics—*presupposes* the Platonic determination of Being as *eidos/idea*.

Heidegger explains this quite thoroughly to Jünger.

Not (as some have rumored, imagining that such rumors could serve as an argument) in order to wrest Jünger, in a vaguely complicitous gesture, from the space of nihilism; but, on the contrary, in order to mark the fact that he belongs fundamentally to nihilism, though he claims to have "crossed the line" or claims to have "surpassed" it. And this by recognizing in *work* and the *figure of the worker*, despite whatever step Jünger might have taken beyond Nietzsche's "going astray" in the "biologico-anthropological," the decisive feature of the will to power as the "total character," in the modern epoch (in the epoch of technology), of the "reality of the real."[9]

But it is precisely because he mobilizes, if we may say so, the concepts of *work, figure* (or *form*), and *mastery* (or *domination*)—*The Worker* (*Der Arbeiter*), one of the two books by Jünger that Heidegger points to here, is subtitled *Mastery and the Figure* (or *Domination and Form/Die Herrschaft und die Gestalt*)—that Jünger remains caught within the very language and the articulation of the "master-words" of nihilism. That is to say, of metaphysics. The concept of *Gestalt*, in particular, although Jünger opposes it to the "simple idea" (in the modern sense of *perceptio*, of the representation by a subject), retains within itself, insofar as the figure is accessible only in a *seeing* (a *Sehen*), the essential element of the "optical," "eidetic," or "theoretical" overdetermination that is constraining throughout the whole of Western ontological discourse. And especially since Plato. Indeed, what is at stake in Jünger's *Sehen* is precisely that *seeing* "which the Greeks call *idein*, a

9. See *The Question of Being*, p. 59.

word that Plato uses for a look that views not that changeable thing which is perceivable through the senses but that immutable thing, Being, the *idea*."[10] *Gestalt*, therefore, is the final name of the Idea, the last word designating Being as "theorized" in its difference from beings—that is to say, transcendence, or the meta-physical as such. Thus, there is not the least accident in the fact that, just as Plato happens to think of what produces, in transcendence or in transcendental production (in the *Her-vor-bringen* of the pre-sent (the *An-wesende*) by presence (*Anwesen*), of being by Being), in terms of the "type" or the "seal" (*tupos*), Jünger thinks "the relation of form to what it brings into form," *Gestaltung* (figuration), as "the relation between stamp and impression" (*Stempel/Prägung*).[11] In both, and answering to the eidetic ontology as such, to onto-ideo-logy, there appears in its contours what must be called, in all rigor, an *onto-typo-logy*. With the difference that in Jünger, impression (as *Prägen*) is interpreted in the "modern" sense as "bestowing meaning"—the *Gestalt* is the bestowal of meaning. This is why "the metaphysical representation belonging to *The Worker* distinguishes itself from the Platonic and even from the modern, with the exception of Nietzsche."[12] For the figure, as the bestowal of meaning—*in order* to be the bestowal of meaning—must be the figure of a *humanity*. To man as figure belongs the role of giving meaning—to man, that is, as worker. Which amounts to saying that onto-typo-logy in Jünger still presupposes, at the foundation of being in its totality, a humanity already determined as *subjectum*: "the preformed figural presence [*die vorgeformte gestalthafte Praesenz*] of a type of man [*Menschenschlag*] (*typus*) forms [*bildet*] the most extreme subjectivity which comes forth in the fulfillment of modern metaphysics and is (re)presented [*dargestellt*] by its thinking."[13] In this way, we can explain why onto-typo-logy, thus inflected, that is, thus "reversed" and brought back to the "subjectal" sphere, finally proceeds from a "modification of

10. Ibid., p. 51.

11. Ibid., p. 53. As concerns Plato, Heidegger here makes reference to the *Theaetetus*, 192–194b.

12. *The Question of Being*, p. 55.

13. Ibid., p. 55. "The appearance of the metaphysical figure [*Gestalt*] of man," says Heidegger on the following page, "as the source of what gives or presents meaning is the final consequence of establishing the essence of man as the determining and measuring [*massgebend*] *subjectum*." That is to say, the final consequence of Cartesianism, of the Cartesian "reversal." This is essentially why "the metaphysical seeing of the figure [*Gestalt*] of the worker corresponds to the projection of the essential figure [*Gestalt*] of Zarathustra within the metaphysics of the will to power" (p. 55).

transcendence," that is, from the transformation of transcendence into "rescendence" (*Reszendenz* or *Rückstieg*), wherein transcendence itself founders and disappears: "A rescendence of this kind, through the figure, takes place in such a way that its state of being present is represented [*sich . . . vorstellt*] and is present again in the imprint of its stamping."[14] A representation that is the mastery/domination of the worker as a "new and special kind of will to power."[15]

Having said this, we can see that the relationship between the metaphysics of the *Gestalt* and Plato is not a simple one, even if the so-called metaphysics of the *Gestalt* is unthinkable in any *form* other than that of a reverberation *après coup* of Platonic onto-ideo-logy. It would be fruitless, therefore, to identify them. And to mark their co-belonging, that is, their commonality of origin, is not the same thing as to identify them. For, from one to the other, more is required than the "subjectal" (let us say, "Cartesian") reversal; Hegel is also needed. Indeed, the Nietzschean or post-Nietzschean *Gestalt* does not arise immediately from nothing—or from the mere *idea* merged (by what miracle?) with the subject as humanity. Especially when the *Gestalt* is that of the worker and destined to *account for*, or provide a *reason* for, nothing less than the appearance of technology itself. It is necessary that somewhere *Gestalt* and work should have been thought together. And, here again, whatever the difference separating the Hegelian *Gestalt* from the "figure of the worker," it is still in Hegel that Jünger's onto-typo-logy originates in the final instance. The proof of this is given to us by the title of the second book by Jünger that Heidegger refers to here— *About Pain* (*Über den Schmerz*)—inasmuch as it is necessary to grasp it in its most profound unity with *The Worker*, and to bring to light the "intimate reciprocal implication" that it appears to organize between *work* and *pain*. It is obvious that Heidegger is extremely prudent here (limiting himself to only "questioning") and that he remains quite elliptical toward what could well be the essential, namely, the "intimate implication" between *work, pain,* and *Gestalt*. That is, toward the relation between *work* and *pain,* on the one hand, and (*re*)*presentation by figure, gestalthafte Darstellung,* on the other. That is, yet again, toward

14. Ibid., p. 57.

15. Ibid. The demonstration, in relation to Rilke, is nearly the same, although it is of course developed with other motifs and passes through other relays; it will suffice to note here, anticipating a further development of this question elsewhere, that in technology, it is essentially a question of the monetary and market economy rather than of work or production.

the relation between dialectic and *Darstellung.* The question of *Darstellung,* here, must give way—and finally in a strange manner. For it is precisely what is involved, though between the lines, when Heidegger's analysis as a whole closes infallibly upon the referral of Jünger to Hegel—and of Hegel to the Greeks:

> In order to be able to delineate more clearly the relations which carry the connection between "work" and "pain," nothing less would be necessary than to think through the fundamental trait of Hegel's metaphysics, the uniting unity of the *Phenomenology of Spirit* and of the *Science of Logic.* The fundamental trait is "absolute negativity" as the "infinite force" or reality, that is, of the "existing concept." In the same (but not the identical) belonging to the negation of the negation, work and pain manifest their innermost metaphysical relationship. This reference already suffices to indicate what extensive discussions [*Erörterungen*] would be necessary here in order to do justice to the matter. If anyone indeed dared to think through the relationship between "work" as the fundamental trait of being and "pain," moving back past Hegel's *Logic,* then the Greek word for pain, namely *algos* would first come into speech for us. Presumably, *algos* is related to *alego* which, as an intensive of *lego* signifies intimate gathering. Then pain would be what gathers in the most intimate. Hegel's concept of the "concept" and its properly understood "strain" say the same thing on the transformed terrain of the absolute metaphysics of subjectivity.[16]

Taking into consideration the Cartesian "reversal," and then Hegel, the fundamentally Greek (and Platonic) origin of onto-typo-logy is indisputable.

But where does all of this lead us?

As far as possible, we might suspect, from Rohde's suspicion about the origin or model of *Zarathustra.* That is to say, in fact, to the suggestion that the *Gestalt,* the metaphysics of the figure (*Zarathustra* included), is simply the metaphysics wherein there is programmed, according to a very determined echo of Platonism, the technological era. Wherein this era is programmed and not where it *thinks* itself. No doubt, Jünger has the merit of recognizing that, as Heidegger had decisively announced, the essence of technology is not, by itself, "anything technical." But the kind of "step back," *Schritt zurück,* that he performs in relation to the last phase of nihilism (in relation to technology) remains insufficient because it does not lead beyond the (Nietzschean) implication of *Gestalt* and the will to power. In all of this,

16. *The Question of Being,* pp. 69 and 71.

what remains "unthought" is the essence itself of the *Gestalt*. Whence the question around which the Heideggerian commentary, at bottom, never ceases to turn—and in terms of which the whole of onto-typology is strictly circumscribed and delimited, that is to say, *criticized*, as belonging to nihilism: "Does the essence of *Gestalt* arise in the area of origin of what I call *Ge-stell?*"

But we touch here, as it were, upon the "neuralgic" spot (the logical knot?) of Heidegger's text—and it is appropriate to read, in its entirety, the passage in which such a question is formulated. All the more so since this question will occupy us for some time:

> It seems to me that the following questions can scarcely be avoided: May we consider the *Gestalt* of the worker as *Gestalt,* may we consider Plato's *idea* as *eidos* even more primordially in terms of the origin of their essence? If not, which reasons forbid this and demand instead that *Gestalt* and *idea* be taken simply as the ultimate for us and the first in themselves? If so, along which paths can the question as to the origin of the essence of the *idea* and of *Gestalt* move? To say this formally, does the essence of *Gestalt* arise in the area of origin of what I call *Ge-stell?* Does the origin of the essence of the *idea* accordingly also belong within the same area from which comes the essence of *Gestalt* which is related to it? Or is the *Ge-stell* only a function of the human *Gestalt?* If this were the case, then the *essence* of Being and the Being of being would be completely the making of human representation. The era in which European thinking believed this is still casting its last shadow over us.[17]

We touch the "neuralgic" point here less because this series of questions puts at risk all the thinking that decides upon the essence of technology, that is, in a certain way, *thought* as such (we know that the most fundamental question, here, the question bearing on "the *essence* of Being," has also already received its "answer"—precisely because it is posed in these terms, and regardless of the status we accord to the interminable *deferral* wherein such questioning must maintain itself), than because what is proposed here, explicitly, is the "thinking word" (*das denkende Wort*) for what is fundamentally involved in *Gestalt*—and thereby in technology, that is, *Ge-stell.* The problem is essentially the following: either *Ge-stell* designates that which allows us to think *idea* and *Gestalt,* in their essential filiation, *together* (in other words, what allows us to dis-cern the entire history of metaphysics—from Plato to its "closure" in the technological era); either, therefore, *Ge-stell* is *a*

17. Ibid., p. 63.

word for the forgotten | withdrawn | concealed essence of Being—or else *Ge-stell* itself depends on a certain determined *Gestalt* of humanity (that is, the essence of Being depends, each time, on the power of human representation, on the figuring or figurative power of human representation), and any possibility of "disconnecting" from (the history) of metaphysics is then prohibited. The problem is therefore the following: What *governs* here—is it *Ge-stell* or *Gestalt*? What comes first and what dominates? In which direction does the derivation go?

It goes without saying that this is a false question, or a false alternative—that language, in every way, has (always) already answered or decided (that there is always, at least, an "etymological direction" of derivation), etc. This is certainly true, but it remains to be seen if it is at all important. In other words, would not the important thing here be instead the possibility that the *site* (for it is a place, a topos) from which both Plato and Nietzsche—or Plato and Jünger—are supposed to be thinkable (situatable, localizable) might be a *word,* and that this word might be a *word for Being*? One could say that it is hard to see the difference, that here or there the same "etymologism" (the same "ontological" overdetermination of etymology) is still at work. Of course. But what then? In other words: this being admitted, what exactly is happening here? How does it happen, for example, that it should be precisely in this word here, in the "exhumation" and circulation of this word, that there is *decided* the refusal to consider, as regards the Nietzsche/Plato relation, a *different* type of filiation—of the kind, once again, that caught Rohde's attention? How does it happen, in the same way, that there should be organized in and around this word—as we saw a moment ago in Heidegger's relatively elliptical treatment of Jünger's relation to Hegel—a certain obstinately observed silence regarding the relation that might *also* exist, in Nietzsche as in Rilke, or in Jünger (after all, all three are "writers"), between the representation of Being as figure (the metaphysics of *Gestalt*) and *Darstellung,* (re)presentation—or, if you will, exposition or "literary presentation"?

What *exactly* happens, then, with the word *Ge-stell*?

Here, we must not move too quickly.

And, above all, we must not be too quick to translate the word *Ge-stell*. We know, moreover, that it is nearly untranslatable. But even if we could find an approximate equivalent for it—even if we could succeed, as has been the case for quite some time, in convincingly "glossing" the word, we would still not have gained very much. It is not a question here of knowing what *Ge-stell* "means." Or, at least, this is wholly secondary. The real question here is one of knowing how the word *Ge-stell* works, how it functions—what use it serves.

What happens, then, with *Ge-stell*?

In the first place, this: since out of *Ge-stell Gestalt* can be derived, and *idea* and *Gestalt* can be thought together (since the essence of *Gestalt* is only accessible, in both its difference from and identity with the *idea*, after the prior elucidation of *Ge-stell*), *Gestalt* is not reducible to the mere figure, no more so than *idea* can be confused with the "mere idea." We know, then, that at least this much happens: the *Gestalt*, essentially, *is not the figure*.[18] Neither in the rhetorical or poetic sense of the term, nor in the "plastic" sense. Let us say that the *Gestalt* is not a figure in the *Latin* sense. Neither *figura* nor *fictio*.

The consequence is that *Zarathustra*, essentially, is not poetry (it is neither *Poesie* nor *Dichtung*), even if it proceeds, as we will see, from what Heidegger calls the "poetifying" or "poetizing" "essence of reason," *das dichtende Wesen der Vernunft*. Or, if you prefer, *Zarathustra* is not a *figura*. To ask, "Why and how within modern metaphysics does a thought become necessary which represents [*vorstellt*] Zarathustra as a *Gestalt*?"—and this is, of course, the question—requires, precisely, at least if it is to be a question of *thinking* the thing, that we avoid posing this question in the philosophically overloaded terms of "criticism" or "poetics": "The oft-given statement that Nietzsche's thinking had fatally turned into poetry [*ins Dichten*], is itself only the abandonment of the questioning of thought."[19] This is why "we must first learn to read a book such as Nietzsche's *Thus Spoke Zarathustra* in the same rigorous manner as one of Aristotle's treatises."[20] No doubt, it is also necessary that we "translate" *Zarathustra*, which is to say, in fact, submit it, whether we may want to or not (and whatever weight we give to the word) to an *allegorical* treatment. But as we do with any philosophical book (or almost). And what we must "translate," in any case, is never of the order of "poetic ornament," of *poetische Ausschmückung*,[21] and still less of the order of "expression." But rather, as it finally comes out, of the order of the *unthought*.[22] So that if "Zarathustra"—besides establishing the *Gestalt*, in the onto-typo-logical sense of the term, for

18. From this point of view, Gérard Granel is right to translate *Gestalt* by "form."
19. *The Question of Being*, p. 55.
20. *What Is Called Thinking?* p. 70.
21. "Who Is Nietzsche's Zarathustra?" p. 78.
22. *What Is Called Thinking?* p. 76: "We do not hear it rightly [the language of thinkers], because we take that language to be mere expression, setting forth philosophers' views. But the thinker's language says what is. To hear it is in no case easy. Hear-

the philosophy of the modern age—still "figures" something, it is because he is, as the spokesman for Dionysus and the master who teaches
the Eternal Return and the Overman, the *Gestalt* of the thinker who
has thought metaphysics at the stage of its completion: one who has
nothing to do, we can easily imagine, with some subject by the name
of "Nietzsche," but everything to do with a certain *answer*, which is
"his" word, to what had to come about and declared itself through him
(to a silent, voiceless—but echoing—"sending" [*envoi*] of the voice of
Being in its withdrawal). Allegorism, at first inevitable—one must ask
about the meaning of Dionysus, about what the eagle and the serpent
represent, etc.—ends by emptying itself out and destroying itself from
within, progressively eroding the gap (from which, as with all allegorism, it proceeds) between "figure" and "concept," but in such a way
that neither the "figure" nor the "concept" escapes this sapping, this
process of wear and disintegration. To the extent that this might be
compared with anything *philosophical*, it is no doubt to Schelling's *tautegorism* that such a movement should be related. But to a *negative* version of such a tautegorism—a little like when we speak of "negative
theology"—which for this reason, would be nothing other (in a still
more obvious way than in Schelling), and at the most extreme limit of
hermeneutics as such, than an *absolute allegorism*.[23]

I ("I") will not return here to the way in which Heidegger, in a
single move, eliminates (or *sublimates*), for the sake of a primary *destination* of the unthought [*l'impensé(e)*] in Nietzsche (i.e., in "Nietzsche"),
at one and the same time the question of the "poetic" or "fictional"
("literary") character of *Zarathustra*, the question of a certain dispersion or breaking up of the Nietzschean "text" (more difficult to get
around, however, than "the absence of the work"—a capital work—
wherein the un-*thought* itself *would organize itself* with the essential "articulation" of a few fundamental words), and, finally, the question of
Nietzsche's "madness." Elsewhere, it seemed to me possible to show—

---

ing it presupposes that we meet a certain requirement, and we do so only on rare
occasions. We must acknowledge and respect it. To acknowledge and respect consists in
letting every thinker's thought come to us as something in each case unique, never to be
repeated, inexhaustible—and being shaken to the depths by what is unthought in this
thought. What is unthought in a thinker's thought is not a lack inherent in his thought.
What is *un*-thought is such in each case only as the un-*thought*."

23. As for Heidegger's "installation"—of course never a simple one (that is to say,
one that is always at the same time deconstructive)—in the domain of the allegorical (or
the symbolic), see in particular the opening pages of "The Origin of the Work of Art,"
in *Poetry, Language, Thought*, pp. 17ff.

but to be honest, it was a bit obvious—that these three questions are really only one, or more exactly, that they all gravitate around a single, central question, at the same time always in view and always thrust aside (constantly proposed, moreover, in terms unacceptable to *thought:* metaphysically marked, and therefore constantly condemned—without "appeal"), and this is the question of the *subject.* The question of the "subject of enunciation," let us say, or of "writing"—nothing, in any case, that might be simply, that is, immediately, assimilated or *identified* with the subject of the "metaphysics of subjectity," under any form whatsoever.[24]

In fact, Rohde's suspicion, as we can easily understand, *finally* refers precisely to such a question. And we understand just as easily that Heidegger could fail to attend to it, simply pass right by it—or even pretend not to notice it. For beyond the mistrust that Heidegger always displays toward any problematic of subjectivity (beyond even his declared hostility, all the way through to his later texts,[25] to the problematic of enunciation, of *Aussage;* a problematic which he held responsible, ever since his introduction to *Being and Time*—paragraph 7, section B—for the covering over or "homoiotic" forgetting of *aletheia*), it is no doubt possible to track down, in the whole of the procedure Heidegger follows when dealing with *Zarathustra,* and already in the very positing of the question that governs it ("*Who* is Nietzsche's Zarathustra?"), a kind of vast movement turning around a question that Heidegger well knows cannot be avoided or eluded (in any case, Heidegger never avoids anything) but that he judges must be "cut off from its support," and taken from behind, in order to neutralize its power.

But why does Heidegger's maneuver here go by way of *Gestalt?* Why does it even go beyond *Gestalt* in search of *Ge-stell?*

Once again, what happens with (the word) *Ge-stell?*

This—in the second place, then (but we are not changing places here, and we will soon realize that with respect to the "first place," it amounts to the same): that from *Ge-stell,* among other things, not only *Gestalt* but *Darstellung* itself ((re)presentation, exposition, *mise-en-scène,* etc.) can be derived. Or, more precisely, *Gestalt* and *Darstellung*

24. Allow me (once more) to refer here to one of my own essays from a work-in-progress on Heidegger, which has appeared under the title "L'Oblitération," in *Le sujet de la philosophie* (Paris: Aubier-Flammarion, 1979), pp. 111–184.

25. See especially "The End of Philosophy and the Task of Thinking," in *On Time and Being,* trans. Joan Stambaugh (New York: Harper and Row, 1972), pp. 55–73.

can be derived together from *Ge-stell,* among other things, even though Heidegger never, unless I am mistaken, explicitly marks this relationship, and to see it we must link together, and in the same turn make homogeneous, several relatively independent texts. Even though, in fact, everything happens here as if the commonality of origin, the *homogeneity* of *Gestalt* and *Darstellung*—symptomatically left unmentioned, we must insist, when it was a question of folding Jünger back upon Hegel—were, in one way or another, something very troublesome.

Because in effect Mimesis is at play here. And because in Mimesis, *in effect,* there is something troublesome.

Act 2, then: *the same characters.* Enter Mimesis.

The set represents . . .

The Stele

Spiegel: noch nie hat man wissend beschrieben, was ihr in euerem Wesen seid. (Mirrors: no one has ever knowingly described you in your essence.)
—Rilke, *Sonnets to Orpheus,* II, 3

Dichtung: das kann eine Atemwende bedeuten. Wer weiss, vielleicht legt die Dichtung den Weg—auch den Weg der Kunst—um einer solchen Atemwende willen Zurück? Vielleicht gelingt es ihr, da das Fremde, also der Abgrund *und* das Medusenhaupt, der Abrund *und* die Automaten, ja in einer Richtung zu liegen scheint,—vielleicht gelingt es ihr hier, zwischen Fremd und Fremd zu unterscheiden, vielleicht schrumpft gerade hier das Medusenhaupt, vielleicht versagen gerade hier die Automaten—für diesen einmaligen kurzen Augenblick? Vielleicht wird hier, mit dem Ich—mit dem *hier* und *solcherart* freigesetzten befremdeten Ich,—vielleicht wird hier noch ein Anderes frei?

Die Kunst erweitern? —Nein.

Sondern geh mit der Kunst in Deine allereigenste Enge. Und setze dich frei.

Ich bin, auch hier, in Ihrer Gegenwart, diesen Weg gegangen. Es war ein Kreis.

Die Kunst, also auch des Medusenhaupt, der Mechanismus, die Automaten, das unheimliche und so schwer zu unterscheidende, letzten Endes vielleicht doch nur *eine* Fremde—die Kunst lebt fort.

(Poetry: that can mean a change of breath. Who knows, perhaps poetry takes the path—also the path of art—for the sake of such a change of breath? Perhaps it succeeds here, since the strange, that is, the abyss *and* the

Medusa's head, the abyss *and* automatons, seem to lie in one direction,—perhaps it succeeds in distinguishing here between strange and strange, perhaps it is here that the Medusa's head shrivels, perhaps right here the automatons break down—for this unique brief moment? Perhaps here, with the I,—the I liberated and astonished *here* and *in this way*—perhaps here yet an Other is freed?

Expand art? —No.
Rather, go with art into that corner that is most properly your own. And free yourself.
Even here, in your presence, I have followed this path. It was a circle.
Art, and thus also the Medusa's head, mechanism, the automatons, the uncanny and so difficult to distinguish, and yet in the end perhaps only *one* strangeness—art lives on.)
—Paul Celan, *Der Meridian*

The set, if you will, is the constellation or chain of some of the major concepts of metaphysics, all of which can be derived from *Ge-stell:* from this unique and philosophically unheard-of word, a word that has never sounded, or ever been employed—although it is very old and in general use in the language—anywhere in (the entire history of) metaphysics, in any metaphysical place (discourse, text, idiom) whatsoever.

It is a very long chain, and it would be futile to want to cover or go back over all of it: there is *stellen* (to summon, to challenge verbally, "to stop someone in the street in order to call him to account, in order to force him to *rationem reddere*"),[26] there is *bestellen* (to cultivate or appoint), *vorstellen* (to represent), *verstellen* (to dissimulate), *darstellen* (to portray, to (re)present), *herstellen* (to produce), *nachstellen* (to track or be after, to avenge),[27] etc.—and still others that will perhaps appear in due time. This chain is a veritable lacework, a sort of vegetal labyrinth proliferating around (or out of) a single root. The "set," then, is this semantic lacework, this network of derivatives—"centered," of course, "anchored" upon a primary "etymon," but also of such exuberance that it is perhaps ultimately impossible to get an overview of it, to "describe" it, or to oversee all of its ramifications.

Hence one inevitably runs the risk of getting lost somewhere—or of losing all continuity of derivation. For example, *between* two or three

26. Heidegger's marginal note to A. Préau's translation of the lecture on technology, in *Essais et conférences* (Paris: Gallimard, 1958), p. 26. See also *The Essence of Reasons,* especially ch. 3.

texts, in the area of (the question of) *Darstellung;* or, to be more precise and to keep hold of the thread that we have already begun to follow, in the area where (the question of) *Darstellung* is, in effect, connected with Mimesis.

In the beginning, however, everything goes rather well. And in fact, when it appears, *Ge-stell* comprises or carries *Darstellung* along with it, almost immediately. This happens, as we know, in Heidegger's lecture on technology (*Technik*). Introducing the word, Heidegger writes:

> The word *stellen* in the name *Ge-stell* not only means provocation [*das Herausfordern*]. At the same time it should preserve the suggestion of another *Stellen* from which it stems, namely, that producing and (re)presenting [*Her- und Dar-stellen*] which, in the sense of *poiesis*, lets what presences come forth into unconcealment [unveiling, *die Unverborgenheit*].
>
> This *Herstellen* that brings forth [or produces: *hervorbringend*]—for example, the erecting [*das Aufstellen*] of a statue in the temple precinct—and the provoking order [*das herausfordernde Bestellen*] now under consideration are indeed fundamentally different, and yet they remain related in their essence. Both are ways of dis-covering [*Entbergen*], of *aletheia*. In *Ge-stell*, that unconcealment comes to pass [*sich ereignet*] in conformity with which the work of modern technology reveals the real [*das Wirkliche*] as standing-reserve [*Bestand*].²⁸

In order to catch a glimpse of what such a text seeks to posit (or does not allow itself to posit), it is necessary to recall, at least briefly, what it follows from and where it comes in. In the preceding pages it has been a matter of "questioning" the essence of technology, inasmuch as, as everybody knows, "the essence of technology is in no way anything technological." Which is to say, it has been a matter—the two movements are indissociable—of deconstructing the very technical (in)determination of technology, its "instrumental and anthropological" conception, according to which technology is a *means* (in view of certain ends) and a human *activity* (practice). Whence the necessity of proceeding through a deconstruction of its etiology. Indeed, Heidegger's deconstruction has here crossed through the entire infrastructure and prehistory of the *principium rationis* in order to arrive at both the

27. Cf. "Who Is Nietzsche's Zarathustra?": *nachstellen* there designates what Nietzsche calls "the spirit of revenge," *ressentiment*—whose first (or last) victim, as we know, is Nietzsche himself, in Heidegger's interpretation. (*Ecce Homo*'s last words—"Have I been understood? *Dionysus versus the Crucified*"—are read by Heidegger as the sign of a (re)lapse into *ressentiment*. See pp. 70 and 77.)

28. "The Question Concerning Technology," p. 21.

Aristotelian (in origin) doctrine of the four causes (material, formal, final, "efficient") and Plato. It has shown—and I note here only the most indispensable aspects of the argument, even at the risk of distorting the analysis a bit—that its etiology presupposes a theory of production (*poiesis, Hervorbringen*) that answers, in its turn, insofar as this producing is a "bringing forth" or a "letting come about" (a *Ver-an-lassen*), to the "aletheic" predetermination of the essence of Being, of presence or of truth. This can be seen in the Platonic definition of *poiesis* as *aitia* (*Banquet*, 205b: "he gar toi ek tou me ontos eis to on ionti hostooun aitia pasa esti poiesis"), for which Heidegger proposes the following translation: "Every occasion for whatever passes over and goes forward [*über- und vorgeht*] into presencing from that which is not presencing is *poiesis*, is *pro-duction* [*Hervorbringen*]," indicating that producing, in this sense, "bringt aus der Verborgenheit her in die Unverborgenheit vor" ("Bringing-forth brings hither out of concealment, forth into unconcealment")—and "comes to pass only insofar as something concealed comes into unconcealment."[29] The essence of technology (*poiesis* involving all production, "natural" or not) is therefore *aletheia*. On the condition, however, that we take into account the metaphysical (in general) and modern (in particular) inflection that *aletheia* suffers, in the forgetting or non-thinking of its essence. Technology is no doubt itself a mode of "discovering" (*Entbergen*). But the "discovering that holds sway throughout modern technology does not unfold into a bringing-forth in the sense of *poiesis*. The discovering that rules in modern technology is a provocation that puts to nature the demand that it supply energy that can be extracted and stored as such."[30]

This is precisely where the root *stell* intervenes—if it is indeed a question of a single, simple root (and presuming consequently that the network of *Ge-stell* does not immediately split and proliferate at the point of its etymological "anchoring"—in which case, there would still be much to say about Heideggerian "etymologism").[31]

29. Ibid., pp. 10 and 11. Heidegger plays here on the word-pair *herausfordern* (to provoke) and *herausfördern* (to extract).

30. Ibid., p. 14.

31. Heidegger in fact plays constantly on the drawing together (if not the pure and simple "assimilation") of *stehen* and *stellen*, even while maintaining a certain difference between them. It is as if he identified the *stal* of *stellein* (which means "to equip," but also "to send word," "to send for") with the *sta* of *stele*, column or stele (cf. *istemi* or, in Latin, *sto, stare*)—thus proceeding (as is so often the case in Heidegger) finally more by philological *Witz* than by any true etymologism. In any case, this is what we are almost obliged to suppose, even though in a text very close to the one that concerns us pri-

In effect, through a general mutation affecting the "causal" domain (the domain of "responsibility" or "efficiency"), this modification of unconcealment, this metamorphosis of *producing* into *provoking* is a transformation of *Bestellen*. It is a transformation of "culture," if, as Heidegger here insists, this is the oldest meaning of the word. For the appropriating and appropriated work of the peasant who cultivated in the sense of "to take care of" and "to maintain" (in the sense in which we say in French—or in Latin—"to establish," "to establish oneself," to construct a "stable," etc.), an entirely different mode of *Bestellen*—of in-stalling, let us say[32]—is substituted. This latter is essentially a *Stellen*, a claiming (a commanding, a committing, a summoning, a challenging), in the sense, this time, of both provoking and extracting (*ausfordern, ausfördern*).

Perhaps this mutation is to be thought of as the passage from the pure and simple *stal* [*étal*] or *display* [*étalement*]—which, after all, would render fairly well one of the senses of *logos* privileged by Heidegger[33]—to all the modern forms of *installation* or *establishment*, from the State (its *constitution* and its *institutions*) up to the generalized *show* (*étalage*) of the market economy. Changed into "provoking installation," *poiesis* would become the unrestrained pursuit of that which has always sustained it and which it perhaps no longer has (of which it perhaps no longer *disposes*), namely of a being "set upright," of the *stable* and the *static* (*Stand, station*), of the place in which to stand up (*Stelle*), and posture or position (*Stellung*), which it identifies with the "standing reserve" (with consistency or with the *store, Bestand*) by which the mode of presence of the present is determined in the modern age—the present itself being thought, for this reason, as object (*Gegenstand*) according to the dominating orientation of the metaphysics of subjectivity.

These analyses have been gone over so much that it is perhaps un-

---

marily here (namely, the "preparatory" lecture to the lecture on technology: "Science and Reflection"), Heidegger notes, in passing, that the Greek word *thesis* (which derives from the—simple—Indo-European root *dhe*) can in German be translated at the same time by *Setzung, Stellung* and *Lage* (see *"The Question Concerning Technology and Other Essays,"* p. 159).

32. Which we should therefore try to understand in the double sense of "to equip" and "to establish," as also in the sense of both "to set up" and "to erect."

33. Cf. the equivalence mentioned above between *Stellung, Setzung,* and *Lage.* Moreover, the *Ge-* of *Ge-stell* implies just such a "gathering and collecting" *leguein* (see *Essais et conférences*, p. 26). On the question of *logos*, see, in the same "collection," pp. 249ff.

necessary to paraphrase any further. In any case, it will undoubtedly suffice to retain from them (but everything is in this statement) that the essence of technology entails, by way of *Be-stellen,* a sense of Being as *stance, stature, station*—as, in "Greek," *stasis* or *stele*—which is and which has always been, in the West, the sense of Being itself. "Being" (as it happens, this word has at times been written *ester*) means *to stand*.[34] Installation, in technology, is therefore both provocation and stele. And it is in this double sense, at least, that one must understand *Ge-stell* (literally, the shelf [*l'étagère*], the *pedestal*) if, besides the *Ge-* of "gathering" and "collection," besides even the relation that *Ge-stell* entertains with the principle of reason (and that gives us "reason" to translate *Ge-stell* by *arraisonnement* [hailing and examining], this word is supposed to "account for" provocation insofar as it "sets upon [*stellt*] man to order [*bestellen*] the real as standing reserve [*Bestand*]."[35] But it goes without saying that this double sense is double only inasmuch as we try to make audible in provocation a deformed echo of the Greek production, of *poiesis.* What predominates and what joins *poiesis* (or even *techne*) and technology—in a common, though unequally, un-

34. On this point, see also *An Introduction to Metaphysics,* ch. 2, "On the Grammar and Etymology of the word 'Being,'" trans. Ralph Manheim (New Haven: Yale University Press, 1959). For the relation between *stehen* and *stellen,* see in particular pp. 63–64.

35. "The Question Concerning Technology," p. 20. A justification is proposed on the same page for this rather surprising use of the word *Gestell.* We must read it, if only in order to note the appearance of Plato and, as if by chance, the *eidos:* "According to ordinary usage, the word *Gestell* means some kind of apparatus, e.g., a bookrack. *Gestell* is also the name for a skeleton. And the employment of the word *Gestell* that is now required of us seems equally eerie, not to speak of the arbitrariness with which words of a mature language are thus misused. Can anything be more strange? Surely not. Yet this strangeness is an old usage of thinking. And indeed thinkers accord with this usage precisely at the point where it is a matter of thinking what is most high. We, late born, are no longer in a position to appreciate the significance of Plato's daring to use the word *eidos* for that which in everything and in each particular thing endures as present. For *eidos,* in everyday speech, meant the outward aspect [*Ansicht*] that a visible thing offers to the physical eye. Plato exacts of this word, however, something utterly extraordinary: that it name what precisely is not and never will be perceivable with physical eyes. But even this is by no means the full extent of what is extraordinary here. For idea names not only the nonsensuous aspect of what is physically visible. Aspect (idea) names and is, also, that which constitutes the essence in the audible, the tasteable, the tactile, in everything that is in any way accessible. Compared with the demands that Plato makes on language and thought in this and other instances, the use of the word *Gestell* as the name for the essence of modern technology, which we now venture here, is almost harmless." We find, but this time in regard to syntax, an analogous motif in the introduction of *Being and Time* (paragraph 7, *in fine*).

thought [*impensée*] of *aletheia*—is precisely the *static* determination of Being. *Ge-stell* is primarily and fundamentally the *stele*. In fact, the text we were just reading an instant ago marked this in an entirely explicit fashion. And if we let ourselves be carried in what is now called the "circulation of the signifier," this *an in-stant ago* could not "fall" any more appropriately, if all of this amounts to saying that *Ge-stell* is a word for *presence*—with presence here interpreted as stele or, since it is always necessary to conjugate everything with (the forgetting of) *aletheia,* unconcealment interpreted as erection.

Whence we can understand that *poiesis* should be translated by *Her/ Darstellung* or that *Ge-stell* should also be a word for *poiesis*. I will return to this later.

But what becomes clear now, above everything else, is the way in which Heidegger, from the vantage point of *Ge-stell,* can consider *idea* and *Gestalt* together—the idea and what we should perhaps now translate as *statue* rather than *figure*.

There are two motifs here.

In the first place, the essence of the *idea* is static. The *idea* is always posited (*gesetzt*); or at least each time he evokes it, Heidegger never fails to recall that *idea* designates the *aei on*, the "perduring," *stability* itself.[36]

But in the second place, and this is the most important, the *idea*, as *Gestalt,* is the product of what Heidegger calls "the poetizing essence of reason," *das dichtende Wesen der Vernunft*. This is not the "poetic" (*dichterisch*) essence of reason—given the way in which Heidegger understands *Dichtung*—but rather the "fashioning" or "fictioning" essence of reason, inasmuch as *dichten* (which has never meant "to condense") is practically synonymous, especially in the compounds *erdichten* and *ausdichten* used by Heidegger, with *bilden*.[37]

What is the fictioning essence of reason, then?

Heidegger explains it in terms of the relation that "Nietzschean

36. Cf. *Essais et conférences,* p. 41, *Nietzsche,* vol. 1, p. 173, etc.: the "idea" is determined, as a general rule, as *Beständigkeit*.

37. In which case, *Dichtung,* if it has, as Lacan would argue, some relation to the "operations" of the unconscious, would be closer to what Freud calls *Darstellbarkeit*. On the distinction that Heidegger carefully draws between "poetry" and "fiction," see *Nietzsche,* vol. 1 (Pfüllingen: Gunther Neske, 1961), p. 585: "This way of speaking about reason's poetizing essence most certainly does not refer to a *poetic* [*dichterisches*] essence. For no more is all thought thinking [*denkerisch*] than all poetization, all fictioning [*Ausdichten*], is poetical."

schematism" bears to Kant and Plato. As regards "Nietzschean schematism," he supports his argument with a fragment from *The Will to Power* (No. 515), a fragment which he comments upon at length at the end of his 1939 course "The Will to Power as Knowledge": "Not 'to know' [*erkennen*], but to schematize—to impose as many regularities and forms on chaos as are necessary to satisfy our practical need . . . (The arrangement, the fashioning [*das Ausdichten*] of the analogous, of the same—this process by which all sensible impressions pass—is the very development of reason.)"[38] "Schematism" thus defines here the essence of reason as the "positing of the same" (*Setzen des Gleichen*), that is to say, as *Erdichten und Ausdichten des Gleichen,* the fashioning and fictioning of the same. The schematizing essence of reason is the *constitution* of the same as the thingness of the thing, on the sole basis of which the thing, whatever its mode of appearance may be each time, is each time thinkable as such. In other words: schematization, the constitution of the same, fashioning and fictioning, is *categorization* in the Aristotelian sense (no doubt a new and final occurrence of the *Stellen* if *kategorein* means first of all to challenge in a public place in order to call to account, to accuse, to commit, etc.) or *idea* in the Platonic sense: "That which is fictioned in such a fiction is categories. That which properly appears to us and shows itself under its aspect: this same thingness of the thing—what in Greek would be referred to as 'Idea'— thus created, is originally fictioned."[39] Idea, category, and schema are consequently owing to the same fictioning power of reason, that is to say, to what Kant ("who for the first time had properly discerned the fictioning character of reason") called precisely the "forming force" (*die bildende Kraft*) of reason or transcendental imagination (*Einbildungskraft*). And just as in the analysis of *Gestalt,* what is involved here is purely and simply transcendence itself. That is to say, less (as we might expect) the *analogical* as such, than that whose matrical form Platonic meta-physics in fact produced:

> The fictioning essence of reason commends all human, i.e., rational, knowing unto a higher origin; "higher" means: lying essentially beyond the everyday habitual seizing and copying [*Ausgreifen und Abschreiben*]. What reason perceives, being *as* being, cannot be appropriated simply by finding it. In Platonic terms, being is that which is present, the "idea."

38. *Nietzsche,* vol. 1, pp. 551ff (German edition).
39. Ibid., p. 584.

When Plato, for example in the dialogue "Phaedrus," tells the myth of the descent of the "idea" from a place above heaven, *hyperouranios topos,* into the human soul, this myth is, in the metaphysical sense, none other than the Greek interpretation of the fictioning essense of reason, that is, of its *higher origin.*[40]

We are now in a position to understand how the derivation of *idea* and of *Gestalt* (but also, though less directly, of category and schema) is carried out, proceeding from *Ge-stell:* it is a matter, each time, of *poiesis,* of the ontological power of *poiesis.* A matter, in other words, through the "application" of *poiesis* to thought or to reason, of the fictioning (idealizing, imagining, categorizing, *statutory,* etc.) essence of the "theoretical." Indeed, up to and including the reversal of Platonism and the mutation of onto-ideo-logy into onto-typo-logy, thought as *stabilization* corresponds to Being as *stele.* Something like an *onto-steleo-logy* sustains, *stays* or *shores up* [*étançonne*], throughout its unfolding, the history of metaphysics—and delimits this metaphysics as the space (this would nearly pass today for a "novelty") of "theoretical fiction" in general. (Metaphysical) thought, *theory,* is, in its fictioning essence, *in-stalling.* That is to say, as well, *standardizing* (hence, of course, the "thought by values," programmed since long ago), since what is at stake here is always the same "word," or even *stylistic* (hence, again of course, a certain obsession of Nietzsche's—and of a few others). Philosophy, then, will have always been a matter of *erection.* And that's what "fiction" is.

It is in this sense, obviously, and in this sense only, that *Zarathustra* is "poietic"—and not poetic, *dichterisch. Zarathustra* is poietic in the same way that Plato's myths are. With, however, something extra which is the modern effectuation of the *idea* as *Gestalt,* or, if you prefer, a certain "realization" of *Ge-stell* still absent in Plato (this is why we cannot properly speak of a Platonic *Gestalt*). But allowing for this difference, *Zarathustra* functions quite as a Platonic myth. In other words, if it is "thought in a metaphysical way," *Zarathustra* is "nothing other than the [*modern*] interpretation of the fictioning essence of reason." Zarathustra descending from his mountain and the soul descending from the *hyperouranios topos* are, at bottom, the same thing: the same movement of transcendence (or, already in its most modern version, the same movement of rescendence). In both cases, fictioning signifies

40. Ibid., p. 585.

transcendental installation, the production (*Herstellung*) and erection
(*Aufstellung*) of the stable (of the Same), without which nothing can
be grasped or thought.

But at the same time we see that fictioning has, finally, nothing to do
with *Darstellung*, exposition, or *mise-en-scène*. No more than the myth
of the "Phaedrus" contains, according to Heidegger, its own *mise-en-
abyme* or is implicated in the very thing of which it is the "interpretation" (namely, as "fiction")—no more than this does the "gestaltist"
onto-typo-logy of *Zarathustra* involve the still very particular *Darstellung* of this "song," "poem," "dithyramb," non-"sacred book," etc. *Fictioning does not lead into its own abyss* [*ne s'abyme pas*]. In any case,
nowhere in Heidegger is there ever the least question of such a thing.

Nevertheless, something is lost, paradoxically(?), in this very lack of
abyss.

Something—it goes without saying—that the *mise-en-abyme* must
always reflect in order to ensure (re)presentation (*Darstellung*): namely,
reflection itself *as* (re)presentation. The loss of *Darstellung* can scarcely
be a simple matter. For it is not simply a question of something that
falls out and that we forget to pick up, or even finally whose fall we fail
to *remark*. In fact, as soon as we consider the abyss, as soon as the suspicion arises that the abyss is always in one way or another implied in
Darstellung (and inversely, that *Darstellung* always gives rise to a *mise-
en-abyme*), it is still necessary to agree on the status of the *Darstellung*
in question and, consequently, the exact nature of the abyss itself.
What, for example, is happening here with this "lack of the abyss," or
this inattention to the abyss? For the difficulty doubtless derives not
only from the inevitable distance that opens up between the Heideggerian commentary and the text or texts that this commentary covers.
It is not enough here to say that Heidegger is not concerned with the
abyssal, and that he thus fails to see what is involved in the problematic
of *Darstellung*, etc. The difficulty derives perhaps also, and especially,
from the structure of the abyss "itself," inasmuch as what is reflected
there (though if not by "figure," *imperceptibly*) is fictioning, that is to
say, the fiction whereby the fictioning essence of reason or of thought
must itself be (re)presented and exposed.

It is surprising, however, that of all the derivatives of the root *stell*, it
is *Darstellung* that should be lost: for we have seen Heidegger explicitly translate *poiesis* by *Herstellung* and *Darstellung*. And in one of the
most fundamental texts devoted to Platonic *poiesis* (the last sections of

his first course on Nietzsche, "The Will to Power as Art"),[41] the same (double) translation is maintained, or rather, respecting chronology, produced for the first time. But in the lecture on technology, as we have seen, the *Herstellen/Darstellung* couple immediately breaks apart to the benefit of *Herstellen* alone. In fact, *Darstellung* disappears in two lines. Let us reread these lines more carefully: "The word *stellen* in the name *Ge-stell* not only means provocation. At the same time it should preserve the suggestion of another *Stellen* from which it stems, namely, that *Her-* and *Dar-stellen* which, in the sense of *poiesis,* lets what presences come forth into unconcealment. This *Herstellen* that brings forth—for example, the erecting of a statue in the temple precinct . . ." In the course on Nietzsche, we find precisely the same gesture, but this time magnified to the dimensions of a general interpretation of art as understood by Plato (and consequently by Nietzsche). We find, therefore, the same gesture again, but this time coupled with, or followed by, noticeably clearer and above all graver effects with respect to the question that concerns us here. For it goes without saying that what is at issue is not simply the disappearance of a *word.* It is *at least* that of a *concept,* if not that of a whole *motif*—of a whole philosophical (and textual) stratum or chain, where, as everyone knows, nothing less is involved, under the heading of the "question of art" (or of *poiesis*), than the question of the *status*—not to say the *stature*—of Mimesis, and thereby, inextricably linked to and entangled with this question, the status of philosophical *Darstellung* itself.

How, then, is *Darstellung* lost? And what is the consequence of this loss for the interpretation of mimesis?

Contrary to what we might believe, the loss is not so easy to perceive. For here again things begin rather well. Asking what the "holy dread" that Nietzsche claimed to experience before the discord or the difference (*Zwiespalt*)[42] between art and truth might signify within the framework of the inversion of Platonism, Heidegger poses the double question of the essence of art in Plato and of the relation it holds with truth. There are two texts on the program: the *Republic* and the *Phaedrus.* But it is obviously the commentary on the *Republic* that we must examine here.

If things (again) begin well, it is because Heidegger begins by pro-

---

41. *Nietzsche,* vol. 1, pp. 162ff.
42. Ibid., p. 163.

viding a framework for the Greek concept of art, that is, *poiesis,* and because the *stell* immediately unveils itself: *poiein* is *to set upright.* But this time particular mention is made of the semantic inflection of *poiesis* (that is, the "poetic" crystallization of the word)—and we are on the edge of *Darstellung:*

> Finally, if by "art" we mean *what is brought forward in a process of bringing-forth* [*das Hervorgebrachte eines Hervorbringens*], what is installed in installation [*das Hingestellte eines Herstellens*], and the installing itself, then the Greek speaks of *poiein* and *poiesis.* That the word *poiesis* in the emphatic sense comes to be reserved for the designation of the installation of something in words, that *poiesis* as "poesy" becomes the special name for the art of the word, poetic art [*Dichtkunst*], testifies to the primacy [or "prestance," *Vorrangstellung*] of such art within Greek art as a whole. Therefore it is not accidental that when Plato brings to speech and decision [*Entscheidung*] the relationship of art and truth he deals primarily and predominantly with poetic creation and the poet.[43]

These circumlocutions of course point to the *Republic,* and, in the *Republic,* to the entire debate in Books II and III on the subject, let us say provisionally, of "mytho-poiesis." But this does not at all mean that it should be here, in Books II and III, that the question of the relation between art and truth is "brought to decision." On the contrary—and here the text is without any ambiguity whatsoever. What is essential is not to be sought in the direction of poetry (or of "poetics"). One or two pages later, moreover, after having recalled in what "political"— that, is ontological[44]—context such a question "comes to language," Heidegger hastens to add the following—by which he permits himself to dispense with a commentary on Platonic "poetics," but at the same time leaves himself open to the danger of retaining nothing of the problematic of *Darstellung:*

43. Ibid., p. 165.

44. *Political*—in the sense this word has in Plato, according to Heidegger—does not mean "political" in a restricted sense (in opposition, for example, to "theoretical" or to "aesthetic"); rather, it means, fundamentally, *theoretical.* No doubt the *Republic* poses questions about the State as a "fundamental structure" (*Grundgestalt*) of the "communal existence" of man. But this questioning, insofar as it is philosophical, is organized on the basis of a theoretical design, that is, on the basis of an essential knowledge of *dike*—which is Being itself as the joining (*Fügung*) of being in its totality. Philosophy, then, is the knowledge of *dike,* of the laws of the ontological joining. This is why the question of politics is the question of truth—and why the philosophers should rule the city-state (see *Nietzsche,* vol. 1, pp. 165–166).

In the pursuit of such inquiry [*concerning the essence of the State, of communal existence* [*Gemeinwesen*], *of the education required for such communal existence*], the following question emerges, among others: does art too, especially the art of poetry, belong to communal existence; and, if so, how? In Book III (1–18) that question becomes the object of the discussion. Here Plato shows in a preliminary way [*aber erst vordeutend*], that what art conveys and provides is always a *Darstellung* of beings; although it is not inactive [*untätig*], its installing [*Herstellen*] and making [*Machen*], *poiein*, remain *mimesis*, counterfeiting [*Nachmachen*], copying and transforming [*ein Ab und Um-bilden*], poetizing [*Dichten*] in the sense of fictioning [*Erdichten*]. Thus art in itself is exposed to the danger of continual deception and falsehood. In accord with the essence of its activity [*Tun*], art has no direct, definitive relation to the true and to true being.[45]

Which means—if one may be permitted to sharpen the contours a bit:

1. That, in the beginning of the *Republic*, the question of art appears *among other questions*. It is therefore not the major or central question. It is a question subordinated, twice subordinated: on the one hand, to the question of education,[46] then, on the other, like the question of education itself, to the question of the essence of the State or of "communal existence."

2. That this question of art, thus subordinated, and what is more, restricted to the sole question of poetry, is properly treated only in Book III, 1–18 (that is, 386a–412a). We must therefore conclude that the entire end of Book II (17–21, *at least*—that is, 376a–383c) is not essentially concerned with this question. Yet it is there that the debate is instituted, and in such a way, moreover, that the separation between

45. Ibid., p. 168.
46. That is, to what in Plato, again, "prefigures" onto-typo-logy, inasmuch as *paideia* must be referred to *Bildung* (and if this word is wrested from the "false meaning" to which it fell victim "at the end of the nineteenth century"). For *Bildung* "has two meanings. It is first a forming [*ein Bilden*] in the sense of an impression that imprints a character upon a thing, following which the thing then develops [*im Sinne der entfaltende Prägung*]. But if this 'form' *informs* [imprints, *prägt*], it is because it at the same time conforms (shapes) the thing to a determining [*massgebend*] aspect that is, for this reason, called a model [*Vor-bild*]. 'Formation' [or more commonly: education—*Bildung*] is thus at once the impression (of a character) and guidance received from a model [*Geleit durch ein Bild*]." "Plato's Doctrine of Truth," trans. John Barlow, in *Philosophy in the Twentieth Century*, ed. W. Barrett (New York: Random House, 1962), vol. 3, p. 256.

Books II and III does not appear to correspond to a fundamental articulation.[47]

3. That Book III takes up the question of art only by way of notice, in anticipation. It has no other object than to delimit or circumscribe (*eingrenzen*) the role of art in communal existence and to submit its activity, its *Tun*, "to certain demands and directives that derive from the guiding laws of the being of the State."[48] The essential takes place in Book X—the essential being the "bringing to decision," *zur Entscheidung bringen*, of the relation between art and truth: the *critique* itself of art. But we must follow Heidegger's demonstration here:

> At this point [*starting from Book III*] we can see that a decision may be reached concerning the essence of art and its circumscribed essentiality in the State only in terms of an original and proper relation to the beings that set the standard, only in terms of a relationship that appreciates *dike*, the matter of order and disorder [*der Fug und der Unfug*][49] with respect to Being. For that reason, after the preliminary conversations about art and other forms of achievement in the State, we arrive at the question concerning our basic relation to Being, advancing to the question concerning true comportment toward beings, and hence to the question of truth. On our way through these conversations, we encounter at the beginning of the seventh book the discussion of the essence of truth, based on the Allegory of the Cave. Only after traversing this long and broad path to the point where philosophy is defined as masterful knowledge of the Being of beings do we turn back [*in der Rückwendung*], in order to ground those statements that were made earlier in a merely provisional

47. As concerns the *Republic*'s "poetics"—that is, its examination of the "logic" of *music* in general (*mousike* in its broadest sense, as it is said), of that which music entails in the way of language or discourse—the most important articulation is made, rather, within Book III (392c), in the movement from the examination of *logos* to that of *lexis* (let us say, to that of "diction"). The end of Book II, on the other hand, coincides (within the discussion of the *logos*) only with the end of the examination of the "theological" content of myths.

48. *Nietzsche*, vol. 1, p. 168.

49. This opposition between what is orderly and what is disorderly—or, according to Klossowski's translation ([Paris: Gallimard, 1971], p. 155), between reason and unreason—is of course to be related to the ontological definition of *dike* as *Fügung*, as the essential joining of being in its totality. *Fug* and *Unfug* mean, respectively, "joined" and "disjoined." Political evil, then, for Plato, is "disjunction." That is to say—if we recall that Heidegger also uses the word *Fügung*, especially in his commentary on Schelling, to designate "system" (*sy-stase*) in its most fundamental sense (see *Schellings Abhandlung über das Wesen der menschlichen Freiheit* [Tübingen: Niemeyer, 1971], p. 34)—the fact of being "out-of-system."

manner [*vordeutend*], among them the statements concerning art. Such a return transpires in the tenth and final book. Here it is shown first of all what it means to say that art is *mimesis*, and then why, granting that characteristic, art can only have a subordinate status [*Stellung*]. Here a decision is made (but only in a certain respect)[50] about the metaphysical relation of art and truth.[51]

The moral—and this is the sole lesson of this overview and "reorganization" of the *Republic:* it is only after the elucidation of the essence of truth, in Book VII, that the essence of mimesis, the "truth" of mimesis, can be decided. The mimetology of Book (II and Book) III, then, does not reach this far. Or, if you prefer, it is not in the Platonic "poetics" that mimesis is to be reached or grasped. "Poetics" is not *decisive—critical* in the strongest sense.

4. That despite everything, Book III demonstrates that the artistic product, the *poietic,* is always simply the "*Darstellung* of what is." Mimesis is thus first of all *Dartsellung.* But this proposition (in which we recognize the equation, though not the translation, ventured by Herder and Solger in the last years of the eighteenth century)[52] is admissible only on the condition that we grant it its full weight. *Darstellung* is there, in fact, only for the *stele,* or—which amounts to the same thing—in order not to say *Nachahmung,* imitation. This is why *Darstellung* immediately calls up *Herstellung,* production or installation, in the most "active" sense of the word (whence the insistence on "activity," *Machen, Tun*), even if it is necessary to limit or restrain the autonomy of this "activity" by conceding that what is proper to it (supposing that it has any property whatsoever), that is, fashioning or fictioning (*Umbilden, Erdichten*), is of the order of counterfeiting (*Nachmachen*) or reproduction (*Ab-bilden*)—and thus of a certain "passivity." This is confirmed, moreover, a few pages later, by the "definitive" definition that Heidegger, calling this time upon Book X, proposes for mimesis: "*Mimesis* means counterfeiting [the 'making-after,' *das Nachmachen*],

50. Heidegger here makes reference to another Platonic problematic of art—the one taken up in the *Phaedrus,* for example, which is discussed in his next chapter.

51. *Nietzsche,* vol. 1, pp. 168–169.

52. Cf. Karl Wilhelm Ferdinand Solger, *Vorlesungen über Ästhetik,* pt. 2, ch. 3: "Von dem Organismus des Kunstlerischen Geistes," sect. 1: "Von der Poesie im Allgemeinen und von ihrer Eintheilung." This equation of terms has been rediscovered in numerous subsequent philological works, particularly (and to name only one of the most recent) in Oswald Koller's *Die Mimesis in der Antike: Nachahmung, Darstellung, Ausdruck* (Bern: Francke, 1954).

that is, *dar-stellen* and *her-stellen* something in a manner that is typical of something else [*d.h. etwas so dar-stellen und her-stellen, wie ein Anderes ist*]. Counterfeiting is done in the realm of *Herstellen,* taking this word in its broadest sense."⁵³ Mimesis, inasmuch as it is for Plato, for all of metaphysics, the essence of *poiesis* (including, no doubt, "natural" *poiesis*), is a mode of *installation* in general. For this reason, *Darstellen* means fundamentally "to install," "to statute." And thus it is better to say *Herstellen.*

These four fundamental traits (the "exclusion" of Book II, the displacement of what is essential to Book X, the relatively subsidiary character of the problematic of art, the twisting of *Darstellung* into *Herstellung*) indisputably orient Heidegger's commentary on the *Republic* and, at the same time, his entire interpretation of mimesis. They are of course indissociable: they constitute a whole. And the hermeneutic *system* they compose has a center. The latter, in its turn, coincides, as is *normal,* with the middle of that non-acephalous animal—standing (upright) on its feet, like every *logos*—which is the *Republic:* in other words, with Book VII (the myth of the cavern), whose commentary, although undertaken elsewhere, is here presupposed.⁵⁴ In other words, everything answers necessarily, as is said openly, to the precondition of the question of truth. That is, to be more precise, to the *Fragestellung* itself, on the one hand—to the positing of the initial question (what can be said of the relation of art to truth in Plato?), which is obviously a question bearing as much on the essence of truth in general as on its Platonic determination; and, on the other hand, to the already established interpretation of the properly Platonic mode of the forgetting of *aletheia* in (and as) onto-ideo-logy. Everything is a function then—some discovery—of the place given to *aletheia.*

Perhaps this is not really a discovery, but in any case it accounts for the major statement around which the whole of Heidegger's commentary pivots (and whose principal proposition, moreover, Heidegger himself underscores)—a statement that is somewhat surprising (we will see in a moment why it is impossible to give it a true translation, that is, a translation without remainder): "*The interpretation of Being as eidos, presencing in outward appearance [Anwesen im Aussehen], presup-*

53. *Nietzsche,* vol. I, p. 173.

54. Cf. "Plato's Doctrine of Truth," where, we should note, at no moment is the "mythical" character of Plato's text on the cave—a "mythical" character that is nevertheless suspect to Heidegger, if we may rely on the quotation marks that never fail to enclose his use of the word "Gleichniss"—put into question, in any way whatsoever.

poses the interpretation of truth as aletheia—Unverstelltheit. We must understand this if we wish to grasp the relation of art (*mimesis*) and truth in Plato's conception correctly, which is to say, in a Greek manner. Only in such a realm do Plato's questions unfold. From it derives the possibility of receiving answers."[55]

Even incompletely translated, the matter is clear.

And, as is glaringly obvious, it is exactly here that the loss of *Darstellung* comes to be inscribed. *Aletheia, a certain determination of aletheia,* obscures *Darstellung.* Scarcely having entered the scene, painfully hoisted onto the stage, the pedestal (*Gestell*) barely *installed,* then, Mimesis literally *falls away* [*détale*]. It drops, it takes a (bad) fall, or, in Greek, it *declines*—to find itself at once in bed (*kline*), that is, in the "clinic" of Book X.

How does all of this happen?

Everything here rests upon the translation, surprising in fact, and rare (if not unique), that Heidegger proposes for *aletheia: Unverstelltheit.* We expected the "veil," "covering over," "withdrawal," "forgetting," "obscuring"—we could expect anything, and yet it is the *stele* that wins out. Of course, *Unverstelltheit,* in its most banal sense, "means" *non-dissimulation* and can pass for as good an equivalent of *Unverborgenheit,* for example, as any other term. Moreover, it is in this sense that one must first understand it, since, a few lines earlier, *Unverstelltheit* is coupled with *Offenheit* ("being open"), which like *Offenbarung* ("disclosure") is one of the master words of the "ontological" vocabulary, and because everywhere else, *aletheia* is *Unverborgenheit. Unverstelltheit,* then, designates "unveiling," "dis-occultation." But it does not translate *aletheia.* If it translates anything (or can, above all, even be translated), it would be rather *non-displacement, remaining-standing,* or *not-falling, non-instability.*[56] In fact, by playing on certain possibilities in French (as it happens, though, they are quite slight), we could venture *désenvoilement* (from *s'envoiler, envoilage, envoilement*—where, by analogy with the curve of a sail, the warping of steel being tempered is designated).[57] This would have the merit of allowing *aletheia* to be heard, but the inconvenience of leaving the *stele,* so to speak, to the *oubliettes.* As a matter of fact, no possibility is very satisfying, and it is

55. *Nietzsche,* vol. I, p. 173.

56. But we must not forget that *verstellen* ("to disinstall," "to displace," "to disarrange," "to mix up," etc.) can also mean "to counterfeit" or "to disguise" (one's voice, one's gestures, one's writing).

57. This translation has been suggested to me by Mikkel Borch-Jacobsen.

probably better to resign ourselves to not translating the word at all. For there is something more important here.

What is more important is that this word arises, indeed *only* arises, in connection with mimesis. This is no doubt necessary: mimesis, as *poiesis* in general, "moves within the realm of *Herstellen* in its broadest sense." But this does not explain everything. And in particular it does not explain how the *stele* can be used for unveiling (even if only to designate unveiling). In other words, this does not explain how, when it is a question of mimesis, there could be an identification or confusion of erection and unveiling.[58] For the appearance of the word, here, in no way signifies any subordination of *aletheia* to *installation*. On the contrary, its function is to submit the *stele* to the law of unveiling—and in such a way that all *Stellung,* in whatever form (beginning with *Darstellung*), can be interpreted only in terms of the initial (always prior) determination of the essence of truth as *aletheia. Stele* is only a name for truth because truth is unveiling. And not the inverse. To put this in very precise terms, it is not the erection that unveils, but the unveiling that erects. Understand this as you will, all interpretations will hold. Because *aletheia* can be said to be *Unverstelltheit,* all *installation* is properly an inauguration, the unveiling of a *stele* or a *statue.* Or—what amounts to the same thing—all *installation* is an *establishing,* that is to say, a production.

So it is that the essence of mimesis is not imitation, but production "in its broadest sense"—and that it can be definitively circumscribed, in the *Republic,* only in Book X: that is, from the moment when it is explicitly determined as production, fabrication, *demiurgy. Only the demiurgic interpretation of mimesis* permits the disengaging of its essence, which is installation, or more precisely, "disinstallation." But what is a demiurge? He is a *Stellmacher,* an installer:

> Whoever produces/installs [*herstellt*] furniture [beds and tables taken as examples from the beginning of Book X of the *Republic*] is therefore called a *demiurge,* a worker [*Werker*], a manufacturer [*Anfertiger*], and maker [*Macher*] of something for the sake of the *demos.* In our language we have a word for such a person, although, it is true, we seldom use it

58. An analogous identification can be found in the passage from *An Introduction to Metaphysics* to which I have already referred, but this time (and undoubtedly not by accident), in connection with the way in which the Greeks thought the essence of language on the basis of a consideration of written language (of the letter as it is set up in the domain of the visible); that is, on the basis of a *grammatical* determination of language whose master words are *ptosis* (*casus,* case—fall) and *egklisis* (*declinatio,* declension).

and its meaning is restricted to a particular realm: the *Stellmacher* (the wheelwright), who constructs frames [*Gestelle*], meaning wagon chassis [*Wagengestelle*]. That furniture and *Gestelle* are made by a *Stellmacher*— that is no astonishing piece of wisdom! Far from it. All the same, we ought to think through the simplest things in the simplest clarity of their relationships. In this regard, the everyday state of affairs by which the *Stellmacher* installs and produces *Gestelle* gave a thinker like Plato something to think about.[59]

In any case, it gives a thinker like Heidegger something to think about.

The entire reading of Book X—which must be understood as a *con-firmation* of Plato's demiurgic mimetology—in fact proceeds from the assimilation of *aletheia* to *Unverstelltheit*. The reading is organized according to a movement which is essentially the reverse of the one that governs Heidegger's interpretation of the myth of the cavern. Just as in "Plato's Doctrine of Truth" it is a matter of showing that Plato (already) no longer understands the essence and meaning of *aletheia*— presuming it was ever, being so "self-evident" to the Greeks, in the least accessible—but instead begins to interpret it in terms of *homoiosis*, adequation (in terms of the justice or rectitude (*orthotes*) of a seeing or saying), thus preparing the ground for the future metaphysics of subjectivity and representation (*Vorstellung*),[60] to this same extent, then, the commentary on Book X strives to relate, by way of the *stele*, this subordination to rectitude (or erection)—upon which all of onto-ideo-logy grounds itself—to the "pre-supposition" of *aletheia*. Within the general economy of Heidegger's *Nietzsche*, the meaning and function of this gesture are clear: it is, in more or less the long run, the sole means of maintaining the version of the inversion of Platonism, that is, the story of Nietzsche's undivided submission to Platonism. If the question of the relationship between art and truth in Plato is inscribed in the last *instance* within the horizon of *aletheia*, we can indeed scarcely see how Nietzsche could have in any way displaced (*verstellen*) the position (*Stellung*) of this question. And in fact we have seen that he

59. *Nietzsche*, vol. 1, pp. 174–175.

60. Cf. *Questions* II, pp. 152ff. This is the famous thesis of the "subjugation" of *aletheia* by *idea*, by evidency or aspect (*Aus-sehen*), bringing about, according to the model of the correction of enunciation—that is, according to a problematic of the lie— a "displacement" of the essence, as well as the *place*, of truth: "As unveiling, truth is still a fundamental trait of being itself. But as the rectitude of seeing, it becomes the characteristic of a certain attitude of man toward the things that are" (pp. 153–154).

did not displace anything about it, at least fundamentally. But it is indispensable to recognize that this gesture corresponds precisely to the loss (or the "letting go") of *Darstellung*—that way of "systematically" minimizing everything that does not belong to the space of demiurgic mimetology: everything that does not stand out against the ground of production or *installation* and, because of this, does not immediately allow us to understand mimesis as *fall*.

In other words, the whole operation presupposes that mimesis can only be (that is, "be") *declination, instability, "disinstallation."*

Two major features of Heidegger's reading confirm this.

On the one hand—but we have already had occasion to notice this— we have the *insistence* with which Heidegger *stabilizes* the idea, that is, the insistence with which he progressively gives precedence, as regards the *eidos/idea*, to the *stele* over the aspect or manifestness, over the *Aussehen*. Or, to be more precise, the way in which Heidegger subordinates seeing (the theoretical) to the *stele*, itself understood as *aletheia*.[61]

But, on the other hand, and above all, we have Heidegger's commentary on the famous "paradigm of the mirror." And in this text the operation is doubled and reinforced by a "secondary" operation that affects the essence of demiurgy itself.

We know how this paradigm is introduced in Plato. Socrates, using the example of the bed and the table, situates the demiurge as the one who fabricates such furniture by keeping his eyes on the *idea* that they essentially are. It has thus been demonstrated, says Heidegger as he follows the text step by step, how the making, the *poiein* of the demiurge, is always, in relation to the idea, a counter-feiting (a *rendering after*). Consequently, the insurmountable limit of all "practice" has been shown, its internal limit, which is "inscribed *precisely in that which 'practice' needs* in order to be 'practical.'"[62] But this subordination of the *poiein*, adds Heidegger, has its other side. *Poiesis* is *at least* "ambivalent"—not only because it holds within it both art and technology (in their modern difference). It is also "ambivalent" because, as the whole tradition has ceaselessly repeated, in spite of appearances it "reveals" *physis* itself, it unveils unveiling—it illuminates *aletheia* and brings it partly out of its "crypt," disclosing that it is there (or that it *is* this crypt). *Aletheia,* that is to say (even under the cover of the idea), *Unverstelltheit:* "For the Greeks the 'Being' of fabricated things was defined, but differently than it is for us. Something produced/installed

61. See especially *Nietzsche*, vol. 1, p. 173.
62. Ibid., p. 175.

[*das Hergestellte*] 'is' because the Idea lets it be seen as such, lets it come to presence in its outward appearance, lets it 'be.' Only to that extent can what is itself be said 'to be.' Making and fabricating therefore mean to bring the outward appearance to show itself in something else, namely, in what is fabricated, to 'in-stall' the outward appearance, not in the sense of fabricating it but of letting it radiantly appear. What is fabricated 'is' only to the extent that in it the outward appearance, Being, radiates."[63] It is here that we turn to the question of the mirror. Here is Heidegger's translation:

But how would it be if there were a man "hos panta poiei, hosaper heis hekastos ton cheirotechnon" (596c), *who installed everything that every other single craftsman was able to make?* That would be a man of enormous powers, uncanny [*unheimlich*] and astonishing.[64] In fact there is such a man: "hapanta ergadzetai," *he installs anything and everything.* He can in-stall not only implements, "alla kai ta ek tes ges phuomena hapanta poiei kai zoia panta ergadzetai," *but also what comes forth from the earth, installing plants and animals and everything else:* "kai heauton," *indeed, himself too,* and besides that, earth and sky, "kai theous," *even the gods,* and everything in the heavens and in the underworld. But such an installer, standing above all beings and even above the gods, would be a sheer wonderworker [*Wundermann*]! Yet there is such a *demiourgos*, and he is nothing unusual; each of us is capable [*imstande*] of achieving such an installation. It is all a matter of observing "tini tropoi poiei," *in what way he installs.*[65]

63. Ibid., pp. 175–176. *Herstellen* thus means *erscheinen lassen*, "to let appear"—which also renders the German word *herausstellen*.

64. Heidegger translates Glaucon's reply ("Deinon tina legueis kai thaumaston an-dra") in the following way: "you speak there of a clever and admirable man." Later on, *thaumastos aner* is translated as *Wundermann*. I will return later to the translation of *deinos* as *unheimlich*.

65. Ibid., p. 176, emphasis added. We should note here that Heidegger translates the Greek word *ergadzetai* by *herstellen*, and not, as we might have expected (and, more-over, as he has done elsewhere), by *wirken* ("to work"). It is almost as if he feels it neces-sary to prevent *worker* from being heard within "demiurge": that is to say, as we will see in a moment, a problematic of *work* within the question of *poiesis* and *mimesis*. This is perhaps his way (more or less, and subtly) of dealing with Marx—especially in his in-contestable link with Platonism and Aristotle. We can already see evidence of this in the way in which he "dialogues" about the *worker* with Jünger (and about the market econ-omy with Rilke), or the way in which he restricts all his variations on the motifs of *work* and *thought* to his determination of the "work of thought" as *Handwerk*—as "surgery" or "handling" [*manoeuvre*], as craft (see especially *What Is Called Thinking?* pp. 14ff.). But this can be still better seen in the first of his "Munich lectures," that is, in his lecture on science, where he attempts—in order to make explicit the definition he wants to pro-pose for science, namely, "science is the theory of the real" (*des Wirklichen*)—to

Heidegger's commentary: "While meditating on what is installed, and on installation, we must pay heed to the *tropos*." The delimitation of demiurgy, of demiurgic *poiesis* (and consequently, of mimesis) rests essentially upon the *tropos*—on what we ordinarily translate, "correctly but inadequately," as "way," "fashion," "mode," and so on (*Weise, Art*). Everything depends on the way. The "wonder-worker" in question, for example, draws his uncanny (*unheimlich*) and astonishing powers from the *tropos* that he puts to work: to give himself the power to install anything and everything, he need only take a mirror and point it in all

---

"make clear," by relying on etymology, what *das Wirkliche* means, in its double meaning of "doing" and "working": "'To work' means 'to do' [*tun*]. What does 'to do' mean? The word belongs to the Indo-European stem, *dhe*; from this also stems the Greek *thesis*: setting, place, position [*Setzung, Stellung, Lage*]. This 'doing,' however, does not mean human activity only; above all it does not mean activity in the sense of action and agency. Growth also, the holding-sway of nature (*physis*), is a doing, and that in the strict sense of *thesis*. Only at a later time do the words *physis* and *thesis* come into opposition, something which in turn becomes possible only because a sameness determines them. *Physis* is *thesis*: from out of itself to lay something before [*vor-legen*], to place it here [to install, *her-stellen*], to bring it hither and forth [*her- und vor-bringen*], that is, into presencing. That which "does" in such a sense is that which works; it is that which pre-sences, in its presencing. The verb 'to work,' understood in this way—namely, as to bring hither and forth—names, then, one way in which that which presences presences. To work is to bring hither and forth, whether something brings itself forth hither into presencing of itself or whether the bringing hither and forth of something is accomplished by man . . . *Wirken* belongs to the Indo-Germanic stem *uerg*, whence our word *Werk* and the Greek word *ergon*. But never can it be sufficiently stressed: the fundamental characteristic of working and work does not lie in *efficere* and *effectus*, but lies rather in this: that something comes to stand and to lie [*zu stehen und zu liegen*] in unconcealment (unveiling). Even when the Greeks—that is to say, Aristotle—speak of that which the Romans call *causa efficiens*, they never mean the production of an effect. That which consummates itself in *ergon* is a self-bringing-forth into full presencing; *ergon* is that which in the genuine and highest sense presences [*an-west*]. For this reason and only for this reason does Aristotle name the presence of that which actually presences *energeia* and also *entelecheia*: a self-holding in consummation (i.e., consummation of presencing) . . . Ever since the period following Aristotle, however, this meaning of *energeia*, enduring-in-work, has been suppressed in favor of another. The Romans translate, i.e., think, *ergon* in terms of *operatio* as *actio*, and instead of *energeia* they say *actus*, a totally different word, with a totally different realm of meaning. That which is brought hither and brought forth now appears as that which results from an *operatio*. A result is that which follows out of and follows upon an *actio*: the consequence, the out-come [*Er-folg*]. The real is now that which has followed as consequence. The consequence is brought about by a thing [*Sache*] that precedes it, i.e., by the cause [*Ursache*] (*causa*). The real appears now in the light of the causality of the *causa efficiens*." ("Science and Reflection," pp. 159–161.) All of these analyses coincide exactly with and confirm Heidegger's interpretation of *poiesis* in *Nietzsche*.

directions. The trope, in this case, is the reflection—and the fact of using it. It is the utilization of the reflection.

But, says Heidegger, this is not exactly a trope: "*Tropos* means how one is turned [*gewendet*], in what direction one turns [*sich wendet*], where one stops, or where one is turned [*sich verwendet*], where one turns to [*gewendet*] and remains bound, and with what intention one does so."[66] In short, *tropos* is *Wendung*, the turn or the way things are turned [*tournure*]. Everything is in the turn. Which does not exactly mean that everything lies in a "turn of the hand," since then the distinction that Plato attempts to make here would not go beyond the difference between the shoemaker and the woodworker: two handicrafts, in other words, two "surgeries" (*kheirourgia, Handwerk*). The way of turning, here, must be understood in relation to *poiesis* as it is thought by the Greeks, that is, in relation to installation: "If we understand installation [*Herstellen*] in a Greek manner, in the sense of the assistance [*Beistellen*] of the Idea (or of the outward appearance) of something in something else, whatever else, then the mirror *does* in this particular sense in-stall the sun."[67] Consequently, mimesis—on the condition that we interpret *poiesis* in its truth and do not confuse it, in the modern way, with fabrication (that is, with the *work* of an active, efficient subject, etc.)—is linked to a certain turning of *Herstellung*, of installation, inasmuch as this installation is itself already a *Bei-stellung*, the idea's "being-installed-with" (something other), its *assistance* or *attendance* to something else. Mimesis is the *diversion* of (demiurgic) *poiesis*. That is to say, it is a *displacement*, a "*disinstallation*," in which, contrary to what takes place in installation properly speaking, the *Beistellung* (the eidetic or ideal attendance-to) can happen ultimately in any way whatsoever and in such a way that it proves difficult, if not impossible, to refer the thing thus installed to its truth or Being, to its idea. The relation of the thing to its idea, then, the eidetico-ideal *appropriation* (what is scholastically called "participation") is what is affected and touched by mimesis. This is why the *stele, aletheia*, takes a blow from it. What mimesis "produces," what it (dis)installs ([*ver*]*stellt*), does not in truth appear, does not unveil itself—even if, as is the case in specular reflection, it is indeed the aspect that appears in the reflected thing (in other words, even if the *assistance* is handled correctly, with rectitude or rightness—"faithfully"). For the only rigorous rectitude is one founded in *aletheia*. Moreover, Plato calls the "product" of mimesis, the mi-

66. *Nietzsche*, vol. 1, p. 176.
67. Ibid., p. 178.

meme, a *phenomenon:* "phainomena, ou mentoi onta ge pou tei aletheia," says Glaucon. Heidegger, instead of translating (?) this line as
"apparent objects, but without any reality,"[68] restores it in the following way: "But what shows itself in the mirror 'only *looks like* [*sieht* nur
so aus wie], *but all the same is not, something present in unconcealment*
[*Unverborgenheit*],' which is to say, something non-disinstalled/non-
dissimulated [*unverstellt*] by the 'merely outwardly appearing as,' i.e., by
semblance [*Anschein*] . . . Mirroring does install beings, indeed as self-
showing, but not as beings in un-concealment, not-being-disinstalled
[*das Nichtverstelltsein*]."[69] Mimesis, in this sense, therefore only "produces" the "phenomenal"—or disinstalls the ideal inasmuch as it is an
unveiling, or even as it is unveiled in ("natural" or demiurgic) *poiesis.*
Mimesis is the decline of *aletheia,* the "lying down" or "stretching out"
of the *stele:* Mimesis is the "easy lay" [*la Marie-couche-toi-là*] of truth.

From this point on, everything is set. The *difference* can be established, mimesis can be criticized and is subject to decision. Indeed, it all
becomes very easy. We must no doubt recognize, as Heidegger suggests, that "Plato is here wrestling [*ringt*] with the conception of the
differing *tropos,*" that all of this is not done all by itself, and that it is
necessary for him to risk a dangerous identification between "good"
and "bad" *poiesis,* between demiurgy and mimesis. But as Heidegger
also immediately recognizes, "the more firmly we hold onto the self-
sameness, the more significant the distinction must become." [70] In combat of this kind, in this "ring" (if we can be allowed to weave the
metaphor in a dubious way), one's adversary is expected to *take a fall.*
It's just a matter of setting the price. At least, this is how it goes when
it is Heidegger who speaks through the mouth of Plato—or who re-
writes him. And it is in this way that Heidegger gives us the last word
of the story, which is without even the least ambiguity, and wherein
stele and *aletheia* are necessarily conjugated one last time:

> *Mimesis* is the essence of all art. Hence a position of distance [*Fernstel-
> lung*] with respect to Being, to immediate and non-disinstalled/non-
> dissimulated outward appearance, to the *idea,* is proper to art. In regard
> to the opening up of Being, that is, to the exposition/apparition [*Her-
> ausstellung*] of Being in the unconcealed, *aletheia,* art is subordinate . . .

68. Lacoue-Labarthe is referring to the translation by Emile Chambry (Paris: Belles-
Lettres, 1967).—*Editor*
69. *Nietzsche,* vol. 1, p. 178, emphasis added.
70. Ibid.

Such diminution [*Verringerung*] of the way of installing is here an obscuring [*Verdunkelung*] and disinstallation/dissimulation.[71]

At least we could say that there is no ambiguity here if throughout this conclusion (which of course presupposes the commentary on what follows the "paradigm of the mirror," the three beds, etc.) there did not happen to reappear, against all expectations—*Darstellung* itself. Confirming the Platonic hierarchy of *poiesis* (the god, the demiurge, the zoographer—the painter), confirming therefore the distance of mimesis, *thrice removed* in relation to *aletheia*, and the reality of its "disinstalling" power, Heidegger recalls that what art "installs is not the *eidos* as *idea* (*phusis*), but *touto eidolon*"—simply the idol. And, exploiting the word, he adds that the idol, here, "is but the semblance [*Anschein*] of pure outward appearance. *Eidolon* means a little *eidos*, but not just in the sense of stature. In the way it shows and appears, the *eidolon* is something slight, small, or negligible [*geringes*]. It is a mere residue [*Rest*] of the genuine self-showing of beings, and even then in an alien domain, for example, color or some material of *Darstellung* [the material of (re)presentation, *Darstellungsstoff*]."[72]

Why does *Darstellung*, with *idol* as intermediary, return here?

Clearly, it returns first only out of necessity and in a restricted way. Things would have been fine without it. For if it returns so long after being "let go," it is only, as is abruptly indicated when Heidegger takes *material* into consideration (with which he was in fact little preoccupied until now), in order "to cover," hurriedly and furtively, what in all of this (in Plato's text as well as in the commentary on it offered by Heidegger—ultimately more Platonic than Plato himself) constitutes a hiatus and remains infinitely problematic: namely, the *deduction* of painting from the "paradigm of the mirror." What do pointing a mirror in all directions and painting on some surface really have in common?

When the passage from the mirror to painting takes place, Plato says (still in Heidegger's translation): "For I believe that the painter too belongs to this class of installers—that is, to the class of *Spiegelers*, of mirrorers [?]."[73] But it is Heidegger who here specifies further and names the kind of demiurge involved in the "paradigm of the mirror." Plato, for his part, is content to say, "For I take it that the painter too belongs to this class of demiurge" (596e). Glaucon, as expected of him, had re-

71. Ibid., p. 186.
72. Ibid.
73. Ibid., p. 179.

acted to the story of the mirrors by saying that nothing is ever yielded in this way but "phenomena." To which—according to Heidegger—Socrates responded by saying: "Fine, and by saying that you go to the heart of what is proper (to the matter, [*Sache*])."[74] For painting belongs to this type of demiurgy. And therefore, we find the painter among this kind of demiurge, among the *Spiegelers*.

But what does this mean? Does it mean that the mirror itself is a demiurge, an installer? According to sound logic, we would have to believe this if the painter is to be said to do the same thing as the mirror (re-produce, let's say). But since when can a mirror pass for a craftsman? If not, so to speak, by figure, by some rhetorical *turn*? By *trope*? And even in this case, moreover, supposing that we "personify" the mirror, how would such a craftsman-mirror be capable—as Plato's text repeats twice—of reflecting itself, of producing or installing itself [*heauton, sich selbst*]? Where have we ever seen mirrors reflect themselves? Where or when have we ever seen them enjoy the—Hegelian—privilege of absolute speculation (or reflection)? Except (empirically) by being two, face to face? Consequently, we must conclude that the *demiurge* to which the painter can (or should) be related is not the mirror, but he who carries it. But in what way is carrying a mirror a demiurgic act? What is it about carrying a mirror that involves a "making," a *poiein*? In truth, nothing much: it is enough simply to hold the mirror. We can admit that here *poiein* does not mean *to fabricate,* but rather *to install.* We can admit that the Greeks did not know the "meaning of work." But, when compared to a wheelwright, to a *Stellmacher*—when compared to a carpenter, or "even" a painter, the mirror-carrier has it pretty easy. One might say that this *also* is to be established: that one must lower the value of the painter, show that he does not install much, etc. But this cannot mean that he does not work—that he has not wrought [*ouvrager*] or worked [*oeuvrer*] (*ergadzetai, wirken*).[75] On the contrary. That he does is indisputable—and moreover not very interesting. But we cannot say as much for the carrier. For even if we admit that he has some role in the act of installation (and we are obliged to admit this), his contribution is reduced simply to *permitting* that *determinate* installation that is the specular installation. He is not the one who has produced the mirror—or the reflection (which is produced anyway, as soon as there is a reflecting surface somewhere,

74. Ibid., p. 178.
75. See note 65.

whatever it might be). At most, he is responsible (*aitios*)—though touching, ultimately, the very limit of pure passivity—for the mirror's orientation. At most, he is the pseudo-"author" (and in fact, as we will see in a moment, *pseudos* itself, the lie, is not far off) of a certain *Darstellung* of what is—of a certain (re)presentation of what is, requiring all the less work or activity as the *Darstellungsstoff* (here, among other things, the polished metal) does all of the work by itself. Or almost.

The "paradigm of the mirror" is therefore—in fact—a paradigm of *Darstellung*.

But it is rigged, a trick paradigm—a trap consisting of an artfully masked hole into which Heidegger, in a certain way, cannot avoid falling. And it is a mimetic fall—if there ever was one—since he falls for the trap while trying to outdo Plato. This can be "seen." I ("I") mean that all of this is perfectly legible: there are signs, and the "accident" does not occur without leaving traces.

The first of these traces is Heidegger's attempt (before or after the fall?) to fill in the hole, that is, to specify the demiurge to which the painter should be compared. A *Spiegeler*, he says. But what is a *Spiegeler*? Is it a *miroitier*, as Pierre Klossowski has translated it? A *Spiegelmacher*? A mirror merchant? A mirror-carrier? What kind of installer is he? One who works or one who doesn't? And why wish to designate, assign, or name him when Plato is careful not to? As is immediately evident, the trace here is the return or persistence of the two questions that Heidegger constantly "represses":[76] namely, the question of manufacture or *work* (insofar as it is a modern, non-Greek question), and the question of the *subject* (insofar as this is *the* modern question par excellence—and, moreover, the question upon which the modernity of the preceding question depends). "Who *works/manufactures what?*" This is the question we must not read in Plato—that is, not without risking the breakdown of the entire critico-hermeneutic "system" of the delimitation of (the history of) metaphysics. This question—"Who works what?"—must remain the post-Hegelian question, that is to say, the question of the post-Hegelian Nietzsche-(Marx)-Jünger "apparatus." Not that of Plato's thought, or even that of Platonism.

This is, however, just the question that Plato *also* poses. Except that he poses it in the form of the question, "*What is?*" (What is installed?) And if he poses it in this form, it is certainly because he is Greek; but it is also because this is the only way of deciding as regards mimesis. It is

76. To say nothing, of course, of the question of the *Stoff*, of material.

a "ruse," a *turn*—something Greek again, a classic trick, and, ever since the *polytrope,* one of the most illustrious among them. The turn—this trope of the mirror (the reflection trick)—consists in effect of speaking of *Darstellung* in terms of *Herstellung.* The second trace, then, is the resurgence *in extremis* of *Darstellung.* We discover here, after the fact, that the trick has consisted in speaking of the producing "subject" (of the producer) in terms of the product. It has consisted in *displacing* the emphasis from the producer to the product, in minimizing this product (hence the idol—and its declination, stuntedness, its distance from truth, etc.) in order to be done with the producer, that is, with the "producer."

But which "producer?" The painter? The painter-artist? Yes, if you will. But he is not really the target here. The victim of the trope is in fact the *tragic author,* the "poet." For he is the "true" mimetician, that is to say, the dangerous mimetician. And it is he who must be excluded, banished. Philosophy has an old account to settle (a great struggle to carry out—608b) with him (with *poiesis*—in the sense that he embodies it); there is an ancient discord, a long-standing difference (*palaia diaphora*—607b) between them.[77] Heidegger, moreover, is obliged to admit this. Indeed this is precisely why, when reintroducing *Darstellung* in "conclusion," he cites the very passage wherein Plato deduces, from the entire specular-pictorial operation, the subordination of the tragic poet (he is third in relation to the king—to the philosopher), at least "insofar as he is a mimetician." *Ut pictura poesis . . .*

But in Plato, at least, this was foreseeable because it was explicitly announced. This is the entire aim of the opening of Book X (595a–c). In Heidegger, however, we have nothing like this. Everything comes as a surprise. And for good reason, since Heidegger has in fact not read this opening. Instead, multiplying precautions and excuses (one can't read everything; I summarize; I'm going right to the heart of the matter, but one should follow the argument in its detail; and so on), he has taken his point of departure one page later—at which point, the ques-

---

77. See *Nietzsche,* vol. 1, p. 189, where Heidegger nevertheless refuses to consider the possibility that the *diaphora* between art and truth that Plato speaks of—although *diaphora* signifies more than simple difference—can be assimilated to discord in its proper sense, to what Nietzsche means by *Zwiespalt;* this for the excellent reason that "if a discordance prevails in Nietzsche's inverted Platonism, and if that is possible only to the extent that there is discordance already in Platonism; and if the discordance is in Nietzsche's view a dreadful one; then for Plato it must be the reverse, that is to say, it must be a severance that nevertheless is concordant."

tion of *poiesis* having been put back into place, we come upon the question (at the end of 595c): What is mimesis?

It is here that the trick begins—a "turn" all the more difficult to circumvent because we still don't know who exactly its author is. Who poses the question (or who has it posed)? It is a matter of trope, of the "way of going about it." How does Socrates go about it? What is it that makes him go about it in this way? *Who* makes him go about it in this way? The question of the trope (and there is something necessary in this) redoubles itself immediately; it implies its own duplication—it is at the same time a question of *Darstellung*. Still, in order to see this, we must not disregard even in the "insignificance" of its detail a certain *fictioning* of the text (of the dialogue, if it is one), a certain *Erdichtung* which is its *Darstellung*. In other words, we must not hasten simply to *identify* (for example) Socrates with Plato (page 171: "Socrates (i.e., Plato) says in that regard . . ."), as elsewhere Zarathustra is identified with Nietzsche (immediately, and even though the question is asked, "*Who* is Nietzsche's Zarathustra?"); a gesture, moreover, that fits well, in both cases, with the selective or obliterating reading that organizes itself around the fundamental words or principal propositions, in other words, with that "hermeneutism" pushed to the extreme that governs (but also *undoes*—and in this, today still, lies its incommensurable greatness) all of Heidegger's work.

What in fact happens here? Plato (that is, Socrates)—"Plato"—*displaces* the question. He installs it differently. It is again a matter of a *Verstellung*. Put more precisely, this displacement is even a substitution, what in German can be called—and this is a word Heidegger never uses in any of his variations on *stele*—a *Stellvertretung*. In place of the question, "*Who is the mimetician (the tragic poet)?*" the question is posed, "*What is mimesis?*"—and the ruse is accomplished. For this immediately allows a return to the old, established habits, to sure ground where we know how to go about things, where to pass, what "path" to follow. In other words, this opens up "the eidetic." One can then speak of what is seen and of what is not seen, of what appears and of what does not appear (or not so clearly), of what shows itself (upright, erect) and of what dissimulates itself, of what gives itself to be seen as this or that, just as it is or not, etc. In short, we can be installed within the visible realm: we do *theory*. All of which seems in fact, since we're speaking of theater, to force itself upon us—on the condition, however, of our not being too "watchful," precisely since nothing more is said about it.

Then, once installed in this way in the theoretical realm, an additional turn can be played out—and as a matter of fact, this is the real turn: *the theoretical itself is placed "en abyme."* A mirror is installed, right in the middle where everything comes to be reflected without exception, "theorized" and "theorizing": the whole of the theoretical realm (the totality of what is) in which we have been installed—indeed, ever since the episode of the cavern. This includes the "subject" who has installed (himself in) the theoretical realm and performed the operation, since the mirror allows one to reflect oneself, and since nothing at all prohibits now—on the contrary—that it should be "Plato" who thus watches himself over Socrates' shoulder or over that of his brother Glaucon (who is here "his" interlocutor and who is overwhelmed by such a "wonder"). It is, strictly speaking—that is, in Hegelian terms— *speculation:* absolute reflection and theory of theory.

But this mirror is not a mirror—or a false mirror, or a two-way mirror. It is there *for* the mimetician. It is only a certain means, a trope, for (re)presenting (*darstellen*) the mimetician. We have here, then, a strange mimetician: a mimetician who is frozen, fixed, installed—theorized. One that has become perfectly visible (and "revealing" himself as "working," of course, in and with the visible). But we hold on to him now, we have our eye on him. Indeed, the mirror is an absolute instrument, as has been known ever since (at least) the story of Perseus: it is the apparatus for gorgonizing Medusa, a fabulous "machine." It allows every possible turn, and is of a formidable—and, moreover, disquieting—efficacy. But nothing is too strong here, and all means are permitted in "capturing" the mimetician. The main thing, perhaps, is to render him, in effect, *unheimlich,* as the image in a mirror, the double, the living being made into a thing (the animated inanimate)—or even (why not?) as that other kind of double that deceives regarding its "life": the mechanical doll or automaton. The trick is perhaps one of those we attribute to *magic* (but isn't Socrates just a bit of a *sorcerer?*), by which the "subject" is "torpedoed," immobilized, put into catalepsy—just as Socrates, as it happens, falls into it *sua sponte* (*dixit* Plato, at least, whose advantage is certainly served by this).[78] Or perhaps, but

78. At least if we suspect, behind the Platonic *Darstellung* of the "Socratic figure," a "manipulation," that is, an entire strategy of mastery on the part of Plato himself in relation to his own "master"—in relation to the one whom he *institutes* as the master-philosopher and in relation to whom, for reasons that will appear shortly, it is a matter, in writing (him), of regaining mastery.

in reverse, it is one of those puppet tricks with which *thaumatopoioi* produce wonders and, as in the cavern, are capable of making one take shadows for being. Or perhaps again, and still in the reverse sense (in terms of mortification), it is a tremendous Daedalian artifice, in the genre of the "living statue" (an animated *Gestalt*)—Socrates, we remember, is fond of speaking of them.[79] In any case, though, one must understand that the "trick of the mirror" is a turn or trick of conjuring or illusionism (*thaumatopoiia,* from *thauma, thaw,* cf. *theaomai*):[80] *theo-*

79. See Pierre-Maxime Schuhl, *Platon et l'art de son temps* (Paris: Presses Universitaires de France, 1952), pp. 50 and 94ff., and in particular for the opposition between "animated statues" (the living statues of Daedalus or of Pygmalion) and "inert images" (for example, the "mute paintings" that serve to designate writing in the *Phaedrus*). See also, on the myth of Daedalus, H. Damisch, "La danse de Thésée," in *Tel Quel* 26 (1966): 60–68. One should also show here, in detail, with other texts by Plato, that what unsettles him, in the plastic realm or in "fiction" (whatever form it might take), is, as P. M. Schuhl has suggested, *simultaneously* that the inanimate being should give itself as something alive and that this (falsely or illusorily) living thing should never be sufficiently alive, that is, it should always let death show through too much (in other words, "brute" death, the bad death that the sensible world holds—and not that death that marks the "separation of the soul and the body" as the beginning of the true "life of the spirit"). The *deinon,* the *Unheimliche* (as the ex-patriation or exile of the soul, as well) is this unassignable, this "neither dead nor alive," that disturbs, or always risks disturbing, the fundamental ontological opposition (between the present and the non-present). This is mimesis, the "disquieting strangeness" of fiction: undecidability "itself."

80. But etymology against etymology, perhaps it is time to recall that Heidegger's mistrust of the *theoretical* is all the weaker (and consequently his "fulfillment" of the Platonic gesture, of Platonic mimetology, is all the more marked) for the fact that *theoria,* at least initially, is not unrelated to *aletheia.* In fact, in his lecture on science, as he tries to clarify the meaning of the term *theory,* Heidegger writes the following: "The word 'theory' stems from the Greek verb *theorein.* The noun belonging to it is *theoria.* Peculiar to these words is a lofty and mysterious meaning. The verb *theorein* grew out of the coalescing of two root words, *thea* and *horao. Thea* (cf. 'theater') is the outward look, the aspect, in which something shows itself, the outward appearance in which it offers itself. Plato names this aspect in which what presences shows what it is, *eidos.* To have seen this aspect, *eidenai,* is to know [*wissen*]. The second root word in *theorein, horao,* means: to look at something attentively, to look it over, to view it closely. Thus it follows that *theorein* is *thean horan,* to look attentively on the outward appearance wherein what presences becomes visible and, through such seeing, to linger with it . . . [But] the Greeks, who in a unique way thought out of their language, i.e., received from it their human existence, were also able to hear something else in the word *theoria,* and this in accordance with the supreme rank that *theoria* occupies within the Greek *bios.* When differently stressed, the two root words *thea* and *orao* can read *thea* and *ora. Thea* is goddess. It is as a goddess that *Aletheia,* the unconcealment from out of which and in which that which presences presences, appears to the early thinker Parmenides.

rization is a *thaumaturgy,* but one in which the *thaumaturge* himself is the victim (according to the "Cretan law," if you will, to which Daedalus succumbs). Indeed, what is involved is an anti-thaumaturgic thaumaturgy (a *mise-en-abyme* that neutralizes the mirror), destined to contain the thaumaturge, to master that *deinos kai thaumastos aner* (that *unheimliche Wundermann*) who is the mimetician, to reduce his disquieting and prodigious power by simply *revealing* that it rests only upon a play of mirror(s) and is therefore nothing—or nearly nothing: a mere sleight of hand, a *Stellvertretung.* This latter would consist in doing everything without doing anything, in pretending to know how to do everything when one does not work and is content to imitate or "double" (or, in the language of the theater, *stellvertreten*) the one who does something by fraudulently substituting oneself for him and by using, in order "to produce" the illusion, a material that lends itself to this in advance (or that others have already prepared in advance) and that one need only *divert* from its own *proper* use, or use generally and *improperly.* In the face of the *Unheimliche*—the improper—mastery becomes possible only by taking it still further, by outdoing it with the *Unheimliche.* This is what speculation is.

Apparently, it makes the decision possible. At least, Heidegger does everything he can to make it allow it. And it is true in any case that everything ends well. From the mirror we pass to painting, from there—now that we have a hold on mimesis in general—to poetry, and the matter is settled. One must recognize, however, that this movement takes some time and that things are perhaps not so simple as they appear. In particular, the passage from the painter to the poet does not seem a matter of course, and one must still close one's eyes somewhat to the status or function of painting. For if painting consists, with regard to each thing, in "miming" it [*mimétiser*] such as it appears, and in producing, in conformity with its specular essence, the "phantasm," if,

---

We translate *aletheia* by the Latin word *veritas* and by our German word *Wahrheit* [truth].

The Greek word *ora* signifies the respect we have, the honor and esteem we bestow. If now we think the word *theoria* in the context of the meanings of the words just cited, then *theoria* is the reverent paying heed to the unconcealment of what presences. Theory in the old, and that means the early but by no means obsolete, sense is the *beholding that watches over truth.* Our Old High German word *wara* (whence *wahr, wahren,* and *Wahrheit*) goes back to the same stem as the Greek *horao, ora, wora*" ("Science and Reflection," pp. 163–165).

in this way—although in miniature and under the form of the idol—painting can make anything (that is, make everything the other *demiurges* make) it is hard to understand why its privileged function would be to paint "a shoemaker, a carpenter, or any other craftsman without knowing any of their trades," and consequently, what commits it to representing all the bodies of tradesmen, as is said in the *Republic* at 598b–c. We thought the painter painted a bed, and instead he paints a carpenter. Soon, he'd be painting himself . . . But the passage is finally made (always on the condition of our not watching too closely)—or at least it costs us nothing to believe this.

It still remains tenuous, though; and it is laborious. For as the passage to poetry reveals, speculation (the *mise-en-abyme,* the theoretical reduction) does not happen all by itself. It remains fragile. And, in fact, if the entire operation consists in trying to go one better than mimesis in order to master it, if it is a question of *circumventing* mimesis, though with its own means (without which, of course, this operation would be null and void), how would it be possible to have even the slightest chance of success—since mimesis is precisely the absence of appropriate means, and since this is even what is supposed to be *shown*? How do we appropriate the improper? How do we make the improper appropriate without aggravating still further the improper? If one must become more of a mimetician than the mimetician "himself" (who?), how can we ever be done? Specularization ("the trick of the mirror") has precisely this function: it assigns to mimesis its means. It makes of mimesis a "theoretical" practice that organizes itself within the visible. It delimits mimesis as (re)presentation/reproduction, as "imitation," as installation with a character of veri-similitude (the true here being determined in terms of idea and *aletheia*). And from the point of view of posterity at least, we know to what extent this trick has succeeded: we are far from having gotten over it. But as regards "Plato," what exactly happens here? Is the infinitization of the *mise-en-abyme,* its "hyperbolic" character, enough to compensate for the appropriation of mimesis, for its onto-ideo-logical reduction? Is the use of *a* mimetic means enough to conjure mimesis? Can this means be the means of all means? Is it essentially a question, in mimesis, of *reflection*?[81]

81. It has been indicated to me that the preceding discussion comes very close to the analysis of Platonic mimesis proposed by Eugen Fink, in *Spiel als Weltsymbol* (Stuttgart: W. Kohlhammer, 1960); see especially ch. 2, sect. 8. So noted then—despite the difference (which is clear enough) in our "intentions."

The Unstable

Os aneplasse Platon [o] peplasmena thaumata eidus.[82]

—Timon, cited by Diogenes Laertius, III, 26

Zwischen den epochalen Gestalten des Seins und der Verwandlung des Seins ins Ereignis steht das *Ge-stell.* Dieses ist gleichsam eine Zwischenstation, bietet einen doppelten Anblick, ist—so könnte man sagen—ein Januskopf. Es kann nämlich noch gleichsam als eine Fortführung des Willens zum Willen, mithin als eine äusserste Ausprägung des Seins verstanden werden. Zugleich ist es aber eine Vorform des Ereignisses selbst.[83]

—Heidegger, "Protokoll zu einem Seminar über den
Vortrag Zeit und Sein"

If these questions are inevitable, it is first of all because it is difficult not to recognize that in the *Republic* Plato must try twice to reach (if he does reach) a decision on mimesis—*to establish a difference.* Of course, secondarily, it is also because this double attempt is apparently not rewarded with the degree of success necessary to exempt Plato from having to start over again, in another place, any number of times. But let us stay with the *Republic,* with the (simple) repetition in the *Republic* of the anti-mimetic operation: the repetition in itself gives us suf-

82. The verse from Timon, formed upon a play on words (a "paragram," says Diogenes), associates Plato's name with the verb *plassein* (in Attic, *plattein*): "to model," "to fashion"—and also "to imagine," "to feign," "to simulate," and so on (compare the Latin *fingere, fictio*), in short *to fiction* (compare the French *plastique*). Its *witzig* character obviously makes it impossible to propose a satisfactory translation for it. Starting from an English translation by R. D. Hicks (Cambridge, Mass.: Harvard University Press, 1925), Genaille tries to restore the verse's "sonorous correspondence" (its *parisosis*) and comes up with: "Comme Platon plaçait de plastiques paroles" (compare the English version, which is even more awkward: "As Plato placed strange platitudes"). Cobet's Latin translation (Paris: Firmin Didot, 1862), although closer to the meaning of the line, fails to restore anything at all: "Ut conficta Plato astutus miracula finxit" (that is, word for word: "As the astute Plato fictioned fictive wonders"). But it is obvious that translating *eidos* by *astutus* takes away a good deal of the line's philosophical "salt."

83. The passage from Heidegger can be translated—approximately—as follows ("approximately" if only because *Ereignis,* both "event" *and* "appropriation," is "properly" untranslatable): "Between the epochal figures of Being and the transformation of Being into *Ereignis* stands the *Ge-stell.* The *Ge-stell* is an in-between stage, so to speak. It offers a double aspect—one might say, a Janus head. It can be understood as a kind of continuation of the will to will, thus as an extreme imprint of Being. At the same time, however, it is a prefiguration of *Ereignis* itself." From *Zur Sache des Denkens* (Tübingen: Niemeyer, 1969), pp. 56–57.

ficient reason to return and look more closely. Perhaps this repetition is even the true sign that the anti-mimetic operation is necessarily doomed to failure, that it can never succeed: at least—since it was not without efficacy for the "others" (and in particular for what will end by being called "literature")—where it takes place, and for the one who produces it. Perhaps, then, this repetition is the true sign of what would have to be thought, if this were not absurd in principle, as the "constitutive undecidability" of mimesis—an undecidability such that there is no philosophical ruse (and especially not the specular/speculative one) capable of overcoming it, or the least critical gesture ("political," for example) able to elude the strange power of contamination that it contains in and of "itself."

Heidegger, as we have already seen, neglects this repetition, even though Plato does not fail to emphasize it. But, undoubtedly, to be interested in these things is to yield to mere "philology."[84]

How, then, despite everything, does Plato emphasize this repetition?

Simply by opening Book X with a kind of preliminary declaration in which Socrates unequivocally affirms that of all that has been thought on the subject of the State—on the possibility of a State whose establishment or function is characterized by an unparalleled rectitude—the most important thing is unquestionably what has been thought about poetry. That is to say, what has been decided regarding the exclusion of "mimetic poetry" (595a). One could not more clearly designate the result achieved as early as about the first third of Book III, at the end of what we can thus think of as Plato's "poetics" (in its narrow sense—which does not include "musicology"; see 398a–b). There, for the first time—that is, before such a gesture is confirmed in Book X itself (607a–608b)[85]—Socrates gives the poet-mimetician (and only him)

---

84. On the limits of Nietzsche's philological reading of Plato, see *Nietzsche,* vol. 1, pp. 155–156. Heidegger argues there that despite the correction of Schopenhauer's deformation of Plato which Nietzsche's philological competence makes possible, Nietzsche touches the heart of Plato's thought only in his understanding of the essence of nihilism, thus realizing the philosophical desire that was initially obscured by professional obligation.

85. Although it is accomplished here in a much less trenchant, decisive way. In fact, it is more of a "reluctant" separation, like that of "lovers who recognize the fatal consequences of their passion." If (imitative) poetry, then, managed to justify itself (to justify the utility or political necessity of both the charm that it exerts and the pleasure that it provides), it would be "open-heartedly" brought back into the city. This strange "erotic" relation that appears throughout Book X between the philosopher and the poet displaces and complicates the classical filial or fraternal rivalry.

a send-off, though not without having rendered homage to him as a sacred (*ieron*), prodigious (*thaumaston*), and ravishing (*hedun*) being, and not without having surrounded this expulsion with an entire ritual (perfume on the head, wrappings) which obviously recalls—is this an effect of mimesis?—the ritual of the *pharmakos*. If we are to believe Socrates (or "Socrates"), this expulsion would manifestly be the most decisive gesture as regards the "foundation of the State," the gesture upon which the uprightness of such a foundation would essentially depend. Political (re)dressing, then, would be a function of the expulsion of mimesis. That is to say, the political "system" (the State, its institutions, its hierarchy of positions, the status of its activities, and so on) would be organized upon this exclusion; it would be erected upon this empty place or installed around it. If one relates, as does Heidegger, *orthotes* to *Unverstelltheit*, to the *stele*, if one conceives of political *orthopedics* as an "aletheic" practice or, more immediately, as an "ideo-logical" practice, that is, as *theory*,[86] then what is at stake in the expulsion of mimesis is *dike* (that is, Being), the just installation and joining (*Fügung*) of being in its totality: *systematization* itself.[87] Heidegger, moreover, says it in nearly the same terms himself,[88] thus proving that the "philological" reading in this case would not have added much.

But this is not so clear.

To say, as Socrates does, that the essence of the political question is played out in this refusal of mimesis is clearly not to say that in the course of the *Republic*'s first few books the question of art happens to be raised only *among other* questions. It is to say that the question of art is the central question of the *Republic*—or of the republic. To indicate, moreover—and again this is what Socrates does (595b)—that the tripartition of the soul elaborated in Book IV was meant to reinforce the exclusion of mimesis is not only to suggest that, from one discussion of mimesis to the next, there is a link that is not exactly Book VII (the Cavern, the setting in place of onto-ideo-logy), but it is also to note, in the clearest way, that the question of mimesis has something to do with what must be called a *psycho-logy*—which, as we know, is proposed in this instance as a "psychology" of desire (*epithumia*) and aggressivity (*thumos*), that is, a "dualism of drives" in relation to which it is necessary to define and calculate the strategy of the *logos*. We also know that what is at stake in this "psychology" is precisely *dike*—ac-

86. See *Nietzsche*, vol. 1, p. 166.
87. On the "translation" of *sustema* (or *sustasis*) by *Fügung*, cf. note 49 above.
88. See ibid., p. 166.

cording to the famous "psychologico-political" analogy—that is, the just division of roles or the keeping of everything (men or "aspects" of the soul) in its *proper* place. It is a question of an *appropriate(d) installation,* of appropriation in general—as is confirmed in Book IX by the entire lengthy discussion on the forms of pleasure (on the tripartition of pleasure), and by what goes along with it (the "removal"—calculated in "base 3," of course—of the tyrant, the denunciation of bestiality, that last, or almost last form of depropriation, etc.), without forgetting Book IX's mimetic episode, the strange *fictioning,* using the model of mythological monsters, of that "image of the soul" intended to convey the effects of injustice. It is true that this resumption of "psychology" (which thus programs the return to the question of mimesis) presupposes, as Heidegger would say, the ontology of Book VII, that is—at least—the determination of the *philosophical* relation to truth. But ontology, also, is *always* presupposed. It is true as well, no doubt for this same reason—and because, ever since the Cavern, the philosopher has been installed—that Socrates speaks in Book X's opening pages of the imprescriptible respect owed to *aletheia*.[89] But the most important thing here is to decide whether this reference to *aletheia,* supposing we credit it with a very strong ontological charge, comes belatedly to support or second a gesture that has not been successfully carried out (and which must therefore be repeated), or whether it was already foreseen from the very beginning that we would pass through (the eidetic interpretation of) *aletheia* and carry out a long ontological detour in order to secure what, as was already known, could not be secured in any other way.

This is a question obviously related to the problem of the *Republic's* "composition." The problem is a classic one: Was the *Republic* written all at once or not? Where would a first version have ended? In what way could he have rewritten it? Or even—and this is a Nietzschean question: How did Plato (or "Plato"), in general, compose his works? A classic problem, then, but one which, precisely because of a lack of "philological" competence, I ("I") will refrain from taking up—but not without suggesting, in passing, that it is no doubt insoluble by

---

89. See 595b–c: "I must speak out [on the reason for which Socrates condemns poetry], although a certain love [*philia*] and reverence [*aidos*, a certain modesty] for Homer that has possessed me ever since I was a boy would stay me from speaking . . . Yet all the same we must not honor a man above truth." We can find an almost identical statement at the end of the examination of the question of mimesis ("it would be impious to betray what we believe to be the truth"—607c)—and again in an analogously "erotic" context (see note 78).

purely philological or historical ("empirical") means, and that, as such, it is probably devoid of all interest. Or rather, the uninteresting thing here would be to subject empirical enquiry to verification—and empiricism in general to certitude. To do so would be to leave the space of a questioning suspicion, or to make empiricism run counter to suspicion. But, as Nietzsche has taught us, it is necessary to maintain empiricism's suspicious acuity. And, in fact, even if we learned for certain that Plato rewrote the *Republic* two, three, or even four times, that he spent a certain number of years doing it, and so on, this would only confirm what everyone has already known for a long time (one need only, as they say, hold a pen—or even simply speak), namely that the result would be the same if he had written the book in two months and in his first attempt—because no one can master even the *merest* statement, whatever it might be, and nowhere, in text or speech, do we have to do with anything the least bit homogeneous. Even if we learned "empirically" that Plato did not write the *Republic,* or that the "original" text went through an incredible number of alterations or successive recastings; or even, as in the stories of Borges, if we had to attribute paternity to several writers (contemporaneous or not)—the problem would not change one iota. For reasons that "Plato himself" knew, denied, and betrayed *perfectly* (and which, as we will soon see, are not unconnected to his fear or hatred of mimesis), it is impossible, in principle, to assign a textual "property"—that is, first of all, to identify an author with certainty. In even the *merest* utterance, equivocity *at least* is the rule. *Pater semper incertus est.*

Fortunately, the question can be approached in a different way; after all, there is a philology in the "broad" sense.

For example, it goes without saying that this question can be approached as a question concerning the status, in all of this, of "psychology." And a question also concerning, by the same right, the exact contents of the said "psychology." It is curious that when Socrates refers to it in the beginning of Book X, he describes in the following way its consequences for mimetology itself: "psychology" shows, he says, or allows us to understand, that all things of the mimetic kind (and first of all tragedies) "seem to be a corruption of the judgment [*dianoia*] of all *listeners* [my emphasis] who do not possess as an antidote [*pharmakon*] a knowledge [*eidenai*] of things as they are" (595b).[90] I will return later (or elsewhere) to this "listening" to mimetic things, though we already

90. Lacoue-Labarthe is using in this passage a slightly modified translation of the *Republic* proposed by Léon Robin (Paris: Gallimard/Pléiade, 1959).—*Editor*

understand—keeping in mind the "specularization" of the mimetic—
what kind of significance this might have. The word "corruption" is
translating here the Greek word *lobe*—which means "outrage" ("shame
and dishonor"), but also "mutilating violence," "ruin," "destruction,"
and even (in Euripedes) "unreason" or "madness." The only remedy
for such an injury, for such a mutilation of *dianoia* (in this case, for
such *anoia,* such *de-mentia*) provoked by mimesis, is ontological contemplation, that is, *theory:* one must correct the (vulnerable) hearing
with the sight, and unreason by knowledge—let us say, just to play, by
(in)sight [*(sa)voir*]. Hence, we can see that Book X's entire "speculative" demonstration will have as its object the preparation of this
onto-ideological remedy (or the use of it on Glaucon, for example—
the most sensitive of ("Plato's") two brothers when it comes to being
fascinated by mimesis). The "trick of the mirror," in this sense, belongs
to pharmacology—but as is the case with any *pharmakon* or any "drug,"
it carries its share of reversibility, that is to say, here again, its "constitutive undecidability."[91] One could say, putting aside the consideration of undecidability, that this is also what is confirmed, at least up to
a certain point, by Heidegger's "ontological" analysis. Certainly. Nevertheless, we still need to understand why it is "psychology's" role to "reveal" the disastrous power of mimesis, and why it is psychology that
reinforces the will to decision in its regard.

How does "psychology" contribute to mimetology?

There can be no question here of embarking upon a commentary of
Books IV and IX of the *Republic.* We would never finish. However:
knowing, as everyone does, that what is being played out in the "psychology" of the *Republic* is the "logical" subjugation of desire and the
no less "logical" control of aggressivity (hatred, violence, irascibility—
which are to be diverted, transformed into courage and "heart," and
conditioned, at least insofar as the "guardians," the politico-military
apparatus, are concerned, so that they can be used for the internal and
external protection of the State);[92] knowing that the whole question is
therefore one of assuring the dominance of the rational part of the
soul, as it is said, over the dangerous conjunction of these two drives
out of which emerges the violence (injustice, *adikia*—"disjunction")

91. I refer here, and may this single mention suffice, to Jacques Derrida, in particular, as goes without saying, to "Plato's Pharmacy" and to "The Double Session," both in
Dissemination, trans. Barbara Johnson (Chicago: University of Chicago Press, 1981),
pp. 61–119 and 173–286, respectively.

92. See *The Republic,* II, 376.

that threatens the "installation" of the communal existence and risks poisoning—literally—all political life; knowing these things, perhaps we have some basis after all for suspecting that "Platonic psychology" is in fact a "psychology" of *desiring rivalry,* of the endless reciprocal hatred implied by the very stuff of desire itself—precisely by its *mimetic* nature.

Here we recognize the fundamental hypothesis upon which rest René Girard's now famous analyses: every desire is desire for the desire of the other (and not immediately desire for an object); every structure of desire is triangular (entailing the other—mediator or model—whose desire desire imitates); every desire is thus from its inception infused with hatred and rivalry. In short, the origin of desire is mimesis—mimetism—and no desire is ever forged that does not at once desire the death or the disappearance of the model or "exemplary" personage that gave rise to it. This is why, for Girard, "*mimesis* meets violence and violence redoubles *mimesis.*"[93] This is also why, in general, every culture (every society whatsoever) is built violently upon the ground—and the threat—of a *generalized* state of competition. The law of desire (the Law?) is that of reappropriation, of "recovery" from the primitive alienation that governs it. Desire wants difference and autonomy, the proper and property; it is the very will to *decision:* the *Same* (identity, identification, undifferentiation) is its terror and the evil that gnaws at it. Because desire's obsession is originality, desire wants its origin negated and its essence forgotten.

There is little need to linger here on what, in such a hypothesis—that is, in this "de-objectivation" of desire—distinguishes itself from (and is therefore rooted in) the Hegelian dialectic of self-consciousness; or, at the same conjuncture, from Nietzsche and Freud. What is essential, for the moment, lies in this belonging-together, of the kind we have just observed, of mimesis, desire, and rivalry. What is essential is the violent power of mimesis, not only inasmuch as desire is mimesis but, much more fundamentally perhaps, inasmuch as mimesis provokes desire. For it is finally an intuition of this sort that animates Plato's "psychology." It is really no coincidence if the mimetology of Books II and III arises with regard to the "pedagogical" problem raised by the guardians, that is, all those members of the social organism whose "natural violence" must be converted—a violence, as we shall

93. "System as Delirium," in *To Double Business Bound* (Baltimore: Johns Hopkins University Press, 1978), p. 93.

confirm shortly, that is desiring violence itself. Just as it is also no coincidence when Socrates relates the question of mimesis explicitly (indicating both that the question proceeds from it and helps to establish
it) to the tripartition of the soul, that is, more precisely, the basic bipartition of the "impulsive" [*pulsionnel*] and the "affective." In short, there
would be, in Platonic "psychology," a "psychology" of mimetic desire
and rivalry, constituting a clear doctrine of what such a desire and such
a rivalry lead to in the long run—not only "tyranny" but also reciprocal destruction, violent internal crisis, generalized undifferentiation
(for which the model is furnished, naturally, by familial war).[94] A "psychology" consequently, that is seeking to produce the *pharmakon* destined to ward off desire and rivalry, or seeking at least to bring about
the admission that it is urgent to adopt—with respect to those whose
entire occupation (their "trade": poets, artists of all sorts) is to ag-
gravate the mimetic illness, to propagate "examples," and so on—the
ritual procedures for the expulsion of the *pharmakos:* the entire politico-
religious protocol for excluding the scapegoat, whose function is to
resolve what Girard calls the "paroxysm" or the mimetic "crisis."

It is true that Girard denies Plato the privilege of having posed the
question of mimesis in these terms. But in so doing, he may be in his
turn, like Heidegger (although for other reasons, and in spite of the
prejudices he entertains with regard to Heideggerian "ontologism"),[95]
a victim of a certain reading of the *Republic*. It remains necessary, as
they tell us in school, to introduce some "nuances." For if Girard can
say here and there, for example, that only the "great writers (Cervantes, Stendhal, Dostoevski, Proust, etc.) have developed the quasi-

94. Plato's first examples, in Book II, of myths that furnish bad models (*tupoi*) and
thereby provoke "unjust" behavior are those of the castration of Uranus and the murder
of Cronus, fratricidal warfare, and so on. The stakes are clearly recognized, moreover,
when Plato remarks that stories based upon such models should not be told to children
(378c–d): "Still less must we make battles of gods and giants the subject for them of
stories and embroideries, and other enmities many and manifold of gods and heroes
toward their kith and kin. But if there is any likelihood of our persuading them that no
citizen ever quarreled with his fellow citizen and that the very idea of it is an impiety—
that is the sort of thing which ought rather to be said by their elders, men and women,
to children from the beginning and as they grow older, and we must compel the poets
to keep close to this in their compositions."

95. See especially *Violence and the Sacred*, trans. Patrick Gregory (Baltimore: Johns
Hopkins University Press, 1977), p. 308, where Girard, against the ontological inter-
pretation of Heidegger, reinstates the classic version (Nietzschean, for example) of
"Anaximander's words" on vengeance, punishment, and expiation.

theory of mimetic desire, absent in Plato and in antiquity, and once again suppressed in the modern period,"[96] or else that mimesis inspires in Plato an "ill-defined fear"[97] (doubtless because Plato, unlike Aristotle, whose theory of catharsis is clearcut, was "closer in time and spirit to the [mimetic] crisis"),[98] he is also quite ready to recognize that Plato does not speak of anything else and that he is capable in particular of noticing the boundless danger or threat toward which tragedy points. Except that—and here is Girard's major complaint—the strategy adopted by Plato proceeds from a simplification (that is, as we shall see, also from a misapprehension): for he is in effect content with *turning back* against the tragic poet the ritual expulsion of the *pharmakos* that grounds the tragic catharsis itself—and he does this because in fact "he resembles," in his idea of mimesis, "those ritual systems for which the maleficent aspects of nature remain inexorably maleficent and that seek to eliminate all trace of them. Plato does not imagine that tragic disorder, tragic violence could ever become synonymous with harmony and peace. That is why he rejects with horror the stirring of parricide and incest that Aristotle, on the contrary, and following him all Western culture, psychoanalysis included, wants to make again a 'cultural value.'"[99]

In other words, Plato is accused of *deciding* with respect to mimesis. And of deciding on the *model* (which he does not analyze, but which fascinates him) of the tragic decision itself. Of deciding without seeing or knowing, or desiring to do either, that from the very fact of (re)presentation, from the very fact of the vicarious structure (this with respect not even to sacrifice—which is already "theatrical"—but to a real, an actual collective murder)[100] of the tragic *Darstellung*, from the

96. "System as Delirium," p. 89. See also *Deceit, Desire, and the Novel: Self and Other in Literary Structure*, trans. Yvonne Freccero (Baltimore: Johns Hopkins University Press, 1965).

97. Ibid., p. 104.

98. *Violence and the Sacred*, p. 292.

99. Ibid., p. 295.

100. Ibid., primarily chs. 1 and 2. See also "Discussion avec René Girard," in *Esprit* (November 1973)—for example, this passage: "Ritual always has something paradoxical in it. It makes men relive the very thing—more or less reduced to a simulacrum, perhaps, but nevertheless analogous—whose return it seeks to stem or avoid . . . My hypothesis justifies both the function—the rite is the weakened reproduction of the original catharsis—and the genesis: if the community is again afflicted with violence, if it is afraid of falling back into violence, it is normal to have recourse to the remedy that cured the illness previously." (p. 538). This is why Girard's whole hermeneutics sup-

fact, in short, of the substitutive, doubling, supplementing nature of the *Stellvertretung* inherent in theatricality, tragedy (as, moreover, *already* ritual itself) compounds with the evil it denounces and proves to be incapable of containing it and "purifying" it. Tragedy would be no more, as Bataille remarked of sacrifice,[101] than "comedy," catharsis that is feigned, acted out, simulated, *mimed*—borrowing its means from (and making the borrowing depend upon) the very thing it seeks to rid itself of. What Girard disputes, fundamentally, is the usage, in regard to mimesis, of a homeopathic medication *based upon representation;* one which, for this reason, turns out not to be really homeopathic and remains *inadequate.* Consequently, Girard objects to the view that mimesis entails representation and can be controlled by a process of representation—or (re)presentation. This is why, if the structure of representation, whatever it is (*Vor-* or *Dar-stellung*), necessarily occasions the uncontrollable proliferation of doubles (of doubles that do not know themselves as such, caught up as they are, in effect, in the *re*presentative mechanism), if "as in every universe that veers toward tragedy there remain only *anti-heroes,* and the city, with which each one identifies himself in turn against the adversary of the moment, is in truth betrayed by all," then it is understandable that in tragedy—as in its philosophical double, Platonic dialogue—"it is the decomposition of the *polis* that we are given to decipher" and that Plato [his "philosophical text"] "functions, at a certain level, as an attempt at expulsion, perpetually renewed because it never reaches completion."[102]

This actually means two things.

On the one hand, it means that Plato does not avoid the trap of a

---

poses, beneath the ethnological or poetic text, an empirical reality whose "empirical character is not verifiable empirically . . . Even if innumerable intermediary stages exist between the spontaneous outbursts of violence and its religious imitations, even if these imitations are all that one can ever observe directly, it is necessary to affirm the real existence of the founding event" (*Violence and the Sacred,* p. 309).

101. See "Hegel, la mort et le sacrifice," *Deucalion* 5 (1955): 21–43. Bataille's well-known critique (if it is a critique) of Hegelian logic, dialectic, and the *Aufhebung*—of the impossibility for Hegel of "exiting" from representation—is articulated in terms of this sacrificial comedy; see Jacques Derrida, "From Restricted to General Economy: A Hegelianism without Reserve," in *Writing and Difference,* trans. Alan Bass (Chicago: University of Chicago Press, 1978), pp. 251–277. From this point of departure, it would be necessary to raise the question—and we will take this up a little later on—of Girard's (paradoxical) refusal to deal directly with Hegel.

102. *Violence and the Sacred,* pp. 295–296. On the basis of this analysis, Girard subscribes to a reading such as "Plato's Pharmacy."

determination or fixation, of a *representation* of the scapegoat—which he removes, as ritual and tragedy already do, from the arbitrariness that presides "in reality" or "originarily" over his "selection." On the other hand, and for this very reason (unless it is the inverse), it means that he cannot do otherwise than carry out mimetically the expulsion of mimesis—which amounts to not expelling it at all or to *repeating* indefinitely and *spectacularly,* as in religion or the theater, its vain expulsion.

Such an analysis could be indisputable, if it did not presuppose (and indeed this is what hides behind the apparent—and willful—"empirical naïveté" of the appeal to the *reality* of the primitive collective murder) the idea that the scapegoat is necessarily arbitrary at the beginning, and if, correlatively, in regard to Plato, it did not rest itself—curiously, but in a flagrant manner—upon a *Stellvertretung,* a substitution of scapegoats, whereby, as if by chance, nothing less than the whole question of the *Darstellung* of the Platonic text—as well as a certain relation of substitution, indeed of supplementation and doubling, implied by that same *Darstellung*—is evaded. For one can credit Girard with having called into question, after Bataille (though with much more brutality), the simulated character of sacrifice and of tragedy, and one can also give him credit for having delimited, after Derrida, the meaning of the Platonic reduction of the undecidable (that is, the impossibility, from Plato's position, of a real expulsion of mimesis);[103] yet, even while acknowledging these points, it is no less difficult to follow him when it becomes clear that the whole operation is sustained, not (as in Heidegger) by the simple identification of Socrates with Plato, but, more subtly—and as a result of a displacement that is, moreover, necessary—by the identification of Socrates with a tragic hero and of the Plato/Socrates relation with the Sophocles/Oedipus relation. Now this is just what Girard does. It is even the essential argument on which he bases the charge of insufficiency or misunderstanding that he brings

103. Bataille, though invoked just once, unless I am mistaken, in *Violence and the Sacred* (p. 222), continually underlies the Girardian problematic. Of course, Girard qualifies this presence with a sort of permanent and implicit rectification concerning Bataille's submission to modernity, i.e., to be more precise, to the *paradoxical* figure of a Hegelian romanticism (as Girard understands it). Bataille, in other words, is not naïve enough, he gives too much credit to representation, he lacks sufficient belief in the actuality of empirical violence, and so forth. *Mutatis mutandis,* the same criticism is addressed (concerning the motif of the interminable) to another crucial reference for Girard, that is, to Derrida. In sum, Derrida as well as Bataille—because of their (Hegelian and/or Heideggerian) sense of the closure of representation—carry out and fulfill the ritual and the religious, the law of repetition.

against Plato and, by the same token (but indirectly), against the entire Western tradition, found guilty, from Greek classicism right up to modern times (from Sophocles to Freud—or even to Deleuze-Guattari)[104] of a strange weakness in regard to the (myth of) Oedipus:

> Under the guise of the true strictures he addresses to the poet, implicit behind the literary and moral arguments, Plato cannot fail to define himself as the *enemy brother* of the poet, a veritable double, who, like all true *doubles,* is oblivious to the relationship. Toward Socrates, whom the city—unwilling to defile its hands by contact with an impious creature— asks to do away with himself, Plato's sympathy is every bit as suspect as that of Sophocles for his *pharmakos*-hero.[105]

The only trouble is that Plato is absolutely not unaware of himself as a double and rival of the poet,[106] and that this charge, which therefore touches upon the question of the "literary form" of Platonism (and, in general, upon the rivalry between "literature" and philosophy), con-

104. See "System as Delirium" on *Anti-Oedipus,* and Chapter 7 of *Violence and the Sacred* on Freud. The critique also applies, though to a lesser extent, to the Hölderlinian interpretation of Sophocles, which in fact covers over, as Girard sees it, the mimetic problematic as it arises factually, biographically, in Hölderlin's correspondence, that is, in relation to the figure of Schiller (see *Violence and the Sacred,* pp. 157ff.). Note, however, that within this vast panorama of the Occident's "culpable weakness" (with the exception of Aristotle—see pp. 290ff.) in regard to Oedipus, Girard does not take into account either Hegel or Schelling (or Nietzsche, at least the Nietzsche of *The Birth of Tragedy*), that is, the *philosophical* interpretation of Oedipus (Oedipus as the prefiguration of self-consciousness, as the incarnation of the Greek desire for knowledge, etc.). (As concerns Hegel, see his discussion in the *Philosophy of History* of the passage from the Oriental world to Greece—along with all of the corresponding texts in the *Aesthetics* and in the *Philosophy of Religion.* Compare also the different analyses dispersed in the *Aesthetics* (on the subjects of tragedy, heroism, conflict, love, etc.) and in the *Philosophy of Right* (in particular, section 118 and the corresponding "Note"). With regard to Schelling, see his analysis of tragedy in the *Philosophie der Kunst* (II, 2, c) as well as the tenth of his *Philosophische Briefe über Dogmatismus und Kritizismus.* In all of these texts (as in a good number of Nietzschean aphorisms), each of which would demand a careful reading—we would find something quite other than the fascination that Girard finds for the "stirring up of parricide and incest," which, on the contrary, is regularly and carefully evaded, passed over silently, minimized—or "sublimated." Finally, the way in which Girard aligns an entire Western tradition with Freud—paradoxically, which is the least we can say—would certainly not stand up to such an analysis.

105. *Violence and the Sacred,* p. 295.

106. Through the intermediary of Socrates, in any case, the rivalry is constantly noted, from the famous episode in the *Phaedo* of Socrates' renunciation of poetry (followed, as Nietzsche emphasized, by its well-known *return*) to the signs of love displayed in the *Republic,* and between them the great triangular scene in the *Banquet* that unites and divides Socrates, Agathon, and Aristophanes, and in which Socrates' mastery

flates Socrates and the tragic poet, and both of them with the tragic
hero himself. The validity of such a reduction is not quite self-evident.

A number of apparently heterogeneous elements (at least two) enter
into a relation of mutual implication here. But the matter is really
simpler than it might seem. For the tragic contamination—the "Oedi-
palization" of Socrates, according to Girard, or if one challenges this
point, the dramatization of philosophical discourse, its obligatory passage through the rival "form"—depends essentially on a single phenomenon, which is the previous fixation, the *representation*, of the
scapegoat. This is to say, the properly religious misunderstanding (but
has there ever been any other kind?) of the mechanism of violence—
and of the essence of mimesis.

For the misunderstanding occurs with the advent of the ritual.

The rite, being a repetition that is institutionalized and codified, the
re-presentation and dramatization of the effective resolution of the violent mimetic crisis (of the collective murder of an arbitrary victim),
functions like any representation (any spectacle): it closes off and masks,
effaces the "thing itself" that it represents. The representation, con-

---

(in every sense of the word) is quite explicitly at play (we will return to this elsewhere).
At the same time, we should not forget the famous passage of the *Laws* (VII, 817) that
closes the analysis of the position of art and mimesis in the city: "For our tragic poets
and their so-called serious compositions, we may conceive some of them to approach us
with a question couched in these words or the like: May we pay your city and its territory a visit, sirs, or may we not? And may we bring our poetry along with us, or what
decision have you reached on this point? What would be the right answer to give to
such men of genius? Why this, I believe. Respected visitors, we are ourselves authors of
a tragedy, and that the finest and best we know how to make. In fact, our whole polity
has been constructed as a dramatization of a noble and perfect life; that is what *we* hold
to be in truth the most real of tragedies. Thus you are poets, and we also are poets in the
same style, rival artists and rival actors [need one underscore this?], and that in the
finest of all dramas, one which indeed can be produced only by a code of true law—or
at least this is our faith." I interrupt here this explicit—and abyssal—text. Not without
regret; for what follows would confirm again what is at stake here, what Girard—perhaps for want of sufficient attention to the complexity of the abyssal Platonic mechanism (we shall come back to this)—does not wish to see: Plato's exceedingly clear
posing of the very problem raised by Girard, all the clearer, we might say, because the
solution adopted (the expulsion of the poet in order to redeem the error of Socrates'
expulsion) is not very clear-cut and never achieves a *veritable decision* (if only because of
the *mise-en-abyme* and the abysses embedded in one another successively or superim-
posed). Yet Girard knows quite well that this is more or less willful and calculated indecision (at least as calculated as it is merely suffered) is, in a certain manner, "decisive."
But not in the same sense in which Girard believes in the possibility of a decision—or of
a revelation. This, as we shall see, is the kernel of the whole question.

strued as secondary, signifies the loss of the originary effectivity, of the origin itself—and that is what Girard, in an entirely classical manner, disapproves, though it is also, in an equally classical way, the entire underpinning of his hermeneutics and of its incontestable power of *decision*.[107] This leads back, as one might suspect—and as it happens, Girard has never made any mystery of it—to this primary intuition: only an originally non-religious predication, doing without sacrifice, only (in Girard's eyes) *Christianity* could reveal the essence of mimesis and of violence. For in this context to "reveal" means to make manifest the violent foundation of sociality, a foundation that, in general, remains foundational and (more or less) efficacious precisely insofar as it does not appear as what it is. To reveal is thus simultaneously to *present* the origin and the mechanism of sacrifice (to make manifest the simply repetitive and representational nature of the sacrifice), to trace the ritual back to the reality of the murderous primitive violence, and, by that very move, to designate openly, to show—and to refuse—the reciprocal violence, the mimetic competition, and so forth that the system as a whole is charged with containing or somehow forestalling. In other words, revelation is possible, and it is the *law of love*.[108] Prefigured (or glimpsed in advance) by Antigone—but tragedy, a deliberate representation of sacrificial representation, is also a "start towards a 'deconstruction' of the religious"—this law is realized only by and in Christ, following a movement which (one cannot avoid noting) recalls the Hegelian logic of a sublation [*relève*], through revelation, of Greek thought and (pre-Christian) religion; providing, it is true, we forget among the great precursors, Socrates.[109]

107. See especially "Discussion avec René Girard," pp. 549ff.

108. Ibid., pp. 551ff. Here is one example: "The Kingdom is perfect reciprocity, nothing more or less. As long as men ask for accountings from one another, there is no good reciprocity; good reciprocity comes only at the price of a total renunciation of violence, i.e., with the offering of oneself as victim. This is to say that, in the universe inaugurated by Christ, a universe in which revelation, even when not understood, little by little corrodes the structures of all society, acting like a slow but inexorable plague, we are always moving toward the moment at which there will no longer be any choice except between total destruction and this total renunciation of violence for which Christ offers the example."

109. Ibid., p. 555: "Christ must die because he is the only one to follow the requirement of absolute non-violence in a world that remains violent. In him, then, violence holds a victim who is no longer arbitrary, but extremely significant since he has opposed the order of violence. Up to this point, the logical movement is the same as in *Antigone,* as Simone Weil noticed. The refusal to yield to Creon's orders, i.e., to recognize the slightest 'difference' between identical beings, the enemy brothers, must lead Antigone

The whole question is consequently whether or not mimesis is *revealable*.

Girard, who is so hard on Plato for this, believes a decision on the matter is possible. Moreover, this is why the question always arises for him in terms of an alternative. And the decision, of course, is always positive.

But what does this suppose?

There are at least two points.

On the one hand, it supposes that revelation comes forth from a place which is not itself comprised or compromised in the mimetic economy—that is, from words or deeds which do not give in to the whirl of violence or to fascination with the sacred, and which, for this reason, do not allow themselves to be caught in the trap of ritual. Thus, it is necessary that there be nothing mimetic or sacrificial in the destiny of Christ: not the slightest "quotation" (in the sense in which Thomas Mann, for example, made use of this concept),[110] or the slightest

---

to death. One can even say that Antigone also announces the Kingdom when she indicts the gods of vengeance and affirms: *I was born to share not hate but love.* One can see in her, as in Christ, the greatest violence and no more violence at all since she deprives men of the aid of violence, of all sacrificial assistance. But Antigone is obviously just a prefiguration without any relation to the effectiveness—mainly negative henceforth yet always more formidable—of Christianity, on the cultural and planetary level." We can find entirely analogous propositions in Hegel, especially in the *History of Philosophy.* Antigone will have always been, as Hegel enjoys repeating in practically each of his courses, the "most sublime [figure] in the history of humanity"—the most authentic prefiguration of Christianity. But the most important thing to note, however, is that propositions of this kind find their place, in the *History of Philosophy,* in the chapter on Socrates, where despite his clear consciousness of the ambiguity of this figure (for Socrates is one), Hegel makes of the dying Socrates—and not without relating him to Christ—the hero who incarnates the tragic conflict between two laws and who expresses, against an era of the world spirit already completed, "the superior principle of the spirit" (trans. E. S. Haldane [London: Routledge and Kegan Paul, 1955], vol. 1, esp. pp. 443ff.). There would be much to say about these texts. But the strangest thing here, to get back to Girard, is the silence he observes—comparing Antigone and Christ in finally a perfectly classic manner—toward the third figure with whom they are usually associated. Which explains perhaps, elsewhere, the conceptual *hapax* represented, in relation to Socrates, by the idea of a *pharmakos* who consents in advance (*Violence and the Sacred,* p. 295). We will come back to this later.

110. See *Freud et l'avenir,* trans. F. Delmas (Paris: Albin Michel, 1960), pp. 240ff. Thomas Mann, moreover, proposes in passing that we read the death of Christ on the basis of the cry "Eli, Eli, lamma sabacthani," as a quotation from Psalm XXII from which the formula for the call is borrowed.

carrying-out of a "role," or the slightest scapegoat function (rejected and sanctified, humbled and uplifted, etc.). Girard may not be wrong in objecting to a Butlmannian style of "demythologization," but it is still necessary for him, in turn, to have recourse to something that closely resembles it.[111] For there is obviously no possible revelation except from the standpoint of an *absolute difference,* of *the* absolute difference—that is, of a "type of divinity" in Christ that is *entirely other.* And here—since apparently a faith is involved—we should no doubt renounce debate, were not a certain paradox evident in such a formidable machine of persuasion, totally occupied with denouncing the *claim to difference,* wherever it occurs, as the symptomatic vice par excellence of mimetic rivalry, organizing its own power—willing itself to be unique and subject to no possible comparison—upon the assertion that somewhere a difference came into being that was (and remains) immune to the mimetic contagion.[112]

But on the other hand, the idea of a possible revelation of mimesis also supposes that it is possible to return to the hither side of represented mimesis, that is, to the hither side of the sacrificial (ritual) "imitation" of the primitive murder. Thus, it also supposes that mimesis in general, beginning with that in which reciprocal violence (namely, desiring mimesis itself) takes root, is *anterior,* in some way or other, to representation. This, moreover, is precisely what Girard takes as one postulate, if not the postulate on which the whole edifice rests:

111. See "Discussion avec René Girard," p. 554. This does not at all prevent Girard, for example, from "demythicizing" in his own way, as he does some pages earlier, the theme of resurrection. For it is, of course, "Eli, Eli, lamma sabacthani" that is here called upon: "But the resurrection, you say. Is it not what marks anew the eternal play of sacralization, the death that springs from life and the life that springs from death? This is only true in appearance. Simone Weil was not mistaken here. She has found in *'Eli, eli, lamma sabacthani'* one of those words that makes the Gospels a founding charter unlike any other. This word . . . is decisive in that it makes the death of Christ the same as ours, a death wholly separated from and without relation to resurrection. Christ does not play with life and at death in the way of the phoenix, the aztec gods, or Dionysus" (p. 552).

112. This is where Christianity—whose entire force and cunning (as Nietzsche would have said) lies in the refusal, to which it has always clung, even at the apogee of its "liberalism," to let itself be situated by comparison—comes to support the solitude, itself incomparable, out of which Girard—literally—*prophesies.* (And in so doing, never misses an opportunity to distinguish himself violently from the competitive agitation of the modern "intelligentsia," in which he sees one of the premonitory signs of the apocalypse that menaces us all.)

At the outset, it is necessary to posit the principle of a mimetic desire, of a desiring *mimesis* on the hither side of every representation and every object choice. In support of this principle, we could refer to direct observation as well as to the works just mentioned [masterpieces that "range from Greek theater (and for this occasion, Plato) to Dostoevski and Proust, passing through Cervantes and Shakespeare"], and to many others. But we can be content to consider it simply as a postulate capable of generating not a linear theory of desire, but a logical development, which is at the same time a historical process with a remarkable explanatory power in the most diverse and sometimes most unexpected domains.

What desire "imitates," what it borrows from a "model," is desire itself, on the hither side of gestures, attitudes, manners, and everything to which one always reduces mimesis by never apprehending it except on the level of representation. It does so in the mode of a quasi-osmotic immediacy necessarily betrayed and lost in all the dualities of the modern problematics of desire, including that of the conscious and the unconscious.[113]

Desire "imitates" desire. Or perhaps, better yet, it *mimes* desire. Desire, if you will, desires desire. Granted. That is, after all, an old story. But if one is not content with this "quasi-osmotic immediacy," or if one has some trouble with it—if only because of its "soporific virtue" aspect— one might ask: What does that mean? Does it necessarily mean that desire does not pass by way of representation? If it is undeniable that desire draws on something that is previous to the visible, external, exhibited *Stellung* of the model (gestures, attitudes, and so on), does that suffice to prove that it does not represent to itself in one way or another the desire that it mimes or desires? Is there no representation except for one caught up in the visible and perceptible? Or, inasmuch as the second has almost always been reduced to the first, is representation always *"theoretical"*?

The question here bears upon the nature and the status of representation. Of representation in general.

Would mimesis, *in the very sense in which Girard uses the term,* not require precisely a rethinking of representation? That is, prior to the classical "theoretical" representation (to the dualism of the present and the represented), a thought of representation in which the *re-* of *repetition* would govern—and carry away—any presentational value (any sense of "objective" exhibition, derived or secondary externalization, spectacle for a subject, and so on)? In other words, would not mimesis,

113. "System as Delirium," p. 89.

this first and constitutive mimesis, not oblige us to form the hypothesis of "another stage"—still a stage, to be sure, but not yet that of a spectacle, one that is separated from any enclosed theater, from any space perhaps, inaccessible, in any case, to any perception whatsoever—on which the prescribed scenario of desire, unbeknownst to the supposed "subject," would be played every time? "Another stage" of which the stage itself, of the world or of the theater (set in whatever manner; this is not important), would never, owing to the constraint exerted by the primitive repetition, be anything other than an external lining [*doublure*] and the effectively secondary repercussion (of a secondariness comparable, for example, to the secondariness of Freud's "secondary processes"), probably linked to the illusion—which no "subject" ever gives up entirely—of a possible mastery of desire and of access to some originality or singularity?

The strangest thing about Girard's thought—the source, moreover, of all its force and its incredible power of conviction—is that, like all the critical "monisms" that go no further in relation to the classical dualisms than the monist affirmation (than anti-dualism), it constantly ends up running into and stiffening against what by every possible means it strives to induce and put across: namely, that representation—that is, repetition—is "originary." This, as we have just begun to see, obviously is "tenable" only, if there is ever the slightest chance that it be so, on the condition that we break down as much as possible the solidarity between representation and its classical concept—that of subjective representation (in the psychological or metaphysical sense), as well as that of specular representation (reflection, the mirror stage, and so on),[114] or, of course, that of "representation" in the theoretical-theatrical sense of the term. It is consequently "tenable" only on the condition that representation be torn from the ground of both *ideology* and of *subjecti(vi)ty,* in which philosophy has rooted it—and that we shake, fundamentally, the concept, indeed the "theorem," of the *sub-*

114. Girard sketches, however, in the "Discussion" in *Esprit,* a critique of the mirror stage which, although it rushes to link Lacan to Rank, and on the basis of a hasty and univocal interpretation of Freudian narcissism, would certainly deserve further development: "I do not believe in the mirror stage. It seems to me that there is an impasse there, a perpetuation of the effective solipsism that marks the Freudian conception of narcissism, or that of Rank in *Don Juan and the Double.* One always takes the *double,* starting from the individual subject, as a phantom, a phantasm, or as imaginary, instead of starting from two, i.e., from concrete relations. This seems to me important for the critique of the philosophical foundations of psychoanalysis which never starts out from the relation, but always from the isolated individual" (p. 542).

ject. For this reason, then, it may perhaps be necessary to begin search-
ing for the aforementioned "originary representation"—whatever may
be, in fact, the cumbersome philosophical surcharge of the concept of
the unconscious—in the direction of what Freud had occasion to
think, once the death instinct (repetition) was introduced, in the form
of a sort of "primary identification,"[115] or of what Nietzsche tried,
doubtless in vain, to thematize for quite a long time in terms of theatricality—as, for example, in this (programmatic) note of 1871 on the
primitive "tragic author-actor," in which there is nevertheless already
forming the suspicion of an "internal representation" preceding scenic
externalization and imitation, reflection, and self-consciousness, and
which would lie at the origin of sociality in general:

> What is the capacity to improvise on the basis of a foreign character?
> As such, it is not a question of *imitation,* for it is not reflection that is at
> the origin of such improvisations. In effect, it is necessary to ask oneself:
> how is the entry into a foreign individuality possible?
>
> It is first the liberation from one's own individuality, thus the act of
> immersing oneself in a representation . . . Each character is an internal
> representation. This internal representation is manifestly not identical to
> our conscious thought about ourselves.
>
> This entry into a foreign individuality is also artistic pleasure . . . This
> originary representation that constitutes the character is likewise the
> mother of all moral phenomena.[116]

115. See Chapter 7 of "Identification" in *Group Psychology and the Analysis of the Ego,*
in Freud, *The Standard Edition of the Complete Psychological Works* (London: Hogarth,
1953–1966), vol. 18, pp. 105–110. There Freud attempts, even if he cannot help "identifying" the figure of identification with the father figure, to "de-objectivate" desire (as
Girard would say), or at least to deduce the first "fixation" of desire on the mother from
this still prior identification. Furthermore, this is exactly why Girard, in relation to the
"later" Freud—in particular, the Freud of *Totem and Taboo*—constantly hesitates between a critique of Oedipalism (which Freud certainly did not "give up") and the recognition, inevitable for anyone who reads at all attentively, of the deep traces of a precise
questioning of this Oedipalism in Freud's last great texts (see *Violence and the Sacred,*
ch. 8). But here, as Girard hints ("Discussion," p. 542), it would be necessary to consider
the entire relation of Freud to Nietzsche.

116. This text, which must doubtless be read in its relation to the reformulation
Nietzsche will try to impose—beginning with *The Birth of Tragedy*—on the Aristotelian conception of catharsis, programs in large measure the Nietzschean doctrine of
"identification" that will lead, in a complex way, as Girard recognizes in the strongest
terms, to the "delirium" of the end ("System as Delirium," pp. 90ff.). We will return to
this elsewhere. (The text may be found in the edition of the *Werke* edited by Giorgio
Colli and Mazzino Montinari [New York: Walter de Gruyter, 1978], Abt. 3, Bd. 3,
p. 324.—*Editor*)

In these few propositions, actually heterogeneous in their scope as well as in their provenance, but which, for this very reason, may lead as far as it is possible—even today—to advance, there is certainly something to which Girard could subscribe. But it is also true—and, unlike most others, Girard does not fail to recognize it—that, pushed to its limit, if it is possible to do so, such a questioning of the originary and of identity, of presence, is probably, beyond the accepted (negative and critical) meaning of this word, *atheism*.

It is here, as Girard would say, that the apparent insufficiency of Platonism "tips over into its opposite." Or, to put it more precisely—and because the figure of reversal is, in this instance, inadequate—this is where Plato's forceful entry into the difficulty of mimesis (let us continue calling it, for the sake of economy, the specular/speculative operation), far from betraying an "ill-defined," obscure, and archaic fear, may just be able to provide, paradoxically, a precious insight into this "originary representation" that is perhaps the—abyssal—"ground" of mimesis.

First, given that the operation in question gets underway, in Plato, with the choice of the poet as the privileged figure of mimetism in general, it allows us to understand what Girard can only deny: namely, that the determination of the scapegoat, the selection of a *representative* of mimesis, is strictly inevitable from the moment when an act of expulsion (differentiation and rejection) is involved and when what is to be expelled—because it is nothing other than mimetic representation "itself," that is, mimesis as the *unassignable* danger that representation [*le représentatif*] might be primal, or, what amounts to the same thing, the danger of an originary absence of subjective "property" or "propriety"—can only be the externalized, scenic, spectacular mimesis. For it is quite necessary, in the rejection of the "bearer of mimesis," that the victim incarnate in one way or another this impropriety, this lack of being-proper necessarily supposed, as Plato knows very well, by the mimetic fact. That is to say, not only the undifferentiation and endless doubling which threaten the social body as a whole, but, on an underlying level and actually provoking them, *mimetism* itself, that pure and disquieting *plasticity* which potentially authorizes the varying appropriation of all characters and all functions (all the roles), that kind of "typical virtuosity" which doubtless requires a "subjective" base—a "wax"—but without any other property than an infinite malleability: *instability* "itself." It is therefore entirely necessary for the scapegoat to incarnate what Girard points to *under* the name of the "undifferentiated," which is the general absence of identity—or rather (we shall see why) the primitive, native lapse or default of identity. This is why the only recourse, with mimesis, is to differentiate it and to appropriate it, to identify it. In short, to *verify* it. Which would without fail betray the essence or property of mimesis, if there were an essence of mimesis or if what is "proper" to mimesis did not lie precisely in the fact that mimesis has no "proper" to it, ever (so that mimesis does not consist in the improper, either, or in who knows what "negative" essence, but *ek-sists,* or better yet, "de-sists" in this appropriation of everything supposedly proper that necessarily jeopardizes property "itself"). Which would betray its essence, in other words, if the "essence" of mimesis were not precisely absolute vicariousness, carried to the limit (but inexhaustible), endless and groundless—something like an infinity of substitution and *circulation* (already we must again think of Nietzsche): the very lapse "itself" of essence.

Because of this it is perhaps not abusive to suggest that the victim is always, whatever his status, a *mimos.* That is, in effect, anyone at all, but a "just anyone" who signals himself (if we can use this kind of expression) as "such," who exhibits "his" non-identity, who brings along in "his" history (Oedipus) or "his" function (the king), in "his" *ethos* (the fool) or "his" trade (the actor, the artist),[117] the dreaded evidence of the primal status and undivided rule of mimetic confusion. The victim is not arbitrary. The choice of a representative of mimesis—of a "better-qualified" representative of mimesis, a "specialist"—always bears in fact on the one who *shows himself* (i.e., shows "himself") as being at once everything—and nothing. The *pharmakos,* individual or collective, is always a *monster* (it is well known that every society maintains or creates such monsters). And his selection, taking no account of the fear and projection onto the "other" of what someone dreads (or desires) in himself, is always guided and constrained by what in the mimetic representation can be seen or perceived—that is, what visibly, *manifestly,* redoubles the mimesis. Hence the oldest and most constant

---

117. Oedipus confuses the familial roles; the king represents all the functions; the fool mixes up words and deeds; and the actor represents ethical and ethological virtuosity, in the sense in which the Greeks spoke of "ethological" mimes. To this list one might add, by way of example, thinking of a famous passage from *The Gay Science* (Aphorism 361), "the" Jew and "the" woman: in short, everyone (and history has ceaselessly confirmed this in a terrifying way) of whom "one" can say that they do not have visibly—do not manifest—any property, that they always offer themselves *as* (something they "are" not). Thus all of those, as well, to whom "one" denies, in the very name of proprietary defensiveness, the right to property. As we know, an entire economy of fear (and consequently of stupidity) is at play here.

gesture vis-à-vis mimesis, which is the attempt to circumscribe it "theoretically,"[118] to put it on stage and theatricalize it in order to try to
catch it in the trap of (in)sight [*(sa)voir*]. Far from covering up or
masking mimesis, theatricality "reveals" it—which means that it fixes
it, defines and "presents" it as that which, in all events, it never is on its
"own." More rigorously, to mask and to reveal, regarding mimesis, to
betray and to unveil: these are—as finally we could never hope to say
better—to go *from like to same* [*du pareil au même*]. Mimesis is always
from like to same. For such is the law of representation—or of (re)pre-
sentation (*Vorstellung* and *Darstellung*, here more than ever, are indissociable): there is "presented" in it what does not present itself and
cannot present itself, that is, there is represented in it what has always
already represented itself. This is why there is only one remedy against
representation, infinitely precarious, dangerous, and unstable: representation itself. And this is also why ritualization and dramatization—the
tragicomedy of sacrifice and of the spectacle—never end. To postulate
that there is, prior to religious or artistic repetition, a real violence, a
true murder, a "cruelty"—and in fact what would prohibit this?—does
not change a thing. No matter how much one invokes the suffering,
the injury, the wounds and death, all the thing's *physicality* (and this
exists; it is *really* inescapable), it will still be impossible to deny—
Bataille, for example, *experienced* this obstinately and tenaciously—that
there is never any factuality [*effectivité*] that is not from the "start" hollowed out and eroded by representation—if only, as we know, by language. Everything "begins" *also* by representation, and religion, in one
way or another, cannot be done with it.[119]

"I" pause here for a moment.
For in the long run all of this might insidiously lead us, finally, to

118. This always presupposes that the theoretical domain embraces the whole of
what is perceptible, or, if you prefer, that all of the "phenomenal," all of the sensible in
general, has already been reduced to the "visible." This may be the philosophical gesture
par excellence, though in no case can it be made into a simple one. For this reason, it
would be useless to see beneath the distinctions that are becoming operative here only
the very classical opposition between the visible and the invisible, and in particular between the visible and the audible. For not only is the audible always subject to a theoretical account but also a substantial portion of the visible does not fail to escape the
theoretical grasp. Let us say, provisionally, even though this is much too simple, that it
is a matter of attacking the optic, scopic, theatrical model of (in)sight, the exemplarity
of the eye—but not, however, with the idea of reaching any hither side of representation. An untenable position, if you will—but one that must be probed.

119. It is finally on the question of representation, in its relation to factuality, that

suspect that nothing in fact more *resembles* mimesis than *aletheia*. Or, if you prefer, and because this translation imposes itself somewhat in our classical memory, nothing more resembles truth than the veri-similar, verisimilitude. And this poses a few more problems.

To be more precise, then, mimesis resembles *aletheia* because *aletheia* does not resemble *itself* and cannot resemble itself, but rather—as either unveiling or non-disinstallation—endlessly withdraws, masks itself, de-sists. *Aletheia*—a woman, as everyone imagines knowing—*undresses "herself" and steals away ["se" dé-robe]* (the word has its resources

---

Girard's system constantly meets confusion. That a sacrifice, for example, might imply a real death and real horror, or, inversely, that a spontaneous collective murder should in fact involve an already theatrical mechanism—these are possibilities that Girard cannot manage to account for. Hence the relative naïveté of the hypothesis of an original founding act that is really "violent," and the relative naïveté of the concept of *violence* that is here put into play. The entire question is finally one of knowing if there can be a pure violence that is not the "abstract negativity" of Hegel. In a certain way, and we always come back to this, Girard fails to come sufficiently to grips with Hegel—*and* Heidegger. This is what Bataille, for his part, never refused to do (even when it is a question, whatever commentators have made him say, of Heidegger). For it is not enough to affirm in the mode of belief that there is something "anterior" to representation if one is to "overcome" the *logic* of the said representation, which is, rigorously speaking, the interdiction of revelation. The religious, which has never been fortuitous, is tough to eliminate—under whatever forms it takes—philosophical, aesthetic, and especially political. We can even ask ourselves if the denial of representation is not what maintains it in the most efficacious manner (for what is this denial except belief?). In any case, it will persist all the more if one fails to recognize [*méconnaît*] the logic or *law* whereby revelation is prohibited precisely in being called upon, or that authorizes revelation only in already having betrayed it: the logic or law that authorizes presence, epiphany, parousia, but only, and always, as *not-such in itself,* and no doubt—as Heidegger (we will return to this) never ceases to remind us—according to an "inadequation," well prior to the opposition between adequation and inadequation or between presence and absence. Christianity, whatever we might say, has not remained a religion by chance, or, by a bad turn of fortune, a historical "accident." It has been subject to this very law—and perhaps we must risk saying once and for all that it is nothing other than that law that Heidegger will end by thinking as the un-thought of Western thought, the "aletheic" law itself, the law of the withdrawal—which is incommensurable with that which appears or disappears—of the presence of the presentable in general. A law to which, necessarily, Girard is still subject, although—no less necessarily—without his knowing it, and in such a way that he reintroduces, without noticing even the least paradox, the very thing he begins, like every "religious" thinker, by contesting and challenging: religion itself. And to recognize as he does that the revelation finally *fails* does not change much, for "succeeding on the level of the text, which is always there and to which we can always refer," it warrants unfailingly the entire hermeneutic enterprise. (See "Discussion avec René Girard," pp. 556–557.)

after all). This is why—read *The Gay Science*—she always involves semblance or appearance and thus only "shows" the *instability* (but not the
absence) of the true. And this is why, as she slips away, Mimesis appears in "her" place. "The appearance," we say, in order to reassure
ourselves, but in fact nothing or no one that might be recognized or
identified, differentiated—a figure (*Gestalt*) that is always displaced,
de-stabilized (*verstellt*), without features or a visage proper to it. A
faceless figure [*sans figure*]: the *same* Aletheia.

That is to say, as well, Aletheia as *no one*—*in person* [*en personne*].

We can perhaps begin to suspect, then, that mimesis is a matter of
masks and words—and of an anonymous voice: *me* (who?), *Aletheia*,
"I" am speaking. Which does not necessarily make for a character . . .

But there is no use anticipating. At this point, having said all of this,
it should be clear that the entire question of mimesis (and consequently
the entire reading of Plato) is caught within the confrontation or conflict between two interpretations of truth. That is to say, more accu-
rately, between two ways of identifying and revealing mimesis, between
two ways of deciding on it.

We have, then, a double, but asymmetrical, critique—and not only
because Heidegger gives Plato the credit that Girard appears to refuse
him. Or even because the second affects the form, more or less super-
ficially, of an "anthropology" that the first has definitively dated and
rendered obsolete in both its philosophical presuppositions and its
general scope. Rather, this asymmetry has to do with what is *at stake*.
For it is surely the same goal in either case: to deliver mimesis from
imitation (which is the derivative interpretation, deforming and, historically, all the more active and powerful the more reductive, spontaneous, and easy it is) and consequently to wrench mimesis away from
the *classical* problematic of (in)adequation in order to back away from
the bi-millennial erring for which philosophy has become responsible.
But in the two cases the goal is neither situated nor posed in the same
way. At least in its consequences. Or rather, once the rectification of
mimesis is played out, the stakes are no longer the same. It would be
absurd to imagine, with the pretext that Girard refers to the Gospel,
that in this instance it is only a question of the banal conflict—not as
clear-cut, all the same, as it is always said to be—between Christianity
and (neo-)paganism,[120] or even between Hellenism and Judaism. As re-

120. This is one of the accusations made by Girard against all of modern philosophy
after Hegel insofar as it returns to the Greeks, appears to ignore (or mistrust) Christianity, finds its clearest inspiration in mythology or tragedy, and displays its propensity for

gards the essential, it is certain that this opposition is more deeply buried, and probable that it divides at the same time—although, yet again, in an unequal way—each of these "two" areas or histories.

Since it is certainly necessary to be more precise, even at the risk of striking once more on the same nail, we must ask: What is this all about?

Simply, this: in Heidegger's case (where it is linked to *aletheia*, to the "stele"), mimesis is thought, in accord with Plato (but in a movement that carries him to the limit, if it does not simply carry him beyond himself), as *disinstallation*, that is, simultaneously, as fall, decline, diminution, obfuscation, and so on. From which we can understand, moreover, why mimesis could then also be interpreted (*after the fact*, but in Plato himself), at the "same" time, as (in)adequation, (dis)similitude, that is, false adequation, false similitude, a degraded copy, and so on. It goes without saying, however, that this divergence in relation to truth does not seriously revise the traditional position of mimesis (mimesis is *decidedly* irrecuperable), and especially that it is incommensurable with that fundamental and absolute "inadequation" of the aletheic withdrawal in regard to any opposition between the adequate and the in-adequate, between presence and absence, etc.—incommensurable, in other words, with that (dis-)distancing [*Ent-fernung*] of the truth that is the inexhaustible and unfathomable abyss of its "very" proximity.

By contrast, in Girard's case (where it is linked in an apparently intra-philosophic manner to desire—to the *subject* of desire), mimesis is thought of more as an *assimilation* (primitive doubling, general reciprocity, undifferentiation, etc.), but in such a way that all the values associated with the opposition adequate/in-adequate are perverted (beyond redress, so to speak), and such that the proper is engulfed in it without there being the least chance, ultimately, for any sort of reappropriation: again we have disinstallation, but this time in the form of a generalized *instability*, actually much more threatening because it is irreducible to a simple decline or fall. It is still necessary to recognize, though, that this can scarcely be argued unless Girard is pushed to the limit, unless the adherences of his interpretation to the philosophic register (even if disguised on this occasion as a "religious" one) and, finally, the moorings of his system (for it is a system) are unfastened. It must still be recognized, then, that such an argument can be made only on the condition that we play off against Girard, against his treatment

---

the great figures of Oedipus, Dionysus, etc. (See for example, "Discussion avec René Girard," pp. 561–563.)

of Platonism and his hope for a revelation of mimesis . . . Heidegger. But not the Heideggerian interpretation of Plato. Something else in Heidegger; let us say—in order to illustrate a bit what this is all about—a Heidegger who would himself be read in the light of a suspicion coming from . . . Girard.

Such a strategy—such an operation—is *sophistic* only in appearance. At stake is an enormous question (truth, of course), and there arises from it, if we know how to deduce it, again a quite simple result. A surprising result, and—today—certainly difficult to confront head on, but nevertheless simple: namely, that mimesis, as Plato experiences it (but not necessarily thinks it, even when he "theorizes" about it), requires the supposition that something governs or precedes *aletheia* itself, or more precisely, *de-stabilizes aletheia*—something that is not unrelated, strange as it may seem, to that determination of truth that Heidegger always endeavored to consider as secondary and derived (the determination of truth as *homoiosis,* as adequation, similitude, or resemblance), but that would in its turn be *displaced,* in any case removed from the horizon of accuracy and of exactitude (of e-vidence), never being rigorously where one expects to see it or precisely what one wants to know. In other words, an unstable *homoiosis* that *circulates* endlessly between inadequate resemblance and resembling inadequation, confounding memory as well as sight, upsetting the play of *aletheia* and indeed carrying its breakdown right up to the very means of signifying its difference—so inapprehensible (imperceptible) is the agitation that this unstable *homoiosis* imparts to the Same.

The reason for such a result is again very simple: it is that the "question of mimesis"—which comes from a dizziness, an uneasiness, a malaise, from whatever you like in the face of this prodigy (*thauma*) that is mimesis, but certainly not, initially, from what is "properly speaking, philosophical wonder," from *thaumazein*—actually forces us to reintroduce the question of *aletheia* within that of language (of *enunciation, Aussage*), insofar as what is at play there is, in effect, nothing other than the question of the "subject." Or rather, the obsession with the "subject."

And this is precisely what Plato (i.e., "Plato") experiences: what *happens* in "Plato." It is, if you will, the moment, *in fact* interminable (ultimately "all of Plato"), wherein *aletheia* and mimesis resemble each other and are, literally, *in homoiosis.* This does not mean that Plato would be aware of it or that we can find in him a theory of this unthinkable resemblance. But he does *know it,* which is not at all the same thing. He suffers it, is perhaps even afraid of it—and if only because he, Plato, perhaps confuses "himself" [or is confused—*"se" confond*] (once again, the *reflexive* is undecidable) with anyone, the first charlatan he meets in the street or the last of the poets or sophists. And to such an extent, moreover, that if he philosophizes we can well suppose that it is finally with no other intention—and initially the most urgent—than to stabilize this alarming circulation of resemblance and "to fix this vertigo"[121] where "he," he who is named Plato, loses "himself." But it must be said that we would not have the least chance of understanding this if, at the other end of the chain, someone who spoke halfway incomprehensibly of an Eternal Return had not proclaimed himself to be definitively breaking away from philosophy while taking himself for Badinguet, Dionysus, or Caesar. And which we would also not understand if it were not precisely the "same" who, in order to engage the process, had previously undertaken to substitute a figure of his own invention—a figure fictioned with strokes made of Platonico-Aristotelian reminiscences—for a famous, reportedly unique, and supposedly "real" philosophical figure (Socrates); and done so after having suffered, for nearly the whole of his intellectual life, the domination of an overwhelming rival-model (Wagner), and before attempting in extremis, but vainly, to regain himself and to (re)present himself according to his true measure and in his authentic, unmistakable figure (*Ecce Homo*).[122]

For this is the sign: fictioning and (re)presentation, *Darstellung,* including—even primarily—*Selbstdarstellung,* auto-(re)presentation or autobiography. In other words, "mimesis." What neither Heidegger, as we know, nor even Girard (who simply takes Plato for Sophocles) wishes to recognize. Or, moreover, can recognize, because, as we could have expected for some time now, it is in fact the very place of *indecision*—that is to say, the place where, in Plato, according to an *indiscernible, double* movement, there is played out the "losing game" of an impossible seizure of mimesis at the same time that the gesture of reappropriation and stabilization is prepared, a gesture which is already the theoretical gesture, that theatricalization which the specular/speculative operation will later have to (struggle to) reinforce. In other words, what *happens*—in Books II and III of the *Republic*—when, under the

121. The expression comes from Rimbaud via Genette, who uses it in a strictly analogous instance in relation to Robbe-Grillet. See Gérard Genette, "Vertige fixé," in *Figures* (Paris: Seuil, 1966).

122. To bring this fully to mind, one may refer to P. Klossowski's reading in *Nietzsche et le cercle vicieux* (Paris: Mercure de France, 1969).

critical pretext par excellence (the settling of accounts with the whole of the poetic tradition and corporate body), Plato stages the programming of *non-mimetic* discourse. This in such a way that underhandedly, and according to the double or triple deformation of a *false mise-en-abyme* (though it is characterized), one finds expressed, but through an interposed person, by means of the discourse of a spokesman for the supposed subject of this discourse, the very law (not) governing this discourse, at least inasmuch as it never ceases to propose "itself" as philosophical discourse proper, that is, as the *anti-mimetic* discourse.

Later, Nietzsche will simply say that Plato clearly betrays his own principles in the *Republic.* But in truth, there can be no question of claiming any longer that there is anything simple about this. Or even of entertaining, probably, the hope of a possible fixation of what *happens* [*se passe*] within the limits of a commentary. The economy of such an operation is too complex—too little "economical." What *happens* here in fact passes beyond the powers of discourse, even (as is the case—unequally—in Girard and Heidegger) that of deconstruction. It endlessly displaces the critical hold and destabilizes the indispensable modicum of theoretical assurance. It unbalances and makes precarious any historical or historial economy, any attempt at delimitation whatsoever. And it does so despite everything, that is, even if everything in it is open to a hermeneutic seizure, to a critical appropriation. This is no doubt why—supposing we can respond, in however small a way, to this kind of dubious irrevelation of mimesis (or of truth), to this loss that is never a pure loss—one should practice something like a (de)-construction, something more positive than critical, something, as it were, *not very negative.* Credit should be given, in other words, to the philosophical even in its very lapsing, in its exposure and failure, in the default of its so-called (or rather self-proclaimed) infallibility. Indeed, one should *sustain* to the end the philosophical *thesis* itself, the thesis according to which—always—truth and knowledge *are needed* [*il faut* la vérité et le savoir*]. But how does one discourse on such an "economy"?

The difficulty here is not that throughout this episode mimesis is never explicitly thematized by Plato in precisely the terms of an economy of appropriation and depropriation. On the contrary. What Plato "knows," once again, he says, he lets be said. This is the entire object of "his" discourse, and all the more so if—in order to draw his profit from it and not lose himself in it—he takes the ambiguous risk (perhaps a little too visibly calculated) of using a delegate to whom he can consign the impasses of this discourse and of producing a fiction which would be responsible, in this case, for assuring the difficult and always questionable fixation of the mimetic evasion. The obstacle upon which the specular reduction stumbles, we recall, is the impossibility of pictorially translating what the mirror could still represent analogically (by either trope or figure), that is, the *polytechnic* "essence" of mimesis. Unless, of course, we imagine a genre of painting aimed entirely at (re)constituting a kind of encyclopedia of the respective bodies of the trades or a gallery of portraits of workers (after all, such a painting does come to exist, and "Platonism" does have something to do with it). But this obstacle arises precisely because the question of mimesis has for a long time been posed in terms of property. Indeed, from very early on, at the opening of the discussion on justice in Book I, injustice is thought of as an absence of proper qualities—or, if you will, as a plasticity whose entire "art" could be defined simply as the "art of appearing just" (361a). And we know that soon after, when under pressure from Glaucon Socrates ceases to dream of the ideal poverty of his primitive city and sees himself forced to envision a "real" State, mimesis is immediately introduced (with the throng of imitators, painters, sculptors, poets, rhapsodes, actors, dancers, theater agents, make-up artists, and fabricators of feminine adornments [II, 373ff.]) along with the market economy's procession of plagues (money, goods for consumption, prostitution, the multiplication of trades, domestic and external violence, and so on). Mimesis has always been an economic problem; it is the problem of economy.[123] From the very moment that money intervenes, there is generalized depropriation, the risk of a polytechnics or of an uncontrollable polyvalence, the exacerbation of desire, the appetite for possession, the triggering of rivalry and hatred. In fact, almost "Capital"; and the entire political orthopedics has finally no other object than to reduce (economically) this senseless expense of the proper that comes along with the "general economy," that is, the mimetic economy.[124] This orthopedics begins, moreover, with the edu-

123. See Jacques Derrida, "Economimesis," *Diacritics* 2 (Summer 1981): 3–25. (Included originally in *Mimesis: Des articulations*.)

124. We thus return to Bataille, to the problem of economy as a problem of death, to the mimetic nature—but abyssally mimetic and not simply imitative, as Girard would have it, of the original event—of sacrifice. And consequently, to the problem of mastery. We could follow this trail and show, since J. M. Rey has already marked the path for us, how the economic or mastering dramatization of the Socratic figure functions in the *Republic* and elsewhere (see "Nietzsche et la théorie du discours philosophique," in *Nietzsche aujourd'hui*, vol. 1 [Paris: Union Générale d'Editions, 1973], pp. 301–321)—and

cation of the guardians—that is to say, as we know, with the conversion of aggressivity and the restriction of desire—and just after the
major principle of the necessary and inviolable repartition of roles and
functions (to each his own task), which must govern the whole enterprise, has been formulated (II, 374).

An economy, then. A catastrophic economy thought in terms of fall,
decline, decadence, and so on. But it is not sufficient unto itself, and
indeed is sustained by something else altogether. This historical entry
of mimesis, in the *Republic,* in fact paves the way for an entire pedagogical debate (the famous education of the guardians) wherein the
haunting preoccupation with the economic will find its reason in the
problematic of mimetism—a problematic that is not, as is repeated
endlessly, principally a problematic of the lie, but instead a problematic
of the *subject* (one can scarcely see what other word to use), and of the
subject in its relation to language.

What is involved, in fact, when it comes time to program the education of the guardians? Quite simply, it is a question of preparing, for
the use of those destined to this function (and to this *sole* function), the
education bequeathed by tradition and now established in Greece—
especially since (and this is spelled out) it would be difficult "to find a
better one" (we should hear: a more appropriate one). This education
is double: gymnastics for the body, and music—in its most general
sense—for the soul. As is well known, it is an education that is both
sensible and "intelligible." But we will begin, says Socrates, with music. At least this is what he has his interlocutor grant "spontaneously."
And of course this concern with the order of exposition (which therefore applies to the "real" order) is not, as they say, entirely innocent.
For as soon as it is admitted—because this is the way that things are
done traditionally—that one should first enter into an examination of
music, music is again distinguished in its narrow sense (in its properly
musical sense: singing, melody, rhythm, etc.) from the "discourse,"
that is, from the verbal part of music. This, in its turn, divides in two,
since there are two forms or two aspects, two "ideas" of discourse in
general, of the *logos:* the true (*alethes*) and the untrue (*pseudos*). But this

---

how, therefore, mimesis is at play in it ever since the scene of death, for example, or the
scene of "erotic" competition (the *Banquet*). It would remain necessary, however, to
show how an economy, *stricto sensu,* the question of money, production, exchange, etc.,
always invades anti-mimetic discourse and retraces the fragile boundary, within the
"economimetic" system, between gain and loss or failure.

bipartition inevitably prompts once again a question of order or precedence: Where do we begin? With what, in reality, do things begin? But
this time what comes up is the question of mimetism. For education
begins with the "imitation" of what language conveys:

> And tales are of two species, the one true and the other false?
> Yes.
> And education must make use of both, but first of the false?
> I don't understand your meaning.
> Don't you understand, I said, that we begin by telling children fables
> [*muthoi*], and the fable is, taken as a whole, false, but there is truth in it
> also? And we must make use of fable with children before gymnastics.
> That is so.
> That, then, is what I meant by saying that we must take up music be-
> fore gymnastics.
> You were right, he said.
> Do you not know, then, that the beginning in every task is the chief
> thing, especially for any creature that is young and tender? For it is then
> that it is best molded [*plattetai*] and takes the impression [*tupos*] that one
> wishes to stamp [*ensemenasthai*] upon it?
> Quite so.[125]

Things begin, then—and this is what "imitation" is all about—with
the "plastic" (fashioning, modeling, fictioning), with the impression of
the *type* and the imposition of the *sign,* with the mark that language,
"mythic" discourses (whether they are true or not matters little; this
becomes a relatively secondary and subordinate question when the essential thing, as is said explicitly, is that such discourses are fictive),[126]
originally inscribe in the malleable—plastic—material of the infant

---

125. *Republic,* 376e–377b.

126. See 377b: "Shall we, then, thus lightly suffer our children to listen to any chance
stories fashioned [*plasthentas*] by any chance teachers?" No doubt, a certain distinction
throughout this text between poiesis and "plastic" might already seem to overlap the
distinction between truth and falsity. But this would be discreetly, and above all, would
not fit in with the almost obligatory metaphorics of poiesis, which is, until the *Timaeus,*
typological. In fact, the true distinction passes instead through the difference between
activity and *passivity,* which embraces the difference between, on the one hand, matter/
receptacle/matrix/malleable wax, and, on the other, seal/imprint/stamp/stylet, and thus
straightaway reintroduces a certain sexual—so to speak—modelization of onto-ideo-
typo-logy. In a certain way, what is at stake in Plato's anti-mimetic strategy is, at whatever "level" of the problematic, the possibility of the reversal of passivity into activity, of
the transition to virility. This holds true especially, perhaps, for the strange relationship
implied by the extremely complex "manipulation" of the Socratic figure.

soul. That is to say, of course, of the soul that is yet *in-fans*. The delay
in coming to speak (and to consciousness), something like the "prematuration" of the child, leads to this vulnerability to fables that is
nothing but the natural submission to maternal or feminine discourse
in general. For myths, here, are what "mothers and nurses" (377c)
tell—not exactly "old wives' tales," but rather those narratives taken
from mythological poetry (the "primordial language" or "the *epos* as
such," says Hegel) which furnish the Greeks with the principal materi-
als for the first familial education, and by which acquisition of the
"mother" tongue is also accomplished. And let us not be surprised here
if we begin to see Lacanian terminology coming progressively to double
Plato's lexicon: there is, there will perhaps always have been, in the *theorization* of mimesis—from the *Republic* to "The Mirror Stage," and
whatever recognition might be given (despite everything and in different ways) to the ineluctability of the fact of mimesis—a kind of virile
stiffening and anxious clenching as well as a resentment against the
original maternal domination and original feminine education, these
being always the sign, for the subject, of its constitutive incomplete-
ness, of its belatedness (impossible to overcome) with respect to its
"own" birth, and of its natural incapability of engendering itself (or at
least assisting in or attending its own engenderment). *Anti-mimesis* is
what will finally be revealed in the last, Hegelian dream of philosophy:
absolute (in)sight, the subject theorizing its own conception and engendering itself in seeing itself do so—the speculative.[127]

Mimesis is consequently grounded in this *original* dependency and
subjection of the "speaking-being." It is, as we habitually and lazily say,
a matter of "influence." But stated more rigorously, mimesis is the
effect of the *typo-graphy* and (if we may venture this *Witz*) of the fundamental "in-semination" which at bottom define the essence of the
paideia (of formation or of *Bildung*) and by which what we call the "subject" is (not) engendered as being necessarily of the order of the figure
or of the fictive in general. An entire Western *discourse* on the subject—
a discourse that after all could well be Western discourse itself—right
away seems to find its limit here; a limit that would lie less, as Heidegger has nevertheless had reason to say, in the supposition of a *sup-
positum* [*suppôt*], of a matrical identity or substantial *hypokeimenon*,
than—on the very borders, perhaps, of the possibilities of *discourse*—in

127. As well as "primary" narcissism, and thus, in a certain way, death. In any case,
nothing that would "eliminate" mimesis "itself."

*the necessary reversibility of the motifs of engenderment and of the figure, of
conception, and of the plastic,* or, if you will, in this kind of reciprocal and
insurmountable metaphorical (figural) exchange between the concepts
of *origin* and *fiction.* What other resource can be drawn upon to signify
engenderment, conception, origin, procreation, creation, etc. but the
lexicon of the plastic and of fictioning, of figuration, of typography and
insemination? And, inversely, how can we think "fictiveness," under all
its forms, if not by reference to engenderment, to the sexual relation, to
conception and nutrition, to hereditary transmission, to education as a
"second birth" or as a supplement to birth, and so on? What discourse
could avoid this endless reference, through constant and overlapping
mention, of "sexuality" in general and of "the mystery of childbirth" to
figuration? What discourse could avoid naming fiction as an origin or
speaking of the origin in terms of fiction (if not in a fictive way)? How
would it be possible for the figure of engenderment to have not always
figured the engenderment of the figure? Or vice versa? Perhaps it is
fundamentally impossible to delimit, as Heidegger has attempted, the
space of onto-typo-logy. Perhaps, at the very root of onto-steleo-logy,
under the rhythms and melodic variations of the history of metaphysics, indeed under the quasi-permanence of "aletheic" withdrawal and
forgetting, there is a kind of continuous or persistent bass in the insuperable formalism (or "figuralism") of the endless repetition of the
typographical motif. As also—through the hollow depths of the "question" of writing and on the threshold of the vertigo of dissemination—
in the *obsession* with the "subject."

In any case, mimesis originates there—and confirms, even as it unsettles, typography. The "character"—if, between *ethos* and *tupos,* this
is what is really involved in every discourse on the "subject"—struck
from the outside, derives from the always anterior circulation of discourses. There is, as Lacan would say, a "preinscription of the subject"
in the structure or order of the signifier that marks the symbolic order's
first domination of the subject. But the "subject," traversed from the
very beginning by a multiple and anonymous discourse (by the discourse of the others and not necessarily by that of *an* Other), is not so
much (de)constituted in a cleavage or a simple *Spaltung*—that is, in a
Spaltung articulated simply in terms of the opposition between the
negative and presence (between absence and position, or even between
death and identity)—as it is splintered or dispersed according to the
disquieting instability of the improper. Whence the obsession with appropriation that dominates through and through every analysis of mi-

mesis, of mimetism, and that works to create—well before a concern is shown for the problematic of the lie—its full economic (and consequently political) bearing. This explains, in fact, why the pedagogical difficulty in which the examination of mimetism is anchored should arise in relation to the "trade" of arms (to the establishment of a "professional army" or of a permanent militia), that is, when it is a matter of settling the delicate question of the Athenian citizen-soldier. The analysis is conducted according to the major principle of appropriation (the very principle of *dike,* the ontologico-political law par excellence): "it is impossible for one man to do the work of many arts well" (374a)— just as it closes, at the moment of the ceremonial expulsion of the poet-mimetician, with a reaffirmation of the same principle ("there is no twofold or manifold man among us" [397e]). What is threatening in mimesis, understood in these terms, is exactly that kind of pluralization and fragmentation of the "subject" provoked from the outset by its linguistic or "symbolic" (de)constitution: an effect of discourses, the "self"-styled "subject" always threatens to "consist" of nothing more than a series of heterogeneous and dissociated roles, and to fraction itself endlessly in this multiple borrowing. Thus, the mimetic life is made up of *scenes from the life of one who is suited for nothing*—or of a Jack-of-all-trades. Let us say that the "subject" *de-sists* in this, and doubly so when it is a question of man (of the male), since there the roles, which are themselves fictive, are moreover passively recorded, received from the mouths of women. In short, what is threatening in mimesis is feminization, instability—*hysteria.*[128]

Hence the urgent need for a serious purification of language and a rectification of fiction. Moreover, it is clear that if it is absolutely necessary to redress discourse in order to install it within truth, it is not first of all because it is a lie—but more fundamentally because it is fiction that *writes* the "subject," that models it and assigns it an identity. Here is the classical problem of *exemplarity:* it is the *critical* problem par ex-

128. The two major risks in Platonic mimetism are feminization and madness. The opening of Book III, in the *Republic,* is explicit in this regard. These are, of course, the two risks between which "Nietzsche" oscillates, that is, Dionysus (Wagner again) *and* "all the names of history," etc. As regards the "question of woman," we are passing very close here (as has been indicated throughout this essay by the motif of the specularization of mimesis) to the trail followed by Luce Irigaray, in *Speculum, de l'autre femme* (Paris: Minuit, 1974). This is also the trail of hysteria; that is to say—for ancient medicine—that incomprehensible disorder occasioned by the untimely displacements of that "unstable animal," the uterus. See Ilya Veith, *Hysteria: The History of a Disease* (Chicago: University of Chicago Press, 1965), chs. 1 and 2.

cellence, so much a part of posterity that perhaps no other discourse will have ever pursued "literature," will have ever tormented fiction (the "romanesque") itself, like the one deploring the pernicious "influence" of books. For "literature," far from simply reflecting (as Girard always seems somewhat tempted to think) a prior generalized mimetism, is on the contrary what provokes mimetism. All of *Don Quixote* is inscribed in Plato, as is the Dante of the episode of Paolo and Francesca.[129] As is the great novel of the nineteenth century, from *Madame Bovary* to *Remembrance of Things Past,* the Freud of the *Family Romances,* and the critical work of Marthe Robert. But perhaps above all, on the negative side of the affair, the entire Christian condemnation of fiction—and the substitution for the romanesque of *The Imitation of Jesus Christ:* "We must begin, then, it seems, by a censorship over our story-makers [the mytho-poets], and what they do well we must pass [*egkriteon*] and what not, reject [*apokriteon*]. And the stories on the accepted list we will induce nurses and mothers to tell to the children and so shape [*plattein*] their souls by these stories far rather than their bodies by their hands. But most of the stories they now tell we must reject."[130]

There then begins, as we know, the entire (very) long critique of traditional mythopoiesis—of Homer and Hesiod, above all. That is, the entire critique of the formidable exemplary power of the mythic "theologies," of the divine and heroic fictions. It is conducted in the name of that principle that demands—if the function of myths is to be, as Thomas Mann says, *re-cited*[131] (or if life, as Novalis says, is a novel)— that we purify myths of all *bad examples,* which are of course always examples of *depropriation* (adultery, a lack of virility or else a weakening of heroism, impiety, disrespect toward the just repartition of functions, ravaging laughter, furious madness, unworthy behavior, and so on). Indeed, can it be wholly an accident—for us—that the first "example" of fiction that Plato proposes for censure is the Hesiodic myth of the castration of Uranus? In other words, is it an accident that the question of mimetism *also* arises as that of parricide and castration? Let it not be

---

129. See Girard, "De la *Divine comédie* à la sociologie du roman," *Revue de l'Institut de Sociologie* (Université Libre de Bruxelles, 1963; series titled *Problèmes d'une sociologie du roman,* under the direction of Lucien Goldmann).

130. *Republic,* 377b–c.

131. See note 110. On the influence of such a re-citation on narrative [*le récit*] itself and the novel in general, one may refer to Gilbert Durand, *Le décor mythique de "La Chartreuse de Parme"* (Paris: Corti, 1961); and to Marthe Robert, in particular, *L'ancien et le nouveau* (Paris: Grasset, 1963).

said that Plato does not know what he is getting into here. For it is surely not without "knowing" a little something that he should resign himself to recognizing the truth of such fictions and should confess, when faced with such a frightening truth, to having just barely the possibility of relying on sacrifice (on the worst form of sacrifice) and taking refuge behind Mystery:

> There is, first of all, I said, the greatest lie about the things of greatest concern, which was no pretty invention of him who told how Uranus did what Hesiod says he did to Cronus, and how Cronus in turn took his revenge, and then there are the doings and sufferings of Cronus at the hands of his son. Even if they were true I should not think that they ought to be thus lightly told to thoughtless young persons. But the best way would be to bury them in silence, and if there were some necessity for relating them, only a very small audience should be admitted under pledge of secrecy and after sacrificing, not a pig, but some huge and unprocurable victim, to the end that as few as possible should have heard these tales.[132]

All of this, though, is still not enough. And if, as we see, the problematic of the lie is indeed subordinated to the question of fictioning and fiction (all fiction is at bottom a "lie"—even *true fiction*), it is because mimesis actually begins effectively to be at play in the very production of fiction. That is to say, as one might expect, at the level of *enunciation*.

In fact, the critique of the *logos*, of the "content" of mythopoiesis—a critique that is minute, patient, exhaustive (we might almost believe that Plato tries to make his pleasure last or to postpone indefinitely its expiration)—displaces itself constantly, and moreover for the most banal of reasons: for it is not clear by what means such a critique could avoid moving back from the statement [*énoncé*] to enunciation, that is, to the question of what Plato calls *lexis*. For no matter how well one is able to sift critically the better part of the great founding myths, to show to what extent they lie or deform the truth, to compare them with what the correct theo-logy teaches of the divine, to denounce them in their effects and pernicious exemplarity, one will not have achieved anything with respect to what is essential, which is after all to seize the essence of fiction (of the "lie") and to understand the reason for its fictioning, mimetic power. Why, in reality, and on what conditions, can we say that myths lie? Where, exactly, does their power come from? How is it that they (re)present an image of man so little appro-

---

132. *Republic*, 377–378a.

priate and that the lessons they teach are only, so to speak, "lessons of depropriation"? Upon what, finally, can the ethical condemnation of myths be founded? And why defend truth? These questions are all the more pressing in that the lie, in itself, is not strictly condemned. It is judged at any rate inevitable—politically inevitable—when, for example, it is a matter of the "interest of the State," of safeguarding what has been installed, of truth [*Wahrheit*] in its proper sense.[133] In other words, these questions are all the more pressing in that the lie is a *pharmakon* that must be handled delicately ("it is obvious that such a *pharmakon* must be reserved for physicians and that laymen should have nothing to do with it" [389b]) and something whose usage—that is to say, whose conversion into a political remedy—requires that one know what to abide by; it is a *pharmakon,* if you will, which can be manipulated only if we have already decided its case.

This is why the *origin* of "lying," of fiction has to be sought actually in the direction of what is properly called enunciation. It must be shown that the "mythic lie" proceeds essentially from poetic *irresponsibility,* that is, from a fundamental perversion of poietic practice, indeed—ultimately—*of linguistic practice in general.* It is because they put themselves out of reach and do not come to answer for their discourse, it is because they do not assist or attend their productions but instead do everything to give them the appearance of autonomy (of truth), it is because, finally, the author in them disappears and thus gives free reign to the circulation of language, that poets "lie" and "show" themselves to be incapable of decision before the natural *equivocity* of discourse.

We know upon which major principle the Platonic analysis of *lexis*—or, if you prefer, the Platonic poetics of genres[134]—is in fact constructed. There is only one criterion: the dissimulation or non-dissimulation (the *Verstellung* and *Unverstellung,* therefore) of the author in his fiction or of the subject of enunciation in the statement he produces. Either the poet *himself* speaks in his own name, without seeking to mislead us or to pass himself off for another (without playing at being the other and, in particular, without relying on the direct quotation of another's words), and we have what Plato calls *haple diegesis,* the "simple narrative." Or else, inversely, the poet hides behind the one he (re)presents (*darstellt*), he makes himself "apocryphal" in order to slip into the oth-

133. Compare Hegel's as well as Heidegger's association of *bewahren* ("to safeguard," "to guard") and *Wahrheit.*

134. For the analysis of Platonic "poetics," let me refer to Gérard Genette, "Frontières du récit," in *Figures II* (Paris: Seuil, 1969), pp. 49–69.

er's identity and so mislead us—in order to make animate what cannot (and should not) be; he presents himself as what is not, exposes himself as other than he is, and depropriates himself—and then we have mimesis. That is to say, essentially, dramatization, *Darstellung* in its proper sense, inasmuch as it presupposes *Stellvertretung*, or substitution.

Mimesis thus "appears" in *enunciative depropriation*.

Such is the origin of the lie. And what in the last instance explains the fictioning power of myths—or of language. What Plato catches a glimpse of, but immediately reduces to a "literary" problem, is that discourses would not have any fictioning power if dramatization were not inscribed in discourse as a constant possibility (indeed, as its very presupposition), thus opening the space of "subjective" exchange and substitution—the entire space of mimetism. This is why, as Socrates claims, the "genre" "most pleasing to children, to their tutors, and to the greatest part of the crowd," is in fact the *mixed* genre, a *diegesis* that includes mimesis: the genre par excellence—in the very difference that constitutes it—of the instability of the subject of enunciation.[135] But it is also the most spontaneous, the least forced or "artificial" mode of the simple act of speaking. Story telling, prior to any literary codification, is done in a semi-dramatic mode. The most elementary *lexis* implies this difference between *at least two* subjects—and, as Plato is always on the verge of confessing, neither the "indirect style" nor pure dramatization is at bottom "natural." The cleavage(s) of enunciation is a law of language. Short of controlling rigorously the procedure of enunciation (which is the very philosophico-political task that the *Republic* essentially assigns itself), there is in language, from the very beginning, from the simple fact of the position (*Stellung*) of the speaking subject, every risk of mimesis. Hidden in it and always imminent, there is the risk of the *disinstallation* of the "subject." Whether we look at it from the side of *logos* or from the side of *lexis*, mimesis is always related to the preinscription of the "subject" in language.

Of course, there is drawn from all of this, besides a normative poetic, the affirmation—and this time, we might believe, certain—of the "law of the proper." For apparently, a decision has been reached. The criterion of *Verstellung* seems to suffice. We exclude the mimetician and keep only the simple narrative, the sole form of discourse or fiction seen to be capable—since it is always guaranteed by a subject who declares himself (or, as we might imagine, a *patent* subject)—of "imitat-

135. See *Republic*, 397d.

ing" (virile) virtue and mental health, themselves defined not otherwise
than by simplicity, non-duplicity, and non-multiplicity, and by the
manifestness of "subjective" property.

Why then begin again? Why will it be necessary to reuse the same
criterion, though displaced from the domain of what can be said to
that of the visible? Why redo, specularly, speculatively, the same operation? What does such an operation *lack*?

Simply what it (already) has in surplus.

That is to say, the ruse or trope in which the very will to capture the
mimetic evasion simultaneously marks and betrays itself, is caught in
its own device and recovers itself. This operation *already* has a mirror,
a theoretical trap—a "thaumatic" machine—in it. An extra one. And
because of this, everything is also lost and swallowed in an abyss.

The *mekhane* is, as we know, a *mise-en-abyme*. But, as we also know,
it is a *false mise-en-abyme*, (in this instance) a *deforming* mirror—if only
because Plato is the first to betray, in the very text wherein he establishes them (the *Republic* is in fact a mixed narrative), the norms that he
has himself prescribed and that govern, in his eyes, good fiction *as* a
discourse of truth. But in fact the set-up is much more complex. Not
only because Plato does not respect the law that he decrees, not only
because an other, Socrates (who speaks in *his* name, in the first person)
represents him and speaks in "his" name,[136] not even simply because

136. Consequently, Plato's manipulation of Socrates is of the mimetico-dramatic
order. The whole question is one of knowing whether the dramatic model privileged by
Plato is, strictly speaking, that of tragedy. This is what Girard thinks, as we have seen,
and he will even go so far as to infer from it a kind of Oedipal scenario (unless the
inverse is true, and Girard, little concerned with questions of poetics, in fact begins by
reading "directly" such a scenario) in the Platonic (re)presentation of Socrates. The entire Girardian reading of Plato—that is to say, despite the credit he accords to the undecidability of mimesis that Derrida has brought out, the charge he makes against the
Platonic *decision*—depends on this point. It remains to be determined, however, whether
the model that Plato adopts is consistently or simply tragic. It is not a matter—let us be
clear—of contesting the notion that tragedy has represented for philosophy a formal or
thematic matrix. Tragedy is *already* philosophical. This commonplace, dating not from
yesterday but from at least 1800, is irrefutable. Nor is it a matter of under-estimating the
relation of rivalry (that is, the mimetic relation) that links Plato—in a hostile fraternity
or that sort of more or less blind twinship described by Girard—to the tragic writers
(or to Homer), and Socrates to Euripides. Although it would probably be necessary to
look also in the direction (as Hegel suggests, with some precision, in *The History of
Philosophy*) of the comic writers, and Aristophanes in particular (if only on account of
the *Banquet* and the *Apology*), or even other less "noble" forms of dramatic mimesis,
such as mime. (See on this subject, in addition to Aristotle's *Poetics,* the famous theses of
Eugène Dupréel, and above all Herman Reich's *Der Mimus* [Berlin: Weidmannsche

this entire pedagogical program, in which the question of mimesis and of fiction is debated, is itself presented as a myth,[137] but because in reality Plato—and this is the height of the paradox—does not speak one word of the *philosophical discourse itself.* Unless this be *indirectly*—by what play of mirror(s)?—and insofar as we may consider the redressing and verification of fictive discourse to be regulated by the model of true discourse, in the form of the discourse of philosophy. But in the *text* it is Socrates, "his" *mimos,* the mimetic part of "himself," who speaks philosophically. The philosopher is here a figure. As for Plato—the one named Plato or (who knows?) the one named "Platton" (the Greeks themselves did not miss the *Witz*)—he *fictions,* content, perhaps, with playfully re-marking his "own" name or the at least double sense that an (assumed) proper name can always take on. If only by an "astute" pun.

As regards an author's dissimulation, the splitting of enunciation, subjective depropriation, etc., we must recognize that it is difficult to

---

Buchhandlung, 1903], especially Chapter 5 on the "mimetic element in Plato" and the relation of Socrates the "ethologue" to the "ethologico-mimetic" art of Plato.) But in fact this is still not the question. Rather, the question is one of knowing whether, from the moment when the end explicitly pursued by Plato is the expulsion of mimesis, and, in particular, of the most overwhelming form of mimesis (tragic mimesis), the strategy such an end imposes is the pure and simple repetition of tragedy, or whether, on the contrary, the redoubtable character of mimesis being clearly recognized, the entire operation attempted by Plato does not consist in taking the risk of *miming mimesis,* specularly redoubling it, with the hope of fixing its disconcerting mobility. This would in any case explain the difference—for there is one—between tragedy and philosophy. But also the fact that it is no accident that Plato chose Socrates—a provocative and voluntary *pharmakos* (and not solicited and consenting), the first great incarnation, according to Hegel, of self-consciousness—for the protagonist of this *parody,* this *diversion* [*détournement*] of tragedy (which is neither a comedy nor a satyric drama) that are the *Sokratikoi logoi.* Nor is it an accident that it is to Socrates, but never to himself, Plato (even as interlocutor—it is, for example, his two brothers who answer Socrates in the *Republic,* while, as the *Phaedon* tells us, he himself is never there), that he entrusts the task of marking the jealous proximity of the philosopher to the poets, the secret love that "he" has for Homer, the pride that is "his own" in having renounced poetry, etc. The least we can say is that a manipulation of this kind is far from being innocent and that, if we had to compare it to something, perhaps it would be better to compare it, finally, with the art of the puppeteer [*marionnettiste*], the *thaumatopoiikos,* to whom "Plato" multiplies allusions each time the question of mimesis is brought up. (See, on this point, Diès, *Guignol à Athènes,* in *Bulletin de l'Association Guillaume Budé* [1927], no. 14/15).

137. See *Republic,* 376d: "Come, then, just as if we were telling stories or fables [*osper en mutho muthologountes*] and had ample leisure to do so; let us educate these men in our discourse."

find anything, *already,* more explicit. But we have still to understand why this is so. And to understand what could have led a philosopher— not one of the least important—to engage these questions in such formal *sophistications* or such writing games. What has generally been neglected is that if the Platonic "poetics" is essentially grounded, as is that of Aristotle, on an analysis of texts handed down by tradition, it nevertheless, as normative (unlike, perhaps, Aristotle's), never regu- lates more than *oral discourse.* To be more precise, if such a "poetics" did not in the last analysis refer to speech and to the conditions of oral enunciation, there would not be the least chance of drawing from it any *decision* whatsoever or any *critical* position. For the criterion of dissimu- lation or substitution is by right inoperative in the case of written enunciation—and for the simple, *elementary* reason that an author can never be there, in person, in order to guarantee the identity of the one who wrote "I," of the one who expressed himself in the first "person." It is impossible to authenticate a written text. The *identification* of a speaker is authorized only in the exercise of living speech—at least in- sofar as (but this is what Plato *wants* to believe) the presence of the speaker is visible or perceptible, insofar as it is always possible "theoret- ically" to rectify the dramatization, or insofar as the speaker (the sub- ject of the *utterance*) can be made to coincide with the "subject" of the enunciation. But in fact nothing, *in principle,* can ever guarantee such an agreement. A "subject" never *coincides* with *itself.* This is why the decision regarding mimesis concerns and can only concern theatrical mimesis alone—or whatever we can conceive in terms of this model. But this is also why *the decision never really takes place,* and why it can never be made. In any case, nothing can ever be established or *shown* here [*s'y avérer*]. For to reduce what is in question in mimesis—and what is, in effect, situated on the side of *Darstellung*—to staging or simple theatricality is necessarily to expose oneself to the possibility of missing the imperceptible play by which a "subject" is always, and without knowing it, already fabricated by fiction. That is to say, "written."

However, read "Plato": you will see that writing *works.*

But writing—and this is hardly surprising—is the last avatar of *Stellung.* It is, consequently, still a mode of installation—but a limit- case, and such that the *stele* threatens to offer itself no longer to sight, to unveil itself no longer, as itself, standing upright, erect.

It is not "my" fault if in German—which is far from being "my" maternal tongue—writing can be referred to as *Schrift*stell*erei,* or if this word can also designate what we call "literature."

That writing can be designated with this name defines no doubt its belonging or its subordination to *Unverstelltheit,* to *aletheia*—Heidegger would have no trouble showing this. But as Heidegger is also the first to know, this subordination holds only to a certain extent.[138] Let us admit that it holds for that part of writing that can be phenomenally installed under the aspect of the mere trace, the trace that is visible, perceptible, present to the eye, unerased. But, as we know, this is not the case when it is a question of *writing before the letter,* a writing that is neither of the order of the visible nor even of the (in)audible—but is perhaps that by virtue of which the order of what can be said is installed (if it is ever installed), *(dis)installed,* imperceptibly, but only as though already hollowed out, corroded, undermined by an unassignable gap, a kind of hiatus or gaping hole that nothing can ever close or fill up since it is anterior to any opening, any virtuality, any potency and any energy, any possible reception of a future presence. —Since it will, as they say, have always already "taken place." We might understand, then, we might begin to understand why, if this is what the writer Plato (at the limit of "his" powers and "his" knowledge) cannot avoid speaking of, he must again and again repeat in vain his attempt to capture mimesis and its "subject." For writing, in this last sense, does not infinitely reflect itself (place itself *en abyme*). By definition, it escapes specula(riza)tion. A text does not theorize *itself;* no aspect or idea of a subject, no unveiling (no matter how furtive) can compensate for or stabilize an evasion that is always unnoticed, not even felt, and whose movement elides itself, as it were, even before it is produced, leaving only an impossible trace—the scar, perhaps, of no wound.

"I" do not know what relation all of this has, or can have, with death, time, or forgetting. All "I" can make out, because it is constantly legible in Plato (as "Plato"), is that the act of writing desperately confronts these, in (im)pure loss. Moreover, this is precisely the reason why theorization, for the one who writes, is not only inevitable but absolutely *necessary.* It is at bottom always impossible not to convert the enunciator into a speaker, the speaker into an actor (a character, a figure, ultimately, a pure "voice")—and the sayable into the visible or the audible. It is even impossible, because this conversion is never suffi-

138. See the analysis, proposed by Heidegger in *An Introduction to Metaphysics* (ch. 2), of the Greek theorization of language (of grammar) on the basis of the "model" furnished by written language.

cient or *truly* successful, not to strive always to accomplish one more theoretical turn—to use the trick of the abyss. There is always, whether it is referred to or not, whether or not it is "shown," a mirror in a text ("Every poet is a Narcissus," said one of the two Schlegels), for this is the only conceivable means of overcoming the inevitable delay of the "subject" in relation to "itself" and of stemming, at least to some extent, that inexorable lapse or failing in which something is said, stated, written, etc.

At least until the day—coming back now to our opening questions—when belief in it collapses, when it has become impossible to repeat (at least *without ridicule*) the same old ruse whose effects, in the end, have been exhausted. It is first of all the theoretical edifice itself that cracks under the pressure of seeking with all its power to complete or accomplish itself. What begins to move, then, in the depths of the mirror, behind its shattered surface (behind the debris of the idea, of the immortality of the soul, of anamnesis, of the subject and of the living present, etc.), is the very terrorizing instability that the mirror was supposed to freeze. Mimesis returns to regain its power. The story is well-known; it is, *for example,* the story of a professor of Greek philology who is obsessed by the demon of writing and who wants to make a name for himself in philosophy. He believes seriously in *himself,* he takes *himself* seriously for a genius, he sets *himself* up as a rival of the greatest figures of thought and letters—he even undertakes, seriously, to imitate Plato.

We know that the consequences foreseen by the said "Plato," when he spoke of imitation, will not delay in coming. Indeed, let us admit that it is a question—this is at least what interested me at the outset—of madness. This would mean, therefore, that mimesis leads to madness, and that madness is a matter of mimesis. Or perhaps even that madness is imitated—or that it imitates "itself." But putting aside all mistrust with regard to the somewhat tiring complacency shown today toward madness, who can guarantee that we have to do here with a *result?*

But in a certain sense, in any case, "I" "here" *decline* all responsibility—all authority in the matter. I simply wanted to see, "me" too.

"Philippe Lacoue-Labarthe"

2

The Echo of the Subject

It must be confessed that the self is
nothing but an echo.
—Valéry, *Cahiers*

I propose to take up in the following pages something (a question, if
you will) that not only remains for me, I admit, without any real answer, but that to a certain point I am even unable to formulate clearly.

What I want to understand, in fact, are two propositions or statements, two *declarations,* that for a long time now "speak" to me or "say"
something to me—consequently, intrigue me—but whose meaning has
always been very obscure. The two declarations remain nearly impenetrable, and thus, in a sense, too difficult, at least for what I feel are my
capabilities. They mark in this way the frontier (where, like everyone, I
constantly stand) of that properly placeless and undefined domain of
all one "knows" only in semi-ignorance, by furtive presentiments,
vague intuition, etc.

The two declarations are more or less alike.

The first is from Hölderlin. It probably dates, if "authentic" (and
this is plausible), from the period of his so-called madness. Like many
others of the same kind, it was reported by Sinclair to Bettina Brentano (Bettina von Arnim), who mentions it in a famous chapter of her
book *Die Günderode.* It runs as follows: "*All is rhythm* [*Rhythmus*]; *the
entire destiny of man is one celestial rhythm, just as the work of art is a
unique rhythm.*"[1]

---

1. Bettina von Arnim, *Die Günderode* (Leipzig: Insel Verlag, 1983), p. 294. One also
finds among the statements reported by Bettina: "Only *the* spirit is poetry, the one that
bears in itself the mystery of an innate rhythm; and it is by this rhythm alone that it can
become visible and living, for rhythm is its soul" (p. 291).

The second comes from Mallarmé, and it too is very well known. It appears in *La musique et les lettres.* Mallarmé is speaking of the *vers libre,* and says simply, in the turn of a phrase, ". . . *because every soul is a rhythmic knot.*"[2]

Propositions of this type are to be found elsewhere, of course: in Nietzsche, for example, or in others. (Still, these others are few; although the idea may be an old one, it is only the rare writer who has known how, or been able, to take it up.) But I will limit myself to these two, and with no other justification, for the moment, than the obsessive hold they have had on me, and continue to have.

Such statements are a kind of emblematic formula. Or better, they are *legends.*

I have ventured to inscribe them here, liminally, in order to indicate the horizon of the problematic. This amounts to positing: these are the phrases that have dictated this work; this is the enigma that oriented it. Nothing more.

This is why the question from which I will start remains still at some distance from these phrases, and from this enigma.

Subject (Autobiography, Music)

With regard to theories which pretend to reduce all art to imitation, we have established concerning the latter a more elevated conception; and that is, that it is not a servile copy but a presentation of objects mediated by the human mind and marked with its imprint. Similarly, with regard to music, we have established that its principle is sensation in a less material sense, namely as a general relation of representations to our own state and quality of internal sense.

—A. W. Schlegel, *Lessons on Art and Architecture*

My point of departure is the following: What connection is there between *autobiography* and *music?* More precisely, and to make things a bit more explicit: What is it that ties together autobiography, that is to say, the autobiographical compulsion [*Zwang*] (the need to tell, to confess, to write oneself), and music—the haunting by music or the musical obsession?

Such a point of departure is abrupt and has every appearance of being arbitrary. I can also imagine that the very use of terms such as

2. Stéphane Mallarmé, *Oeuvres complètes* (Paris: Gallimard, 1945), p. 644.

"autobiographical compulsion" and "musical obsession" might be surprising. Let me quickly justify them.

Because it appeals first of all to the notion and the fact of autobiography, the question proposed here belongs to the more general problematic of the *subject,* and in this case, the writing subject. Or rather, though this can come down to the same thing if we attend to the ambiguity of the reflexive construction (and allowing the accentuation of a certain "desistance," to which I will return), the subject that writes itself [*s'écrit*]: that writes about the subject, that is written about, that is written—in short, the subject that is one, "one," only insofar as it is in some way or other *inscribed.*

Taking advantage of what can be condensed in the genitive and in the double sense (at least) that adheres to the word "subject" in our language, I might say simply: *the subject of writing.*

As advanced here, this general problematic of the subject is an extension of what I have elsewhere designated as "typography."[3]

It is based obviously on the irreversible displacement to which the thought of writing, quite removed from the reigning formalism or from its opposite, submits the "modern" relation between literature and subject (or discourse and subject, text and subject, and so on; the various denominations are unimportant here)—a displacement that comes about, beyond Heidegger and classical psychoanalysis (from Freud to Lacan, let's say), if only through this thought's shaking of such philosophemes or conceptual assemblages as signification and meaning [*vouloir dire*], identity, integrity, auto-affection, self-presence, and alienation. Or if only through its shaking of a term such as "subject," since it still holds firm, be it as divided subject, split subject, absent, emptied, etc.

But this problematic of the subject implies above all that if one attempts to follow the path opened by Heidegger and test the resistance of the concept of the subject (especially in that part of metaphysics that still survives indefinitely under the name of "the human sciences"), it is necessary to go by way of a deconstruction of the area of greatest resistance. Now, this area of greatest resistance—at least this is my initial

3. This work was proposed as a continuation, in a minor key, of "Typography," but it also draws upon some of the analyses presented in "L'Oblitération" (published with "L'echo du sujet" in *Le sujet de la philosophie (Typographies I)* (Paris: Flammarion, 1979), pp. 111–184. It is a revised and amplified version of a text that served as the basis for a seminar in 1975–76.

hypothesis—is nothing other than theoretical or philosophical discourse itself, beginning (I'm thinking of Heidegger) with that discourse that takes its orientation from the deconstruction of the concept of subject.

This is nothing other than philosophical discourse itself inasmuch as it exhibits (and cannot avoid exhibiting, though in a manner that is subtle, devious, silent, and almost unnoticeable—even though *authority* is always speaking) a constant and fastidious preoccupation with its own subject. Be this, finally, in the most stubborn denegation. That every philosopher should be inscribed in his (or her) own discourse, that he should leave his mark there, by or against his will, that it should always be possible therefore to practice an autobiographical reading of any philosophical text, is hardly new. Indeed, since Parmenides, this fact has probably been constitutive of philosophical enunciation as such. Nietzsche writes somewhere near the beginning of *Beyond Good and Evil:* "Gradually it has become clear to me what every great philosophy so far has been: namely, the personal confession of its author."[4] Provided we observe the greatest caution in regard to the "psychologism" that inevitably burdens every declaration of this sort, there is for us, today, something incontestable here (and certainly, also, too quickly acknowledged).

More interesting, however, is that, since Kant, since the interdiction imposed upon the dream nourished by all of the Moderns of a possible *auto-conception* (in all senses) of the Subject,[5] the question of the subject in general—and of the subject of philosophical discourse in particular—has fallen prey to a certain *precipitation.* I would even say, thinking here precisely of Nietzsche, its first victim (or its first agent), a certain panic. Examples are not lacking: whether it is in the speculative transgression of the Kantian interdiction, or conversely, in fidelity to Kant (as with Schopenhauer or even Nietzsche); whether in all the attempts to absolutize the subject or else in its most radical and most intransigent critiques; whether in philosophy "proper" or else in its undefined "outside" (its heart perhaps), that is, in literature, according to its modern (Romantic) definition—everywhere, this obsession with the subject leads or threatens to lead to "madness."

4. Friedrich Nietzsche, *Beyond Good and Evil,* trans. Walter Kaufmann (New York: Vintage, 1966), p. 13.

5. I would refer here to Jean-Luc Nancy's *Le Discours de la syncope* (Paris: Flammarion, 1976), and *Ego Sum* (Paris: Flammarion, 1979), as well as to the work we did together in *L'absolu littéraire* (Paris: Seuil, 1978).

This process has its effects probably throughout the entire realm of art (and why not science as well, something that should be examined) and most certainly is not foreign to the social and political configurations we live under (though here it must of course be treated in a carefully differentiated analysis). And yet, though we may name it for economy's sake a process of the *decomposition* of the subject, everything happens as though it produced within itself a strengthening or *reinforcement* of the subject, even in the discourses that announce its dissolution, its shattering, its disappearance.

Speaking only of philosophy, this is fundamentally the entire history (almost a hundred years now) of the "case of Nietzsche." We see it in the quality of exemplarity attached to Nietzsche's "madness," the almost absolute exemplarity deriving from the unprecedented power of fascination that it has exercized. As we know, neither Freud,[6] nor Heidegger,[7] nor, closer to us, Bataille (nor even Blanchot) has been spared. Nor many others, as one can easily imagine. Nothing prevents us from finding in this strange posthumous destiny a verification of Nietzsche's paradoxical, though entirely coherent (if not perfectly concerted) "success": the success of his desperate will (he who, better than anyone, was able to discern philosophy's subterranean conflict and who had pushed as far as possible the critique of the subject, the system, the work, etc.) to erect himself as an incontestable figure of thought and to sanction an "oeuvre" that he knew to be threatened (a work in the process of *unworking* [*désoeuvrement*]), that he had himself frag-

6. If one reads, for example, Freud's correspondence with Arnold Zweig (*Letters of Sigmund Freud*, ed. Ernst Freud, trans. Tania and James Stern [New York: Basic Books, 1960]; see letters 230, 255, 257, 264, 278, and especially 276), one may follow, right on the surface of the text, the outline of a pure process of mimetic rivalry, grafted onto Zweig's project of writing a "historical novel" about Nietzsche. One can see how Freud, having expressed his reservations in minute detail, having served as an unaccommodating intermediary with Lou Salomé, and having discouraged Zweig by every means possible (including bringing up old gossip concerning Nietzsche's syphilis, "contracted in a male bordello in Genoa"), opposes to Zweig another project, or a counter-project, for a "historical novel" (a life of Shakespeare) and then triumphs—belatedly but definitively—in announcing his *Moses*. The "scene" is all the stronger in that Zweig had begun by multiplying precautions and dealing gently with Freud's susceptibility (which he must have feared)—though of course in the clumsiest manner possible, constantly comparing Nietzsche . . . to Freud and suggesting that he was writing or wanted to write such a biography about Nietzsche for want of being able to write one of the same kind about Freud. But this is only one example; one finds elsewhere, in the *Selbstdarstellung*, the correspondence with Lou Salomé, etc., ample material to confirm this point.

7. See "L'Oblitération."

mented, dispersed, broken, and taken to the very limits of the calcina-
tion of text and meaning. In Nietzsche, as after him (and in his wake),
the active destruction of the *figure,* whatever its mode (exhibition or
ostentation, but to an equal extent withdrawal and the cult of ano-
nymity, secrecy, and silence), aggravates against all expectations the
burden of agonistic mimesis in philosophy. The old fascination with
biography, given new impetus by an autobiographical complacency
(*Ecce Homo* underwriting Nietzsche's "madness"), and the old mechanism of exemplarity that was naïvely thought to be inoperative and out
of use like the old myths, continue to function. The desire for "figurality" has never been more powerful or more constraining, thus forcing
us—and this is the least of its consequences—to return once more to
philosophy and to its history, to the "score" and scansion imposed
upon it by those who thought they had passed beyond, if not any
problematic of the subject (or Subject), at least the limits of the historical and systematic field in which the subject held authority.

This is why it is essential that the question of autobiography—that
is to say, once again, the question of the inscription of the subject—be
reconsidered anew. The problem to be dealt with is what I might call,
for convenience, the *closure of exemplarity*. For the moment, at least, it is
insuperable.

But this hardly explains why a second motif should be introduced.
Or why this second motif should be music, the "musical obsession"
[*hantise musicale*]. Isn't the problematic of the subject as envisaged sufficient, and isn't one risking here useless encumbrances and complica-
tions, even the possibility of taking this problematic beyond the point
where, in practice, it can still be circumscribed?

The introduction of this second motif, as I hope to show, answers to
a necessity. But I should add that it derives first from a simple observation. Here again, Nietzsche is involved, as well as a few others.

The question I asked myself is the following: How is it that on at
least two occasions in the (modern) history of philosophy, a certain
auto-biographical compulsion (linked, moreover, to well-known manifestations of pathology and delirium) should have been associated, in
the clearest possible fashion, with what I have resigned myself to calling the "musical obsession"? Obviously I'm thinking here of Rousseau
and Nietzsche. And it will be understood that by "musical obsession,"
I do not mean a penchant or taste for music, even exaggerated and
tending to obsession, but rather a profound frustration, producing in

turn all the pathogenic effects imaginable, of a "musical vocation," of an authentic desire to "be a musician" (and to be recognized as such)— such that henceforth, and under the effect of this "denied" vocation that is constantly at work, music becomes a kind of obsessional theme, or is invested with an exorbitant value, and can on occasion engage the work (and its subject) in an unmerciful mimetic conflict with a "real" musician (Nietzsche *contra* Wagner, for example). Is this merely an accident, a chance conjunction? Or is there some necessity—a constraint inherent in the very being and structure of the subject, in its desire to reach itself, to represent and conceive itself, as well as in the impossibility of capturing or even glimpsing itself—that actually links together the autobiographical compulsion and the musical obsession?

I should note here that I would not pose a question of this sort if it were not that elsewhere, in "literature" (although the boundaries here are still more uncertain than in the case of other domains), a perfectly analogous phenomenon is to be observed with an undeniable regularity. Thus, taking only a few major examples (and without going back to Diderot's *Le neveu de Rameau*, a text that poses more complex problems), one can point to a number of German Romantics (especially Hoffmann), to Stendhal, to Proust, to the Michel Leiris of *L'age d'homme* or the trilogy *La règle du jeu*, or to the Roger Laporte of *Fugue*. And this without mentioning, as the inverse case (or almost), the curious necessity that prompts certain among the most famous representatives of the German *Künstlerroman*, such as Hermann Hesse (in *Gertrude*) or Thomas Mann (in *Doktor Faustus*), to draw upon, directly or otherwise, the autobiographical form.

Let us admit, consequently, that the question *holds up,* and that some reason lies behind it.

The interesting thing about the phenomenon at which it aims, as we can easily see, is that it should make it possible to return, by basing the analysis initially on the intraphilosophical distinction between the visible (the theoretical, the eidetic, and scopic, etc.) and the audible (or the acoustic, and I do not say the verbal), to the *hither side* of the "theoretical threshold" itself. It should make it possible to return to the place where the *theory of the subject* (but perhaps also *the subject of theory*) would see itself, if I may say so, obliged to put into question its privileged apparatus, its instrument, which, from Plato to Lacan, is a specular instrument. And a *speculative* apparatus.

The question, in this sense, would be "infra-theoretical" and would bear upon the pre-specular. More precisely, it would ask, albeit from out of theory itself (which would not be engulfed in this process [*s'y abîmerait*] without a further operation: the infra-theoretical is its orient, not its resource), whether there is, whether there can be, a pre-specular, and what this might mean or involve. To refer to *our* mythology—I mean psychoanalysis—I would like to know (if this can be *known*) what happens when one goes back from Narcissus to Echo. I would ask, then, this simple question: What is a reverberation or a resonance? What is a "catacoustic" phenomenon?

Document

Socrates, make music!
—Nietzsche, *The Birth of Tragedy,* citing Plato

But I am hardly "inventing" such a problematic, at least as regards its principle.

It derives, in fact (down to the very terms of the initial question: what connection is there between autobiographical compulsion and musical obsession?) from the work of Theodor Reik, and from one book in particular to which I shall return shortly. Thus, it is a question *already posed,* already recognized, explored, surveyed, and treated, a question that has already provided space and matter for theory (in this case, psychoanalysis). A question, then, that is *passée,* and probably *closed.* One might say that this is unimportant, and that it is hard to see what would prevent its being taken up again in such a way as to reactivate its particular force and sharpen its edge—applying it, for example, where Reik himself could not have thought of putting it to work: in the philosophical domain and within the general problematic of the subject of philosophical discourse, etc. Why, in other words, not use it as a kind of lever in a reading of *Ecce Homo?*

Besides all the difficulties involved as regards *application* (difficulties compounded in this case, no doubt, in that Reik claims that his work belongs to "applied" psychoanalysis), the question itself, once again, would have to *hold up.* As such, that is; as a question (and here things are not so clear that one might affirm this without hesitation), and *a fortiori* as a theoretical possibility. But it is evident that in extending the power of psychoanalysis to an area where Freud for his part declared himself incompetent (making only brief and prudent incursions into it), Reik not only touched the very limits of theory, but also could not avoid intersecting with Nietzsche's thought on music (for there is no other in the period): that sort of "musical ontology" that everyone sought (and found) in *The Birth of Tragedy.* Nor could he avoid, at least in part, submitting himself to it and suffering its authority.[8] Nietzsche, as we know, is at work in psychoanalysis—and I am not referring only to the "scene" that Freud never failed to make, half tacitly, for his benefit. But he is at work in it secretly. He does not dominate it, and in no way is he master of this theory.[9] Suppose, nevertheless, that he is liable to emerge, surreptitiously or otherwise, to direct it. Could one still move back from the theory thus directed to the direction itself and carry over to Nietzsche a question that he probably did not establish but at least induced? What is the *power* of psychoanalysis (the general question is borrowed from Jacques Derrida and Sarah Kofman)[10] with regard to that of which it would like to be the truth? What is, in this instance, its power over philosophy, over Nietzsche?

There is ample reason, consequently, not to read Nietzsche according to Reik. But at the same time there is no less ample reason to read Reik. This does not necessarily mean reading Reik according to Nietzsche; rather, since it is impossible that Nietzsche should not be implicated here, it would mean reading him in the closest proximity to Nietzsche, in the margins of certain books by Nietzsche, or *between* certain books by Nietzsche. Between *Ecce Homo,* let us say, and *The Case of Wagner* (or *Nietzsche contra Wagner*). As something like a preface, if you will, to the reading of Nietzsche.

To read Reik in this instance, however, is to read above all *one* book by Reik. Not that the others should be without interest—on the contrary. But as will soon become clear, it is necessary to attend here to a single book, or to what was intended as such, even if, by the author's

---

8. *The Birth of Tragedy* has its effect upon almost all the analytic texts devoted to the origin of theatricality, from *Totem and Taboo* through A. R. F. Winterstein's *Ursprung der Tragödie,* including also Reik's work of 1929, "Künstlerisches Schaffen und Witzarbeit," in *Lust und Leid im Witz: Sechs psychoanalytische Studien* (Vienna: Internationaler Psychoanalytischer Verlag, 1929), pp. 59–90.

9. On the contrary, the use of Nietzsche entails always an initial "analytic translation" of his concepts (particularly the opposition Apollonian/Dionysian). In Vienna, Nietzsche is basically thought of as a precursor. See Alexander Mette, "Nietzsches 'Geburt der Tragödie' in psychoanalytischer Beleuchtung," *Imago* 18 (1932): 67–80.

10. More precisely: Jacques Derrida, "Le facteur de la vérité," in *Poétique* 21 (1975): 96–147, collected in *La carte postale de Socrate à Freud* (Paris: Flammarion, 1980), pp. 439–524, and translated by Willis Domingo, James Hulbert, Moshe Ron, and Marie-Rose Logan in *Yale French Studies* 52 (1975): 31–113; and an unpublished essay by Sarah Kofman on Nerval.

own confession, it finally fails in this respect (though of course one is not obliged to believe him . . .).

The book is *The Haunting Melody*.[11] At least this is what we would be referring to if a complete French translation were available. However, only the final part of this large work—and this is never indicated—has been published in our language, under the (uselessly soliciting) title *Variations psychanalytiques sur un thème de Gustav Mahler*.[12] It is true that this part is easily detachable; it does form a whole, as they say, and can be treated as such. So we must resign ourselves. Still, even if this has little bearing on what I will try to demonstrate here, it would not be a bad thing to have at our disposal an honest (if not complete) French edition of this text.

These preliminaries aside, why address ourselves to this text?

Essentially for three reasons. The first reason I am keeping deliberately in reserve—my motives will appear later. It has to do with the fact, quite simply, that the book is a "theoretical failure"—once again, by the author's own confession (although in this case nothing would permit us to doubt him in advance).

The second reason is evident: it is that we have to do here with an *autobiography*,[13] or at least a fragment of an autobiography, since there exists, to my knowledge, a second autobiographical work (*Fragment of a Great Confession*),[14] and since, in addition, a good number of Reik's apparently more purely "theoretical" texts (articles, studies, various essays) readily take the form of autobiographical narrative. We will encounter a few examples. In short, there is definitely in Reik a kind of "autobiographical compulsion," or, to use the title of one of his works, a "confessional constraint," a *need to confess*,[15] of which *The Haunting Melody* is finally only a fragment. Twice detached . . .

11. Theodor Reik, *The Haunting Melody: Psychoanalytic Experiences in Life and Music* (New York: Farrar, Straus and Young, 1953). Subsequent references to this volume will be given in brackets in the body of the text.

12. *Variations psychanalytiques sur un thème de Gustav Mahler* (Paris: Denoël, 1972). For the purposes of this essay, I will retain the title *The Haunting Melody*.

13. This is why it was easy to detach this part from an ensemble that is written in the style of an essay.

14. *Fragment of a Great Confession: A Psychoanalytical Autobiography* (New York: Farrar, Straus and Giroux, 1949; rpt. Westport: Greenwood Press, 1973). The phrase "fragment of a great confession" is from Goethe, who used it to refer to his entire oeuvre.

15. *Geständniszwang und Strafbedürfnis* (1925), translated as *The Compulsion to Confess: On the Psychoanalysis of Crime and Punishment* (New York: Farrar, Straus and Cudahy, 1959). Cf. Reik, *Surprise and the Psychoanalyst: On the Conjecture and Com-*

But "autobiographical compulsion" means here, if the term is even possible (and things begin now to be no longer so evident), "auto-analytic compulsion." This, either because the autobiographical compulsion masks itself and covers itself under the theoretical (and practical) pretext of auto-analysis, still more or less admitted in Vienna in the twenties (and for reasons that are not without interest, as we will see)—or because, inversely, it is a matter of an auto-analytic compulsion (with all this implies, as one might already imagine, in relation to the "founding father" of psychoanalysis) that is able to satisfy itself, that is, accomplish itself, through disguise: by way of an operation of a "literary" type, through *Dichtung*. This, in turn, and as one might expect, is also not without domestic and economic, that is, familial and filial, implications. However this may be, the fact is that Reik, in his own way, deliberately practiced what is today called—according to a very old concept in which the essence of literature is at once determined and lost, but in which the essence of philosophy is probably [*vraisemblablement*] secured—*theoretical fiction*. This practice forces itself upon him with a double necessity, since in Reik's work, as in psychoanalysis as a whole and generally in any theory of the subject, we are dealing quite simply with a theory of the *figure*. I will merely cite as evidence Reik's other great autobiographical work, which predates by a few years *The Haunting Melody*, namely *Fragment of a Great Confession*. This work closes on a note (which happens to be entitled "Rondo finale") in which, by way of conclusion, Reik calls into question the status of the work he has just written (is it a novel or a work of psychoanalysis?) and wonders if there won't one day exist "a new kind of autobiography . . . in which one's experiences are not only told, but also investigated with the methods of modern psychology."[16]

The second reason compelling us to read this work, then, is that we have to do here with an autobiography to the second power (autobiography as auto-analysis, or vice versa), even to the third power, reflect-

---

prehension of Unconscious Processes, trans. Margaret M. Green (New York: Dutton, 1937), regarding communication as a function of the psyche: "[Our psychic material] must aim, among other things, at communicating to us something about the hidden processes in the other mind. We understand this primary endeavour; it does serve the purpose of communication, of psychical disburdenment. We are reminded of Freud's view that mortals are not so made as to retain a secret. 'Self-betrayal oozes from all our pores'" (p. 29). On the motif of confession (and thus also the topic of psychoanalysis as a confession of that of which one is not aware—thus as a theory of confession), one might also consult *Fragment of a Great Confession,* chs. 22 and 23, esp. pp. 446ff.

16. *Fragment,* p. 495.

ing upon itself by an additional theoretical turn (specular/speculative) in such a way as to present itself—we will return to this point—as a theory of autobiography.

The third reason, finally, issues from the decisive feature of the book, namely the manner in which—unlike, for example, *Fragment of a Great Confession,* in which a musical reminiscence provides the occasion for the "autobiographical return"[17]—it associates in a very strict way the autobiographical compulsion and the musical obsession.

But here it is necessary to begin to read.

Music Priming

With me the perception has at first no clear and definite object; this is formed later. A certain musical mood comes first, and the poetical idea only follows later.

—Schiller, cited by Nietzsche in *The Birth of Tragedy*

The association derives simply from the fact that the autobiographical (or auto-analytic) project takes its departure from a psychopathological accident (in the sense of the "psychopathology of everyday life") that is of a musical order, or implies music. It is not exactly an auditory hallucination (Reik may hear the voice—that is, listens to it[18]—but he is not hearing "voices"); rather, it is a reminiscence, the return, in very precise circumstances, of a melodic fragment. Obviously an involuntary return, and moreover one that immediately becomes obsessing or tormenting. What leads Reik into the autobiographical adventure, what he also investigates theoretically, and to the point that this questioning requires the power of his "analytic listening," is finally, in all its banality, the phenomenon of a "tune in one's head" that "keeps coming back" (without rhyme or reason, as they say), can't be identified, and, for a certain time at least, "doesn't go away" or "can't be gotten rid of." This is the phenomenon that I am calling, for want of a better term, "catacoustic," in that it bears an affinity to the perception of a kind of inner echo and is comparable (excluding its obsessive na-

17. Cf. "Age Sixty (A Note Before)," ibid., pp. 1–4.
18. *Fragment,* pp. 249–250; and of course Reik, *Listening with the Third Ear* (New York: Grove, 1948), to which I return below. I should note, however, that the latter book, written in the United States, takes up again and popularizes the theses of *Surprise and the Psychoanalyst,* at the same time correcting surreptitiously and firmly the ideology of American psychoanalysis.

ture, though even so . . .) to all the phenomena of reminiscence, musical or not, that have also been described or analyzed in literature (especially Romantic and Post-Romantic).

Music, then, primes; it sets off the autobiographical gesture. Which is to say, as well, the theoretical gesture.

The same device, used by Reik for getting started in the two autobiographical texts available to us (*Fragment of a Great Confession* and the one that will occupy us henceforth), is found again, in almost identical form, in the theoretical texts. Whereas Freud starts, for example, with the forgetting of a proper name, a disturbance in memory, an art image (or even his own dreams), Reik prefers to *listen*. It is the audible, generally, that awakens his analytic attention. The most striking example (and for good reason, since it is also of interest to musical aesthetics is that provided by the opening of the essay "Kol Nidre," which I cite here in part:

> Some time ago I stayed as a guest in the house of a music-loving family, and there I heard a composition played by a cellist which, although I am by no means musical [!], made a *peculiarly strong impression* on me [my emphasis, because it is obviously a matter of *Unheimlichkeit* and we will have to return to this point]. A particularly solemn and impressive minor passage occurred three times and awakened a feeling of pre-acquaintance in me that mingled curiously with the sombre emotions the melody itself had aroused. I was unable to recall when and where I had heard the melody before, and conquering a disinclination to exhibit ignorance of a well-known composition in such a circle, I asked my hostess the name of the piece. She expressed astonishment that I did not know it, and then told me that it was Op. 47 of Max Bruch, entitled "Kol Nidre," a modern free setting of the ancient melody which is sung in all the synagogues of the world before the service on the Jewish Day of Atonement. This explained to me my feeling of pre-acquaintance; but failed to account for the *strange emotion* [emphasis added] accompanying it and for the subsequent fact that the tune ran persistently in my head throughout the following day.[19]

Reik goes on here to make an immediate association with his childhood, and with the synagogue of his childhood, in practically analogous terms: "I remembered the mysterious trembling that possessed the congregation when the cantor began the Kol Nidre . . . and how I, child as I was, had been carried away by that irresistible wave of feel-

19. See Theodor Reik, *The Ritual: Psychoanalytic Studies,* trans. Douglas Bryan (New York: International University Press, 1946), p. 167.

ing . . . [yet] certainly incapable of understanding the full meaning of the words."[20]

But one notes again the same phenomenon, though in this case it is a second beginning (a "re-priming"), in the text devoted to the shofar and to the origin of music.[21] It is a text in which Reik tells us that he is going to probe into "the most obscure region of the Jewish *liturgy*, a *terra incognita* comparable to a primitive forest, reverently avoided by the science of religion, rich in confusing, mysterious, frequently even uncanny characteristics," and where the musical reminiscence introduces the theoretical question that concerns him: "It is a long time since I heard the sounds of the shofar, and when recently, in the interest of this work, I heard the shofar blown on New Year's Day, I could not completely avoid the emotion which these four crude, fearsome, moaning, loud-sounding, and long-drawn-out sounds produced. I do not attempt to decide whether the reason for my emotion was the fact that I was accustomed to this sound from youth, or whether it was an effect which everyone might feel.[22]

If I point immediately to these texts, even before having covered the first lines of *The Haunting Melody*, it is not simply to clear the ground or set out some guideposts (such as *Unheimlichkeit*, or the purely emotional, affective character of the musical effect). Rather, it is to designate from the outset the difficulty that Reik encounters *theoretically*, and to which, as is suggested by the formal analogy in narrative or discursive procedures, the autobiographical undertaking will be destined to respond. This difficulty involves precisely that which, within the general problematic of an aesthetic "guided by an economic point of view" (as Freud says), or else in relation to the question of the origin of ritual, cannot be called an "acoustic fantasy"—that which, in other words, slips or intrudes *between* the two registers: that point where, in all probability, the Freudian theory of the subject comes apart.[23] On the one hand, there is the register of the *verbal* (the "more than acoustic," if you will), presiding, at least as model, over the description of the operations of the unconscious, of its writing which has been coded

20. Ibid., p. 168.
21. Ibid., p. 226.
22. Ibid., p. 237.
23. This is without taking into account the "sociological" problematic of the origin or emergence of the subject as it is developed in Freud's *Totem and Taboo* and, above all, in his *Group Psychology and the Analysis of the Ego*. But it would not be difficult to show that the two registers in question compete with one another in the context of this problematic and that the theory of the subject is not reinforced by it.

through displacement, condensation, the play of tropes, etc., and above all presiding over the description of the formation of the Ego and the Superego.[24] On the other hand, there is the register which cannot be called simply the figural (despite the concern with *Darstellbarkeit*), but which must also be considered that of the *imaginary* in that it cuts across every stage of the Freudian construction, from the image, through the fantasy and the dream scene, to the ideal. It is as if Reik blurred all the divisions (often strict) to which Freud submits, and plunged into a sort of hole or gap between the "symbolic," if you will, and the imaginary—a hole that is not necessarily occupied by something like the "real," be it consigned to impossibility.

This, of course, has its consequences—even if the theoretical failure is certain.

Mourning and Rivalry

As for me, I think that insanity and madness are that horrible music itself, those few notes that whirl with a repugnant rapidity in those cursed melodies that are immediately communicated to our memory—even, I want to say, to our blood—and which, long after, we still can't get rid of.

—Tieck, *Love and Magic*

But it is time now to open to the first pages of *The Haunting Melody*. The book begins, as we know, with the story of a musical reminiscence.

As to the circumstance, first of all, the "primal scene" or the initial experience, things are relatively simple and the scenario can be briefly recapitulated.

On the evening of December 25, 1925, Freud telephoned Reik (then on holiday in the Austrian Alps) to inform him of the death of Karl Abraham—who, it should be emphasized, had been Reik's analyst (his instructor analyst) and his friend—and to ask him to deliver the funeral eulogy before the Vienna Psychoanalytic Society. This is where it starts. Reik, naturally, is shocked. He leaves his hotel to walk in the night, following a snowy path up into the forest (an appropriately *unheimlich* landscape: "The fir wood, the same in which I walked daily, had an unusual appearance. The trees seemed to be higher, darker, and towered almost menacingly up to the sky. The landscape seemed changed.

24. See Sigmund Freud, *The Ego and the Id*, in *The Standard Edition of the Complete Psychological Works*, vol. 19, trans. James Strachey with Anna Freud (London: Hogarth and the Institute of Psycho-Analysis, 1962).

It was now solemn and sinister as if it conveyed a mysterious message . . . There was only that heavy and oppressive silence around me
and in me. I still remember the dense and numb mood of that walk, but
I don't remember—it is more than a quarter of a century since—how
long I walked on in this mood" [*Melody*, p. 221]). During the walk,
Reik catches himself humming a tune that he initially does not recognize, but soon identifies at the first return or repetition. It is the opening measures of the chorale that forms the final movement of Mahler's
Second Symphony, a chorale constructed upon a poem by Klopstock
that Bach had already used, and entitled *Aufersteh'n*, or "Resurrection"
(from which comes the name of the symphony).

In the days that follow, Reik begins to write the eulogy for Karl
Abraham. In spite of all his efforts, the tune will not disappear, repeating and imposing itself each time he thinks of Abraham. It presents
itself, as Reik says, as the "*leitmotif* of my mourning for my dead friend"
(*Melody*, p. 222). It has, says Reik, a rare haunting power (though this is
not the essential thing here, it does enter into the clinical picture of the
so-called obsessional neurosis), a power all the more evident in that the
return of the first measures seems always to arise against the background of the obstinate forgetting of the following ones. If Reik "hears"
the first lines, or the last ("you will rise again, my dust, after a brief
rest" [*Melody*, p. 222]), he is never able to recover the intervening melody, the second motif, or, of course, the text on which it is constructed
("Believe, my heart, you have lost nothing / Everything you longed for
is yours, yes, yours / You have not lived and suffered in vain" [*Melody*,
p. 223]).

Reik, having tried without success to hold off the return of this tri-
umphal song (though it is nonetheless a song of *mourning*) and having
had no more success in struggling against the forgetting of the motif of
consolation, begins to sketch an auto-analysis that will last no less than
twenty-five years. (The writing of the book begins exactly on December 25, 1925; from which one can see that there is some truth in the
argument that superstition, ritualism, obsession with numbers—in
short, everything that can be classified under the Freudian category of
"belief in the omnipotence of thoughts," or acts—is always associated
with the major characteristic of obsessionality: inhibition). It is thus a
prolonged, if not interminable, auto-analysis whose initial moments at
least must be examined if one is to avoid getting lost in the intricacies
of a relatively complicated *intrigue*.

*   *   *

Contrary to what one would expect, Reik's most spontaneous impulse is not to engage in the analysis of mourning. And yet an enormous question is lying here (but too enormous, too close, in any case, to a Nietzschean question): What exactly links music to mourning? What links it to the work or play of mourning—to the *Trauerspiel,* to tragedy? His most spontaneous impulse is not even to attach the upsurgence of the haunting melody to his own "case," to all the obsessionality he knows to be in himself: the anticipated mourning of his own death, his inhibition, his "failure before success"—all motifs that he always infers elsewhere from such a return of Mahler's melodies.[25] No, the most spontaneous impulse is rather one of a theoretical kind. And for good reason: the spontaneity here is entirely induced by Freud. The move consists simply in seeking in the words of the chorale, in the text of Klopstock, the reason for the obsessional return of the melody. Hence the first attempt, naturally one of *translation,* to reduce the acoustic (and the musical) to the verbal: "I pondered what the motif wanted to convey to me. I heard its message, but I did not understand it; it was as if it had been expressed in a foreign language I did not speak" (*Melody,* p. 223).

Yet despite the recollection of several memories and the rapid train of two or three associations, the motif of "resurrection" persists in *saying* nothing to Reik. Likewise, what is left of a conversation that Reik was able to have with Abraham concerning the Christian faith, the Kaddish prayer, the relation between Egyptian eschatology and Mosaic hope, etc., fails to "speak" to him or to allow any deciphering or decoding whatsoever (all of these important motifs are legitimately invoked here, but they do not weave together for him into a meaning).

Until that moment when Reik, by chance of course (that is, by way of a symptomatic error as to Abraham's native city), relates Abraham's imperviousness to Mahler's music to his Nordic origins.

The decisive association is then produced, more or less according to the following schema. I will break it down here into its components: Abraham does not like Mahler's music, which is too "meridional" for his taste as a man of the north, too Austrian, too "bohemian." Furthermore, and I emphasize this associative element in passing, Abraham spoke an extremely correct, according to Reik "almost literary," German—the opposite of the relaxed pronunciation of the Viennese—and

25. See, in particular, *Listening with the Third Ear,* chs. 1, 3, 4 and 7 (where Mahler is associated with "the voice of the father").

with a strong and clear northern accent. Reik believes it to be a fact that Abraham was a native of Hamburg. But in reality—and here is the error—Abraham was born in Bremen. The error is a "fertile" one, however, since it permits him to pass to Mahler, to make the bridge or the connection. More precisely, it allows him to articulate together (thereby explaining the association) the chorale of the Second Symphony and Abraham's death; for it happens to be in Hamburg that Mahler found, as they say, the "inspiration" for this chorale—at the time of the funeral ceremony which the city had organized in honor of Hans von Bühlow (to whom Mahler apparently served as assistant) and in the course of which the Bach chorale, based on the same poem by Klopstock, was performed.[26]

At this point, the principal actors are in place: the *quartet* (as Lacan says in a text to which I will return) is formed. A scene opens and the analytic drama can begin.

Two characters who dominate the whole, however, are missing. These characters do not expand the initial quartet (Bühlow/Mahler, Abraham/Reik) into a sextet, but rather confirm it as a quartet, frame it. One of them at least, as his role necessarily dictates, can consolidate the set-up and provide the key from behind the scene, permitting the unfolding of the intrigue upon the enframed stage.

This is what happens very shortly afterward: Freud, to no one's surprise, makes his entrance.

From the anecdotal point of view, the essential is played out immediately after Reik has pronounced Abraham's funeral eulogy. Federn, who is presiding over the meeting, commits a slip of the tongue:

> After I had finished my eulogy, Freud, who sat near me, shook my hand, and Dr. Paul Federn, the chairman, closed the meeting with a few sentences. The old, friendly man made a slip of the tongue which made us smile and lifted, at least for the moment, the gloomy atmosphere of the evening. He said, "We appreciate the speech we just heard by Dr. Abraham" . . . Did that slip reveal that he wished me dead or was it an unconscious compliment? Conceited as I was, I unhesitatingly adopted the second interpretation. I could not imagine that anybody could seriously compare my modest accomplishments with those of Karl Abraham, but I must have wished unconsciously to be acknowledged not only as his stu-

26. Mahler's (rivaling) identification with von Bühlow is an identification with the orchestra conductor. It is coupled with an identification with Beethoven as composer, and as a composer of symphonies.

dent, but as his successor. I know from my analysis that I had emulated him, but I had never daydreamed that I could reach a position comparable to his within our science or the psychoanalytic movement. Such thoughts must, nevertheless, have been unconsciously working in me. (*Melody*, pp. 235–236)

What is then set in place is nothing other than the (expected) motif of rivalry—a motif that Reik had himself emphasized in his funeral eulogy (without failing to associate it in passing with Nietzsche):

Why deny it? Some psychoanalysts have believed they could prove their early independence from a teacher, as well as their independence of thought, in getting quickly emancipated from his influence and in becoming emphatically opposed to him. Occasionally one has referred to the sentence by Nietzsche: "You reward your teacher badly when you always remain only his pupil." But whatever may be justified in this sentence, it has nothing to do with the indecent high-speed in which the "conquest" of the teacher often takes place at present. We hope that the students of Abraham are protected against such a possibility by the analytic insight they have obtained from their master. (*Melody*, p. 233)

But this motif of rivalry, which admittedly does not teach us much about the rigid agonistic structure of the closed Viennese context (in any case, we have seen others since), or, to any greater extent, about "homosexual identification" (which would also enter into the picture of obsessional neurosis), introduces the further motif of guilt. The latter is associated, and in a perfectly strange manner, with music. This also happens in the text of the funeral eulogy:

It can scarcely be avoided that every important and grave event entering our lives leads us after some time slowly back to analytic trains of thought. Psychoanalysis has convinced us that all mourning is connected with unconscious self-reproach that can be traced back to certain emotional attitudes toward the deceased. This self-reproach, however typical, is individually different according to the individual relationship to the person who died. Yet there is, I believe, one of a general nature. I was reminded of it the other day by the remark of a little boy. The four-year-old son of a patient [the allusion to practice is obviously not without significance here, since, as we know, Reik was not a doctor but a "layman"] saw a funeral procession on the street and asked what it was. His mother explained to him what death and funeral mean. The child listened attentively and then asked with wide eyes, "But why is there music? He is already dead and does not hear it any more." There is a serious and even a profound meaning for us in the simplicity of the child's question. It

puts us to shame as we become aware of the inadequacy and the impotence of our words in the face of the great silence. But it shames us, too,
because it leads to the question: Must such things happen before we are
able to express how much we appreciate and care for our friends? (*Melody*, pp. 234–235)

Beneath mourning and rivalry, then, there is guilt, that is to say,
shame—and Reik is not unaware of the fact that it is connected with
the "compulsion to confess." But what is important is that the motif of
guilt, associated in this way with the music of the funeral eulogy, is
found associated, when Freud intervenes, with the question of *style*.
This is, once again, strange.

But in fact, Reik has no sooner recalled his spontaneous, advan-
tageous interpretation of Federn's slip of the tongue, than he adds the
following. It too must be cited, in that it also addresses the question of
the native language (the mother tongue, of course), and a certain music belonging to it:

It is sometimes harder to confess feelings of silly vanity or ideas of grandeur than deeds or thoughts one should or could be more ashamed of. I
just now was going to suppress such a trait of my vanity, namely, the
memory that I was proud of a trifling detail of my style in that speech.
The last paragraph runs in German: "Dennoch heisst uns, bevor wir die
uns allen vorgezeichnete Strasse weiterziehen, inneres Bedürfnis gebieter-
ischer als Ziemlichkeit, Karl Abraham zum letzten Mal zu grüssen . . ."
("Yet before we move along that road, destined for us all, inner need
drives us more imperatively than decency to salute . . ."). I still remember that I relished in my thoughts the repetition of the i-vowel in that
sentence. I would have suppressed this petty feature, had not my mentioning the name of Freud admonished me to be more strict with myself.
I remembered, namely, that many years later when I asked Freud for help
in an actual conflict and was in a short psychoanalysis with him, I once
said during a session, "I am ashamed to say what just occurred to me
. . ." and Freud's calm voice admonished me, "Be ashamed, but say it!"
    After the meeting was closed, I accompanied Freud to his home in the
Berggasse. He praised my speech and emphasized that I had not merely
given a laudatory oration, but had also mentioned some of the shortcom-
ings of Abraham, whom he appreciated so highly. He added that we are
still unconsciously afraid of the dead, and because of this hidden awe are
often led to speak of them only in overpraising terms. He quoted the
Latin proverb, *De mortuis nil nisi bene*, as an expression of that unconscious fear, and added a humorous Jewish anecdote which makes fun of
the insincerity of eulogies. (*Melody*, p. 236)

The Style and the Accent: Hearing Seeing

The instinct of the ear imposes a musical
cadence on elocution.

—Cicero, De Oratore

All of this, in its subtle simplicity, is still far from being perfectly clear.

But let us retrace the course of the association. What do we obtain? Bracketing for the moment Reik's continual allusions to what links music—the essence of music?—to mourning and death (by way, essentially, of shame and guilt, and thus by way of an agonistic structure, or what psychoanalysis calls "ambivalence" in the theory of identification), the only relation that exists between Mahler and Abraham is that established by Abraham's *accent*. Likewise, if this relation is in turn connected, again by means of an agonistic relation in which Freud is involved, with Reik's ambition or mimetic desire,[27] then it is a stroke of literary vanity (extremely powerful in Reik), or rather of *stylistic pride,* that allows us to understand it.

In both cases, not only does everything happen at the level of audition or listening, but what is heard and begins to make sense (to "signify," not in the mode of signification but, if one may rely on a convenient distinction, in that of *signifiance*)[28] is not, strictly speaking, of the order of language. Rather, it affects a language, and affects in the use of a language (although this cannot be understood in relation to the Saussurian *parole,* or in relation to linguistic "performance") its *musical* part, prosodic or melodic.

Reik is interested, as we see, in the *voice:* intonation, elocution, tone, inflections, melisma, rhythm, even timber (or what Barthes calls "grain"). Or color. These are all things which are dealt with by ancient rhetoric (that of enunciation and diction, of *lexis*) and which might sustain up to a certain point the attention of a musical theory, as was the case in the long history of the development of the operatic recitative, or even a stylistics. But they do not fall under the jurisdiction of

27. Although *confessed,* as one might expect, and in any case a matter of public knowledge. See Theodor Reik, *From Thirty Years with Freud,* trans. Richard Winston (New York: Farrar and Rinehart, 1940), esp. ch. 3.

28. Lacoue-Labarthe is drawing the term essentially from Benveniste (though it is now commonly used). See in particular Emile Benveniste, *Problèmes de linguistique générale,* vol. 2 (Paris: Gallimard, 1974), ch. 3 ("Sémiologie de la langue").—*Editor*

linguistic distinctions in the proper sense (of the type semiotic/seman-
tic, for example) because, more fundamentally, they escape the metaphysical (theoretical) distinctions that always underlie them (sensible/
intelligible, matter/form, body/spirit, thing/idea, and so on). A phenomenon of this sort is, finally, untheorizable. What is to be made of
the voice, of the *lexis,* and of phonation if they concern not only the
"psyche," desire, or even, as Barthes would have it, "le corps en jouis-
sance,"[29] but equally an investment that is social, historical, cultural,
aesthetic—in short, *ethical,* in the strict sense of the word *ethos?* To
what, exactly, is such a phenomenon to be referred? And how is it to be
integrated into our understanding of the general production of meaning? Reik, at any rate, admitted that he could speak of it only in
(vague) terms of intuition and empathy, and doubted that it might ever
give rise to any science whatever.

Such a phenomenon nonetheless constantly solicited his attention.
He even made such an attention the very index or criterion of good
analytic practice. Well before Ivan Fónagy and "The Instinctual Bases
of Phonation,"[30] Reik hoped to orient psychoanalysis in that direction—unsuccessfully, moreover (Groddeck alone among his contemporaries had perhaps any chance of hearing it). He was thus obliged to
claim it, and not without a certain complacency, as the "auditive" character of his own *habitus.* Thus in *Fragment of a Great Confession* (an
attempt at auto-analysis which is modeled entirely, to put it briefly, on
the famous episode in *Dichtung und Wahrheit* where Goethe abandons
Frederike Brion, and which therefore presupposes that Reik's life is
constructed and copied "by imitation" from that of Goethe), Reik frees
himself, belatedly, from the Goethean imago by emphasizing his extreme acoustic sensitivity. "In contrast to Goethe, who received his
best and most significant impressions through the eye, I was, as the
French psychologists would say, a '*type auditif*.' I was not just blind as a
bat, but most of my impressions and memories were connected with
the ear—of an auditory character."[31] He justifies in this way the constant gesture, his *first* constant gesture, of relating to music (as if music, he says, constituted the "web" of his memories) what is of the
order of literature or quite simply of discourse. (The entire Sesenheim
episode, for example, is inscribed in the "scenario" of the symphony by

29. Roland Barthes, "Le grain de la voix," *Musique en jeu* 9 (November 1972): 57–63.
30. See Ivan Fónagy, *La métaphore en phonétique* (Ottawa: Marcel Didier, 1979),
ch. 6: "Le caractère pulsionnel des sons du langage."
31. *Fragment,* p. 249. On Goethe as a plastic artist, see p. 103.

Beethoven designated "pastoral," whose initial title, as Reik does not fail to remind us on this occasion—and most eloquent in relation to what will concern us shortly—was *Sinfonia caratteristica*.)

One will have recognized here the motif of "listening with the third ear."

We know that Reik borrowed the expression from Nietzsche. It is found in Aphorism 246 of *Beyond Good and Evil*. Nietzsche writes:

> What torture books written in German are for anyone who has a *third* ear! How vexed one stands before the slowly revolving swamp of sounds that do not sound like anything and rhythms that do not dance, called a "book" among Germans! Yet worse is the German who *reads* books! How lazily, how reluctantly, how badly he reads! How many Germans know, and demand of themselves that they should know, that there is *art* in every good sentence—art that must be figured out if the sentence is to be understood! A misunderstanding about its *tempo*, for example, and the sentence itself is misunderstood.
>
> That one must not be in doubt about the rhythmically decisive syllables, that one experiences the break with any excessively severe symmetry as deliberate and attractive, that one lends a subtle and patient ear to every *staccato* and every *rubato*, that one figures out the meaning in the sequence of vowels and diphthongs and how delicately and richly they can be colored and change colors as they follow each other—who among book-reading Germans has enough good will to acknowledge such duties and demands and to listen to that much art and purpose in language? In the end one simply does not have "the ear for that"; and thus the strongest contrasts of style go unheard, and the subtlest artistry is *wasted* on the deaf. —These were my thoughts when I noticed how clumsily and undiscerningly two masters in the art of prose were confounded.[32]

The third ear, as we see, is the "artistic" or "stylistic" ear that discerns in writing, discourse, or a language a fundamental musicality—fundamental, above all, in that it makes *sense*. As Nietzsche continued to insist from the time of his first works on Greek prosody, we have to do here with the very intelligibility of what is said (which is "sensible"). And it will have been noted in passing that this musicality is essentially a rhythmics. We have yet to draw all the consequences from this point.

What does Reik make of this borrowing? Something that is, finally, rather faithful to Nietzsche—if only in the privilege Reik accords to rhythm. But let us not get ahead of ourselves. Before this, the third ear

32. *Beyond Good and Evil*, pp. 182–183.

defines the analytic listening, that is to say, the interpretation of the unconscious from out of the unconscious. It is, says Reik, "the means of detecting the substructures of the soul":

> The analyst has to guess them, to sense them, in using his own unconscious like a receiver of messages, which are at first unrecognizable, but can then be grasped and deciphered. The analyst has to "listen with the third ear" to what his patients say and what they leave unsaid. He has to acquire a fine ability for hearing the subtones of the unconscious processes. But this means that, if necessary, he has to have free access to his own unconscious; that the road to his own deep feelings and thoughts has to be unblocked. He must be able to reach his own experiences, which form a concealed reservoir of emotions and thoughts, a subterranean store room of unconscious memory-traces. These hidden memories secure the means to understand the other person.[33]

Still more precisely, such a faculty of listening should at the most primitive level regulate the simple *perception of the other* as an unconscious perception, one that is capable of offering infinitely greater material, according to Reik, than what is given to us by conscious perception. But while the unconscious perception considered here is perfectly diversified (sight, smell, touch, etc.) and concerns the outer *habitus* or "surface" of the other, it is in reality audition, strictly speaking, that is determinant. All perception is at bottom listening. Or, in other terms that come down to the same thing, listening is the paradigm (not the metaphor) of perception in general. The unconscious *speaks.* And the voice, that is, the *lexis,* is that by which it speaks— which presupposes, in a perfectly classical manner, that language is determined essentially as a language of gesture, a *mimicry:*

> There are certain expressive movements which we understand, without our understanding exactly being at work in that understanding. We need only think of the wide field of language: everybody has, in addition to the characteristics that we know, certain vocal modulations which do not strike us, the particular pitch and timbre of his voice, his particular speech rhythm, which we do not consciously observe. There are variations of tone, pauses, and shifted accentuation, so slight that they never reach the limits of conscious observation, individual nuances of pronunciation which we do not notice, but note. These little traits, which have no place in the field of conscious observation, nevertheless betray a great deal to us about a person. A voice which we hear, though we do not see

33. *Fragment,* pp. 328–329. There are analogous statements in *Surprise and the Psychoanalyst, Listening with the Third Ear,* etc.

the speaker, may sometimes tell us more about him than if we were observing him. It is not the words spoken by the voice that are of importance, but what it tells us of the speaker; its tone comes to be more important than what it says. "Speak, in order that I may see you," said Socrates.

Language—and here I do not mean only the language of words, but also the inarticulated sounds, the language of the eyes and gestures—was originally an instinctive utterance. It was not till a later stage that language developed from an undifferentiated whole to a means of communication. But throughout this and other changes it has remained true to its original function, which finds expression in the inflection of the voice, in the intonation, and in other characteristics . . . Even where language only serves the purpose of practical communication, we hear the accompanying sounds expressive of emotion, though we may not be aware of them.[34]

But it is perfectly clear: while listening is privileged to the extent that it is necessary to consider it as more (or less) than a metaphor for analytic comprehension, it is nonetheless the case that, speech being finally mimic in nature and referring back to a more primitive gesture, listening is quite simply seeing. "Speak a little so that I can see you."

In a certain sense, one might stop at this point. Everything that can, and should, draw us to Reik, everything in his work that makes it more than a simple repetition of Freud—that is to say, its "theoretical failure"—is inscribed on this page.

His theoretical failure, or rather, working through him, the general failure of the theoretical. That is to say, its complete success. For if, despite his apparent "theoretical naïveté," Reik continues to run up against the impossibility of circumscribing the essence of listening, it is because he has *already* theorized it. Hence the obligation to speak, at least provisionally, of a theoretical reduction (eidetic, scopic) of the acoustic, although the distinction between the visible and audible, given the kind of phenomenon (or "thing") in question, is less pertinent than ever. No example better illustrates this than Reik's way of joining systematically and seamlessly the motif of listening with the Goethean motif of *repeated reflections*.

The theoretical reduction is a *specular* reduction. An old secret heritage of Platonism: the voice, diction, the audible in general (and music) are

<hr/>

34. *Surprise and the Psychoanalyst*, p. 21. See also *The Compulsion to Confess* and *Listening with the Third Ear*.

attainable only by speculation. We need not even go through here the extremely complex turns of the "Goethean" auto-analysis; it will suffice to refer to the penultimate part of *Surprise and the Psychoanalyst,* which shows Reik debating once more the possibility of analytic hearing— the possibility of "unconscious communication" or of "reciprocal elu- cidation of unconscious processes." Over long chapters, Reik makes use of the example provided by the analysis of a hysterical patient (ap- propriately manifesting strong feelings of guilt), examining, as he is obliged to do by the associative strata opened up by the listening, the overwhelming effect produced in him ("similar," he says, "to the ef- fects of music") by the final scene of an otherwise mediocre play. The principal theme of this play allows him to understand or to intuit, "by empathy," the discourse of the patient in question. This is precisely the situation of listening with the third ear: what one might call a listening by echo, or catacoustic interpretation—exactly what Reik proposes to conceptualize by calling upon the Goethean doctrine of "repeated re- flections." It comes down, quite simply, to falling back upon the idea of the necessarily mediate character of the knowledge of the Ego:

> I propose to use an expression of Goethe's for this psychological process and call it "repeated reflection" (*wiederholte Spiegelung*). The poet speaks on several occasions of this term which he borrowed from entoptics. In one essay he tells us to consider that repeated reflections "not only keep the past alive but even raise it to a higher existence" and reminds us of the entoptic phenomena "which likewise do not pale as they pass from mirror to mirror, but are actually kindled by it." In a letter about obscure passages in *Faust* (to Iken, September 23, 1827), he observes . . . : "Since we have many experiences that cannot be plainly expressed and commu- nicated, I have long adopted the method of revealing the secret meaning to attentive readers by images that confront one another and are, so to speak, reflected in one another." I believe that the same procedure that was here adopted for literary purposes can, *mutatis mutandis,* be used on occasion in scientific psychological work, in order to reveal the secret meaning."[35]

What is involved here, of course, is the position of the Other in analysis (the concept, as Lacan pointed out, is very much present in Reik), and there unfolds from it an entire *dialectic* that is relatively fa-

---

35. *Surprise and the Psychoanalyst,* pp. 234–235. In *Fragment,* pp. 46–47, Reik cites *in extenso* another text by Goethe bearing the same title, but addressed to Professor August Nake of Bonn, who had traveled to Strasbourg in 1822—like Lenz to some extent—in order to "relive Goethe's youth on the spot in Sesenheim," and who had

miliar to us today. Thus, there is played out in the appeal to the spec-ular (a gesture which Reik thinks of as analogical in character, just like his recourse to music, but which perhaps is not so much so as he thinks) the entire theoretical and practical possibility of analysis, and *a fortiori* of auto-analysis. Because the very hypothesis of the uncon-scious, as Reik says ingenuously, places us before an "antinomy" (ac-cess "to the deepest and most vital region" of the Ego is forbidden to consciousness), any understanding of the Ego "needs to be reflected in another."[36] And thus it is not at all by chance if, in a movement exactly symmetrical with the one we have just observed, it is revealed that one may pass almost immediately from the optical analogy to the acoustic analogy—from the reflection to the echo. Barely two pages later, while attempting to explain how "the other person's unconscious impulse is communicated to the analyst," Reik declares quite simply that on the whole it "is as if some external impression stirred the reminiscence of a well-known melody in us." And he adds, "Say, for instance, that the opening bars were played on the piano. For a person with a musical memory it is not necessary for the melody to be played all through for him to recognize it. After only a few bars, the reminiscence of the whole melody, or at least of its essence, will occur spontaneously to the listener. In like manner, the unconscious memory trace of the induced emotion is stirred as a kind of experimental verification, so to speak, in the analyst."[37] In short, resonance (or echoing) and reflection are per-fectly interchangeable as theoretical or theorizing figures of repetition, of the reactivation of the trace, or of the analytic *reading*, all presup-posed by the complex "graphology" at work in Freud.[38]

"The Novel is a Mirror . . ."

A theory of the novel should itself be a
novel.

—Friedrich Schlegel, *Conversation on Poetry*

---

composed a memoir of his "pilgrimage" that was shown to Goethe. One finds in Goethe's text the following phrase: "Contemplation and the moral reflection of the past not only preserve it as living reality, but elevate it to a higher level of life. Similarly, entoptic phenomena do not fade from mirror to mirror, but are, by the very repetition, intensified.

36. *Surprise and the Psychoanalyst*, p. 237.

37. Ibid., p. 239.

38. I refer, of course, to Derrida's essay, "Freud and the Scene of Writing," trans. Jeffrey Mehlman, *Yale French Studies* 48 (1972): 74–117.

We seem to be quite far from what attracted our attention, our "read-ing," at the outset of the auto-analysis recapitulated in *The Haunting Melody:* the decisive association that brings into play both Abraham's accent or diction and the stylistic trait (alliteration) of Reik's funeral eulogy—in short, the role assigned to *style.*

It is nonetheless in the specular reduction that the question of style is decided (or lost).

Style, as Reik knows, is double. It is first of all a phenomenon of diction or enunciation, whether oral or written (which also implies, as he repeats many times, handwriting).[39] But it is also the "character": the incised and the engraven, the prescribed (or pre-inscribed), the "programmed" in a subject—in other words, he says, the unconscious, and the unconscious as a system of traces, marks, and imprints. This is why style *betrays;* it is, essentially, the *compulsion to confess. Confession* itself—that is to say, speech.[40]

Nonetheless, it is one thing to say: "Psychoanalysis has claimed that we do not live, but that we are lived [we will soon find, though this time from Mahler's pen, an analogous phrase], that is, the greatest part of what we experience is not of our conscious doing, but is 'done' by unknown powers within ourselves." And it is another thing to add, a few lines later: "Freud once varied the saying 'Le style, c'est l'homme' to 'Le style, c'est l'histoire de l'homme.' This was certainly meant in the sense that the style of a man reflects the story of his life, his education, his reading, his experiences. As I read my book with the eyes of a psy-chologist, Freud's rephrasing took on another meaning: the style, the characteristic manner of expression, my choice of words as well as my sequences were a kind of confession, revealing to the attentive reader an important part of my own life story."[41]

39. See *From Thirty Years with Freud,* where Reik reports this remark by Freud: "There is no doubt that one also expresses one's character through one's writing. What a shame that our understanding of it is so ambiguous and its interpretation so uncer-tain. Graphology is not yet a domain of scientific research." (Translated from *Trente ans avec Freud* [Paris: Editions Complexe, 1956], p. 31.)

40. *The Compulsion to Confess:* "In these applications, the words *bekennen* or "con-fess" have not at all that more special meaning which is given them today. And what about the German *Beichte* (religious confession) which is used as a synonym for confes-sion? The word comes from the old German *pijehan* meaning simply to talk. From the old high German *pijiht* there developed the middle high German *begiht* and *bihte* which may be recognized in the modern word *Beichte.* The Latin word *confiteri,* from which the English "confess" is derived, like the German *bekennen* or *gestehen* originally meant merely to say something emphatically" (p. 311).

41. *Fragment,* p. 222–223. Cf. *From Thirty Years with Freud:* "Freud revised the well-

This is another thing, quite another thing, because (with the help of a certain psychologism) all the difference between the *incised* and the *fashioned,* the *type* and the *figure,* or, if you prefer, between *writing* and *fiction,* is marked here. "Prescription" or "programmation" is not "molding," even less the molding provided by experience or life. This is what ultimately separates the *Bildungsroman* from tragedy.

But of course, this is where the theoretical becomes involved— where it counters.

For here, at the point where the question of style surfaces, Reik stops abruptly. The effect of inhibition is enormous, so powerful in his case that it will take him no less than twenty-five years to get over it and to complete (or almost) the task that was nevertheless so quickly begun—to succeed, in any case, in writing this book. One can always attribute such a thing to "obsessional neurosis." But how can one explain the *après-coup,* the retarding, the delay? What "catacoustic logic" is to be inferred there?

It was such a logic that interested Reik. It is hardly by chance that he placed as an epigraph to *Fragment of a Great Confession* this verse from Goethe: "Late resounds what early sounded." And this is clearly what he was hunting for in music. He was seeking, in short, to define a kind of "musical" essence of the subject. Nevertheless, he was not unaware of the fact that to submit to the theoretical was to lose all chance of reaching his goal. This is why the theoretical "failure" is also a "success" and the "inhibition" will never be truly lifted—or will have always been lifted in advance. *The Haunting Melody* concludes with these lines:

> Emerging from those haunted grounds and arriving at the end of this study, I suddenly remember that I often daydreamed that it would become a "great" book. It became nothing of the kind, only a fair contribution to the psychology of unconscious processes. Yet as such it presents a new kind of recording of those inner voices which otherwise remain mute.
>
> In revising this study, I have again followed its themes and counterthemes and their elaboration. I know the score. But, as Mahler used to say, the most important part of music is not in the notes. (*Melody,* p. 376)

I will be returning to the "phonography" to which he alludes here— it is probably the best definition Reik could give of autobiography.

In any case, we have reached the point where the book's organizing

known maxim to "Style est l'histoire de l'homme." By that maxim he did not mean merely that literary influences *fashioned* the style of the individual, but that the development and experiences of an individual do their part in *molding* his style" (pp. 9–10, emphasis added).

mechanism is in place. It is at the very moment in his narrative when Reik marks (that is to say, confesses) the arresting effect of inhibition that there begins to develop, following the *après-coup* logic of composition or fiction, the autobiographical intrigue—or auto-analytic intrigue (why not say, in more economical terms, *autographical?*).

The intrigue is, properly speaking, *novelistic* [*romanesque*]. The autobiography, according to a necessity that must now be analyzed, is a novel.

The mechanism that has set itself in place, is, as we know, specular—doubly specular. It is the classic mechanism of "mimetic rivalry," in Girard's terms, and therefore of the narcissistic conflict whose description Freud sketched out in his theory of identification (itself a sketch, incomplete).[42] It is reframed here, or, what comes down to the same thing, closed upon itself as with a mirror, redoubled. A specular mechanism, then, that brings six characters (in search of an analyst?) face to face with each other according to strictly homologous relations, though they confront each other two by two, in quartets. These characters are, respectively, Mahler, von Bühlow, and Beethoven (from bottom to top along the line of musicians); and along the line of analysts, Reik, Abraham, Freud.[43]

From here, an entire myth (a personal myth) can be organized, or, borrowing Lacan's definition, "a certain objectified representation of an epos . . . of a *geste* expressing in an imaginary way the fundamental relations that are characteristic of a certain mode of being of the human being."

The definition is from a seminar made famous by its more or less clandestine circulation, "The Individual Myth of the Neurotic, or 'Poetry and Truth' in Neurosis,"[44] a seminar in which Lacan in fact insisted on the kind of framing or spacing of the mimetic relation that we have just seen. Before returning to Reik's autobiographical narrative, I would like to pause over Lacan's analysis—my reasons for this detour will appear shortly.

In the second part of his presentation—the first part devoted to a

42. *Group Psychology and the Analysis of the Ego*, ch. 7. In *Standard Edition*, vol. 18, pp. 65–145.

43. Between the two columns, there is always the figure of Goethe, who, more than the "complete artist," represents a kind of "universal genius."

44. Published by Editions des Grandes Têtes Molles de Notre Epoque (without date or place). The text is an uncorrected and unreviewed transcription of a seminar. A

rereading of "Notes upon a Case of Obsessional Neurosis" ("The Rat Man")—Lacan took up again in its general outlines, though implicitly, the analysis that Reik had proposed of the Frederike Brion episode in *Dichtung und Warheit* (found again *in extenso* in *Fragment of a Great Confession*).⁴⁵ Having situated psychoanalysis, as it is important to recall here, *between* science and art—as belonging to what was classified in the Middle Ages under the category of "liberal arts"⁴⁶—and having, in this vein, envisaged the myth in its relation to science as fundamentally the supplement for the lacking truth,⁴⁷ Lacan undertook the necessary task of reworking the constitutive myth of psychoanalysis (Oedipus). This reworking was not only to account for progress recorded in the "analytic experience," but also to elucidate as well how "all analytic theory stretches out within the distance separating the fundamental conflict which, through the intermediary of rivalry with the father, links the subject to an essential symbolic value . . . always in function of a certain concrete degradation . . . between the image of the father and [what Lacan named at this time] the image of the master [the 'moral master']."⁴⁸ Lacan thus returned, appropriately, to the nodal point of Freudian theory (the point where this theory constantly

---

correct version by J. A. Miller has since been published by the review *Ornicar?* (May 1979). The previous citation appears on p. 5 of the seminar transcription.

45. The two examples chosen by Lacan are, each time, cases of obsessional neurosis—the question remains as to what commits this "formation" (as Lacan says) to the mythical and thus also to the mimetic.

46. Because of the way it retains always in the foreground, Lacan added, "the fundamental relation to the measure of man": that is to say, "the internal relation that in some sense can never be exhausted, that is cyclical and closed upon itself—the relation of measure between man and himself . . . which is the use of language, the use of the word" (p. 2).

47. Seeing myth, in other words—and all of this is fairly close to Lévi-Strauss—as "providing a discursive formulation to that something that cannot be transmitted in the definition of truth, since the definition of truth rests only upon itself" (p. 3), and consequently has its proper place within that "art" of intersubjective relations or that very particular kind of anthropology that is psychoanalysis.

48. Lacan, "The Individual Myth of the Neurotic, or 'Poetry and Truth' in Neurosis," p. 4. The passage from which Lacoue-Labarthe is quoting goes as follows: "Toute la théorie analytique est tendue à l'intérieur de la distance qui sépare le conflit fondamental qui par l'intermédiaire de la rivalité au père, lie le sujet à une valeur symbolique essentielle, mais, vous allez le voir, qui est toujours en fonction d'une certaine dégradation concrète, peut-être liée aux conditions, aux circonstances sociales spéciales, de l'image et de la figure du père, expérience tendue donc entre cette image du père, et d'autre part . . . "

exposes itself to the risk of a general revision and even threatens to collapse), that is to say, to the concept of identification—and especially
primary identification.[49] Lacan did not follow exactly the path opened
up (barely) by Freud, who maintained that identification was "possible
before any object choice" and therefore prior, by right, to the Oedipus
complex. Lacan took on the Oedipus complex itself and sought to "de-
triangulize" it by noting a fundamental and necessary discordance—a
matter, he says, of a "defaulting" [*carence*]—between the (real) father
and his (symbolic) function, a discordance which requires the splitting
of paternity as such and the appearance of an "imaginary father" capable of taking on the function. But it is a discordance that requires as
well, as its repercussion, the splitting of the son—the subject "himself"—a splitting constitutive of neurosis (together with, as in the case
of Goethe, all the affectation of transvestism, makeup, and all the
mythic conduct—in other words, the *imitation* of the *Vicar of Wakefield*).
This splitting, or, as Lacan also said—an inevitable word here—"alienation" of the subject "with respect to itself," makes it oscillate vis-à-vis
its double between distancing (where the substitute bears every "mortal" menace) and a "reintegration" of the role (where desire is inhibited). A well-known situation in the "Romantic" or "fantastic"
novelesque forms (that of Hoffmann, for example). In short, Lacan
sketched out, though within psychoanalysis and while retaining the
Oedipus complex, a "mimetology" fairly comparable to the one that
Girard, with quite different intentions, will elaborate later.

This double splitting (or doubling), this "quaternary" system, Lacan
said, is consequently what both defines the "impasses" of neurosis (but
also the Ego's assumption of its function as subject) and makes it possible to envisage "a critique of the entire Oedipal schema."[50] The
"mythical quartet" would take over from the familial triangle and, at
least up to a certain point, would undo the schema of object(al) libido,
prohibited desire for the mother, etc.

All of this did not fail to lead back, of course, to what Lacan characterized as the "second great discovery of analysis"; namely the
"narcissistic relation" itself, "fundamental to the entire imaginary development of the human being" inasmuch as it is connected to what

49. One might recall, among other examples, that in *Group Psychology and the Analysis of the Ego* (ch. 6) Freud introduces identification among the non-libidinal (ante-
sexual) "affective attachments"—which refers one back to the entire problematic (or the
difficulty) of "primary narcissism."

50. "The Individual Myth of the Neurotic, or 'Poetry and Truth' in Neurosis," p. 34.

might be called "the first implicit experience of death."[51] Thus it led back, as one will have guessed, to the *mirror stage*.[52]

> It is one of the most fundamental and most *constitutive* experiences of the subject that this something inside him which is alien to him and which is called the Ego, that the subject first sees himself in an other, more advanced and more perfect than he, and that he even sees his *own image* in the mirror at a period when analytic experience shows him to be incapable of perceiving it as a totality . . . at the same time that he is himself undergoing the original disarray of all effective motor functions that belongs to the first six months after birth [emphasis added].[53]

What was thus constructed, via the Freudian imago and the mirror stage (the text of 1949 ["Le stade du miroir comme formateur de la fonction du Je"], moreover, was fairly clear on this point) was a theory of the *figure* and of *fiction*—a theory of death as figure, of the double, and of the *dead* double as *Gestalt*, in the Hegelian and above all post-Hegelian sense of the term. For the entire analysis ended by organizing itself around the conclusion that the "fourth element" in the quaternary structure (and this time a very Hegelian, perfectly dialectical quaternity) is nothing other than death: the *imaginary* death (of a subject itself imaginary or specular), whose mediation is constitutive, however, of the subject function in general—given that there is no subject, as such, that is not alienated, divided, cloven. The mediation of this "fourth element" would also be constitutive, therefore, bringing back into vigor the eidetic transcendence of Platonism whose logic Heidegger brought forth,[54] of the "giving of meaning" itself, or of what establishes, in its unverifiable truth, as Lacan said, "the measure of man." In which case, and this is indeed what Lacan stated in conclusion, the theory of narcissism is nothing other than the truth of *The Phenomenology*

51. Ibid., p. 33.

52. Which should be reread here and saved from the simplifications to which it has been subjected, especially concerning the role of language (and therefore of the mother) in the initial phase of supplying for the deficiencies of prematuration.

53. "The Individual Myth of the Neurotic, or 'Poetry and Truth' in Neurosis," p. 33. The French text reads as follows: C'est une des expériences les plus fondamentales, les plus constitutives pour le sujet que ce quelque chose à lui-même étranger à l'intérieur de lui qui s'appelle le Moi, que le sujet se voit d'abord dans un autre, plus avancé, plus parfait que lui, et que même il voit sa propre image dans le miroir à une époque où l'expérience prouve qu'il est incapable de l'apercevoir comme une totalité . . . , alors qu'il est lui-même dans le désarroi originel de toutes les fonctions motrices effectives qui est celui des six premiers mois après la naissance."

54. Apropos, essentially, of Nietzsche and Jünger, see "Typography."

of Mind. Or, at least, it is alone capable of "accounting for certain facts that might otherwise remain enigmatic in the Hegelian theory" since "after all, in order for the dialectic of a struggle to the death, a struggle of pure prestige, simply to come about, death cannot be realized, otherwise the entire dialectic comes to a halt for want of combatants; and it is necessary that in a certain manner death be imagined."[55]

In other words (this goes without saying), speculated.

I recount none of this analysis in order to "criticize" it. Everything here is unquestionably right (perfectly accurate), also true (on the basis of truth considered in its essence), and in any case *theoretically* unsurpassable—even if it might eventually be reworked (by Lacan himself, for example). I pause over this text only because it allows us to inscribe in a particularly effective manner the ensemble of problematic elements that has occupied us here within the horizon of *figural ontology* (specular and speculative), or, if you will, *fictional ontology* (Lacan speaks of myth in this text, but it comes down strictly to the same thing).[56] Three reasons for pausing over this text, then:

1. Because (and this was my immediate pretext) this analysis allows us to account for the Reikian mechanism or set-up (which it partially exploits): the doubly specular, quaternary structure—the mirrored square from which is engendered, because it frames it, a fiction that is entirely of the order of a novel, and that will soon be seen to oscillate between auto- and allo-(bio)graphy (a narrative of the life of Mahler and a narrative of the imitation of the life of Mahler, which was previously an imitation of the life of von Bühlow, etc.). This leads us back to something very close to the "family romance," *minus* the *family,*[57] whose model Freud established, and constitutes in fact the first degree of "fictioning" in *The Haunting Melody* (or—at this level of analysis, there is no difference—in that quasi-love story, *Fragment of a Great Confession*).[58]

2. More important, such an analysis defines what is really *at stake* in what Reik, following Thomas Mann, calls the "autobiographical im-

55. "The Individual Myth of the Neurotic, or 'Poetry and Truth' in Neurosis," p. 35.

56. In "The Mirror Stage," *Gestalt* and *fiction* are taken up explicitly.

57. See Marthe Robert, *Roman des origines et origine du roman* (Paris: Grasset, 1972).

58. A love story in imitation of the Sesenheim episode—and in which Reik's first wife is implicated. This cannot be said of *The Haunting Melody,* which does not breathe a word of the love for Alma Mahler (passionate and distant) that Reik bore for a long time. (See J. Palaci, "Remembering Reik," in *Le Psychologue supris,* trans. Denise Berger (Paris: Denoel, 1976), pp. 9–31.

pulse,"[59] and which is coupled here with a subtle auto-analytic impulse. At least, it defines *indirectly* what is at stake. But this suffices to make it possible to locate the inhibition, the double inhibition at work here: both theoretical, by submission, and also literary, artistic ("I dreamed that [this work] would become a 'great' book . . .").[60] Indeed, taking form around the question of the status of analysis (is it a science or an art?), and organizing itself, as is revealed at the end, in relation to the speculative dialectic, Lacan's analysis allows us to postulate—if we relate it openly to Reik, that is, to an *analyst,* and an analyst himself implicated in the "personal myth" and the narcissistic, imaginary, specular, mimetic scenario that he first helped to reveal—that what is at stake in Reik's venture is nothing other than his very *position as analyst.*

By this I mean not his position within the Vienna Society, or the legitimacy of his "lay" status, or even his need for Freud's recognition (although there is *also* this), but rather, at the most acute point of the mimetic conflict, his position as *subject of the theory of the subject* (or as *subject of psychoanalysis*). This means, first of all, the subject, in full, of the analytic *theory* itself—a theory, as we know, that tested itself, following the circular, self-annulling schema of anticipation, by constituting itself directly from the "empirical subject," Freud "himself," whose theory it established (thus repeating, at least in its initial premises, a certain Hegelian reversion from the desire for knowledge to the knowledge of desire, and the circulation, again Hegelian, of *auto-conception*). But because psychoanalysis could not, by definition (that is, as a "science" of the unconscious), construct itself on the model of Hegelian Science (but rather, *mutatis mutandis,* on the divided, equivocal model of a "phenomenology"), it also means the subject, in full, of that *fiction,* that *Dichtung* from which comes necessarily, though always subordinated in advance by the theoretical anticipation, the "narrative," or the "epos" of auto-conception. By figures, or, in Freud, by typings.

This, finally, is why Reik, at the very intersection of the theoretical and the fictive (in their point of internal overlap), becomes involved in the theory of auto-graphy as well as that of music (areas abandoned by Freud), and at the same time "fictions," in a novelistic or autobiographical manner, a book that is to be a "great book." This in the sense that Freud, as Reik is the first to recognize, and thus envy, is a "great

59. *Fragment,* p. 213.
60. This is not to be so clearly found elsewhere, especially not in *Fragment* (where, it is true, music does not come into question).

writer,"⁶¹ comparable to the greatest (Sophocles, Shakespeare, etc.), of whom Freud himself was jealous even as he recognized his debts. Reik, moreover, never fails to recall this last point, superimposing always on Freud (in *Fragment,* but also in *The Haunting Melody*) the tutelary figure of the "great Goethe."

3. Finally because Lacan's analysis takes into account (but it is necessary to continue to "double" the analysis, reintroduce Reik, and fill this lacuna) the subject of the theory of the subject *in its fiction,* in the figural problematic [*figuratique*] through which every theory of the subject passes, as in the fiction where, by a repercussion, the subject of that theory himself cannot avoid becoming implicated (directly or indirectly, as in the case of Freud and Moses).⁶² It takes into account, if you prefer, the text and the *lexis* proper to it; that is to say, not only the difference separating the enunciation from the enunciated (or separating the subject of the one from the subject of the other), but also the fundamental *dissymmetry* of the "quaternary" relation or specular doubling—the dissymmetry whereby, for example (condensing), Reik will never be to Freud what Mahler is to Beethoven, because, not being Mahler (not being an artist), he has even less chance of being Goethe than Freud, to whose theory he submits himself (at play here is all the disparity of status and prestige lying between the theoretical and the fictive, science and art). And thus, because it takes into account this discord that no speculation can dialectize because it is inscribed in the specular relation itself, it is very likely that we are dealing here with a *loss of the subject,* undermining in advance any constitution, any functional assumption, and any possibility of appropriation or reappropriation. This loss of the subject is imperceptible, however, and not because it is equivalent to a secret failing or hidden lack, but because it is strictly indissociable from, and doubles, the process of constitution or appropriation. For this reason, I have already proposed to speak of (de)constitution.⁶³ But this is makeshift. What should be noted here, with and against Lacan, and going back from Lacan to Reik, is that there is a constant though muffled breakdown of the imaginary, of the

61. See among other texts, *From Thirty Years with Freud,* p. 9.

62. Taking into account, in Lacan's terms, the retreat of the mythical itself within the theory of myth and consequently *also* the kind of abyssal separation, in which all narcissistic reassurance vacillates, between the desire for knowledge and the "will to genius"—what Lacan, who refers only to the Reikian analysis of the "case of Goethe," and who gives no reference to its mimetico-autobiographical frame, could not do.

63. I refer here to "L'Oblitération."

resources of the imaginary. The imaginary destroys at least as much as it helps to construct. More precisely, it continually alters what it constructs. This explains, perhaps, why the subject in the mirror is first of all a subject in "desistance" (and why, for example, it will never recover from the mortal insufficiency to which, according to Lacan, its prematuration has condemned it). It explains also the delay, the inhibition, the *après-coup* effects, the deterioration—in short, everything belonging to the deadly repetition that is at work in more than just the so-called obsessional neurosis. We are dealing here not with a pure rupture of the economic in general, but with the slow erosion of appropriation. Undoubtedly death must be "imagined" for the dialectic of recognition to be able to function. But the dialectic of recognition itself does not perhaps function so well, not only because every subject is on its way to death [*"en passe" de mourir*], or even because it is irremediably separated from itself (as "subject"), but simply because it comes to itself only in losing itself.

The "theoretical" consequence (though at the limit of the theorizable): the figure is never *one*. Not only is it the Other, but there is no unity or stability of the figural; the imago has no fixity or proper being. There is no "proper image" with which to identify totally, no essence of the imaginary. What Reik invites us to think, in other words, is that the subject "desists" because it must always confront *at least* two figures (or one figure that is *at least* double), and that its only chance of "grasping itself" lies in introducing itself and oscillating *between* figure and figure (between the artist and the scientist, between Mahler and Abraham, between Freud and Freud). And this perhaps accounts for the logic of the *double bind*, the "double constraint," at least as it is borrowed from Gregory Bateson in Girard's mimetology.

Everything seems to point to the fact that this destabilizing division of the figural (which muddles, certainly, the distinction between the imaginary and the symbolic, and broaches at the same time the negativity or absolute alterity of the "real") is precisely what is involved in the "musical obsession," connecting it, as a result, with the autobiographical compulsion itself.

Agony

AGONIE, 1580 (Montaigne), in its modern meaning as in the expression "death agony"; formerly, "anguish of the soul," XIVe (Oresme, sometimes under the

form a(n)goine), from which the modern meaning is derived. Borrowed
from eccl. Lat. *agonia,* "anguish" (from the Greek *agonia,* prop. "struggle,"
whence "agitation, anguish").

—Bloch and Wartburg, *Dictionnaire étymologique de la langue française*

We must start again, here, from Reik's theoretical failure, or rather
from his theoretical *quagmire,* since "inhibition" certainly has something to do with it.

Why does he get bogged down?

We know now that it is due to Reik's inability, in the proceedings of
mimetic rivalry, in the agon with (Abraham) Freud, to *strike down the
idol,* either by regaining strength on his own terrain (that of auto-
analysis, along with everything that goes with it) or by winning ground
where his competence is lacking (in music).[64]

In both cases, the theoretical floundering—which is in part the same
thing, though only in part, as his pure and simple submission to Freudian theory—is coupled, as is logical, with a *renunciation.* Here, between submission and renunciation, the plot begins to take shape; all
the more so as renunciation coincides in this case with the failure and
blockage of auto-analysis.

The first theoretical renunciation affects the problematic of autobiography. Everything happens very quickly: the theoretical movement
is hardly sketched out before it aborts. Freud, and the overwhelming
theoretical constraint he represents, is not without a role here.

Once again, the episode is linked to the immediate consequences of
the eulogy for Abraham presented to the Viennese Psychoanalytic Society. Reik, it will be remembered, had accompanied Freud to his home,
which had given him the time to hear from Freud's own lips a judgment of his funeral eulogy. Reik continues his narrative as follows:

> The conversation with Freud remained in my memory because it touched
> a subject which had preoccupied my thoughts in the last weeks before I
> went on Christmas vacation. I planned then to write a paper on the pri-
> mal form of autobiography and the motives that made men write the
> story of their lives. I had studied the history of autobiography as far as I
> could gather material [a compulsive gesture that is frequent in Reik—for

64. Reik is perfectly aware of what is at stake in the book. For example: "As silly as it
now sounds, I must have grotesquely exaggerated the importance and significance of
that study in my daydreams and must have attributed a singular place to it in analytic
literature" (*Melody,* p. 370).

example, he had read *all* of Goethe] in presentations of ancient cultures and followed its traces until they were indiscernible in prehistoric times. [There then follows a short treatise on autobiography.]

The first autobiographies were not written, but chiseled into stone. They are to be found in the tombs of the Babylonian-Assyrian and Egyptian civilizations and can be traced back as far as about 3000 B.C. We have autobiographical documents of this kind from old Egypt about great personalities of the court. They have typical features in common and appear as self-glorifications of achievements, as documents of self-righteousness. The craving for fame and a desire to live in the memory of posterity become clear later on. In the inscriptions on tombs, the wish is expressed "to bring one's name to eternal memory in the mouth of the living." Thus, the stones really speak (*saxa loquuntur*) and become monuments for the dead. The desire to be admired and loved seems to reach beyond one's life. There must be other motives of an unconscious kind that propelled men to write autobiographies, for instance self-justification, relief from unconscious guilt feeling and others. Such motives reveal themselves in Rousseau's *Confessions*, in John Henry Newman's *Apologia pro Vita Sua* and in modern autobiographies.

Walking home from the meeting, the conversation with Freud echoed in me and led me back to the subject of the beginnings of autobiography which were originally conceived with the thoughts of one's death and were written, so to speak, from the point of view of one's own memory with posterity, *sub specie mortis*. The desire to live in the memory of later generations, as it is expressed in the tombs of ancient Egypt, must have led to the thought of the weighing of the souls in Egyptian religion. The Judgment Day in Christian eschatology and similar ideas are expressions of a free-floating, unconscious guilt feeling and make men terrified that they will be punished in the beyond. In some artists this guilt feeling concerns their works: they are afraid they have not accomplished enough.[65] (*Melody*, pp. 236–237)

I have cited this piece—this "genealogy" of autobiography—almost in its entirety so that one may fully grasp the movement that carries (and paralyzes) it: namely, the way in which a certain breakthrough, however embryonic, is suddenly arrested and brought back (by way of the themes of a feeling of guilt or the desire for glory and eternity) to the most classical theoretical schema, that of narcissism.

It is quite visible. Examining what he thinks is the archaic, primitive

---

65. See *The Compulsion to Confess*, II, 7, and in particular pp. 306–308, where the assuagement of guilt by confession is directly related to tragedy and to Aristotelian catharsis.

history of autobiography, Reik encounters, in the incision or inscription of the *type* (in a certain *typography*), nothing other than the prehistory of fiction, the prehistory of modeling and of the plastic constitution of the subject (and *a fortiori*, beyond what he knows or means to say, the prehistory of specular or narcissistic recognition). What he encounters is thus what he relates elsewhere, having read Nietzsche and not hiding the fact, to style (or to the "typical," the "characteristic")—quite aware that the whole problematic of the double and of repetition must be subordinated to it. I am thinking in particular of the numerous pages in *Fragment of a Great Confession* where Reik sets out an entire doctrine (I have alluded to this) of destiny or the "demonic."⁶⁶ But having thus touched on the subfoundation of narcissism (and thereby of mimeticism), Reik retreats behind the guilt and obsessional inhibition of the artist—consequently behind a Freudian motif—missing, by the same gesture, what might have authorized his speaking of autobiographical constraint or compulsion: the necessary *re-citation,* though futile and deluded in its desire for recognition, of an inaccessible prescription.

It is almost as if the theory of inhibition inhibited the theoretical breakthrough, that kind of "interior departure"—*out of,* but *within* the theoretical—by which Reik tends to rejoin "empirically," through research and history, the foundation of figurality. This latter is the most hidden layer of ontological discourse; in it, from the *Timaeus* to Nietzsche (passing undoubtedly also through Kantian schematism), the figure of theory is decided, precariously, in the theory of the figure. Precariously: this is a difficult, uncertain discourse. One in which, well before the universal "photology" or the universal "ideology" of philosophical discourse properly speaking, the two metaphorical registers of

66. See *Fragment,* pp. 39 and 78–79 (model and repetition of the model; Sesenheim and *The Vicar of Wakefield*); p. 200 (modeling, style, and the double); p. 222ff. (destiny); and p. 170: "Freud has shown that throughout life men and women repeat a certain experience . . . It is as if destiny compels them to find themselves in the same social or psychic situations. Freud has also demonstrated that in these cases in which a mysterious fate brings about the same course of events, destiny comes in reality from within. The compulsion of repetition is to a great extent determined by unconscious tendencies which work upon the person and direct his actions. It does not matter whether those actions lead to pleasant or unfortunate experiences. The compulsion of repetition operates "beyond the pleasure principle." Before Freud, Nietzsche remarked that a person who has a definite character has also a typical experience that occurs again and again. Goethe observed the same phenomenon long before these two great psychologists. It seemed really as if a demon led Goethe's love relations always to the same negative result in those years which are decisive in a man's life."

writing and procreation (if we are still dealing here with tropes or figures) intersect—everything that mobilizes the motifs of the type, the seal, the imprint, inscription, insemination, the matrix, programmation, etc., and is charged with the task of assuring the schematization of chaos through its organization, everything that makes it possible to think the engendering of the figure.

In short, Reik, who is not a metaphysician, carries on what he calls "psychology" at the edge of such a discourse—a discourse that he cannot maintain, however, and that he always covers over with the very ideology of the double, the mirror, the model and the figure.

This is not only why his theory of autobiography is abortive, but also why the autobiography itself cannot be written. Or can be written only specularly, by an interposed person (or figure), thus following a movement at work everywhere in one form or another, and that makes every autobiography essentially an *allobiography*, the "novel" of an other (be it a double). The novel of a *dead* other, or other dead. Just as Montaigne's essays are a tomb for Etienne de La Boétie and draw upon the great exemplary dying figures of antiquity (beginning with the Socrates of the *Phaedo*), *The Haunting Melody* opens with the death of Abraham and calls up the rival figures of Mahler and Freud. It too is a tomb: its initial form is that of a funeral eulogy. That Reik should "know" what is to be thought about the funeral eulogy in general, even that Freud should suggest it to him, changes nothing. On the contrary: autobiography, the biography of the *dead* other, is always inscribed in an agon—a struggle to the death, and thus also, as Lacan argues, a struggle of pure prestige.[67] Every autobiography is in its essence the narrative of an *agony*, literally. This is why (among other reasons) it is not incorrect to substitute "thanatographical" for "biographical": all autobiography, in its monumental form, is *allothanatography*, if not *heterothanatography* (if the figure is never just one). *Sub specie mortis*, as Reik says.

But here the exemplary dead figure—one of the exemplary dead—is an artist, a musician. *The Haunting Melody* is also nothing other than a "bio"-graphy of Mahler, a *Künstlerroman*.[68] In other words, it is the

---

67. Which suggests—it would at least be worth a try—that we might read *The Phenomenology of Mind* as an "autobiography" of the Absolute as Subject.

68. Or simply an analysis of Mahler. As a backdrop to the entire agonistic engagement with Freud, there is obviously Freud's famous "analysis" of Mahler (in a single afternoon!) that Reik asked Freud to recount to him. (See the letter from Freud cited in *The Haunting Melody*, pp. 342–43.)

180

The Echo of the Subject

narrative of what is "dead" in Reik, or, more precisely, of what determines his *agony:* the obsession with music [*la hantise de la musique*]. Mahler, then, as the name of the subject in agony.

No one will be surprised if we are on the verge of the second theoretical floundering.

Dopo le Parole

Kein Musik ist ja nicht auf Erden,
Die uns'rer vergleichen kann werden.

—Arnim and Brentano,
  Des Knaben Wunderhorn[69]

Here things happen much less quickly, but the renunciation is much clearer.

The narrative recounting this second failure warrants our pausing for a moment, if only long enough to understand how it arises from the inhibition of the auto-analytic gesture. Reik explains it already at the end of the first chapter:

> Psychological interests always had a predominant place in my thoughts, and it seems that my narrow talent is also restricted to this area.
>
> It certainly did not prove itself, however, in this case [auto-analysis on the basis of the episode of a musical reminiscence], because it failed me in the solution of an insignificant minor problem. Looking back now, I am able to put my finger on the spot where my initial and repeated mistake in my experiment in thought associations can be found. When you give yourself to free associations, when you follow without excluding any associations everything that occurs to you, it is necessary to keep in mind the first thought, the point of your departure into that unknown area . . .
>
> [There follows here a discussion of the imperative character of this technical rule and of the labyrinthine wandering (the metaphor is Reik's) to which Reik is condemned for twenty-five years by failing to have held on to this Ariadne's thread. Reik then continues:]
>
> The failure of my attempt did not teach me a lesson in this direction; on the contrary, it led me astray in an even more general manner. Instead of remaining within the realm of inland navigation, having the port before my eyes, I went out into the wide sea when I had lost my way. I tried

69. "There is no music on earth / That can be compared to ours." Poem entitled "The Celestial Life" ("Das himmlische Leben"), drawn from *Des Knaben Wunderhorn*, by Achim von Arnim and Clemens Brentano. This poem makes up the text of the *Lied* with which Mahler's Fourth Symphony concludes.

to solve the special question of why that chorale had haunted me in entering into research on why a certain melody follows people, sometimes for hours. Instead of adhering to the particular problem, I attempted to find a solution for it in following a general line. For many months I concentrated on this subject, read all I could find about it in books and articles and gathered material from the analysis of patients and from self-observation. [Always the same obsessional gesture.] This interest ran beside others during the following years. Excerpts from books and articles were made, notes on theories and observations jotted down, and much time and energy was wasted on an expedition for which I was not equipped. On this wide detour, some of whose stations are marked in the following chapters, I finally returned to the point of departure, to the unconscious meaning of the chorale melody that haunted me between Christmas and New Years, 1925, to the experience to which this volume owes its existence. (*Melody*, pp. 238–239)

To return to the "unconscious meaning of the chorale melody" and to rediscover thereby the "point of departure" come down to the same thing. It is, in fact, to submit purely and simply to the Freudian programming.

Nonetheless, it is not quite so simple either, and we should examine it a bit more closely.

It is true that Freud, despite his declared incompetency, would seem to have said all there is to say about the haunting melody or musical reminiscence. Reik, in any case, refers to him constantly. Moreover, this is what had determined, however he accounts for it himself, his first auto-analytic gesture; that is to say, when he had addressed himself first to the text, to the "words" of Klopstock's poem, in order to account for the tormenting return of Mahler's chorale.

With one exception, the Freudian theory of musical obsession is constant: the phenomenon is explained always by association, and the association itself is always made with reference to the text (or else to the title) of the melody in question.[70] This explains why Freud takes all his examples from the domain of opera or the *Lied* (or from the operetta and the popular song), or else from so-called programmatic music.

Of all the texts cited by Reik, or to which he alludes (drawing from the *Traumdeutung*, in particular), I retain only one (this one, however,

---

70. Or to the author's name, and sometimes also to the circumstances in which it is heard—but this is not specific to music. This is nevertheless the "Ariadne's thread" of Reik's auto-analysis: the identification of Reik's position at the death of Abraham with that of Mahler at the death of von Bühlow.

from the *Introduction to Psychoanalysis*). I choose it simply because it is
the one Reik uses to begin a discussion with Freud. Reik presents it in
the following way:

> There is, as far as my knowledge goes, only a single instance in which the
> phenomenon of the haunting melody is discussed in psychoanalytic
> literature. It is a passage in Freud's *Introductory Lectures*. It is there stated
> that melodies which occur to us are conditioned and determined by
> trains of thought that have a right to be heard and that occupy our mind.
> "It is easy," says Freud, "to show that the relation to the melody is tied to
> its text or origin, but I have to be cautious not to extend this statement
> to really musical people about whom I have no experience." With them,
> he admits, the occurrence of a melody might be determined by its musi-
> cal content [which, in Freud, itself remains perfectly undetermined]. The
> first case is certainly frequent. Freud mentions the instance of a young
> man who was for some time haunted by Paris' song from *La Belle Hélène*,
> a song which, to be sure, is charming. Analysis turned his attention to
> the fact that a girl Ida competed in his interest with another by the name
> of Hélène. This factor was hitherto neglected in the psychological theo-
> ries on the subject, namely, the relation to the text of the melody, espe-
> cially the unconscious connection of this text to the interests of the
> individual. Every psychoanalyst can contribute numerous instances that
> prove this unconscious motivation of the haunting melody.
> [There follows a collection of examples, and Reik then turns again to
> Freud's text with the purpose of "discussing" it.]
> The psychological progress which is marked by the introduction of
> the unconscious factor of thought associations connected with the text is
> so obvious that it makes it almost easier to formulate the criticism of the
> theory. Freud himself already anticipates the objection that the emer-
> gence of the melody cannot be determined only by the text of the tune;
> to the example he quotes, he adds the remark that the Paris song is really
> charming—a hint of its esthetic quality. Freud admits, too, that for really
> musical people the content of the tune might be of great significance. It
> seems to me that Freud's theory emphasizes one-sidedly the determining
> role of the text. The melody itself must be of a much higher significance
> than Freud assumed. The esthetic quality of the musical content need
> not even be very valuable. Did we not hear from H. Schneider, a profes-
> sional musician and piano teacher, that he was haunted by a banal, cer-
> tainly not wonderful tune, *Pony Boy*? And how often do you and I find
> that we cannot get rid of a tune of very questionable or clearly poor
> quality, a vulgar waltz or march! . . . A tune had no words, it was one of
> the *Lieder ohne Worte* and you did not appreciate its musical value highly,
> but it perhaps haunted you for a whole day. (*Melody*, pp. 245–247)

In other words, the hermeneutic procedure based on the textual (or verbal) reduction of the acoustic and the musical is insufficient. And as we see, Reik insists on this all the more in that Freud himself had voiced such a suspicion. For this reason, moreover, the discussion is cut short, even though Reik is perfectly aware that this is where the real problem begins to present itself.

But again, let us not be hasty.

Previously (before evoking this text), Reik had alluded briefly to another text by Freud, this one from the *Psychopathology of Everyday Life*. Here is the opening of the second chapter of *The Haunting Melody:*

> As I have pointed out earlier in this book, the phenomenon that we are sometimes persecuted by a certain melody cannot be clearly and cleanly separated from the more general one that a certain melody occurs to us in the middle of a train of thought, of a conversation or of our daily work. The haunting melody is only different in duration or intensity from the everyday experience when a tune occurs to us, we do not know why. With the exception of an already mentioned very short passage in Freud's *On the Psychopathology of Everyday Life*, published in 1904, no discussion is known to me in psychoanalytic literature. (*Melody*, p. 24)

Now this "short passage" is an interesting one for several reasons. Let us open to the place indicated by Reik in *The Psychopathology of Everyday Life*.[71] The passage in question is a long note near the end of Chapter 9 (in an appendix in the German edition) in which Freud examines the case in everyday life of "symptomatic and accidental acts." He devotes a long discussion to the "loss of objects," especially objects such as presents and gifts—a loss that attests, as one might guess, to the lack of esteem in which the giver is held, but which can also, by associative translation, signify a much more serious loss (we are not far from mourning). There is also the case of the loss of valuable objects and not just "little nothings," a loss that can represent either a repressed idea (a signal, Freud says, "to which we do not lend our ear"), or, principally, that can be the equivalent of a kind of "propitiatory sacrifice . . . to the obscure powers of destiny presiding over our fate and whose cult still exists among us." With this latter possibility, we find ourselves brought back again to the motif of the "demonic," and thereby, eventually, to ritual obsession. In any case, we are on familiar ground.

71. *The Psychopathology of Everyday Life* (on "symptomatic and chance actions"), in *Standard Edition*, vol. 6, pp. 215–216.

It is in this context that the note appears. It is limited apparently, to a fairly disjointed presentation of a collection of examples (although there is much to be said about Freud's technique of using examples). Toward the end, however, one reads:

> If one takes the trouble, as Jung (1907) and Maeder (1909) have done, to note the tunes that he finds himself humming, unintentionally and often without noticing he is doing so [which is thus the first stage of the haunting melody itself, which is nothing other, as we just read in Reik, than the simple amplification of this phenomenon], he will pretty regularly be able to discover the connection between the words of the song and a subject that is occupying his mind.
>
> The subtler determinants, too, of the expression of one's thoughts in speaking or writing deserve careful attention. We believe that in general we are free to choose what words we shall use for clothing [*einkleiden*] our thoughts or what image [*Bild*] for disguising them [*verkleiden*]. Closer observation shows that other considerations determine this choice, and that behind the form in which the thought is expressed a glimpse may be had of a deeper meaning—often one that is not intended. The images and turns of phrase to which a person is particularly given are rarely without significance when one is forming a judgment of him; and others often turn out to be allusions to a theme which is being kept in the background at the time, but which has powerfully affected the speaker. In the course of some theoretical discussions I heard someone at a particular time repeatedly using the expression: "If something suddenly shoots through one's head." I happened to know that he had recently received news that a Russian bullet had passed right through the cap that his son was wearing on his head.

As we see, what resurfaces here is nothing other than the motif of *style,* associated in an apparently inorganic manner with the question of musical reminiscence. Of course, it is treated in the classical terms of a putting into form or image (trope or figure), and of the veiling or disguising of a signified or a "theme." Nevertheless, the motif is taken up in such a way as to concern, as in the case of Reik's first associations, the *lexis* itself or the enunciation of a statement [*énoncé*] that, as such, cannot be enunciated (by the subject).

Two things appear with a certain clarity. On the one hand, the symptomatic nature of the phenomenon (and consequently its *signifiance*) lies in *repetition.* But by examining the "singing" character of a melody, as Freud says, by asking what causes such a melody to "come back" to us, is one not inevitably led back to some *repetitive* essence of music (and not simply in the refrain)—led back to what necessarily commits music to recapitulation and variation?[72] We will return to this point. What also appears, on the other hand, is that the stylistic phenomenon of unconscious repetition—which is far from being unimportant, as Freud notes, when it comes to judging (*beurteilen*) someone or gaining access to "the intimate life of his soul"—is connected to the fundamental determination of the subject as "ethos" or as character.

We find here all the variations on the famous expression "The style makes the man."

There would perhaps be nothing to draw from this textual episode, were it not for the fact that we find here (by way of a certain displacement) precisely the path taken by Reik—though he undertakes, as we know, to challenge the Freudian theory, thus entering, almost deliberately, into an impasse.

As will become clear, we shall pass very close to a certain Nietzsche—at least the Nietzsche of *The Birth of Tragedy*.

In trying to understand how music *itself* (independently of the text, the title, the program, etc.) can signify, and to understand the nature of musical *signifiance*, Reik will first associate music with mood, sentiment, and emotion—in short, with the affect in general: as "repressed," of course.

Shortly before, we remember, Reik spoke of a "tune without words" (one of the *Lieder ohne Worte*), capable, no matter how mediocre, of haunting one throughout an entire day. He goes on:

It must be that this tune was the musical expression of a certain mood or feeling, the adequate or congenial presentation of an emotional attitude you felt at the moment. It is not necessary that the person be aware or conscious of this particular emotion, yes, he can even feel consciously in a different, even in an opposite mood. A patient of mine who broke with a sweetheart after a relationship of long duration, and who felt very sad, became aware that with the inner ear he heard persistently in the middle of his depression a very cheerful march tune. In his analytic session the next day, he had to admit to himself that he must have felt that the breaking off of the relationship was a liberation, as the lifting of an emotional burden, freeing him for certain tasks he had had to postpone on account of it. We have thus to consider that unconscious and even repressed emotions find their manifestations in such emerging melodies. We know that Mozart wrote the great E Flat Major Symphony and the Jupiter Sym-

72. Once again, a Nietzschean question. It is the focus of a long demonstration at the beginning of *The Birth of Tragedy*, when Nietzsche accounts for the strophic form of the *Volkslied*.

phony during one of the most unhappy periods of his life. Mahler's Fourth Symphony was composed in a depressed mood, while the Sixth Symphony, which was called tragic, was written when the composer felt "cheerful . . . and flourishing like a green bay tree," as his wife says. The factor of the musical expression of a certain emotion in the tune, which is conspicuously neglected in Freud's theory of the haunting melody, becomes immediately clear in cases in which there is no text for the composition or in which the text is evidently not known to the person.[73] (*Melody*, pp. 247–248)

In a word, then, music is the expression (or representation) of the *Stimmung* (although Reik does not exactly say how, except to resort—but could one do better?—to the division of minor and major, "unhappy" and "happy"). The tormenting melody is consequently the representation of an unconscious *Stimmung*.

There follows an attempted analysis of musical creation, particularly in the *Lied*, which seems to repeat—in reverse, but with an analogous result—the famous description of poetic creation borrowed by Nietzsche from Schiller, and to which I have already alluded. We will recall how Nietzsche, in Chapter 5 of *The Birth of Tragedy*, draws on Schiller's confession "that before the act of creation he did not have before him or within him any series of images in a causal arrangement, but rather a musical mood (*Stimmung*)."[74] Nietzsche refers to this statement not only to prove the anteriority of the Dionysian (let us say, for the sake of simplicity, the musical) in relation to the Apollonian—concept, image, figure, etc. He cites it also, as demonstrated on the subsequent page, in order to attempt to think the unthinkable passage from chaos to figure, from the originary One ("which is pain and contradiction") to phenomenality in general—and here the *type* will intervene. At the same time, and on the other hand, it is to show out of what abyss of the subject, out of what impossible originary identification with originary suffering is formed (*sich bildet*), through the mediation of the *example* (which is to say, for Nietzsche, the myth, or, if you will, identification in the common sense of the term), the "subject" in its modern definition—that "illusion." Thus, he writes:

73. Cf. *Surprise and the Psychoanalyst*, ch. 28: "The memory [of a melody] can also be completely missing. What rarely fails to appear is the impression made by the melody, its affective content, what the notes are trying to say, to express—and that quite independent of whether I remember the text, or even if I know it at all" (p. 239).
74. *The Birth of Tragedy*, trans. Walter Kaufmann (New York: Random House, 1967), p. 49.

We may now . . . on the basis of our aesthetical metaphysics set forth above, explain the lyrist to ourselves in this manner.

In the first place, as a Dionysian artist he has identified himself with the primal unity, its pain and contradiction. Assuming that music has been correctly termed a repetition [*Wiederholung*] and a recast [*Abguss*— in printing, a "print"] of the world, we may say that he produces the copy [*Abbild*] of this primal unity as music. Now, however, under the Apollonian dream inspiration, this music reveals itself to him again as a *symbolic [gleichnissartig] dream-image*. The inchoate, intangible reflection [*Wiederschein*] of the primordial pain in music, with its redemption in mere appearance, now produces a second mirroring as a specific symbol or example. The artist has already surrendered his subjectivity in the Dionysian process. The image that now shows him his identity with the heart of the world is a dream scene that embodies the primordial contradiction and primordial pain, together with the primordial pleasure, of mere appearance. The "I" of the lyrist therefore sounds from the depth of his being: its "subjectivity," in the sense of the modern aestheticians, is a fiction.

Taking things from the side of the musician (not from that of the poet), and, of course, *mutatis mutandis* (that is to say, without the *onto-typology* that underlies Nietzsche's text), Reik proposes a similar analysis:

> In the musical creative process, the text of a poem provides, so to speak, a stimulus to awaken emotions or moods that had been there before, waiting for the release of expression. The texts have to fulfill certain musical requirements, but, more important, they must be able to stimulate, but are unable to fully express those emotions. The text has, as some composers say, to be "spacious" or "roomy," not satiated with music. If it is not capacious in that sense, the composer has no possibility of expressing and expanding himself. Richard Strauss occasionally remarked that some of Goethe's poems are so "charged with expression" that the composer has "nothing more to say to it." (*Melody*, pp. 248–249)

A Nietzschean, "melocentric" analysis, opening (though this time in a more strict proximity to Nietzsche) onto nothing other than the phenomenon of *musical catharsis*—or, to paraphrase Nietzsche's words in the last chapters of *The Birth of Tragedy*, the discharge of an unbearable affect (of an originary pain or suffering) provoked by music. Music would provoke such an effect in that it is the first reproduction or repetition, the first *immediate* mimeme of the originary One (in which case, its mode of action, the catharsis it causes, is of a strictly "homeopathic" nature; in short, music heals—this is the theme of consolation, of the death it evokes). But it would also provoke such an effect, for this same reason, inasmuch as it engenders mimetic reduplication (the constitution, on the order of the visible and the figural, of the individuated, the Apollonian, theatricality, etc.); so that the subject can be engulfed in it through emotional discharge, but without losing itself irretrievably—drawing from it, on the contrary, that specifically theatrical and tragic form of pleasure that Freud will define as "masochistic."[75] To put this in other terms, music's catharsis is such that it permits the subject to mime the return to the originary One, to the undifferentiated, to chaos (even while preserving itself, thanks to the "protective screen" of the myth or of the example, which, like the representative scission of representation, allows for identification without risk).

Reik, of course, does not go this far.

And yet the enigma of the haunting melody is indeed catharsis, a musical catharsis still conceived of in the classical fashion as "liberating" but whose *evocation* here, in that it touches indirectly on *agony* (on the relation to Abraham and even to Freud—desired "dead") as well as masochistic pleasure, produces the fatal effect of renunciation. Still pursuing his analysis of musical composition and the relation, in the *Lied,* between music and text, Reik comes to write the following:

> If we neglect the psychological difference between the composer and the listener, we dare say that the text must also play a similar role for the person who is haunted by a melody. It is an important point of contact that reminds the person of a similar inner experience or awakens similar emotions or moods as expressed in the text. But the tune expresses something else or more: *the immediate quality of experience. It is an emotional expression much more adequate than words.* In the *relieving* process of singing the tune, *the emotions that move the person are much more discharged by the tune than by the text of a song.* It is also remarkable that it is very rarely that the words of a tune without the music occur to a person and haunt him for a long time. But it is superfluous to enlarge upon this point, because the frequent case of our being haunted by a melody that has no text, by a passage from a symphony, some bars from a violin concerto, proves sufficiently that the text cannot possibly be the only determining factor in the process and that the Freudian explanation cannot be sufficient to understand the phenomenon.
>
> Something not expressed in the text or not adequately expressed in it manifests itself in the melody. When I am singing a melody that haunts me, I am expressing emotions. It has the same meaning as when I am

75. I refer here to my essay "La scène est primitive," in *Le sujet de la philosophie,* pp. 187–216.

laughing, crying, sighing or sobbing. It is the same as tears, sneers or cheers. (*Melody*, pp. 249–250; emphasis added)

This is precisely where Reik renounces. Taking up again the narrative thread, he will pass on, with Mahler as intermediary, to the autobiography, the *allobiography*.

It is a despairing renunciation, the product of a narcissistic retreat—a regression. This is perhaps because Reik has touched upon a phenomenon that, despite the catharsis, begins to exceed and broach the subject's economy, and ruin it from within. Laughter and tears, sarcasm and cheers (Reik speaks elsewhere of the erotic experience),[76] all those emotions—social or "intersubjective," as they say—in which consciousness disappears and the body is in spasms, where there is produced a suspension or a fundamental and rending "caesura," all of them are perhaps of the order of *l'émoi*.[77] Meaning *powerlessness:*

> But where do we go from here? It would now be necessary to present a psychological theory of what comprises the emotional character as well as the esthetic value of music, to probe into the mystery of why certain sound waves affect us this way and others in that way. It means it would be necessary to enter the realm of musical theory, including the science of acoustics. At this point, I again become painfully aware of my incompetence. I am as equipped for entering the glacial areas of abstract music theory as a pedestrian in a summer suit is prepared to undertake an expedition to the North Pole. Dissatisfied, even disgusted with myself, I shall break off the attempt to find a general solution to the problem of the haunting melody. I can only express the hope that a psychoanalyst who has extensive knowledge in the field of musical and acoustic theory, and a wide experience in this area, will pick up the thread at this point and bring the problem to a solution. I must admit to myself [as always . . .] that I have failed again because I have been too ambitious. (*Melody*, p. 250)

Mimesis and Unheimlichkeit

Aristotle, following Plato (*Republic*, X, 606), and basing his work on his clerico-musical experiments and practices, and not on properly medical experiments and practices, applied to tragedy the idea of a *katharsis ton*

---

76. And does not miss the opportunity to recall the anecdote about Anton Bruckner, who could not stand hearing Act 2 of *Tristan* and had to take refuge in the toilets in order to masturbate.

77. A term meaning "agitation" or "emotion." Lacoue-Labarthe is drawing upon the etymology of the term.—*Editor*

pathematon produced by a vehement discharge—not, as recently claimed, by
the calming of the passions through a "reconciling ending."
—Erwin Rohde, *Psyche*

But what, exactly, has been renounced?
Let me venture here, by way of hypothesis, this answer: what Reik
renounces is precisely what could have allowed him to tie together all
of the threads upon which he has drawn from the beginning. Not that
he might rediscover, as he hopes, *the* Ariadne's thread of auto-analysis
capable of bringing him out of the theoretical labyrinth and of orienting him in the "palace of mirrors" of narcissistic rivalry. But it would
have allowed him to attempt to reconstitute the enigmatic motif ("the
figure in the carpet") which has until now been continually unraveling,
a motif in which would be outlined (if he could see it), and from which
he could think *together,* the question of style or accent (of *lexis*), that of
auto(bio)graphical compulsion, and finally, that of musical catharsis
("homeopathic" discharge).

But it happens that in Reik's own text—on one occasion—these
three questions are assembled together. Perhaps without his knowing
it (though I'm not so sure), and in any case without result. As though
it were already too late, and as though the theoretical submission to
Freud prevented Reik from *letting go* to the point of renouncing the
renunciation, a renunciation which, despite everything, determines
his fragile narcissistic *recovery* in the demand for paternal assistance
(whereby theory, here Oedipus, triumphs twice over).
This also happens in the second chapter, a few pages after the
renunciation.
It is at the moment, of course, when Reik, following the logical trajectory of the auto-analytic recapitulation, returns to Mahler's Second
Symphony, still trying to understand what it is in the final movement
(in the chorale) that could have awakened in him such an echo. The
investigation, as we might expect, is meticulous. Reik turns first to the
various statements (letters, things confided, interview responses) in
which Mahler himself explained his intentions. The texts are contradictory, doubly contradictory.
In an initial statement, Mahler rejects any subordination to the text:
"I know that as far as I can shape an inner experience in words, I certainly would not write any music about it. My need to express myself

musically and symphonically starts only where the dark emotions begin, at the door leading to the 'other world,' the world in which things are not any more separated by time and place. Just as I consider it an insipidity to invent music to a program, I feel it is unsatisfactory and sterile to wish to equip a musical composition with a program" (*Melody*, pp. 252–253). This first statement, in which the origin of musical creation is located in relation to the failure of the capacity to speak, as a substitution for verbalization, is followed by two program texts, themselves contradictory.

The exact content of the two programs is unimportant here. Let us say simply that in each case, and following a well-known schema in the musical tradition running from Beethoven to Strauss or even to Schönberg, it is a matter of the life and destiny of a hero (the hero of the First Symphony, Mahler says, having already indicated that it was the artist himself) whose death, of course, elicits fundamental "metaphysical" questions. Such as: Why death? What is the meaning of life? Is life merely a farce after all? It is not too difficult to recognize underneath the pathos of the discourse the style of (obsessional) narcissistic questioning.

But from the formal point of view (and this is where the contradiction comes in), there is the fact that the Second Symphony is considered to be a "narrative"—even a "biography": these are Mahler's terms—and that the biography is already given. It is given first in a classical mode of third-person narration: novelistic or "epic" (it is a "symphonic story," says Reik). But a second time it is given in a much more complex mode.

In Plato's terminology, it is a question of what would be called a simple narrative; *haple diegesis,* a first-person narrative assumed, as such, by its author. (Plato, as we know, defined this as the mode proper to the dithyramb; pure of all mimesis, that is to say, of any dramatic element—unlike, for example, the epic—the dithyramb was taken by him to be the only mode eventually tolerable, presuming of course a strict supervision of its content.) Contrary, though, to what one might have thought, this shift to the simple narrative, this change in the formal set-up, does not at all indicate a sliding from biography to autobiography. Rather, it signals, taking account of the introduction of a mimetic and specular element, a sliding toward *allobiography*—the very set-up of Reik's own book. This, however, Reik does not notice.

Here is how he describes it—I cite the page in its entirety:

In these three months [separating the two versions of the program] the character of this concept has changed. It is no longer a presentation of the hero's life, but its mirroring in the mind of a survivor, a relative or friend who returns from the grave, recalls the story of the deceased's life and is by his recollections led to metaphysical questions in his thoughts: Why did you live? Why did you suffer? What is the sense of life? Questions to which an answer is given in the last movement. In other words, the original concept is now put into another frame. It is as if one's own life and emotions were looked at by an observer, and this onlooker ties metaphysical reflections to a review of this other life. The difference in the technique of presentation becomes transparent by a comparison from the literary field, for instance between a novel in the "I" form and another in which, as in many stories of Somerset Maugham, the storyteller meets an old friend after many years and this man tells him about an experience he has had in the meantime. The "I" form of the presentation is kept, but the storyteller, the I, is only a recorder or observer. Although he sometimes speaks of his own opinions or emotions, he remains an episodic figure, while the often unheroic hero experiences a tragic, comic or tragi-comical destiny. It is psychologically recognizable that this I, this recorder, tells *either a past experience of his at which he now looks from a bird's-eye view, or presents a potentiality of his own which never actually became a reality in his life.*

The psychological advantages of this technique of presentation—not to mention the artistic ones—are that it allows the storyteller a detachment from, and even sometimes a kind of emotional aloofness toward, his own experience of a past potentiality of his destiny. The person of the writer appears, thus, psychologically split into two figures, the I, the storyteller, and the Me, the acting or suffering character. One can assume that this technique of presentation is appropriate to the self-observing or introspective side of the writer. (*Melody,* pp. 254–255; emphasis added)

This is all quite clear and should require no commentary. The "musical scene," as it were, remains still the same: the funeral ceremony (that is, more secretly, the scene of *agony*). But we see now the reason for it: the death of the other (the hero, the rival) is always at bottom my own death. The schema is that of identification along with everything this entails—the death wish and guilt, narcissistic intoxication and the feeling of failure, etc. Mahler at von Bühlow's funeral, Reik in his Austrian forest the evening he learns of Abraham's death. This is why the music laments—music in general laments, be it "joyous," "light," "pleasant" (inverting the lamentation into an exaltation of my immortality). What it laments is always my own death (unpresentable as such, said Freud:

its very inevitability is refused by the unconscious, and the Ego must learn of it through the intermediaries of figure and scene).[78] What touches or moves me in music, then, is my own mourning.

For this reason, what appears here in the description of a situation of indirect narration (which, in addition to the novels of Somerset Maugham, characterizes, for example, Thomas Mann's *Doktor Faustus*), and in the disguised autobiography and the specularization of writing in the first person, is nothing other than the mimetic element, the same that is found, whatever Plato might say or want to think of it, in the "simple narrative," the *haple diegesis*. There is no writing, or even any discourse, that is simply in the first person—ever. Because every enunciation is abyssal. And because I cannot say my dying—even less my being already dead. If all autobiography is an autothanatography, autobiography as such is, rigorously speaking, impossible.

Reik, in his way, demonstrates this flawlessly. But there is more.

For in this first program (reversing the course followed by Plato and moving from *lexis* to *logos*), the second and third movements, following the first, which "recounts" the funeral ceremony in honor of the hero, are conceived of as "interludes" recalling the life of the hero—the second concerned particularly with the "memory of happy times." Now, it is precisely this programmatic description that Reik chooses to cite *in extenso*. The narrator or witness continues to recount, but this time the scene takes on (is this such a surprise?) an *unheimlich* quality.

> It happened that you were at the burial of a person dear to you and then on the way back suddenly the image of an hour of happiness, long passed, emerged. This image has an effect similar to a ray of sun: you can almost forget what just happened. When then the daydreamer awakens from his fantasy and returns to life, it may be that the unceasingly moving, never understandable bustle of life becomes as ghastly as the moving of dancing figures in an illuminated dance hall into which you look from the dark night, from so far away that you cannot hear the music. The turning and moving of the couples appears then to be senseless, as the rhythm clue is missing. (*Melody*, p. 253)

The scene, of course, is not so happy as it promised to be at its outset. It is indeed a scene of "resurrection," in continuity with the first movement: "You awaken; you return to life." In other words, a scene

---

78. Sigmund Freud, "Thoughts for the Times on War and Death," *Standard Edition,* vol. 14, pp. 273–300.

of forgetting. As Freud would say, no one ultimately believes in his own death. The same logic is still at work here. This is why the scene veers toward the *Unheimliche*.[79] It veers in this manner toward the *Unheimliche*, into this estrangement of the familiar, by way of the "musical" *mise-en-abyme* (if this is conceivable), which is itself very *strange* in that music itself is given the role of awakening the awareness of its own absence and of the impossibility of perceiving it. It happens not so much because the sounds themselves are missing, but because of the lack of *rhythm:* "the rhythm clue is missing." The lack of a rhythm that is *heard* renders the distantly perceived scene of the ball "phantomlike" and "senseless"—fantastic—and creates the malaise, the feeling of a distancing of what is close, the quality of "between life and death," and the appearance of automatic panic that are perfectly recognizable and typical.

Rhythm, then, is heard. It is not seen—directly from the movements of the dance, for example, from the repetition and regularity of its figures. On the contrary, without rhythm, the dance (it is a waltz) becomes disorganized and disfigured. In other words, rhythm, of a specifically musical (acoustic) essence here, is prior to the figure or the visible schema whose appearance, as such—its very possibility of being perceived—it conditions. This is why its lack throws off (scopic) perception, and *estranges,* defamiliarizes, disturbs the familiar, the visible, the phenomenal, properly speaking. What is missing, Plato would have said, is an *idea*. For what is missing is quite simply a "participation" (categorization, schematization): in this case the *repetition* or temporal (not topological or spatial) constraint that acts as a means of diversification by which the real might be recognized, established, and disposed. Or more precisely, since in this case we have to do with a dance in which the movements and figures are themselves performed *in imitation* of an (inaudible) music and since rhythm *is* consequently the figure, *essentially* the figure (which itself is perhaps not essentially of the order of the visible), what is missing is the repetition on the basis of which the *repetition of the dance* (the dance as repetition, imitation, and within it, the repetition of figures) might appear. Missing is the repetition from which the division might be made between the mimetic and the non-mimetic: a division between the recognizable and the non-recognizable, the familiar and the strange, the real and the fantastic, the sensible and the mad—life and fiction.

79. See, in Freud's essay "The Uncanny" (*Standard Edition,* vol. 17), everything related to the representation of death and the omnipotence of thoughts (pp. 242 and 247).

The absence of rhythm, in other words, is equivalent to the infinitely paradoxical appearance of *the mimetic itself:* the indifferentiable as such, the imperceptible par excellence. The absence of that on the basis of which there is imitation, the absence of the imitated or the repeated (music, which in its very principle is itself repetition) reveals what is by definition unrevealable—imitation or repetition. In general, nothing could appear, arise, be revealed, "occur," were it not for repetition. The absence of repetition, by consequence, reveals only the unrevealable, gives rise only to the improbable, and throws off the perceived and well-known. *Nothing* occurs: in effect, the *Unheimliche*[80]—the most uncanny and most unsettling prodigy. For in its undecidability, the *Unheimliche* has to do not only with castration (this *also* can be read in Freud), the return of the repressed or infantile anxiety; it is also that which causes the most basic narcissistic assurance (the obsessional "I am not dead" or "I will survive") to vacillate, in that the differentiation between the imaginary and the real, the fictive and the non-fictive, comes to be effaced (and mimesis, consequently, "surfaces"). Without the beneficial doubling (or because, according to Freud, of the change in "algebraic sign" the double undergoes in the development of the Ego),[81] the immediate certitude of "primary narcissism," its confused, blind, ante-specular recognition, is shaken.

In which case, rhythm would also be the condition of possibility for the subject.

But let us not go too quickly; let us remain a bit longer in the vicinity of the Second Symphony.

Although we had reason to anticipate this point, we will understand better now why the section following the *unheimlich* movement (the waltz) in Mahler's program, after a prayer for redemption given to a solo voice—the passage from lamenting to imploring—is a "vision" (Mahler's term) of deliverance and unanimous resurrection snatched from the terror of the Last Judgment: the famous chorale based on the poem by Klopstock, "Aufersteh'n." The return to music, to the song (properly speaking, to the canticle)—the chorale, let us not forget, is here in the position of a citation, referring back to Bach and to the

80. Including the sense Heidegger gives to it in, for example, "What Is Metaphysics?" in *Wegmarken,* in Heidegger, *Gesamtausgabe,* vol. 9 (Frankfurt: Klostermann, 1976); trans. David Farrell Krell in *Martin Heidegger: Basic Writings* (New York: Harper and Row, 1977).

81. "The Uncanny," pp. 234–236.

death of von Bühlow—at last provokes the cathartic discharge. It is not
at all by chance that we have to do here with a chorale: think of
Nietzsche and his admiration for the Lutheran chorale, where the presence of the Dionysian, he says, leaves its mark in German music. It is
the healing dithyramb: the music capable of relieving, calming, even
sublimating "terror and pity"—the obsession with death. Capable also
of healing the ill it provokes, the *émoi* (which can be heard, with the
third ear, as *é-moi:* the caesura of the subject).[82]

Rhythm, Type, Character

Rhythm is the Idea of Music.

—Friedrich von Schlegel, *Ideas*

Rhythm is the delay.

—Pablo Casals

Reik "knows," then, that there is a point where the three questions
(of lexis, of autobiography, and of musical catharsis), are actually connected. In empirical terms, it is the Second Symphony, whose recollection supposedly launched the entire autobiographical enterprise—the
symphony of which Mahler said, "I don't compose; I am composed."
In theoretical terms, if you will, it is the question of rhythm. This latter
is something pre-specular (or even pre-figural), and consequently difficult of access, but it should be possible to understand what links it to
catacoustic repercussion, to resonance or to echo, and to reverberation,
if only because it is definable only on the basis of repetition (the spacing and the division in the Same, the repeated difference-from-itself of
the Same).[83]

82. See Nietzsche, *The Birth of Tragedy;* also Erwin Rohde, *Psyche: The Cult of Souls
and Belief in Immortality among the Greeks,* trans. W. B. Hillis (New York: Harcourt,
Brace, 1925): in particular everything related to the Greek maenads and corybants as
these topics are echoed in Plato and Euripides and the "homeopathic" treatment—
above all by wind instruments (aulos)—of "mania," possession, and sacred orgiastic
frenzy, in chs. 8 and 9. See also H. Jeanmaire, *Dionysos* (Paris: Payot, 1951), pp. 105ff. As
regards the "stylistic" analysis of Mahler's symphonies, and how they might be compared with other literary and philosophical forms, one should read Theodor Adorno's
Mahler, esp. chs. 1–4.

83. One may consult on this point Didier Anzieu, "L'enveloppe sonore du Soi,"
Nouvelle revue de psychanalyse 13 (Spring 1976). In Anzieu's definition of a kind of "acoustic" narcissism, however, there occurs a constant sliding from the acoustic to the lin-

But why does Reik, who "knows," want to know nothing about it? Why does he not even pick up this mention of rhythm in Mahler's statements? Why does he go almost to the point of refusing explicitly to make the connection between the three questions which are nevertheless quite present in his own text?

An immediate and plausible answer: because this would be to tamper with a certain foundation of analytic theory.

A less immediate and less certain answer: because rhythm, holding the very frontier of the theoretical domain, escapes any effective grasp.

As to the first answer, I'm obviously thinking of renunciation—of the repetition of renunciation in Reik. For it is a fact that there is no lack of texts, either on "analytic technique" (*Surprise and the Psychoanalyst, Listening with the Third Ear*) or of a more properly theoretical nature (the essay on the shofar) in which the question of rhythm returns and runs through Reik's concerns. This does not mean that one can find in Reik a doctrine of rhythm. The position of the concept, however, is always revealing, and this is what becomes important. I'll take two examples. If we don't wander, they should lead us to the essential.

The first example is an entire chapter of *Surprise and the Psychoanalyst*.[84] Reik raises here the delicate problem in analysis of knowing when to tell the interpretation to the patient, and seeks the solution in Freud ("Die Frage der Laienanalyse"). The answer is lapidary: "That is a question of tact, which may become much subtler through experience."[85] Then, in strict continuity with a line of inquiry with which we have already dealt (for example, in regard to "repeated reflections"), and which involves "inter-unconscious" communication, there follows a long justification of the Freudian solution organized around the theme of "the relation between tact, measure and time." As might have been expected, the example of music is first called up in order to make us "hear" what is involved:

> Those who still object to this association of tact and time or find it unconvincing, need only think of music. It can hardly be denied that there is the closest connection between music and time, indeed, that the very essence of music can be derived from a function of time. And is not mu-

guistic (to the verbal). Thus, precisely those essential aspects of the classical divisions (double articulation, for example) are maintained that might be challenged by the consideration of musical *signifiance*.

84. Taken up again in part in *Listening with the Third Ear*, ch. 28.
85. *Surprise and the Psychoanalyst*, p. 112.

sic, of all the arts, the most difficult to grasp intellectually? . . . We remember at the right moment that the notion of tact belongs to two
fields, the musical and the social, and that in all probability it has retained something of its temporal character even in the second derivative
meaning.[86]

This linking of the social to the musical by a shift from cadence to
"tact" (in itself not without interest) is what then permits Reik to come
to rhythm. I will leave aside the details of a demonstration that takes its
departure, as should be noted, from a description of the psychopathology of the "lack of tact" (we are here precisely on the "social"
terrain in which the question of style was once debated), and will go
immediately to the portion of the text where the essential is established: namely, the definition of what Reik calls "personal rhythm." On
the basis of this determination, tact can be defined a bit later as social
adaptation, the bringing into conformity of different and heterogeneous rhythms. Before that, however, comes sexual life, a certain "music"
in sexual relations:

> In music, it is a matter of course that questions of "tact" are treated from
> the standpoint of time. For *Takt* means time as counted and consolidated
> in units. The transference of this metrical term from music to social life
> shows that here, too, temporal factors come into play. And here, more-
> over, sexual life may claim to have typical significance. The society of two
> may be taken to represent society in general. The temporal factor, as seen
> in the seasonable beginning and ending of the sexual prelude and in the
> final ecstasy, is decisive in character. A poet has spoken of the ideal of
> love as "two hearts and one beat." Even those who are accustomed to
> regard sexual attraction as a matter of instinct, in accordance with its
> dominant element, cannot escape the conviction that happy love is
> largely dependent upon the temporal concordance of the individual
> rhythm of two human beings.[87]

To each individual or subject, then, there corresponds a rhythm, and
one can consider social life as a whole, at least on the level of the
affective and pulsional, as governed fundamentally—and more or less
regulated, between cohesion and discord—by a general rhythmics.
Reik emphasizes in the latter, calling upon biology and all the well-
known phenomena of periodicity and alternance (waking/sleeping, ac-
tivity/fatigue, etc.),[88] its primitive, archaic, primary character—going

86. Ibid., pp. 114–115.
87. Ibid., p. 119.
88. Even mobilizing, in the background, a physics and a cosmology (seasonal

so far as to suppose a state of pure and simple rhythmic undifferentiation at the origin of human development (which would be identified with the achievement of a complex arrhythmic state). Consequently—and this is what interests Reik—the pulsional process subject to this rhythmic alternance remains infra-liminary, and thus only unconscious empathy is able to grasp it.

But as we see, this long paraphrase of "in the beginning was rhythm,"[89] oscillating as it does between tact (the question of rhythmic agreement or eurythmy) and the general rhythmicity of the pulsional—and oriented by an exclusive consideration of metrics and the temporal factor—does not, rigorously speaking, reach that point where the subject "itself" (if such a thing exists) may be subsumed or thought under the category of rhythm.

For the limits, certain (internal) limits of Freudian theory—the closure demarcated by *Beyond the Pleasure Principle* among others[90]—would thereby be exceeded. Or, to put things in another way (even if this should be a bit surprising near the end of this long path), it would probably be necessary to dissociate as much as possible the question of rhythm from any *musical* problematic. This is, once again, from a problematic that is exclusively one of temporal repetition, energetic alternance, pulsation and interruption, cadence and measure. It would be necessary to be, as it were, more of a "theoretician"—not in order simply to return, without further ceremony, to the eidetic, the specular, etc., but rather in order to attempt to understand how rhythm establishes the break between the visible and the audible, the temporal and the spatial (but also the inscribed and the fictive), thus resisting the hold of such partitions and bearing a relation rather to *archi-écriture* in the Derridean sense of the term.

We know, since Jaeger's remarks in *Paideia*,[91] and, above all, Benveniste's article, republished in *Problems in General Linguistics*,[92] that *rhuthmos* or *rhusmos* (which never derived from *rheo*) means originally, according to the testimony of the tragedians, and to Archilochus and

and astral movements, flux and reflux, etc.)—in short, an entire "general energetics," founded, in a Freudian manner, upon the regulated dualism of forces.

89. Ibid., p. 125. The formula is von Bühlow's.

90. See ch. 5 on the rhythm of the drives of life and death. (See also, on the rhythm of sexual drives, Freud's *Three Essays*.)

91. W. Jaeger, *Paideia*, trans. Gilbert Highet (New York: Oxford, 1939–44).

92. "La notion de 'rythme' dans son expression linguistique," in *Problèmes de linguistic générale*, vol. 1 (Paris: Gallimard, 1966), pp. 327–335.

Aristotle commenting on Democritus in the *Metaphysics* (985, b4), *skhema:* form or figure, schema. In the "materialist" tradition in particular, *rhuthmos* is understood in this fashion as one of the relevant traits of the general differentiation of what is, together with *diathige* ("contact," which is, according to Aristotle, order: *taxis*) and trope (which Aristotle understands in relation to position or *thesis*). This differentiation or distinction is illustrated (but do we still have to do here with an illustration?) with the letters of the alphabet. As Benveniste says with regard to an example drawn from Herodotus, "It is not by chance that Herodotus uses *rhuthmos* for the 'form' of the letters at approximately the same time that Leucippus . . . defines this word with precisely the same example. This is the proof that a still more ancient tradition exists that applied *rhuthmos* to the configuration of the signs of writing." [93] Nor, one might add, is it by chance that Georgiades, as Heidegger reminds us in the 1966 seminar on Heraclitus,[94] chooses to translate rhusmos by *Gepräge:* imprint, but also seal or type. The *character.*

So we are back on familiar ground—in the vicinity, at least, of the question of style, incision, and pre-inscription (even of imprint and impression); a question on the basis of which it seemed to me possible, passing through Reik, to circumscribe the problematic of the subject and writing, of auto-graphy—drawing, in this way, upon resources that are prior to those offered throughout the tradition by the specular or figural grasp. Moreover, as Benveniste notes, from the type to the figure (or, as in Plato, to the image in the mirror),[95] or from the type to disposition (*Stimmung*), to humor and what is not inappropriately called the *character,* there is an uninterrupted filiation.[96]

But once again, we should not rush too quickly over the steps of the argument.

Benveniste insists on this point at some length: *skhema,* in fact, is only an approximation for *rhuthmos.* If *skhema* designates "a fixed, real-

93. Ibid., p. 330.

94. Eugen Fink and Martin Heidegger, *Héraclite* (Paris: Gallimard, 1973), pp. 80–81. Thrasybulos Georgiades, *Musik und Rhythmus bei der Griechen* (Hamburg: Rowohlt, 1958), esp. ch. 2.

95. "Le notion de 'rythme' dans son expression linguistique," p. 332; *metarrhuthmizesthai,* in the *Timaeus* (46a), is used in the sense of "reproducing the form by speaking of the images that mirrors send back."

96. Ibid., p. 331. Cf. also the use of *type* and *frappe* in French argot ["guy" and "little bastard"].

ized form posited as an object" (a *stable* form, therefore a figure or *Ge-stalt*),[97] *rhuthmos,* on the other hand, is "the form at the moment it is taken by what is in movement, mobile, fluid, the form that has no organic consistency." It is, Benveniste adds, "improvised, momentaneous, modifiable" form.[98] Thinking of Kant, one might say that it is the form or figure as broached necessarily by time, or that time (that is to say, probably, repetition in its difference) conditions its possibility. It is thus not so surprising that the later musical determination of rhythm should be the result of a *theoretical decision,* namely Plato's, even if one might think, as a kind of footnote to Benveniste's demonstration, that this new acceptance ("theoretical," as one speaks of "musical theory") refers back as much to "character" and to what the Greeks certainly did not think of as a "subject," as to the changing configuration of dance movements, as Benveniste would have it.

For this appears explicitly in the *Republic.*

The demonstration is given when Socrates, having considered in *mousike* in general its verbal part (the *logos* and the *lexis*), arrives at the examination of music properly speaking and undertakes a *critique* of its mimetic component. Here, the distinction is applied that was used in relation to discourse, and music is dealt with as the equivalent of *lexis,* enunciation. But musical *lexis,* as it were, unlike *lexis* itself, is strictly mimetic, and for the obvious reason that the relation of music and musical form to the *logos* (to the discourse, the text that it accompanies) is itself mimetic. Music, says Plato, must accommodate itself (*akolou-thein*) to the *logos.* It is a matter, consequently, of bringing into agreement, creating a homogeneity between, the musical mode and the discourse—a discourse itself already "censored," of course, purged, corrected, and made to conform to truth. This presupposes that music in itself, independently of the discourse it illustrates, is capable of *signifiance.*

Now, this signifying power is a mimetic power: music (harmony and instrumentation, on the one hand, and rhythm on the other) imitates. It does so according to fixed, traditional criteria, whether these relate (principally as regards harmony) to "ethical" traits (lack of vigor, suppliance, violence, courage), or, in the case of rhythm, to *characters.* This is why, when it comes time to discuss the question of rhythm,[99]

97. See "Typography."
98. "La notion de 'rythme' dans son expression linguistique," p. 333.
99. *Republic,* III, 399e.

the whole problem is to get rid of all rhythmic variety or irregularity
and why it is necessary to call again upon the criterion of *simplicity* as it
determines, in the examination of the *lexis,* the choice of enunciation in
the first person (*haple diegesis*)—the criterion, in other words, meant to
protect against the threat of dissimulation or the dissimilation of the
speaking subject.[100] As a result, only those rhythms are retained that
imitate the life (the style) of an ordered (*kosmios*) and virile man (coura-
geous, *andrios*), and "measure and melody" are obliged to submit
themselves to the words of such a man.

Rhythm (measure and meter, prosody) is therefore judged fundamentally in relation to *diction* inasmuch as this imitates or represents a
character. Rhythm manifests and reveals, gives form and figure to,
makes perceptible, the *ethos.* It brings forth essentially its unity, its simplicity, its whole nature, open and undissimulated (and this is what
Plato calls the *euskhemosune,* the right "schematization," the proper
bearing: in music this will depend on the *eurythmy*); or, on the contrary, it will bring forth its heterogeneity, its plurality or internal complexity, its multiversality and its lack of proper bearing (*askhemosune*),
the ungraspable and fleeting nature that is brought about in general by
an *arrhythmic* state.

To this extent, then, it should perhaps be recognized that rhythm is
not only a musical category. Nor, simply, is it the figure. Rather, it
would be something between beat and figure that never fails to designate mysteriously the "ethical"; for the word (and perhaps already the
concept) already implies—at the very edge of what of the subject can
appear, manifest, or figure itself—the type and the stamp or impression, the pre-inscription which, conforming us in advance, determines
us by disappropriating us and makes us inaccessible to ourselves. A pre-
inscription that sends us back to the chaos that obviously was not sche-
matized by *us* so that we should appear as what we are. In this sense,
perhaps, "every soul is a rhythmic knot." We ("we") are rhythmed.

For this reason, then, the auto-graphic compulsion is indeed connected to the obsession with "music." That is to say, the obsession with
rhythm. This latter obsession, precisely because rhythm is conceived
and theorized as figure (carrying with it, consequently, everything of
the order of modeling, exemplarity, etc.), or because it is felt and spoken
of as pulsation or repetition marked by a caesura, constantly converts
itself in an incomprehensible manner into an obsession with melody.

100. See Lacoue-Labarthe, "Nietzsche apocryphe," in *Le sujet de la philosophie,*
pp. 75–109.

"There is a tune for which I would give . . ." But it is perhaps simply a rhythm in which "I" seek desperately to recognize "myself."

From this point of view, *The Haunting Melody* is the *exemplary* culmination of what we might call the story of a long wandering. One can understand, then, that the theoretical renunciation (as well as the narcissistic retreat) that gives it its form should also constitute its paradoxical success: its too great success—even if Reik, who does not know enough "musical theory," fails. He has had at least the time, as we have seen, to trace out a program and to demonstrate that the return of Mahler's chorale was due simply to an analogy of circumstances, and that it could be interpreted in terms of affective ambivalence, jealousy, identification, the relation to the father (symbolic or imaginary), etc. And he has had the time to prove that the motif of the haunting melody does not exceed in any way the official limits of psychoanalysis.

Maternal Closure

Du bist die Ruh,
Der Friede mild,
Die Sehnsucht du,
Und was sie stillt.

Ich weihe dir
Voll Lust und Schmerz
Zur Wohnung hier
Mein Aug' und Herz.

Kehr ein bei mir
Und Schliesse du
Still hinter dir
Die Pforte zu.

—Friedrich Rückert[101]

Once, however—and I want to conclude with this second example announced above, returning to the same question (that is, the most elementary question: Why does music have such overwhelming power?)— once Reik did suspect that rhythm was not essentially musical.

It occurs in the text he dedicated to the shofar, in other words, to his childhood. He is impelled here by the constraining passion for origins

---

101. The text of *Lied D, 776 (op. 59, no. 3)*, by Schubert. Let me acknowledge that these concluding pages are dedicated to the voice of Gundula Janowitz.

that constantly inspired him, and which as we know is nothing but the echo of the autobiographical compulsion.

Reik examines the myths of the origin of music and discovers two things in succession. He discovers first that the Jewish (Biblical) tradition is the only one that does not attribute the invention of music to a divine gift. He then discovers that the primitive instrument of that invention is not, strictly speaking, a musical instrument. According to an *Encyclopedia of Protestant Theology* that he likes to cite, "no melody can be played on it and . . . it cannot produce different sounds!"[102] We have to do, then, with a kind of noise-making machine, closer to a percussion instrument, to the primitive rattle or the "bullroarer" described by ethnologists, than to the horn or bugle. This is why the emotion that comes from hearing the shofar, comparable, Reik says—because the call has an analogous signification—to the emotion produced by any call to resurrection (let us recall Mahler's Second Symphony), is so enigmatic as to defy analysis:

> Can the unusually strong emotion be due to the three sounds which are produced from the shofar? The three sets of sounds . . . *are only distinguished by change of rhythm* [emphasis added] . . . These highly primitive, long-drawn-out, abrupt and vibrating associations of sound cannot possibly contain in themselves the secret of their effect. The very worst works of our most modern musical composers put these sounds to shame so far as the art of composition and musical value are concerned. The sound of the shofar is more like the bellowing of a bull than music. The only remaining explanation is, that the listeners who are emotionally affected on hearing these sounds unconsciously form an affective association between the sounds of the shofar and something unknown to us, perhaps old events and experiences.[103]

Thus it happens that Reik suspected once that something not specifically musical (or something ante-musical) is conceivable in terms of rhythm and "change in rhythm"; he suspected once that the emotion elicited in us by such an archaic "music" is not a properly musical emotion. But once this suspicion reaches the surface, it is hastily covered over—in this case to the benefit of a myth of the origin of art (of music) that repeats, with only slight differences, the myth offered in *Totem and Taboo* or in *Group Psychology and the Analysis of the Ego*, and leads us back to the now "familiar" topos of *agony*. Art would be the repetition

102. *The Ritual*, p. 226.
103. Ibid., pp. 237–238.

of the originary murder, and the four rough sounds of the shofar would imitate the overwhelming and terrifying cry of the assassinated *Urvater,* his groan of agony, as well as the clamor of terror of the murderers. Music, perhaps the most primitive of all arts, would proceed from this reproduction or imitation of the most ancient moan and would elicit what is probably the most archaic emotion—fright, as Reik insists in *Surprise and the Psychoanalyst.*[104] The ear, said Nietzsche, is "the organ of fear." The entire Reikian notion of catharsis is found again here.

This, however, is an analytic hypothesis competing with the Freudian one that tragedy (or, in *Group Psychology,* the epic) is the originary form of art, the first repetition of the "inaugural" murder. It also competes with the hypothesis proposed by Reik himself in *Artistic Creation and Wit* (or even, surprising as it may seem, in his piece on the shofar) that art would have its origin in *mimicry* or in the *verbal transgression* of fright. But nowhere, as we know now, will there appear what would make it possible to think together, prior to the intervention of specular or catacoustic mimesis (prior, in the same way, to the intervention of the representational, sacrificial, or theatrical break [*coupure*]), mimicry, elocution, and rhythm. On the contrary, and no doubt because such a "before" is in principle unassignable, we are always brought back to the scene and to the theatrical and theoretical schema of Oedipus. We are led back to the hatred (fear) for the father and to the maternal preference that inspires the first hero-poet, as Supplement B to *Group Psychology* explains, the first encouraged by his mother's complete love (sheltering him from paternal jealousy) to undertake fantasmatically the murder, in reality collective, of the *Urvater.* In other words, we are always brought back to the conflict between what Freud calls the two "absolute narcissisms": that of the *Urvater* and that of the infant *in utero.*

Perhaps it is impossible to get beyond the closure of narcissism, even by shaking its specular model. I am almost tempted to add, by way of conclusion, thinking of the "maternal voices" that overwhelmed Nietzsche and even more of the riddle with which *Ecce Homo* opens (which has exerted a constant pull on this essay): "I am . . . already dead as my father, while as my mother I am still living and becoming old"[105]— perhaps it is impossible to get beyond the maternal closure. Of what else, other than the mother, could there in fact be reminiscence? What

104. Ibid., pp. 267–281; *Surprise and the Psychoanalyst,* ch. 20.
105. *Ecco Homo,* p. 222.

other voice could come back to us? What else could echo, resonate in us, seem familiar to us? Let us recall the "place where each of us once dwelled," the "I know this, I've already been here"[106]—and thus, "I've already heard it." Plato thought that mothers are the ones who impose or imprint upon each of us our type. How else, in fact, would we be "rhythmed"? And do we have the means to pass beyond this limit?

This is what leads me, in order not to conclude, to offer simply two texts. Both, each in its way, say this limit. I'm not certain I should allow it to stop me at this point.

The first is by a psychoanalyst (another one): Georg Groddeck—one of the few, finally, to have confronted the problem of music. In an essay of 1927 entitled "Music and the Unconscious," he wrote:[107]

> The psychological data from the period preceding birth, in which the in-fant discovers nothing from his own impressions but the regular rhythm of the mother's heart and his own, illuminate the means used by nature to inculcate in man a musical feeling . . . It is understandable that the child's equilibrium in the mother's body comes into play when the sense of rhythm and measure appear. A much further-reaching consideration is connected to the statement that the musical has its origin before birth: the musical is an indestructible inheritance of the human being. It inhab-its every human being since Adam and Eve because—and this is the core of my proposition—music might make use of noise, but it is just as often mute. It can be heard, but it can also be seen. It is essentially rhythm and measure and as such is deeply anchored in the human being.

The second text is from an American poet, Wallace Stevens. It is a fragment of a poem entitled "The Woman That Had More Babies Than That."

> The children are men, old men,
> Who, when they think and speak of the central man,
> Of the humming of the central man, the whole sound
> Of the sea, the central humming of the sea,
> Are old men breathed on by a maternal voice,
> Children and old men and philosophers,
> Bald heads with their mother's voice still in their ears.
> The self is a cloister full of remembered sounds

106. "The Uncanny," p. 245.

107. In *Psychoanalytische Schriften zur Literatur und Kunst* (Wiesbaden: Limes Verlag, 1964), trans. M. Schneider in *Musique en jeu* 9, pp. 3–6.

And of sounds so far forgotten, like her voice,
That they return unrecognized. The self
Detects the sound of a voice that doubles its own,
In the images of desire, the forms that speak,
The ideas that come to it with a sense of speech.
The old men, the philosophers, are haunted by that
Maternal voice, the explanation at night.[108]

108. Wallace Stevens, "The Woman That Had More Babies Than That," *Opus Posthumous*, ed. Samuel French Morse (New York: Knopf, 1957), p. 81.

3

The Caesura of the Speculative

Alles schwebt.

—Anton Webern

The purpose of these remarks, extracted from work in progress, will
be twofold.

First, I would like to show—but this is scarcely a thesis, so evident is
the point, fundamentally—I would like to show that tragedy, or a certain interpretation of tragedy, explicitly philosophical, and above all
wanting to be such, is the origin or the matrix of what in the wake of
Kant is conventionally called speculative thought: that is to say, dialectical thought, or to take up the Heideggerian terminology, the onto-
theo-logical in its fully accomplished form. It has been known for some
time, or at least since Bataille, that the dialectic—the mastering thought
of the corruptible and of death, the determination of the negative and
its conversion into a force of work and production, the assumption of
the contradictory and the *Aufhebung* [*relève*] as the very movement of
the auto-conception of the True or the Subject, of absolute Thought—
that the *theory* of death presupposes (and doubtless not entirely without
its knowledge) a *theater:* a structure of representation and a mimesis, a
space which is enclosed, distant, and preserved (that is, safeguarded
and true if one hears, as did Hegel, what is said in the German word
Wahrheit), where death in general, decline and disappearance, is able to
contemplate "itself," reflect "itself," and interiorize "itself." This space,
this "temple," and this scene were for Bataille the space of sacrifice—a
"comedy," he said.[1] We all know this celebrated analysis. On the other
hand, what is a little less known—and which I would like to emphasize

1. See "Hegel, la mort et le sacrifice," *Deucalion* 5 (1955): 21–43.

for this reason—is that in the earliest stages of absolute Idealism, we find the speculative process itself (dialectical logic) founded quite explicitly on the model of tragedy. In reconstituting this movement even rapidly (following it, of course, in the very denegation or disavowal of theatricality), one can detect, with a certain precision, the philosophical exploitation (raised to the second power) of the Aristotelian concept of catharsis. So that, presuming this suspicion is justified, it is not simply mimesis, or simply the "structure of representation" that turns out to be surreptitiously involved in the dialectic, but the whole of tragedy, along with what essentially defines it for the entire classical tradition, namely, its proper *effect:* the "tragic effect," the so-called "purifying effect." As might be anticipated, the question in this case would be as follows: What if the dialectic were the echo, or the reason, of a ritual?

But let me add right away that this is not the essential part of what I have to say.

Indeed, I am much more interested in carrying out the "counter-proof" of this hypothesis. For the work from which I have extracted these remarks does not relate *directly* to speculative Idealism, but rather to Hölderlin and to the Hölderlinian theory of tragedy. I am not unaware that between Hölderlin and the other two (by whom I mean those major and almost exclusive protagonists, in their very rivalry, of speculative Idealism: Hegel and Schelling, Hölderlin's ex-schoolmates from Tübingen) the distance is for the most part extremely small, indeed sometimes even nonexistent or imperceptible. I am not unaware of this—in fact, it is exactly what interests me most of all. It is precisely because Hölderlin collaborated in the most intimate manner possible in the building of the speculative dialectic—on the model of tragedy— that his work calls for examination here.

These assertions would seem to create a paradox. I am therefore bound to explain them a bit. In fact, an entire "strategy" (if we still retain this very aggressive and militaristic vocabulary; or let us say more simply, an entire "procedure") is involved here, and it is necessary, if what follows is to be intelligible, that I give some indication of my general direction.

The Hölderlin who seems to me urgently to require examination (and decipherment) today is the theoretician and dramatist (as regards the essential, the one is inseparable from the other). It is the Hölderlin of a certain precise and sure trajectory in the theory and practice of the theater, in the theory of tragedy and the experience or the testing—and this entails translating the Greeks (Sophocles)—of a new kind of dramatic writing. Perhaps simply of a new kind of writing: one which is, as he himself and his epoch said, "modern."

We should recognize that the Hölderlin of whom I am speaking has been generally neglected up to the present day. This is particularly evident in France, which has been in this case a perfect echo chamber for common opinion; even though care has been taken to translate all of Hölderlin's theoretical texts (beginning even with his famous *Notes* on the translation of Sophocles), no one has risked proposing a version, even a problematic one, of Hölderlin's translation of Sophocles, something that is indispensable to understanding what he hoped to accomplish. And even in Germany, where commentaries abound, and despite the appearance of works of great philological rigor (or probity), it seems that no one has wished to see just what was at stake in this dramaturgical work—work, it must be remembered, that occupied the greater part of what is recognized as the "lucid" part of Hölderlin's productive activity (from 1798, if not earlier, to 1804). Only a few practitioners of the theater, perhaps, in Berlin or elsewhere, have attempted to interrupt and take up again, using Hölderlin as their point of departure, the adventure (an "other" adventure, if you like) of tragedy. But this is far, as you might surmise, from indicating a general movement . . .

Yet in saying this, I would like to forestall at once a possible misunderstanding. If it seems to me in fact to be crucial, to be crucial today, to focus upon the work that for sheer convenience I am calling Hölderlin's dramaturgical work, I do not wish to underestimate or put in a subordinate position in Hölderlin's oeuvre the place of lyricism, overturning in this way the perspective of the classical commentaries (in particular, Heidegger's study, which in this respect remains insuperable). On the contrary: it is no less crucial to recognize that all of the texts written between 1798 and 1800 (while Hölderlin's first dramaturgical effort, *The Death of Empedocles,* was marking time), all of those in which a general poetics (that is, a theory of genres) is adumbrated, are quite explicit on this point; in Hölderlin's eyes, the lyric is the modern genre par excellence—or at least, if the question is indeed asked whether or not we are still dealing with a genre (and Hölderlin, probably the only one throughout this time, had some doubts on this point), it is considered that "thing," between poetry and literature, toward which the *Dichtung* (writing) required by an epoch that constituted itself through its imperceptible but violent difference to antiquity had to be directed. If there is such a thing as an oeuvre of Hölderlin, and if, as such, it culminates or finds its accomplishment at some point, then undeniably it does so in the lyric, however lacking in relevance such a category might be here. Heidegger, it should be added, is not the only one to insist rightly on this, and one can find exactly the same motif in the tradition (I am thinking, essentially, of Adorno and Peter Szondi) inaugurated by two well-known texts by Benjamin.[2]

But here is the question: How does it happen that in such divergent and, indeed, mutually conflicting commentaries as those by Heidegger, Adorno, and Szondi (I deliberately set Benjamin apart) the same privilege is found attached to the lyric, and the same interest, as a consequence, is shown in the "last" great poems of Hölderlin—in which is sought what is indeed inscribed there, that is to say, a thought? Starting with the same text and with a similar evaluation of it, how is it possible both to extricate (as is the case, in an exemplary manner, with Szondi) the rigorously dialectical structure of Hölderlin's thought and, as Heidegger persists in doing, decipher the emergence of an interpretation of truth that is no longer reducible to the Platonic-Cartesian interpretation of truth (as theoretical and enunciative adequation) or—already—to its speculative and dialectical reelaboration? Might it not be the neglect of Hölderlin's dramaturgical work, its evaluation as a subsidiary, transient phase, including even his "dialogue with Sophocles" and with Greek tragedy, that has made it impossible to follow, at one time, *both* the way in which Hölderlin rigorously dismantles the speculative-tragic matrix he himself helped to elaborate (and his entire passage through the problematic of tragedy works in this direction) *and* the way in which, in the long and difficult work of the disaggregation and undermining of speculative thought, nothing, finally, could offer him the resources for an "other" thought, or give him the possibility of instituting any difference whatsoever in relation to it?

The question I am posing therefore has to do with the possibility, in general, of a demarcation of the speculative: of the general logic of differentiation, of the ordered contradiction, of the exchange or the passage into the opposite as the production of the Same, of the *Aufhebung* and of (ap)propriation, etc. The question, as you see, cannot be posed simply as follows: How was Hölderlin able to tear himself away or

---

2. Lacoue-Labarthe refers here to Walter Benjamin, "Zwei Gedichte von Friedrich Hölderlin," in *Gesammelte Schriften*, vol. 4, ed. Rolf Tiedemann and Hermann Schweppenhauser (Frankfurt: Suhrkamp, 1980), pp. 105–126; also to Benjamin's remarks on Hölderlin in "Die Aufgabe des Übersetzers," *Gesammelte Schriften*, vol. 10, ed. Tillman Rexroth, pp. 9–21.—*Editor*

break free from this speculative scheme and from dialectical logic? To pose such a question—and, *a fortiori,* to pretend to give an answer—would inevitably reintroduce the very constraint from which one would like to be freed (that is, the constraint of *opposition* in general). Moreover, as is well known, this is why there is a closure of the speculative that is by right insuperable. And it is also this inexhaustible power of reappropriation which always menaced the Heideggerian procedure from within and which does not cease to oblige us, today, to take up anew the question of the relation between dialectical process and the aletheic structure—indeed, between dialectical process and "event-(ap)propriation" in the sense of *Ereignis.*

The question I am asking, rather, is the following—a "limit-question" if you like, since it has finally no proper object and destroys in advance any possibility of an answer, at least in the received forms of the answer (in the positive or negative): How is it that the demarcation of the speculative, in Hölderlin, is *also* its marking (or its remarking)? How is it, in other words, that the speculative (de)constitutes itself—I mean, dismantles itself, deconstructs itself in the same movement by which it erects itself, installs itself and constitutes a system? And what does this imply about the possibility and the structure, about the logic, of truth and of property in general?

*

The problematic as it is set up here presupposes that Hölderlin occupies a rather singular place within a certain history (one not solely empirical, but not ideal or pure either, this being the history of the completion of philosophy). This place is so singular, in fact, that it most probably marks the limit of *critical* power as such. Yet this is not at all to say that we should prohibit ourselves from *reading* Hölderlin (nothing is more alien to the procedure just now mentioned than such a pious renunciation). If by "completion of philosophy" is meant the exhaustion of a program, the realization or effectuation, the *thought* of a bi-millennial questioning of the Same out of which philosophy in its entirety has unfolded; if the completion of philosophy is the thinking of difference in the sense of that "One differing in itself" (*En diapheron heauto*—Heraclitus) which Hölderlin made the most constant, most explicit motif in his questioning of the essence of the Beautiful and of Art, ever since he cited it in *Hyperion;* if, moreover, for reasons that cannot be developed here but that may be presumed familiar enough, the completion of philosophy is the passage over the gap or the closing of the wound (re-)opened, in extremis, by Kant in the thinking of the

Same; if, in short, it is this covering over of the Kantian crisis (the "leap over Kant," as Heidegger puts it) and of the loss of everything this crisis swept with it beyond any power of legislating, deciding, and criticizing—then Hölderlin (this is his singular position, his "case," if you like) will have represented, in this completion which he *too* brings about and to which he "contributes" more than a negligible share, the impossibility of covering over this crisis, this wound still open in the tissue of philosophy, a wound that does not heal and that reopens constantly under the hand that would close it. It is not that Hölderlin wanted it that way—he wanted, if he wanted anything (and for some time he did want something), the resolution of the "crisis," in whatever sense you care to understand the term. And still less is it a matter of his having become the master of this paradoxical gesture (he will have thought of it, in large measure, *as* the tragic, or a certain tragic, at least—but this gesture itself will have carried him beyond any point of control, though I do not say beyond that which one can bear or endure). No: there is no category, as such, that is pertinent here. We cannot speak simply either of lucidity or of failure—what is involved escapes the opposition of power and impotence. And even though he himself should have been wholly engaged in it, it is not an "effect of the subject," it is probably not even "analyzable" in terms of the unconscious, though one could not deny the part played by the repetition compulsion and the silent work of the *Todestrieb* within this obstinate struggle for (in)accomplishment. Only Hölderlin's logic, "his" logic, if it *were* a logic in any specific way and if it could be detached, would offer the possibility of glimpsing the process involved. But the "case" is such, in fact, that despite his obstinate insistence on *self-calculation,* he was not able to give rise to any logic that might have been properly his own and that could have brought about a scission.

*

It is here, then, that I break off and pass on.

Obviously, in the space available to me, I could not give even an approximate idea of the path that should be taken in order to approach the singularity, fleeting and essentially undiscoverable, of such a case. I am thus obliged, whether I like it or not, to proceed by example.

*

So I return to my initial remarks and simply pose the following question: What does tragedy have to do with the birth of speculative thought and of the onto-logic? To what point is one authorized to say that it is tragedy, the reelaboration of the philosophical or "poetic" (Aristotelian) conception of tragedy, that furnished the scheme which is the matrix of dialectical thought?

The entire character of such a question certainly makes it debatable. One could perfectly well demonstrate, and have every right to do so, that it is not primarily within the theory of tragedy that things began to be organized in speculation. At the very least, it would be necessary for us to recall that the step leading to the speculative was first taken through the question of art in general (as inherited from Kant's Third Critique) and, more specifically, through the question of *Dichtung* and the relation between literature and philosophy. Hegel was the first to recognize this and emphasized it in a well-known homage to Schiller at the beginning of the *Aesthetics.*³ The overcoming of the aesthetic (of taste) in a theory of the Beautiful and of Art, the attempt to constitute a grand philosophical lyricism, the recasting of the poetics of "modes" (as Genette says), and thus the systematization of the poetics of genres, the general problematic of the (absolute) work or of the Organon (that is, of the self-engendering, as Subject, of the Work), what could be called, consequently, the "literary operation" (that is, the invention of literature as its own theory or auto-conception), also the will to decision concerning the old (and still open) debate between Ancients and Moderns: all of this was played out in the last decade of the eighteenth century, between Weimar and Berlin (between Schiller's essays on aesthetics and the *Athenaeum,* the lectures of Schelling and the remarks of Goethe)—all of this works to constitute the crucible of speculative philosophy and in all probability takes precedence over all other, more clearly delineated points of transition (such as that of the physics or the *Naturphilosophie* of the time).

This said, it would also not be too difficult to detect, running beneath this complex problematic taken as a whole, the guiding thread of a primary and constant preoccupation, of a single question—none other than that of *mimesis,* at whatever level one chooses to examine it (whether it be that of "imitation," in the sense of the "imitation of the Ancients," of mimesis as a mode of *poiesis,* i.e., Aristotelian mimesis, or even—and this does not fail to enter into play—of mimesis in the sense of "mimetism" or *imitatio*). This is precisely why speculative Idealism opens conjointly and indissociably as a theory of the Subject, of Art,

3. Lacoue-Labarthe is citing the French translation of the 1835 edition of the *Äs-thetik:* G. W. F. Hegel, *Esthétique,* trans. S. Jankélévitch (Paris: Aubier, 1964).—*Editor*

and of History. But this is also why, even though this is not always truly clear, tragedy and the theory of tragedy (from Friedrich Schlegel or Schiller to Hölderlin, or from Schelling to Hegel) orient in a fundamental way this trajectory, which itself merges essentially with an attempt to "overcome" (as they used to say) *mimetology.* Here I am referring less to the historico-cultural reinterpretation of the origins of tragedy (that is, to the entrance upon the philosophical scene of the Dionysian and all its successors) than to the rereadings of the Tragedians themselves as philosophical documents and models—beginning, of course, with Sophocles.

This is why, in following the example offered by Peter Szondi in his *Essay on the Tragic,*[4] I shall first consider a text by Schelling, dating from the period 1795–1796, and which figures in the last of his *Philosophical Letters on Dogmatism and Criticism.*[5] Szondi, who bases his remarks on this text (but also seems to forget the case of Freud—rather difficult to forget), develops the thesis that if "since Aristotle there has been a poetics of tragedy [we should understand here: a poetics of the tragic effect, based upon the doctrine of catharsis] . . . it is only since Schelling that there has been a philosophy of the tragic."[6] My ambition is simply to show that the so-called philosophy of the tragic remains in reality (though certainly in a subjacent manner) a theory of the tragic effect (thus presupposing the *Poetics* of Aristotle), and that it is only the persistent silence which this philosophy maintains in regard to this filiation that allows it to set itself up, over and above the Aristotelian mimetology and theory of catharsis, as the finally unveiled truth of the "tragic phenomenon."

Here is Schelling's text:

> The question has often been asked: how was the reason of Greece able to bear the contradictions inherent in its tragedy? A mortal—pushed by fate into becoming a criminal, himself fighting *against* fate, and nevertheless punished frightfully for the crime, which was itself the doing of fate! The *reason* for this contradiction, what made it bearable, lay at a level deeper than the one hitherto sought, lay in the conflict of human freedom with the power of the objective world, in which the mortal—assuming that this objective power was a more lofty one (a fate)—neces-

---

4. *Versuch über das Tragische* (Frankfurt: Insel Verlag, 1964).

5. A complete translation of this tenth letter is found in F. W. J. Schelling, *The Unconditional in Human Knowledge: Four Early Essays, 1794–1796,* trans. Fritz Marti (Lewisburg: Bucknell University Press, 1980), pp. 192–193. The translation presented below is by Robert Eisenhauer.

6. *Versuch,* p. 7.

sarily had to be defeated, and yet, because he did not go down to defeat *without a struggle,* had to be *punished* for his being defeated. The recognition of human freedom, the *honor* which fell due to such freedom, followed from the fact that the criminal, defeated only by the superior power of fate, was nonetheless *punished* as well. Greek tragedy honored human freedom by *allowing* its heroes to *fight* against the superior power of fate: in order not to exceed the bounds of art, Greek tragedy had to allow the hero to be *defeated,* but, so as to make good upon this humbling of human freedom—a humbling demanded by art—tragedy also had to let him *expiate* his crime, even the one which was committed because of fate . . . A great thought was contained in the hero's suffering the penalty even for an *unavoidable* crime, so that he might prove his freedom through the loss of that freedom itself, and so as to be defeated even as he declared the rights of free will.

You have no doubt recognized the figure of Oedipus here. Since Aristotle (at least explicitly), Oedipus has not ceased to be regularly invoked by philosophy as its most representative hero, the early incarnation of self-consciousness and of the desire to know. This, as everyone is aware, also holds perfectly well for Freud.

Szondi's analysis of this text is incontestable: he shows that the presentation of the conflict or of the tragic contradiction intervenes, at the conclusion of Schelling's *Letters,* in order to offer the possibility (and the model) of a (re)solution, in the dialectical sense of the term, to the philosophical contradiction par excellence, which Schelling calls the opposition of dogmatism and criticism. This latter is the opposition in general of the subjective and the objective, of the "absolute I" not yet conditioned by any object and the "absolute Object" or the "Not-I"— that is to say (so as to remain with the thread of Kantian or Fichtean terminology), of freedom and natural necessity. Indeed, the possibility offered by the tragic fable or scenario is that of the preservation (though to the benefit and in the sense of freedom) of the contradiction of the subjective and the objective, since the tragic hero, "at once guilty and innocent" (as Hegel will also say) in struggling against the invincible, that is, in struggling against the destiny that bears responsibility for his fault, *provokes* an inevitable and necessary defeat and *voluntarily* chooses to expiate a crime of which he knows he is innocent and for which, in any case, he will have had to pay. Culpable innocence and the "gratuitous" provocation of punishment are therefore the solution to the conflict: the subject *manifests* its liberty "by the very loss of its liberty." The negative, here, is converted into the positive; the struggle (be it ever so vain or futile) is in itself productive. And it is easy to see, if one recomposes the pattern of the scheme thus put in place, that the "conciliation," as Schelling says, operates according to the very logic of the "identity of identity and difference." The Oedipal scenario therefore implicitly contains the speculative solution. And everything has been prepared here for that absolutization or that paradoxical infinitization of the Subject within which philosophy will find its completion.

It could be shown that such a scheme exercises its constraint over the entire "Idealist" interpretation (is there any other?) of the tragic—including even that of Hegel himself. Novalis is obeying its logic when he declares that the philosophical (speculative) act par excellence is suicide, and it is incontestably this scheme that first leads Hölderlin, himself desirous of writing a "true modern tragedy," to choosing the figure of Empedocles. This obviously does not mean that it is simply this scheme that led him to undertake the translation of Sophocles and to propose *Oedipus the King* in his later work as the model for modern tragedy. But what is interesting here is that, even with its speculative rehandling (or its transposition, if you prefer, into metaphysical discourse, its ontological translation), this scheme is not basically different from the one Aristotle proposes in the thirteenth chapter of the *Poetics* (1452b), where he examines the question concerning what must be sought or avoided in the construction of the fable if tragedy is to produce "the effect proper to it"—the effect of the catharsis of fear and pity. For Aristotle too, as we know, *Oedipus the King* is the model of the "most beautiful composition"; it is the model of that type of composition called "complex" (as opposed to the simple fable), which implies a *peripeteia*—the sudden turn or *metabole* of the action into its contrary—and a recognition (the reversal from ignorance into knowledge, of *agnoia* into *gnosis*). Now if *Oedipus the King* enjoys such a privilege, it is because, among all the examples that fulfill this double requirement (all of them cases having to do with the "turning about of fortune"), it is the only one able to evoke the two passions which it is the function of tragedy to "purify." "This is the case," says Aristotle, "[of the] man who is neither a paragon of virtue and justice nor undergoes the change to misfortune through any real badness or wickedness but because of some mistake [or lapse, even bad luck or 'misfire'— *hamartia*]."[7] This would seem to be very removed from the articulating principle of Schelling's argument and from what gives it its thematic originality: this being, against the background of the notion

7. *Aristotle's Poetics*, trans. Gerald Else (Ann Arbor: University of Michigan Press, 1967), XIII, p. 38. All excerpts cited in the text are taken from this edition.

of innocent guilt (i.e., the paradox or that sort of structural oxymoron identified of course by Aristotle), the theme of the insurrection of the tragic subject and his assumption, in its very injustice, of the rigors of destiny. But recall the question with which Schelling began his text: How was Greek reason able to *bear* the contradictions of its tragedy? And substitute, for just a moment—while thinking, for instance, of the fear and pity Aristotle speaks of—"passion" for "reason." It is difficult not to see that in both places it is basically a matter of the *same* question and that, bearing in mind the ontological translation to which I just alluded, one can detect in Schelling's formulation the following question: How was Greek reason (that is, basically, How was philosophy . . .) able to "purify" itself of the menace which the contradiction illustrated by the tragic conflict represented? Can we avoid seeing, in other words, that although *hamartia* is in no way equivalent to the provocation of an inevitable defeat (between the two, in fact, there lies the whole problematic of the *Subject* as such), the question bearing upon the *tolerance* or the capacity for tolerance, in general, of the unbearable (death, suffering, injustice, contradiction) governs, in both cases, the entire interpretation?

As a consequence, it is indeed tragedy itself in both cases—the tragic spectacle—which is involved. Tragedy: that is, the mechanism of (re)presentation or of *Darstellung,* the structure of mimesis (which is what Schelling is thinking of when he mentions, though without any further elaboration, the "barriers of art" that Greek tragedy had to respect). Indeed, only mimesis—which in Aristotle's view, as we know, is the most primitive determination of the human animal and the very possibility of knowledge and the Logos, of reason (*Poetics,* IV, 1448b)— only mimesis has the power of "converting the negative into being" and of procuring that paradoxical pleasure, essentially "theoretical" and "mathematical" (moreover, especially reserved for the philosopher), which man is capable of feeling in the *representation,* provided it is exact, of the unbearable, the painful, and the horrible: "Such is the case for example with renderings of the least favored animals, or of cadavers" (*Poetics,* IV, 1448b). Only mimesis gives the possibility of "tragic pleasure." Once they become part of the spectacle, in other words, both death and the unbearable (that is, in 1795, the contradictory) "can be faced." The spirit henceforth, far from taking fright, can take its leisure "sojourning" in their proximity—even derive on occasion a certain pleasure from them, and in any case can purge itself, heal and purify itself, preserve itself from its own fear (perhaps too, from the madness that threatens it and probably also from the pity the spirit feels if, as Aristotle leads us to understand in passing, there can never be pity except in the form of pity for oneself). And if, in fact, the nature of the philosophical operation in general (and of the speculative one in particular) is fundamentally *economic,* the very principle of this economy is offered to philosophy by the specular relation and mimetic semblance, by the very structure of theatricality. The philosophy of Schelling draws from the same source—inaugurating the thought of the tragic, as we see, only by echoing the poetics of tragedy, or even, more distantly, the ancient background of ritual and of sacrifice of which, as we have every reason to believe, Aristotle's catharsis is *also* a philosophical justification and transposition. Or perhaps—and the one need not exclude the other—a logical *verification.*

*

I should now pass to the "counter-proof" mentioned at the beginning of this chapter (though the word seems definitely less and less suitable). There should be nothing simpler, apparently, since, as you know, there also happens to exist (to our fortune, but not by accident) a reading by Hölderlin of *Oedipus the King,* and it should therefore be easy to bring the two texts into some sort of confrontation.

But, of course, things are not so simple.

First of all, a difficulty arises from the fact that Hölderlin's *Notes* on the translation of Sophocles presuppose as their background not only (as has often been emphasized) a general introduction, which Hölderlin announced to his editor but never sent (one that was probably never written and of which, in any case, we have no trace), but also all of Hölderlin's previous work on tragedy. This work itself was left in the form of fragments or drafts at different stages of development, and is thus laconic, rough, and of an obscurity that is at times strictly impenetrable. But the difficulty is also due to the fact that the analysis of *Oedipus,* aside from the fact that it is meant to justify a translation, stands up only on the basis of the very tight relation it bears to the analysis of *Antigone*—just as the converse would, up to a certain point, be equally true.

But only up to a certain point.

This is because the fundamental text for Hölderlin's interpretation of tragedy is, in reality, *Antigone.* It is *Antigone* that represents the most difficult and the most enigmatic of tragedies, of all tragedies. It constitutes in this way the center, albeit (to speak like Hölderlin) an "eccentric" one—a kind of pivot, we might say, which is impossible to center—around which gravitate, though with difficulty, constantly impeded or thwarted in their movement, his repeated attempts at theorization. The reason is that *Antigone* is the most Greek of tragedies (and consequently transformed by the translation, in this case a particularly violent one, in order to "bring it closer to our mode of representation"[8]—to us as moderns—and make it correspond to this "Hesperian" age which defines our historical situation). One should even say: the reason for it is that *Antigone* incarnates the very essence of tragedy, if it be true that tragedy is forever a specifically Greek genre and, in this way, not "reconstitutable"—if not wholly untransposable. Moreover, this is why there cannot be a modern tragedy (at least in the rigorous sense) except in and through the translation of ancient tragedy. And this is also why—a general rule, even if it can be illustrated by only one example—the translation must be all the more violent and transformative in that it involves a text more properly Greek.

At any rate, this is what explains the difference in Hölderlin's treatment of the two Sophoclean tragedies he selects. But it should also be noted, because these things count, that they are presented within an "editorial" arrangement (one apparently chosen by Hölderlin) in which, curiously enough, the translation of *Oedipus the King* (in an initial volume) precedes that of *Antigone*. The most modern tragedy thus comes before the most ancient. Is there an indication here that a tragedy that is properly Greek, provided it be transformed (if not deformed), is really more modern than a Greek tragedy, like *Oedipus the King*, which "tends" toward the modern? "Modern" meaning here that the work's "artistic character," as Hölderlin says, all "Junonian" rigor and sobriety, is opposed to the natural basis of the Greeks (to their holy *pathos,* their Apollonian impulse toward the "fire of heaven") and better corresponds in this way to the proper nature of the Hesperians who, the inverse of the Greeks, are "sons of the earth" (Kant's expression, recalled by Beaufret)[9] and, as such, subject to the "limit" and immured within an essential finitude?

Such a question, it is true, involves the entire problematic of imita-

8. Friedrich Hölderlin, *Werke und Briefe,* ed. Friedrich Beissner (Frankfurt: Insel Verlag, 1969), p. 786. Unless otherwise indicated, all citations of Hölderlin's work will be from this edition.

9. Jean Beaufret, "Hölderlin et Sophocle," in Friedrich Holderlin, *Remarques sur Oedipe, Remarques sur Antigone,* trans. François Fédier (Paris: Union Générale d'Editions, 1965), p. 14.

tion in history, which for this reason *is* not, but *remains* irreducible to the dialectical logic to which it appears to be subordinate. I cannot develop this point any further at this time; but I cannot help thinking that this is perhaps the sign that for Hölderlin there was basically no modern tragedy except in the form of a *deconstruction,* a practical one, of ancient tragedy. Just as there was, undoubtedly, no possible theory of tragedy and of the tragic except in the deconstruction of classical poetics and its speculative reinterpretation. The one inseparable from the other.

But while we are on this point, and because the matter seems to me also important for us as "moderns"—who perhaps must maintain with Hölderlin (this does not mean necessarily: with all of his contemporaries) a relation that is analogous to the one he maintained with Greek authors (this is not to say: with all of the Greeks)—I would like to ask in passing if the "modern" was not for Hölderlin something like the *après coup,* in the strict sense, of Greek art: that is to say, the repetition of what occurred there without ever taking place, and the echo of that unuttered word that nevertheless reverberated in its poetry.

This could explain, in any case, the enterprise of *translation,* and the altering of the scheme of imitation (classicist or dialectical) that it presupposes. And this could undoubtedly explain the secretly and paradoxically greater modernity of *Antigone,* which is, Hölderlin says, more "lyrical" and in which, in fact, Sophocles shows himself closer to Pindar, who was always considered by Hölderlin the "summit" of Greek art (which did not in any way obviate the necessity of *translating* Pindar as well, of commenting upon, analyzing, or indeed *rewriting* him). For it was a matter of making Greek art say what it had not said—not in the manner of a kind of hermeneutics attempting to find the implicit in its discourse, but in quite a different manner, one for which I doubt very much that we as yet have a category. It was a matter of making it say by this means, quite simply, that which was said (but) *as that which was not said:* the same thing, then, in its difference [*en différence*]. *En diapheron heauto.*

Think, for example, of the chiasmic historical scheme to which I alluded a moment ago: it initially presupposed that a certain form of Greek tragedy (which is its regular or canonical form, its truly tragic form, Hölderlin says—at this juncture, the form of *Oedipus the King*) was in a position to define the ground of our own nature. What the Greeks, in effect, achieved against and beyond their nature, their art, delimits exactly what is proper to the moderns: the tragedy of a slow

222 The Caesura of the Speculative

beating down, the "wandering under the unthinkable" (*Werke,* p. 785), and the famous: "There is the tragic for us, that we depart from the world of the living quietly, packed up in some container" (*Werke,* p. 941). Quite the opposite, in other words, of the tragic *sublimation,* the "eccentric enthusiasm" that defines the initial "panic" surge of the Greeks toward the "One-Whole," their brutal and catastrophic transgression, which modern culture rediscovers in its art (the sentimental, in Schiller's sense, or, as Hölderlin would rather say, the elegiac) and its thought (the speculative itself). As Beaufret has emphasized, such a scheme takes up in rigorous fashion the Aristotelian mimetology as it is presented in the *Physics* (II, 8, 199a) and according to which—one finds here the same structure of differentiation—art, if it indeed imitates nature, also has the power of "carrying out" or "bringing to term" (*epitelein*) what nature, by itself, is incapable of "effecting" or "operating."

But now suppose that *Antigone,* once translated and rewritten under the conditions we have seen—suppose the *Antigone* of Sophocles *itself* were at once the most Greek of tragedies *and* the most modern, and that, in order to communicate this difference that repetition implies, imperceptible in itself, one were to transform here or there what it says so as to say better what it says *in truth.* In this case, the historical scheme and the mimetology it presupposes begin slowly, vertiginously, to vacillate, to distort, and to hollow out in an abyssal manner. And if you also consider that the structure of supplementation—defining in sum the mimetic relation in general, the relation between art and nature, is in Hölderlin's eyes fundamentally a structure of aid and protection, that it is necessary if man is to evade "taking flame in contact with the element," then you will not only understand what the stakes were for him in Greek art (it was a matter, finally, of dealing with a "madness" brought about by excessive imitation of the divine and speculation), but you also will understand why in the modern epoch—even though this epoch reverses, in principle, the Greek relation between art and nature—one must indeed repeat what is most Greek in the Greeks. Begin the Greeks again. That is to say, no longer be Greek at all.

I offer these indications, though they are elliptical considering the degree of patience required here, not only for the purpose of marking by way of a kind of relief the place of *Antigone.* Nor do I want to give the quick impression (a false one, at that) that Hölderlin's "theory"— which, unlike that of Schelling, explicitly takes into account the problematic of the tragic effect—might have extricated itself, by who knows what lucidity, from the sacrificial and ritual model of tragedy. As we have seen, Hölderlin did not restrict the function of catharsis only to the art of antiquity; and the preoccupation with ritual was always a constant with him—assuming as undeniable Girard's argument that his obstinate and oppressive questioning ("at the doors of madness") concerning tragedy and mimesis cannot be dissociated from his *biography*, and that what is involved in the process of mimetic rivalry which Hölderlin always more or less knew he was involved in (vis-à-vis Schiller, in particular) is a final attempt to settle or, more precisely, to *regulate* (they are not quite the same thing, and this could well shed light on Hölderlin's *retreat*, too quickly called his "madness") the double bind that structures mimetic identification ("Be like me" / "Do not be like me") and sets in motion the "cyclo-thymic" oscillation. If you like, it seems to me that we can at least acknowledge in Hölderlin that he never denied we have need of art—though hardly, as Nietzsche said, "so as not to be destroyed by the truth": for Hölderlin, rather, all things considered, art was a means of gaining access to truth—provided, obviously, that we not understand truth here in the speculative sense (if this is possible). For it is all too clear that the speculative, which was also, in its very logic, the hope of a possible resolution of the insurmountable contradiction brought on by the "machine" of the double bind (thus offering the hope of a therapy, indeed, of a possible cure), nevertheless remained, in Hölderlin's eyes, the paradoxical and dangerous "second nature" of the Moderns—as paradoxical and as dangerous as their artistic virtuosity had been for the Greeks, and through the fault of which, since the Greeks had left idle their natal (or "native"), the "empire of art" which they wanted to establish collapsed.[10]

If, in truth, I have delayed a bit over *Antigone*, this is not simply because I have been thinking of Schelling's consternation at Hölderlin's translation of Sophocles (which, as he wrote to Hegel, "showed his state of mental derangement").[11] It is because I was thinking of Hegel himself, and of his icy silence: the very one who was nevertheless to write in the year immediately following the publication of Hölderlin's *Notes* the pages of the *Phenomenology of Mind* devoted to *Antigone*, pages that program, up to Nietzsche and Freud (and even to Heideg-

---

10. Lacoue-Labarthe is alluding to lines from a late fragment published in Friedrich Hölderlin, *Sämtliche Werke*, ed. Friedrich Beissner (Stuttgart: Kohlhammer, 1946–1968), vol. 2.1, p. 228.—*Editor*

11. Cited ibid., vol. 7.2, p. 296.

ger), the modern interpretation of tragedy, but which are difficult not to read also as the detailed and prolix rectification of Hölderlin's analysis. Even if, as Derrida has shown in *Glas*,[12] there is played out in these pages, at its limit, the very possibility of the speculative and of the onto-logic—even if it is true that tragedy (as testimony and as genre) will have always represented within this onto-logic the place where the system fails to close upon itself, and where the systematic does not quite succeed in fully overlapping the historical, where the circularity (as Szondi notes) alters itself in a spiraling movement while the closure can scarcely contain the pressure under which it has perhaps already succumbed without anyone's becoming aware of it—even still (I mean to say: there is one more reason for thinking that) the speculative will have *also* emerged from, and (re)organized itself around, this gesture of expulsion. Heidegger, as we know, was particularly attentive to this point. But this is also, perhaps, why he was unable to avoid "sacralizing" Hölderlin.

*

Once again, I am not saying this with a view toward extricating Hölderlin from the speculative and making him, if you will, the "positive hero" of this adventure. The theory put forward by Hölderlin is speculative through and through—beginning with that theory upon which the analysis set forth in the *Notes* is based.

Indeed, the model here is the same, structurally (and even to a certain point, thematically), as the one we found in Schelling. Like Schelling, moreover, and in terms that are rigorously analogous, Hölderlin thought and would have been able to write that tragic drama exists at a "higher level, where unity itself becomes reconciled with conflict, and both become one in a more perfect form . . . the loftiest manifestation of the idea and of the essence of all art."[13] At any rate, Hölderlin maintained that tragedy was "the most rigorous of poetic forms" (letter to Neuffer of 3 July 1799, *Werke*, p. 904) and that it is properly constituted by the fact that it expresses "a more infinite divine" through "more sharply defined differences" ("Grund zum Empedokles," in *Werke*, p. 571). Hölderlin basically shared the idea common to all of Idealism that tragedy is the absolute *organon*, or, to take up the expression that

12. Jacques Derrida, *Glas* (Paris: Galilée, 1974), left-hand column in the vicinity of p. 188.
    13. F. W. J. Schelling, *Philosophie der Kunst*, in *Sämtliche Werke*, ed. K. F. A. Schelling (Stuttgart: J. G. Cotta, 1859), pt. 1, vol. 5, p. 687.

Nietzsche applied to *Tristan* (a work in which Nietzsche found approximately the same thing), "of all art, the *opus metaphysicum*."[14] This is why, in all rigor, Hölderlin's theory of tragedy was at once an onto-phenomenology and an onto-organology. As evidence, this fragment of 1799 in which, assuming we do not dwell too long on the dynamic paradox that it presents (or on its strange syntax), we find, under the name of the tragic *sign*, the *figure* (in the strong sense, the *Gestalt*— Hölderlin also speaks of the symbol) of the suffering hero who is the site of the revelation and the epiphany of what is:

> The meaning of tragedies is most easily understood on the basis of the paradox. Because all power is justly and equally distributed, all that is original appears not, indeed, in its original strength, but properly in its weakness, so that properly the light of life and the appearance belong to the weakness of each whole. Now, in the tragic the sign is, in itself, meaningless, without effect, and yet that which is original is openly manifest. For, properly, the original can appear only in its weakness, but, insofar as the sign in itself is posited as meaningless = o, the original, the hidden ground of each nature, can also be presented. If nature presents itself properly in terms of its weakest gift, then the sign, when nature presents itself in its strongest gift, = o.[15]

There would be a great deal to say about such a text—and it would complicate our reading singularly. I cite it here only for what it offers on a first reading and simply to give a feeling for the kind of logic that is manifestly operative in it. For it helps explain how Hölderlin is able, in another fragment contemporary with it (1798–1800), to define tragedy as the "metaphor of an intellectual intuition" ("Über den Unterschied der Dichtarten," in *Werke*, p. 629): that is to say, the transfer and passage into the nonproper of "being" or of the "union ['the absolute bond'] of subject and object" with a view to its (ap)propriation, for such was the concept, as a text that is somewhat earlier testifies ("Urteil und Sein," in *Werke*, p. 591), of intellectual intuition that he took up from Fichte.

In its turn, however, such a definition (presupposing that what is signified by a work, here the absolute, finds its expression by means of a "catastrophe" and reversal into the "appearance" or the opposing "artistic character") engenders, when it is brought together with the dis-

14. F. W. Nietzsche, *Unzeitgemässe Betrachtungen*, published with a French translation by Geneviève Bianquis in *Nietzsche: Considérations intempestives (III et IV)* (Paris: Aubier, 1954), p. 251.

15. Hölderlin, *Sämtliche Werke*, vol. 4.1, p. 274.

tinction between "tonalities" (naïve, ideal, heroic) inherited from Schiller, a conception of tragedy which we might call "structural," or, if you prefer, a general "system of combination" of what Hölderlin thinks of as the "calculable" in the production of the different poetic genres. Now the logic of such an "axiomatics" is, in itself, dialectical. It gives rise, for example, to those tables or "graphs" by which Hölderlin attempts to schematize, for each genre, the rule for what he calls the "alternation of tones," and where the opposition—in a complex series—of the "fundamental tone" and the "artistic character" (of "signification" and "style") is to find its "resolution" in the "spirit" of the genre or, as the case may be, of the work. It is in this way that tragedy, at least in its canonical structure (the very structure not adhered to by *Antigone*), represents the "naïve" resolution—we should understand here "epic"—of the initial antinomy between its "ideal" fundamental tone (the tone of the subjective aspiration toward the infinite, the speculative tone par excellence) and its "heroic" artistic character (here the tone of discord, of *agon*, and of contradiction). Szondi has flawlessly analyzed all of this, and there is nothing to be added, except perhaps the observation, in echo of some of Adorno's suggestions in his *Mahler*, that this entire dialectic of tones (and, in a certain way, dialectic in general) is undoubtedly not so alien to the mode of composition of the great symphony after Mozart. And it is in this way that we can also understand why Adorno was quite justified elsewhere in comparing the "parataxis" characteristic of Hölderlin's late style with the writing of Beethoven's last quartets.

Now, if things are as I have said and if speculative logic does constrain Hölderlin's theory to the point of submitting it to this sort of "organicist" formalism (so close, in its principles, to what one finds in all the attempts, Romantic or Idealist, to "deduce" the genres, works of art, or the arts in general), how then is it that the analysis of *Oedipus the King,* as presented in the *Notes,* diverges so radically in the essential from that proposed by Schelling, for example? Has Hölderlin been able to extricate himself, by some miracle, from the most powerful of theoretical constraints?

Certainly not.

Need I repeat again? The theory put forward in Hölderlin—and this would apply to more than just those texts which are usually classified as such—*is,* through and through, speculative. At least (and here you may refer again to *Glas,* p. 188) it can always be interpreted in this way, read in this way, and written in this way. For it is probably in just this fashion—above all, when it wished to extricate itself from this constraint—that the theory itself was first read and written. But this is not to say that it *reread* itself and *rewrote* itself in this manner—especially when it did not want to extricate itself from this constraint, in which it also saw its resource, its protection, and, perhaps, its "remedy."

It seems to me, in any case, that in the very difficulty Hölderlin had in theorizing (by this I mean his difficulty in mastering theoretical exposition and carrying it through), a difficulty that is increasingly marked and that also does not spare his poetic production or his lyric poetry (on the contrary, it constantly *disorganizes* them), that in the aggravation of that sort of paralysis affecting his *discourse* (trapping it in ever more rigid logical and syntactic bonds), Hölderlin, by a movement of "regression," if you will (I shall return to this: it is without any pejorative implications), comes to touch upon something that dislocates *from within* the speculative. Something that immobilizes it and prohibits it—or rather, distends and suspends it. Something that constantly prevents it from completing itself and never ceases, by doubling it, to divert it from itself, to dig into it in such a way as to create a spiral, and to bring about its collapse. Or that interrupts it, from place to place, and provokes its "spasm."

How can we describe such a movement? Despite everything, there is perhaps a means open to us in the fact that it necessarily entails a theoretical and discursive component. This is, quite clearly, a makeshift procedure inasmuch as one cannot avoid—as I will be forced to do here—detaching the discursive or the theoretical from what remains, or from its own remainder.

It is in this way that I am led to speak of "regression"—at least as a kind of indication. Let me present the matter schematically, with a minimum of nuance. Whereas the model of speculative tragedy is constructed upon the "denegation" of Aristotelian mimetology and theory of catharsis, Hölderlin, for his part, returns to it insistently, struggling to get back to Aristotle, or, in any case, a general theory of mimesis. But this movement of return, this "step back," leads him beyond Aristotle and the (already) philosophical interpretation of tragedy, at once toward Sophocles (and thereby toward the religious and sacrificial function of tragedy) and toward what *haunts* Plato under the name of mimesis and against which Plato fights with all of his philosophical determination until he finds a way of arresting it and fixing its concept.

All of this, in its way, is quite simple. However, I must hasten to add that the movement of "regression" in Hölderlin does not stop here. First of all, the movement does not take place by itself alone, or all at once. For example, it should be shown, with some precision, how the successive drafts of *Empedocles* and the theoretical reflection accompanying them slowly and laboriously mark the stages of this "regression." This would take considerable time and would not be so easy. Nonetheless, the trajectory appears with a certain degree of clarity as regards its basic principle and its line of direction. For Hölderlin in fact takes as his point of departure a scenario that is overtly speculative: that of the so-called "Frankfurt plan," which underlies the greater portion of the first version. Empedocles is here the very figure of speculative desire and nostalgia for the One-Whole, suffering from temporal limitation and wanting to escape finitude. The drama is then organized (I am simplifying) around the hero's internal debate (a wholly "elegiac" struggle and still rather close to the style of *Hyperion*). Its sole subject, virtually, is the justification of speculative suicide. This is why "modern tragedy," in its initial phase, is at bottom nothing but the tragedy of tragedy or even, in a quasi-Romantic way, the tragedy of the theory of tragedy: a work seeking to be absolute in the power it grants itself to reflect itself and raise itself to the level of Subject.

The question has nevertheless often been asked why Hölderlin abandoned this first version and what reason (philosophical or dramaturgical) prompted him to modify, at least twice, this first scenario—to the point of abandoning the project entirely (the "failure") and passing on to his translation of Sophocles. Beda Allemann[16] suggests that Hölderlin, conscious of a kind of "plot deficiency" generally common to what are known as *pièces à thèse* (as if there were any other kind), had attempted to "motivate" dramatically Empedocles' metaphysical resolution. This is not impossible. In any case, what matters is that when Hölderlin reorganizes the scenario in the second version and, in fact, complicates it, what he essentially introduces is the idea that Empedocles' speculative temptation is a *fault*. As a result, of course, the plot attains a properly tragic register. And generally, the commentators have been right to emphasize this. But what has escaped general notice is that the introduction of the fault here is in effect the setting into place of an "Oedipal" type of scenario: that is, of a sacrificial scenario. Empedocles' fault is that of publicly declaring himself divine in the presence of the entire Agrigentine people. In other words, the philo-

16. Beda Allemann, *Hölderlin und Heidegger* (Freiburg: Rombach, 1954).

sophical transgression has now become a social one, or—what amounts to the same thing (here)—a religious one. Naturally, Empedocles thereby brings upon himself the enmity of the Agrigentines who impute to his lack of measure the fundamental responsibility for the plague which is ravaging the city and who, in order to rid themselves of the defilement, carry out against Empedocles (in a quite explicit and detailed manner) the well-known gesture of the expulsion of the *pharmakos*—a gesture doubled, almost immediately, in the normal (dialectical) manner, by his sacralizing rehabilitation (hence the final redemption of Empedocles, in the style of the conclusion of *Oedipus at Colonus*).

The transformation to which Hölderlin subjects his *Empedocles* thus goes in the direction, as we see, of a "return to Sophocles." The remarkable thing, however, is that such a return satisfied Hölderlin no better than the post-Kantian construction from which he had initially started. This is no doubt why, between the second version and his draft of a third, which was probably abandoned rather quickly, Hölderlin attempted to take his project in hand theoretically in a long, obscure, and difficult essay that evidently had to be written separately because of the renunciation of his original design of a "reflexive tragedy."

Now it happens that this essay ("Der Grund zum Empedokles") presents us in turn with an analogous phenomenon of "regression." But it is now a matter of a philosophical "regression" internal to (the history of) philosophy: that is, the already mentioned "return" to Plato, to the Platonic problematic of the mimetic (or dramatic) mode of enunciation. Nothing might have forewarned us that he was about to take such a problematic into account. Its abrupt introduction (dis)organizes the dialectical scheme of the tragedy.

I quote, for example, the following passage from his essay. Hölderlin addresses himself here to the structure of tragedy in its difference from what he defines, probably, as the essence of the great modern lyric— that is, the "tragic ode":

> It is the deepest interiority that is expressed in the tragic dramatic poem.
> The tragic ode also portrays the inward in the most positive differences,
> in actual oppositions; however, these oppositions are present more in the
> simple form and *as the immediate language of sentiment*. The tragic poem
> veils the interiority in the portrayal still more, expresses it in more sharply
> defined differences, because it expresses a more profound interiority, a
> more infinite divine. The sentiment no longer expresses itself directly . . .
> Thus, in the tragic dramatic poem as well, the divine is expressed which
> the poet senses and experiences in his world; the tragic dramatic poem is

also an image of the living for him, one that for him is and was present in his life; but as this image of interiority *increasingly denies and must everywhere deny its final ground to the same measure that it must everywhere become closer to the symbol,* the more infinite, the more ineffable, the closer the interiority is to the *nefas,* the more rigorously and the more austerely the image must differentiate the human being from the element of his sentiment in order to keep the sentiment within its limits, *the less the image can directly express the sentiment.* (*Werke,* pp. 571–572; emphasis added)

We find here a theory of the dramatic figure (of the personage or of the "character") in its relation to the author, a kind of "paradox of the dramatist," if you will. The reader will also have recognized, in passing, a motif that we have already encountered and that takes the form of the law according to which the style of a work is the effect or the product, the result of the "catastrophe" of its first fundamental tone or of its signification. This is why the more the tragic poet wants to express "the most profound interiority," the more he must pass through the mediation of a "foreign material." And this is nothing other, consequently, than the paradox that founded the speculative interpretation of tragedy and permitted the deduction (or reconstruction) of its organically dialectical structure. However, even on the first reading, it is easy to see that something prevents the pure and simple reapplication of this analysis. For even if Hölderlin, using all the means available to him, and to the point of exhausting his dialectical resources (the text, indeed, loses itself and fails to close with a result of any kind), strives to think the dramatic figure as a means or a mediation for the paradoxically adequate expression of the author or the subject, this dialectical starting device, constantly reengaged, always lacks a principle of resolution. Everything happens, therefore, as though we were dealing with (and with nothing more than) a kind of immobilized attenuation of a dialectical process that marks time in an interminable oscillation between the two poles of an opposition, always infinitely distant from each other. The act of suspension is this: quite simply, the incessant repetition of the engaging of the dialectical process in the—never changing—form of *the closer it is, the more distant it is; the more dissimilar it is, the more adequate it is; the more interior it is, the more exterior it is.* In short, the maximum of appropriation (for the perpetual comparison here originates in a movement of passing to the limit, and proceeds necessarily from a logic of excess—of the superlative) is the maximum of disappropriation, and conversely. "The more infinite the interiority . . .

the more rigorously the image must differentiate the human being from the element of his sentiment . . ."

One can well imagine the analysis that might be undertaken here on the basis of the contradictory structure implied by the mimetic relation—on the basis of the "double bind." This obsession with the near and the distant (or, what amounts to the same thing, peril and protection) runs through, obviously in addition to the poems, even some of the greatest such as "Patmos," all the correspondence (with Schiller, in particular), and constitutes the privileged metaphor—if at this point it can still be considered such—of the detailed description Hölderlin gives of his own cyclothymia. Such an analysis would be perfectly justified; all the more so in that it would inevitably have to touch upon what is progressively articulated, in that inflection to which Hölderlin subjects mimetology, with regard to the general problematic of the subject of enunciation. But by the same token, nothing would prevent us from recognizing in this paralysis affecting (without end) the very movement of the dialectic and the ontologic, and beyond the evident gesture of conjuration, the return effect of mimetology within the speculative, and, consequently, within the general discourse of truth and presence. It is true that Heidegger constantly sought in Hölderlin the possibility of backing up from the assumption in the speculative mode of *adaequatio,* and of "exiting" *from within* the onto-theo-logic. This is why the "logic" of *aletheia* can also be inscribed as the "logic" of *Ent-fernung* [*é-loignement,* or "(dis)distancing"]. But who knows whether this "logic" itself (including, too, what ceaselessly carries it off in its most demanding moments) is not also penetrated throughout by (if not subject to) mimetology? The "logic" of the open-ended exchange of the excess of presence and of the excess of loss, the alternation of appropriation and disappropriation—all that we might baptize, following Hölderlin's terminology (and for lack of anything better) the "hyperbologic," together with everything that holds it still within the framework of the "homoeotic" definition of truth—who knows if this is not the (paradoxical) truth of *aletheia?*

In any case, it is such a "hyperbologic" that evidently underlies the final definition of the tragic proposed by Hölderlin.

Here it is—it is very well known:

> The presentation of the tragic rests principally upon this: that the monstrous, the fact that God and man couple, and the fact that without limit

the power of nature and the innermost of man become one in fury, is
conceived in that the limitless becoming-one is purified through limitless
separation. (*Werke*, pp. 735–736)

It is again a matter of catharsis. It is even much more: a "generalization" of the theory of catharsis, if you will, but one which can be such
only in the abandonment of the terrain upon which Aristotle had constructed his own—that is, the terrain of the "spectacular" relation.
Indeed, such an understanding of catharsis proceeds by taking into account the "subject" of tragedy or of the dramatic utterance. This is why
it carries with it, over and above a simple "poetics," an entire thought
of history and of the world, of the relation between man and the divine
(or between heaven and earth), of the function of art and the necessary
"catastrophe" by which the natural becomes the cultural, and of the
general movement of alternation or of exchange of the proper and the
nonproper. Once again, I cannot go into this any further here. I should
emphasize, however, that only the "hyperbologic" is undoubtedly
capable of accounting for the scheme of the "double turning about"
upon which Hölderlin's last thought is founded and according to which
the very excess of the speculative switches into the very excess of submission to finitude (a scheme in which the "categorical" turning about
of the divine corresponds to the *volte-face,* as Beaufret says, of man toward the earth, his pious infidelity, and his extended wandering "under
the unthinkable," which fundamentally define the Kantian age to which
we belong).

Whatever we might make of such a thought, the lesson, with respect
to tragedy, is as clear as can be: the more the tragic is identified with
the speculative desire for the infinite and the divine, the more tragedy
presents it as a casting into separation, differentiation, finitude. Tragedy, then, is the catharsis of the speculative.

Which means also the catharsis of the religious itself and of the sacrificial—a final paradox, and not one of the least surprising.

What authorizes such a definition of tragedy, first of all, is nothing
other than Hölderlin's reading of *Oedipus the King.* This reading is
based entirely upon a condemnation that could not be more explicit
with regard to the indissociably speculative and religious temptation in
which Hölderlin finds the fundamental motive of the Oedipal "fable"
and the reason for its "composition"—comparable, he says, to the unfolding of a "trial of heresy."

What, indeed, is Oedipus' fault?

It is, Hölderlin answers, to act "as a priest." The response is surprising. But here is the beginning of his analysis—it is impeccably clear:

> The *intelligibility* of the whole rests primarily upon one's holding in mind the scene in which Oedipus *interprets too infinitely* the word of the oracle and in which he is *tempted in the direction of the nefas.* [The transgression, the sacrilege, is thus the excess of interpretation.] For the word of the oracle is:

> > He has clearly commanded us, Phoebus the king,
> > To purify the land of the defilement that has been nourished on this ground
> > And not to nurture what cannot be healed.

> This *could* mean [emphasis added: this is the literal, profane, political translation of the oracle's statement]: . . . keep a good civil order. But Oedipus immediately speaks in a priestly fashion:

> > Through what purification . . . (*Werke,* p. 731)

"And he goes into *particulars,*" adds Hölderlin, meaning to indicate that the movement has from this point on become irreversible, and that Oedipus, indeed, will conduct his own trial of heresy. The tragic fault consists, then, in the religious and sacrificial interpretation of the social ill. The tragic hero *goes under,* as Schelling would say, for wanting to carry out the ritual and for desiring a *pharmakos* in order to remove the defilement which he imagines to be sacred. He is destroyed not by directly provoking the punishment, but by calling up the old ritual of the scapegoat victim. He is destroyed, in short, by his belief in what Girard calls the religious "mechanisms," which are in fact, though with regard to a different concept of religion, "sacrilegious" mechanisms, because they presuppose the transgression of the human limit, the appropriation of a divine position (Antigone will be an exemplary case) and the appropriation of the right to institute difference by oneself (this will be the case of Oedipus just as well as that of Creon, for such a reading of tragedy indeed definitively precludes that one could even conceive of a "positive" tragic hero). Thus, he who desires difference and exclusion excludes himself, and suffers, to the point of irreversible loss, this inexorable, unlimited differentiation that the "hyperbologic" introduces in its doubling of the dialectical-sacrificial process in such a way as to prevent its culmination and paralyze it *from within.* Tragedy, because it is the catharsis of the speculative, presents disappropriation *as* that which secretly animates and constitutes it; tragedy presents (dis)appropriation. This is why Oedipus incarnates the madness of knowledge (all knowledge is the desire for appropriation) and represents, in his tragic course, the "demented quest for a consciousness" (*Werke,* p. 733): nothing other, perhaps, than the madness of self-consciousness.

This reelaboration of the interpretation of tragedy cannot fail, in its turn, to touch the dialectical-structural conception of the organization of tragedy. It results, in any case, in the subordination of the theory of the alternation of tones. Indeed, from the moment the mimetic structure no longer guarantees in principle the reconciliatory and reappropriating "return to the Same"; from the moment the tragic spectacle presupposes, behind it, the irremediable loss of every secure position and determination of enunciation, and sees itself condemned, as a consequence, to represent the process (itself at all times complex and differentiated) of (dis)appropriation, everything then forces the dynamic and productive successivity that structurally organized tragedy to give way to a mechanism of pure equilibrium. The structure of tragedy itself becomes immobilized and paralyzed. Yet this does not in any way prevent this "neutralization" of the dialectical dynamic from being constantly *active.* For the tragic structure *also* remains dialectical, and only the deconstruction of the Sophoclean-Schellingian (or Aristotelian) model of the tragic requires this (de)structuring of tragedy.

This, in fact, comes down to "disorganizing" tragedy in the strongest sense of the term: desystematizing it and disjointing it. It consequently comes down to reconstructing it at the very point where its dialectical organization confirms itself: upon an empty articulation or the lack of all articulation, a pure asyndeton which Hölderlin calls the "caesura" and which suspends the "catastrophic" process of alternation:

> For the tragic *transport* is properly empty and the most unbound. Whereby, in the rhythmic succession of representations, in which the *transport* presents itself, *what in meter is called the caesura,* the pure word, the counter-rhythmic intrusion, becomes necessary in order to meet the racing alternation of representations at its culmination, such that what appears then is no longer the alternation of representations but representation itself." (*Werke,* p. 730)

Such a disarticulation of the work and of the process of succession through alternations that constitutes it as such—by which we pass (and here again, by what effect of "regression"?) from a *melodic* conception of the work to a *rhythmic* one—does not do away with the logic of exchange and alternation. It simply brings it to a halt, reestablishes its equilibrium; it prevents it, as Hölderlin says, from carrying along its representations exclusively in one sense or another. It prevents (a protective gesture, which does not necessarily mean a "ritualistic" one) the racing oscillation, *crazed panic,* and an orientation toward this or that pole. The disarticulation represents the active neutrality of the interval between [*entre-deux*]. This is undoubtedly why it is not by chance that the caesura is, on each occasion, the empty moment—the absence of "moment"—of Tiresias's intervention: of the intrusion of the prophetic word . . .

*

For "tragedy," in German, one says *Trauerspiel*—literally, "play of grief or mourning."

Something different, then, if you will allow me such an association (in fact, not really so free) from the "work of mourning," the sublimating learning of suffering and the work of the negative—the two conditions, as Heidegger has shown, of the onto-logic: *Arbeit,* meaning labor and work (*oeuvre*), and *algos,* that is, *logos.*

Why would we not conclude, then, that in (dis)organizing tragedy in this way, Hölderlin *caesuraed the speculative* (which is not to go beyond it, or to maintain it, or to sublate it) and, in so doing, rediscovered something of the *Trauerspiel?*

At any rate, we know that Hölderlin wrote the following about Sophocles—its simplicity is disarming:

Many sought in vain to say joyfully the most joyful.
Here, finally, here in mourning, it pronounces itself to me.[17]

17. Hölderlin, *Sämtliche Werke,* vol. 1.1, p. 305.

4

Hölderlin and the Greeks

For something to come about, something must depart. Hope first figures as
fear; the first appearance of the new is
fright.
—Heiner Müller

When Hölderlin begins to write, a specter is still haunting Europe:
that of *imitation*.

Though the century born under the sign of the quarrel between the
Ancients and Moderns will come to an end with the French Revolution, the style of this revolution, its *gestus* and *ethos,* is itself neo-
classical—imitated from Rome or Sparta.

And in the thinking Germany of the epoch (which is also to say the
Germany that thinks because it is marking, or believes it marks, an
"epoch" in history), in spite of everything—in spite of the *Hamburgische
Dramaturgie* and *Sturm und Drang* (I cite at random), Herder's *Ideen
zur Philosophie der Geschichte der Menschheit* and the interest in Diderot,
Moritz's cosmopolitanism and aesthetics, especially in spite of (or perhaps because of) the Crisis opened up by Kant, a rent or schism that
nothing and no one can manage to mend—Winckelmann in fact still
rules. Winckelmann, and this sentence, in which he summarizes the
general agonistic in which a whole culture exhausts itself and a nation
probably misses its birth: "The only way we can become great, and, if
this is possible, inimitable, is by imitating the Ancients."[1]

A gigantic historical *double bind,* and the consequent threat of
psychosis.

---

1. Johann Joachim Winckelmann, "Gedanken über die Nachahmung der griechischen
Werke in der Malerei und Bildhauerkunst," in *Réflexions sur l'imitation des oeuvres
grecques en peinture et en sculpture,* ed. Leon Mis (Paris: Aubier, 1954), p. 95.

In any case, nowhere else are the Greeks to this extent an obsession. In the thinking Germany of the 1790s, they cast their shadow on a world that is sharply stratified, rigid and closed, making the Enlightenment [*les Lumières*] more of a twilight. The Modern is late in coming. This also means: Germany is late.

Yet as Hölderlin begins to write, there is talk of a dawn: *Morgenrot*. Jakob Böhme's old word will be very much in circulation, at least where things are decided in this *fin-de-siècle* decade—precisely where Hölderlin will never manage to make a place for himself: Jena, standing under the control of Weimar.

But why does one speak of dawn?

Because, thanks to Kant and in defiance of him, a *theoretical* solution to the fixed and insurmountable contradiction between Ancient and Modern seems possible: a means is glimpsed for setting free the Modern. Or rather, a means for transforming it through the work and the effect belonging to a twist *within* the mimetic machine itself, a means for making the Modern, subject to those inaccessible masters, the Greeks, master of the masters. Everyone now knows that this theoretical programmation of the Modern (but henceforth the Modern will always also be theoretical), which, through and beyond Nietzsche, will govern Germany (and not only Germany), is outlined for the first time in Schiller's aesthetic writings. Hegel, professing aesthetics in his turn, will not fail to credit Schiller for being the first to have taken the step beyond Kant, and to have claimed the speculative fulfillment of truth "even before philosophy recognized its necessity."[2]

The theoretical solution, in other words, is the dialectical resolution. The *Auflösung* itself.

The fundamental text, here, is the triple essay "Naïve and Sentimental Poetry." We know from the analysis begun by Peter Szondi[3] that this essay was initially Schiller's first attempt to settle the question of his relation to Goethe—to the crushing model that Goethe represented in his eyes. A matter of mimetic rivalry, of course; and an attempt, necessarily reflexive and theorizing, to break the indefinitely binary rhythm of identificatory cyclothymia. But the limited double bind of Schiller's relation to Goethe was in this case identical to the

2. Lacoue-Labarthe is citing the French translation of the 1835 edition of the *Ästhetik: Esthétique*, trans. S. Jankélévitch (Paris: Aubier, 1964), p. 87.—*Editor*

3. Peter Szondi, "Das Naive ist das Sentimentalische: Zur Begriffsdialektik in Schillers Abhandlung," in *Lekturen und Lektionen: Versuch über Literatur, Literaturtheorie und Literatursoziologie* (Frankfurt: Suhrkamp, 1973).

general double bind of the relation to the Greeks: Goethe already passed for an Olympian genius, with an aspect as exalted and a stature as imposing as Homer's. A Greek, in short, miraculously rising up in the arid—artificial—West.

But what does "a Greek" mean to the era?

It means, in the wake of Winckelmann and his variations on the "Greek body," and after the divisions introduced by Rousseau, what could be imagined and posited as a *being of nature*. Which is also to say, correlatively, what the modern *beings of culture* could no longer even hope to become again, however powerful their nostalgia, since, as Schiller said, "nature in us has disappeared from humanity."[4] Thus, one considers Greek, or "naïve," the poet who *is nature*, who "only follows simple nature and feeling, and limits himself solely to the imitation of actuality";[5] on the other hand, the poet who *seeks nature* or desires it, as though called by the lost maternal voice, is modern, or "sentimental." For the art to which he is henceforth confined essentially entails dissociation, division, desolation—contrary to nature, which harmonizes and unites (man with the world and man with himself). These motifs—or rather, these theses—are well known.

It is generally less frequently remarked, however, that these theses finally come down to a historical translation, or "historicizing," of the Aristotelian definition of art, of *techne*. This was undoubtedly Schiller's decisive gesture. "Generally speaking," a canonical text of the *Physics* says, "on one hand techne accomplishes what phusis is incapable of effecting; on the other hand, techne imitates phusis."[6] Interpreted historically, this double postulation can yield this result: art, so far as it imitates nature, is specifically—and following Winckelmann—Greek art: mimesis is Greek. On the other hand, it is up to the Moderns to accomplish—to see through or bring to term, to complete—what nature cannot carry out. Consequently, it is up to the Moderns to go a step beyond the Greeks—to "accomplish" them.

That is to say, also, to surpass or surmount them.

A number of years later, in terms that he probably also considered anti-Rousseauistic and which, as in the case of Schiller, were actually in a direct line with Rousseauism, Kleist will say in his essay "On the

4. Friedrich von Schiller, *"Naïve and Sentimental Poetry" and "On the Sublime,"* trans. Julius A. Elias (New York: Friedrich Ungar, 1966), p. 103.

5. Ibid., p. 115.

6. Cf. Francis M. Cornford's translation in Aristotle, *The Physics,* vol. 1 (Cambridge: Harvard University Press, 1957), p. 173.

Marionette Theater": "But Paradise is locked and the cherubim behind us; we have to travel around the world to see if it is perhaps open again somewhere at the back . . . we would have to eat again from the Tree of Knowledge in order to return to the state of innocence."[7] This is exactly what Schiller, in his own words, had wanted to say, and what he had said: "We were nature . . . and our culture, by means of reason and freedom, should lead us back to nature."[8]

In these lines, as elsewhere (one might also use the examples of Schelling or Schlegel) the scheme we find—which is the very matrix for the scheme of the dialectic—is constructed on the basis of a rereading, explicit or not, of Aristotelian mimetology. And consistently, the operation has a cathartic end or function. The speculative resolution is perhaps still a mode of catharsis. In other words, a good use of mimesis.

We know furthermore that the opposition of Naïve and Sentimental involved a whole series of oppositions for Schiller, not only historical (Ancients and Moderns), geographical (as for Winckelmann: South and North), or aesthetic (plastic and poetic, epic and lyric), but also properly philosophical. They are borrowed, in this instance, from Kant: intuitive and speculative, objective and subjective, immediate and mediate, sensible and ideal, finite and infinite, necessary and free, or, to shorten the list (but we are gathering here all of metaphysics itself), body and spirit. In strict Kantian orthodoxy, or, as Hölderlin will say, in strict fidelity to Kant, these oppositions should have remained oppositions, and as such, irreducible. But as is clear in each line of Schiller's text, the whole demonstration organizes itself around nothing other than the desire or the will to reunite these oppositions and to produce, as Hegel will say, reconciliation.

I quote, almost at random:

> If one now applies the notion of poetry, which is nothing but *giving mankind its most complete possible expression,* to both conditions, the result in the earlier state of natural simplicity is the completest possible *imitation of actuality*—at that stage man still functions with all his powers simultaneously as a harmonious unity and hence the whole of his nature is expressed completely in actuality; whereas now, in the state of civilization where that harmonious cooperation of his whole nature is only an idea, it is the elevation of actuality to the ideal or, amounting to the same

7. Heinrich von Kleist, "On the Marionette Theater," trans. Christian-Albrecht Gollub, in *German Romantic Criticism,* ed. A. Leslie Willson (New York: Continuum, 1982), pp. 241–244.

8. *"Naïve and Sentimental Poetry,"* p. 85.

thing, the *representation of the ideal*, that makes for the poet. And these
two are likewise the only possible modes in which poetic genius can express itself at all. They are, as one can see, extremely different from one
another, but there is a higher concept under which both can be subsumed, and there should be no surprise if this concept should coincide
with the idea of humanity . . . This path taken by the modern poets is,
moreover, that along which man in general, the individual as well as the
race, must pass. Nature sets him at one with himself, art divides and
cleaves him in two, through the ideal he returns to unity.[9]

Of course, Schiller immediately adds that, because the ideal is infinite and thus inaccessible, the being of culture "can never be perfected
in its kind." We encounter here the theme of asymptotic completion; it
is common to the entire epoch, up to (but not including) Hegel: to the
Fichte of *Über die Bestimmung des Gelehrten* (practically contemporary
with Schiller's essay), to the Schlegel of Fragment 116 of the *Athenaeum*
on progressive poetry (that is, Romantic poetry), and even to the
Schelling of the *System des transzendentalen Idealismus*. All the same,
infinitizing means, in addition, absolutizing. It also means effectuation,
Verwirklichung—or "organization," in the rigorous sense of the term.
And moreover, when he tries to think the law thus "put into work,"
Schiller will outline in potential form the movement of dialectical logic:

> For the reader whose scrutiny is critical I add that both modes of percep-
> tion [the naïve and the sentimental, the ancient and the modern] consid-
> ered in their ultimate concepts are related to one another like the first and
> third categories, in that the last always arises by the combination of the
> first with its exact opposite. The opposite of naïve perception is, namely,
> reflective understanding, and the sentimental mood is the result of the
> effort, *even under the conditions of reflection,* to restore naïve feeling ac-
> cording to its content. This would occur through the fulfilled ideal in
> which art again encounters nature. If one considers those three concepts
> in relation to the categories, one will always find *nature* and the naïve
> mood corresponding to her in the first; *art,* as the antithesis of nature by
> the freely functioning understanding, always in the second; the *ideal,* in
> which consummated art always returns to nature, in the third category.[10]

If Sentimental is opposed to Naïve (or Modern to Ancient), we
must also think that the Sentimental (the Modern) is always beyond
itself—containing in itself already a step [*le pas en lui*] outside itself; it
is the internal transgression that at once cancels and preserves the op-

9. Ibid., pp. 111–112.
10. Ibid., pp. 154–155.

position or the contradiction that gave birth to it. The Sentimental *aufhebt*—sublates—the opposition of the Naïve and the Sentimental, of the Ancient and the Modern.

Hölderlin will not be too far off on this point. While he is still corresponding with Schiller, he constantly reflects back to him the image of this incontestable triumph. Schiller was announcing the actual possibility of a modern art:

> Out of discontent with myself and with what I am surrounded by, I have thrown myself into abstraction; I try to develop for myself the idea of an infinite progress of philosophy; I try to prove that what we should insistently demand of any system, the union of subject with object in an absolute I (or whatever you want to call it), is undoubtedly possible in an aesthetic manner, in intellectual intuition, but is possible in a theoretical manner only by way of infinite approximation.[11]

And this in effect will be the rigid, strict framework which, throughout the first years in which he undertakes to write, Hölderlin will be unable—or will not dare—to transgress. Again we find mimetic submission. But more serious this time, and leading almost to an impasse because it is redoubled: the necessity reigning in the agonistic relation dictates that Schiller should be even more (hopelessly) inaccessible to Hölderlin than Goethe was to Schiller.

Proving the existence and defining the exact configuration of this dependence or theoretical obedience with regard to Schiller would require lengthy analysis. Moreover, it is not simple; it is not a mere dependence. It does not preclude, for example, a more rigorously philosophical work (I am thinking of the critique of Fichte, which will mark so decisively Schelling's path of thinking, and will be of such consequence in the construction of speculative Idealism); nor does it preclude a poetological production (especially a theory of genres), stricter and, in what remains of it, more systematic than anything analogous one can find in Schiller. But it is a dependence all the same. And one strong enough, we know, to have hindered Hölderlin's theoretical work for a very long time, if not permanently. And not only his theoretical work.

Thus, it would not be incorrect to say that until about 1800–1801— until the failure and abandonment of the "modern tragedy" that *Em-*

---

11. Letter to Schiller of September 4, 1795, in Friedrich Hölderlin, *Werke und Briefe*, ed. Friedrich Beissner (Frankfurt: Insel Verlag, 1969), p. 846. Subsequent references to this work will be given in the body of the text.

pedocles was to be—Hölderlin remains, except in a few minor respects
(and even though the Greeks are not, for him, one question among
others, but, from the beginning, his only question), generally faithful
to the Schillerian (and the Winckelmannian) vision of the Greeks, and
to the philosophy of history that structures it or derives from it.

The point where things will begin to shift—a new understanding of
the Greeks making its appearance, an entirely different thought of history emerging—is that moment when Hölderlin, persisting with his
project to write a "modern tragedy," will conclude from the failure of
his *Empedocles* that it is necessary, or that *there remains*, to translate
Sophocles. The point where things will begin to shift, consequently, is
when Hölderlin takes on, with one and the same gesture, the problematic of the theater (is tragedy still possible?) and the test of translation
(do the Greeks still speak to us, and can we make them speak?). Another way, but ever more rigorous, of working across the terrain of
mimesis.

To the extent that this shift can be situated (though the gesture is
altogether precarious), we may consider that from the moment of his
trip to Bordeaux, to that French Midi or "Provence" strangely identified with Greece—brief, blinding exile and catastrophic return—
Hölderlin's final thinking on the Greeks is cast.

The latter is found, at least as concerns his discourse (but the poems
say nothing else, as Benjamin noted), in some letters—to his friend
Böhlendorff, to his editor—and in the enigmatic, or elliptical, *Notes* on
the translation of Sophocles. Perhaps also in some commentaries, no
less elliptical, on Pindar.

In spite of their almost unassailable difficulty, what can we make of
them?

Behind a thematic still largely dependent on Winckelmann and Schiller
(even if Hölderlin constructs entirely new categories), we find one
thing, first of all, that is completely unprecedented in the age: namely
that *Greece* [la *Grèce*], as such, Greece *itself,* does not exist, that it is at
least double, divided—even torn. And that what we know about it,
which is perhaps what it was or what it manifested of itself, is not what
it really was—which perhaps never appeared. In the same way, correlatively, the modern West—what Hölderlin never identifies simply
with Germany but calls, more generally, Hesperia—does not yet exist,
or is still only what it is not.

It is certain that Schiller had already had a hint of this fold internal to each of the extreme sites of history when he became aware, for example, that Goethe could be thought of as "naïve" only within the very space of the Sentimental. The division between natural and cultural (or between natural and artistic-artificial) that articulates the difference between Ancient and Modern could, in other words, fold upon itself and traverse each of the terms it separates. But this was no more than a suspicion. For Hölderlin, on the other hand, it is perfectly evident and fundamental. If you like, the tension that Aristotle introduced into *techne,* and that Schiller, whether he knew it or not, translated historically, is made by Hölderlin, without going back on this irreversible historicization, the very essence of each culture.

This tension is located with the categories of the proper and the non-proper, the "national" (natal or native, which is a most rigorous interpretation of the Schillerian Naïve) and the foreign. But a firm law—a destiny—governs it: any culture (any nation or people, that is, any community of language and of memory) can appropriate itself as such, return to itself—or rather come to itself, attain itself and establish itself—only if it has previously undergone its otherness and its foreignness. Only if it has been initially disappropriated. This means that disappropriation (difference) is original, and appropriation, as Hegel will say—and if it can take place—is its "result." Excepting this question (can appropriation, as such, occur?), we can see to what extent a logic like this resembles, almost to the point of being indistinguishable from, Logic itself—in other words, the speculative logic. This exception, however, precludes reducing Hölderlin's very singular logic simply to the dialectical procedure.

For the originary differentiation, the uprooting or the estrangement—*Unheimlichkeit* in the strict sense—is probably irreversible. At any rate, the movement of appropriation, as Hölderlin continually repeats, is what is most difficult and what holds the greatest risk. Thus, the first of the two letters to Böhlendorff specifies that "the proper [*das Eigene*] has to be learned just as well as what is foreign"—but only to add almost immediately: "The *free* use of the proper is the most difficult" (*Werke,* p. 941).

Indeed, the destiny of Greece provides a first example.

The Greeks, as Hölderlin imagines them, are natively mystical: in his terms, "sacred pathos" is innate to them; their proper element is the "fire of heaven." Beneath the measure and virtuosity, the skill of Greek art, Hölderlin sees a primitive Greece, prey to the divine and the world of the dead, subject to the Dionysian effusion or the Apollonian fulguration (he does not distinguish between them)—a Greece that is enthusiastic and sombre, dark, from being too brilliant and solar. An Oriental Greece, if you will, always tempted in the direction of what Hölderlin calls the *aorgic* in order to distinguish it from the *organic*. More violent than that of Schlegel, the Greece Hölderlin invents is finally what continues to haunt the German imaginary up to our time, and what will at any rate traverse the whole of the text of philosophy from Hegel to Heidegger, passing through Nietzsche. Moreover, if we were to translate philosophically the categories used or forged by Hölderlin—something that is always possible and necessary, although not sufficient—we would say that the proper of the Greeks is speculation itself, the transgression of the limit that Hölderlin, via Kant, thinks as the limit assigned to a human Reason that is nevertheless condemned to the "metaphysical drive." The transgression of finitude. And by the same token, one might understand, at one and the same time, why a modern tragedy could not be built around a mystical hero (such as Empedocles) desiring fusion with the One-Whole, and why it is indeed a hidden fidelity to Kant, the "Moses of our nation" (*Werke*, p. 889), as Hölderlin wrote to his brother, that will have always paralyzed the speculative temptation—impeded it and diverted it—opening up the possibility of an "other thought." This is what must be said, I believe, to do justice to the Heideggerian reading in its essential *philosophical* objective (which does not necessarily mean, for example, its political objective).

The Greece thus discovered by Hölderlin is, in short, *tragic* Greece— if the essence of the tragic is, as the *Notes* say, the monstrous coupling of god and man, the limitless becoming-one and transgression of the limit (hubris) that tragedy (a remote echo here of Aristotle) has the function of purifying.

Tragedy—that is to say, tragic *art*. For the Greeks, something foreign to which they had to apply themselves and through which they had to pass, according to the law stated above, if they were to have the least chance of appropriating what they properly were. It was therefore their destiny not only to turn away from heaven and to forget, in all faithful infidelity, the divine which was too immediately close to them, but also to organize this henceforth sober and sobered life and to maintain it within a proper measure. Hence the fact that they built an "empire of art" and excelled in heroism of reflection and calm vigor— "strong tenderness," Hölderlin says (*Werke*, p. 945), thinking of the "athletic body" described by Winckelmann—as in what the technical rigor (the *mechane*) of their poetry allows us to call "clarity of exposition" (*Werke,* p. 940). As the first letter to Böhlendorff says: "The Greeks are less masters of the holy pathos, because it was innate to them, while on the other hand, from Homer on, they are superior in the gift of representation, because this extraordinary man was soulful enough to capture for his Apollonian realm the occidental *Junonian sobriety* and thereby truly to appropriate that which is foreign" (*Werke,* p. 940).

The Greek Naïve is consequently acquired. And it is nothing that one might relate, in any way whatsoever, to something natural.

But this acquisition was also what caused the ruin of the Greeks. A poetic sketch almost contemporary with the texts to which I allude here says that, precisely because of their artistic mastery, "the native (or the natal) was left idle" and that "Greece, supreme beauty, foundered."[12] Something, then, stopped the Greek people in their movement of appropriation. Something difficult to assign, but in which is hidden, perhaps, the enigma of the impossible approximation of the proper—that is, the enigma of what Heidegger thought as the law of *Ent-fernung, é-loignement:* the approach of the distant which yet remains the distancing of the near. Or what one might think in this context as the law of *(dis)appropriation.*

Perhaps, too, it is necessary to relate this thing to what Hölderlin calls, in writing of *Oedipus Rex,* and with a word that is not accidentally taken from Kant, the "categorical turning away" of the divine: "Since the Father," the elegy *Brot und Wein* says, "turned his face from men and since mourning, with good reason, began on earth."[13] When the Greeks, in the tragic moment of their "catastrophe," forgot themselves by forgetting the god—properly the moment of the *caesura,* of the gaping or interrupting articulation around which Sophoclean tragedy is organized, but which also perhaps (dis)articulates history itself—the divine probably withdrew definitively, definitively turned about, itself forgetful and unfaithful, but as such appropriating itself in its very distancing (it is of the god's essence to be distanced—*é-loigné*) and forcing man to turn himself back toward the earth.

For since the Greek catastrophe, such is in fact the lot of Western man. *Notes to Antigone:*

12. See Chapter 3, note 10.
13. Translated by Michael Hamburger in *Poems and Fragments* (Cambridge: Cambridge University Press, 1980).

For us—given that we stand under a Zeus more properly himself, who not only *holds a limit* between this earth and the savage world of the dead, but also *forces more decisively toward the earth* the course of nature eternally hostile to man in its path toward the other world, and given that this greatly changes the essential and patriotic [*vaterländischen*] representations, and as our poetry must be patriotic, such that its material be chosen according to our view of the world, and its representations be patriotic—Greek representations vary in that their principal tendency is to be able to grasp and compose themselves (because this is where their weakness lay), whereas the principal tendency in the modes of representation of our time is to be able to strike something, to have address; for the absence of destiny—the *dusmoron*—is our weakness. (*Werke*, p. 788)

This is why Hölderlin can say that the Modern—the Hesperian or Western—is the inverse of the Ancient, of the Oriental. What is proper to us is sobriety, clarity of exposition. Because our reign is that of finitude. Also of slow death, if one thinks of what the modern tragic must be ("For this is what constitutes the tragic for us, that we leave quietly the realm of the living . . . and not that, consumed in flames, we atone for the flame that we were not able to subdue"—*Werke*, p. 941); slow death, or "wandering under the unthinkable" (*Werke*, p. 785), as in *Oedipus at Colonus* or the end of *Antigone*. Dereliction and madness, not a brute, physical death; the mind touched, and not the body.

But this proper, even should it escape a tragic catastrophe, is still the farthest thing away for us—the most near/distant. On the other hand, what we excel in is "sacred pathos," the desire for an infinite and mystical transgression: the "Sentimental," in the strongest sense of the word, the one given to it by Schiller, or "speculation," in the sense of Idealism. But to no less an extent, subjective Poetry, in the Romantic sense.

This is why, if we must undergo the experience of this foreign element (go to Bordeaux, for example: cross France "prey to patriotic incertitude and hunger"),[14] nothing, in what is accessible to us of the Greeks—that is, nothing in their art—can be of any help to us whatsoever. Because they never appropriated what was their proper, nothing of the Greek being—irretrievably buried, lost, forgotten—could ever be recovered. *The Greeks' proper is inimitable because it never took place.* At the very most it is possible to catch a glimpse of it, or even perhaps deduce it from its opposite—art. And then introduce it, *après*

14. In a letter to Casimir Ulrich Böhlendorff of autumn 1802, Hölderlin speaks of the men and women of southern France who have grown up "in the anxiety of patriotic uncertainty and hunger" (*Werke*, p. 945).—*Editor*

coup, into this art. Hence the work of *translation* (and I am thinking more particularly of the translation of *Antigone,* conceived as the most Greek of Sophocles' tragedies), which consists in making the Greek text say what it said endlessly *without ever saying it.* Which consists, then, in repeating the unuttered of this text's very utterance.

But the fact that the proper being of the Greeks should be lost, and consequently inimitable (what the Nietzsche of *The Birth of Tragedy,* as we can see, will not have heard), does not in the least mean that we might imitate what *remains* to us of the Greeks—that is, their art, that by which they tend to be, in all impropriety and strangeness in relation to themselves, near to what is for us, still so distantly, proper. Greek art is inimitable *because it is an art* and because the sobriety that it indicates to us is, or should be, nature for us. Our nature (sobriety) can no more take its bearing from their culture than our culture (sacred pathos) can take its bearing from their nature—which was never carried into effect.

In the chiasmic structure that shapes history, then, there is no longer any place, anywhere, for an "imitation of Antiquity." "It is probably not allowed for us," says the first letter to Böhlendorff, "to have with the Greeks anything *identical*" (*Werke,* p. 940).

Greece will have been, for Hölderlin, this inimitable. Not from an excess of grandeur—but from a lack of proper being. It will have been, therefore, this vertiginous threat: a people, a culture, constantly showing itself as inaccessible to itself. The tragic as such, if it is true that the tragic begins with the ruin of the imitable and the disappearance of models.

5

Diderot: Paradox and Mimesis

Who states the paradox?

Who, in general, states, is able to state a paradox? Who or what is the *subject* of a paradox?

But also, because the word has given the title: Who, in this particular text attributed to Diderot, in "Paradoxe sur le comédien," states the paradox? Not: Who declares its law or certifies its exactitude and truth? But very simply: Who is the author of it and responsible for it? Who takes, or can take, the responsibility for saying: "I am the subject of this statement, a paradox"?[1]

*

Toward the end of Diderot's text, toward the end of this *dialogue* which is the "Paradoxe sur le comédien," the two antagonists, whom in principle we know only by the indications "First" and "Second," appear to have almost exhausted their arguments. More precisely, their discussion, that false oratorical joust dominated by the First, ends by turning to the latter's advantage. The Second, who until then, it seems, could hardly do more than cue his partner, but who in reality has constantly forced him to speak, now proposes a test. He says, in essence: You have just developed at length a *theory* on the art of the actor which offends common sense, and to which, as you see, I cannot subscribe; let us move on to the *theater*, and see if we can verify it.

1. As in almost every case in this volume, *énoncer* is translated as "to state," and "*énoncé*" as "statement." It should be noted, however, that "to state" or "statement" bears a propositional or declaratory connotation that is not necessarily conveyed in the French terms, particularly as they are defined in linguistics. "To utter" and "utterance" would therefore also be appropriate alternatives in many cases, though they have not been used here for reasons of consistency.—*Editor*

Thus, the dialogue proper is interrupted (to resume only in extremis). As the antagonists agree to pass on to the theater, it passes to *narrative*.

This is how the episode is presented:

> Our two interlocutors went to the playhouse, but as there were no places to be had they turned off to the Tuileries. They walked for some time in silence. They seemed to have forgotten that they were together, and each talked to himself as if he were alone, the one out loud, the other so low that he could not be heard, only at intervals letting out words, isolated but distinct, from which it was easy to guess that he did not hold himself defeated.
>
> The ideas of the man with the paradox are the only ones of which I can give an account, and here they are, disconnected as they must be when one omits in a soliloquy the intermediate parts which serve to hang it together. He said: . . .[2]

There follows, indeed, a long "soliloquy" that is interrupted by the narrator's incidental remarks and that turns quickly, conforming to a practice long claimed by Diderot, into a true "interior dialogue." But it is an interior dialogue that is spoken "aloud." Thus, it fits into the whole of the dialogue as its exact counterpart, *en abyme;* in a manner so perfect that the First himself will be taken into the illusion and imagine that he has "continued to dispute," when in reality he has both asked the questions and answered them—and the Second has not listened but only dreamed.

This movement is clearly not without interest, and even if it is not very new or very "modern," it probably merits study. But this is not what prompts me to recall the episode.

The real reason (I will put it in the form of a question) is this: Why is the subject who takes charge of the narrative here, and exhibits himself as such, in the first person, able to say that "the ideas of the man with the paradox are the only ones of which I can give an account"? Is it simply because it has just been mentioned—in an initial narrative sequence, it will be noted, assumed by an impersonal subject, a neutral voice, ("from which *it* was easy to guess . . .")—that the First's soliloquy or monologue is spoken "aloud," and that the narrator, having heard it from his position as witness, is able to record his words? Or is

2. The translation of "Paradoxe sur le comédien" cited here is found in Diderot, *"The Paradox of Acting" and "Masks or Faces?"* ed. Wilson Follett (New York: Hill and Wang, 1957), p. 65. All subsequent page references given in the text are to this edition.

it because the I-narrator confesses in this manner to being the First, thus capable only of reporting his own thoughts, and also obliged to forgo the reconstruction of the other's discourse—of which, at any rate, he has heard at best only snatches?

Nothing, absolutely nothing, allows us to decide.

Both versions are plausible: the first, according to the rules of "verisimilitude" and the conventional logic of narrative; the second, because since the beginning of the dialogue, the author, the text's enunciating subject (necessarily withdrawn from the text, "apocryphal," as Plato would say, because we are dealing with a pure dialogue), has constantly given indications meant to identify him as the First. Or the inverse. On two occasions, in any case, the First has reminded his interlocutor (anonymous, even if some critics have identified him with d'Alembert) that he is the author of *Père de famille;* twice he has referred his interlocutor to his *Salons* for further details concerning the "speculative principles" of his aesthetic; and he has not even refrained from designating himself by name in reporting by way of anecdote that he once found himself accosted by Sedaine with "Ah! Monsieur Diderot, you are splendid!" ("Paradox," p. 34).

The author—Diderot—thus occupies two places simultaneously (that is, in the same text). And two incompatible places. He is the First, one of the two interlocutors. Or at least he has presented himself as such. But he is also the one who, putting himself overtly in the position of author or general enunciator, sets himself apart from the First, or is able, if only as a game, to set himself apart from him and to constitute him as a character.

It goes without saying that a simple break in the form of exposition does not explain this double position, this contradictory double status. The fact that the text passes from a dialogic (or mimetic) mode to a narrative mode (or diagetic—simple or mixed) does not oblige the enunciator of the first mode—who must then *appear, show himself* in one manner or another, as again Plato would say, but who could perfectly well continue to identify himself as one of the two speakers—to take that sort of "step back" that leads him to deal with the two antagonists from an equal distance, in the third person. No *formal* law can impose or justify such a gesture. Nothing, for example, prohibits the author from openly acknowledging his identity when he passes to direct enunciation of the narrative. It would have sufficed to cast the narrative in the first person from its beginning: We went to the theater, but as there were no places to be had we turned off to the Tuileries . . .

We are dealing, then, not with a phenomenon of exposition but with one of *enunciation*. Moreover, the effect produced is disturbing and dizzying in a way that is certainly different from that of the dialogue's return *en abyme* within the soliloquy, which follows in such a perfectly controlled and virtuoso manner, and which is undoubtedly only a consequence (if it is not simply a means of "arresting the vertigo").

The intrusion of the "I," in other words, far from signifying the author's appropriation or mastering reappropriation of the text, far from being a "signature" effect or the effect of what I have elsewhere called *autography*,[3] represents rather the moment in which the status of the text (the entire book) vacillates. This is why it unsettles the thesis itself. Who states the paradox? Who is its guarantor? At the same time excluded and included, inside and outside; at the same time himself and the other (or each time, one must suppose, himself as an other—hence the dialogic constraint, even in the monologue). The enunciating subject occupies in reality no place, he is unassignable: nothing or no one. A discursive stance [*instance*] that is unstable and without status—all the more exterior to the statement for whose enunciation it is responsible in that it finds itself reimplicated in it and subject to what from that moment can no longer be considered its own enunciation. The author's "apocraphy" here is even more formidable than what Plato feared.

One might say that we are simply dealing with the fact of enunciation in general. This is quite possible, but it is not specifically what interests me here. I am trying to work at another question, of more limited scope. It would take the following form: Would not this impossible position of the subject or the author be the effect of what he himself (which is to say?) is charged with stating, namely a paradox? Would not a certain logic inherent in the paradox necessarily carry the enunciation of any paradox beyond itself, sweep it away in a vertiginous movement that would finally engulf, endlessly and irremediably, its subject?

In other words, would not the enunciation of a paradox involve, beyond what it has the power to control, a paradox of enunciation?

*

What, then, is a "paradox"? And what is its logic?

Though Diderot, after the fashion of his epoch (and in particular—this is hardly astonishing—of Rousseau), makes abundant use of the word, he is undoubtedly not the one to whom we should look for an

3. See "The Echo of the Subject."

answer, at least not directly. Most of the time, in fact, he follows the received, traditional meaning of the term. The definition given in the *Encyclopédie,* as Yvon Belaval has indicated, offers a fairly good model: "It is a proposition that appears absurd because it contradicts received opinions, but which, nonetheless, is fundamentally true, or is at least able to take on an air of truth."[4]

Yet on another level, Diderot always held another conception of paradox (the classical commentaries have clearly established this point). In referring to the "Rêve de d'Alembert," for example, in which one finds, among others, the very thesis of the "Paradox," he speaks of "madness" and "extravagance." Not apologetically, but rather in making these the sign or index of the greatest philosophical profundity, of wisdom itself: "It is not possible to be more profound and more mad," he says.[5] Or again: "This is the greatest extravagance and at the same time the most profound philosophy."[6] The paradox is thus not only a contradicting or surprising opinion (out of the ordinary and shocking). It implies a passing to the extreme, a sort of "maximization," as is said in logic nowadays. It is in reality a hyperbolic movement by which the equivalence of contraries is established (probably without ever *establishing* itself)—the contraries themselves pushed to the extreme, in principle infinite, of contrariety. This is why the formula for the paradox is always that of the double superlative: the more mad it is, the more wise it is; the maddest is the wisest. Paradox is defined by the infinite exchange, or the hyperbolic identity, of contraries.

Elsewhere, in regard to Hölderlin, for whom this will be (whether or not we are dealing here with an influence)[7] the privileged mode of thinking, particularly in his theory of theater and tragedy, I have proposed to call such paradoxical logic, for convenience, *hyperbological.* It is not just devious or tortured, as we see, but properly abyssal—to the

---

4. Cited by Yvon Belaval in *L'esthétique sans paradoxe de Diderot* (Paris: Gallimard, 1949), p. 168.

5. Cited in Belaval, *L'esthétique,* p. 168.

6. Ibid.

7. See Chapters 3 and 4. In any case, we know from Roland Mortier's famous work *Diderot en Allemagne* (Paris: Presses Universitaires de France, 1954), that the manuscript of the "Paradox" had circulated in Germany during the last decade of the eighteenth century (thus, well before its publication in France in 1820), and that it almost certainly passed through the hands of Goethe and Schiller. From this point of view, it would not be absurd to think that something could have reached Hölderlin—by means, for example (one among others) of Schiller's long note on the theater in the first part of his essay "Grace and Dignity."

point of implicating itself in its own definition. And this is probably what explains the fact that nothing is able to stop the hyperbological in this movement by which it coils indefinitely about itself and envelops itself. Nothing can hold it, and in particular no dialectical operation, despite its strange proximity to speculative logic (the incessant, or at least regular, alteration of the same, the passage into the opposed or contrary, etc.). The hyperbological is unceasing, endless. Which also means: without resolution.

But these preliminaries aside, with what paradox are we dealing in "Paradoxe sur le comédien"?

Two questions should be distinguished.

There is first of all the fact that the very thesis of the "Paradox"—the so-called thesis of the insensibility of the actor, or of the artist in general—is in flagrant contradiction to what is apparently one of Diderot's most constant themes, and in particular to the thesis complacently developed in the second of the "Entretiens sur le fils naturel" (another important component of Diderot's dramatic aesthetics, along with the "Discours sur la poésie dramatique"). This is the well-known thesis concerning enthusiasm. One will remember: "Poets, actors, musicians, painters, singers of the first order, great dancers, tender lovers, the true devout, this whole enthusiastic and passionate troop feels vividly, and does little reflecting."[8] The "Paradox," however, affirms exactly the opposite: "Great poets, great actors, and I may add, all great imitators of nature, whoever they may be, beings gifted with fine imagination, with broad judgment, a fine tact, and sure taste, are the least sensitive of all creatures" ("Paradox," pp. 17–18).

From here it is a short step to conclude that the paradox (of the "Paradox") is reducible to this contradiction—a step taken, I believe, by most critics, whose major concern appears to be resolving such a contradiction and, for example, reconstituting, according to the classical presuppositions of an "organicist" reading (committed to the homogeneity and the finality of a work), an "aesthetic without paradox."[9]

I do not at all want to claim that such a problem does not exist—or even that one can entirely avoid this kind of reading. But I want to note that there exists also, in itself, the thesis of the "Paradox"—namely the paradox.

---

8. "Entretiens sur le fils naturel," in Diderot, *Oeuvres*, ed. André Billy (Paris: Gallimard, 1951), p. 1252.

9. Lacoue-Labarthe's immediate reference here is Belaval, *L'esthétique sans paradoxe de Diderot.—Editor*

But in what way is the paradox, in the "Paradox," paradoxical? Is it because it runs up against a prevalent opinion about actors (and prevalent among actors themselves—fortunately not all of them), contesting basically the old myth of the actor's identification with the character he plays? Or is it first of all, and more essentially, because it obeys this hyperbologic that I have just attempted to describe? We need to take a closer look.

How, then, in the "Paradox," does the paradox set itself in place?

It appears quickly, as early as what one might isolate as the second sequence of the text. The First has indicated his reluctance to state his feelings about a pamphlet by a certain Sticoti, which serves here as a pretext: "Garrick ou les acteurs anglais" (this provides the occasion, moreover, for an "overture" that is also paradoxical; I lack the space to consider it here, but would note that in it we see the First play at his self-love and the esteem given to him in a way that follows the most traditional agonistic relation). But he ends finally, under pressure from the Second, by resolving to speak: the work of Sticoti is a bad work and a useless work: "A great dramatic artist will not be a bit the better, a poor actor not a bit the less inefficient for reading it" ("Paradox," p. 12).

The demonstration then begins. It is a first long development (where everything, practically, will have already been said) leading to the following statement, which might be considered as one of the two or three major statements of the paradox itself:

> But the important point on which your author and I are entirely at variance concerns the qualities above all necessary to a great actor. In my view, he must have a great deal of judgment. He must have in himself an unmoved and disinterested onlooker [one could not be, in fact, more paradoxical, at least in the terms chosen]. He must have, consequently, penetration and no sensibility, the art of imitating everything, or, which comes to the same thing, the same aptitude for every sort of character and part. ("Paradox," p. 14)

But this statement itself is only a conclusion. It draws the consequences from two propositions that appeared in the course of the exposition. The first appeared immediately: "It is nature which bestows personal qualities—appearance, voice, judgment, tact. It is the study of the great models, the knowledge of the human heart, the habit of society, earnest work, experience and acquaintance with the theater, which perfect the gifts of nature" ("Paradox," p. 12). The second proposition, a little further on, simply backs up the first with an argument that is properly aesthetic and dramaturgical—or, if one may risk the word, "dramatological": "How should nature without art make a great actor when nothing happens on the stage as it happens in nature, and when dramatic poems are all composed after a fixed system of principles?" ("Paradox," p. 13).

What is involved in this series of propositions?

The first states that if "it is nature which bestows personal qualities," it is study, work, experience, apprenticeship, the practice of the profession—in short, everything that can be acquired and that can be encompassed by the broadest conception of art—"that perfects the gifts of nature."

It is not too difficult to detect here an echo, however faint, of the Aristotelian definition of *mimesis,* the relation between art and nature. That is, an echo of Aristotle's fundamental mimetology, or we should perhaps say his "onto-mimetology"—"Aristotle" being here not the name of a doctrine, but the site of a generative schema, a matrix, and the index of a historico-theoretical constraint.

I am referring, obviously, to the famous passage in the *Physics,* which Jean Beaufret has appropriately used to support his analysis of Hölderlin's dramatology.[10] Aristotle says first (194a) that in general "art imitates nature": *he tekhne mimeitai ten phusin.* Then, a little further on (199a), he specifies the general relation of *mimesis:* "On the one hand, *techne* carries to its end [accomplishes, perfects, *epitelei*] what *phusis* is incapable of effecting [*apergasasthai*]; on the other hand, it imitates." There are thus two forms of mimesis. First, a restricted form, which is the reproduction, the copy, the reduplication of what is given (already worked, effected, presented by nature). And this first meaning of the term is of course found in Diderot (as in everyone). In any case it grounds what has been called, perhaps a bit hastily, Diderot's "naturalism."

Then there is a general mimesis, which reproduces nothing given (which thus re-produces nothing at all), but which *supplements* a certain deficiency in nature, its incapacity to do everything, organize everything, make everything its work—*produce* everything.[11] It is a

10. See Beaufret, "Hölderlin et Sophocle," in Hölderlin, *Remarques sur Oedipe, remarques sur Antigone* (Paris: Union Générale d'Editions, 1963), p. 8.

11. The English verb "supplement" suggests a compensating for a deficiency, or a completing. It does not quite capture the French *suppléer,* which can bear the sense of the

productive mimesis, that is, an imitation of *phusis* as a productive force, or as *poiesis*. It accomplishes, carries out, *finishes* natural production as such. "Perfects it," Diderot says. This is why, in the "Paradox" itself, Diderot can speak of "the magic of art," or elsewhere—and all the more easily in that he draws upon a subjective conception of being and of nature, in perfect conformity with the metaphysics of the Moderns—reverse the traditional relationship between art and nature and decree the first, in its very function of supplementation, superior to the second. We know what consequences this will have in the theory of genius and in that of the "ideal model," which guide both his dramatic aesthetics and his pictorial aesthetics.

In the second proposition, however, Diderot introduces another kind of consideration. He asks, in essence, how art (dramatic art and the art of the actor) could do anything other than supplement nature, since there is a stage, a theater, a representation—and rules or "principles" for that representation (a literary or dramatic "convention," he will specify later when evoking Aeschylus: "a protocol three thousand years old"—"Paradox," p. 22).

But what does this argument signify, if not, apparently at least, that Diderot justifies the necessary supplementarity of art (that is, general mimesis) by resorting to the restricted concept of mimesis, simple reproduction or representation: "Nothing happens on stage as it happens in nature"?

It is true that on the one hand this comes down to positing that there is never any pure and simple *imitation*. The argument is of the following kind, and it is an old one: since the stage is in any case not life, it is difficult to see how mere re-presentation, and a simple reliance on the natural, could produce art. It is an uncompromising critique of the *naïve* conception of art: of art as native and natural, immediate and spontaneous (taking "naïve" in the strict sense of the term, thinking of Schiller and a whole tradition of German aesthetics that will find in these analyses certain resources).

But on the other hand, and this is of quite another importance, this argument comes down in reality to positing that it is essentially the theater—the fact of theater or theatricality—which accounts for the general function of supplementation that devolves to art. I believe one

English term, or suggest the notion of replacing or substitution. "Supplement" is used here in order to retain the echo of Jacques Derrida's development of the notion of *supplément. —Editor* might even argue (to continue following my guiding thread here) that fundamental mimetology is perhaps only a projection, or an extrapolation, of the conditions proper to dramatic mimesis. At the very least, and because it represents the function (or even the fact) of supplementation in general—the function, or the fact, of *substitution*—it is necessary to think that the theater exemplifies general mimesis.

Theatrical mimesis, in other words, provides the model for general mimesis. Art, since it substitutes for nature, since it replaces it and carries out the poietic process that constitutes its essence, always produces a theater, a representation. That is to say, *another presentation*—or the presentation of *something other,* which was not yet there, given, or present.

Hence the privileged role Aristotle accords to the theater, and the exorbitant role Diderot accords to the actor, the great actor. The latter is the artist par excellence, superior even to the poet, and barely inferior, for being confined to the stage or enclosed in this or that specific theater, to the courtier—that player in the "theater of the world," or that great social actor.

For Diderot, following a movement that can also be found in Hölderlin (though Diderot perhaps inaugurates it), actually moves back behind Aristotle, and constantly has recourse, whether he knows it or not, to a more ancient, more archaic determination of mimesis; that same determination, for example, that prompts, at the beginning of the *Republic,* the Platonic condemnation of the dramatic poet-actor, the mimetician as such, and his philosophic-ritual expulsion.

We have arrived at the paradox itself.

Let us reread: "In my view he [the actor] must have a great deal of judgment. He must have in himself an unmoved and disinterested onlooker. He must have, consequently, penetration and no sensibility, the art of imitating everything, or, which comes to the same thing, the same aptitude for every sort of character and part."

"No sensibility?" is the astonished reply of the Second, who can hardly believe his ears. And in general, the paradox is reduced to this lapidary verdict—as if the paradox had no other purpose than the redistribution of the requisite qualities of the actor, when in fact it is concerned precisely with the absence of any *proper* quality in one who intends to take up (or proves suited for) representation and production. The logic of the statement is perfectly clear, and the rest simply follows: the requirements of judgment, coldness, penetration; the systematic valorization of "artistic" or nonnatural qualities (intelligence, work, technical skill in construction); the assignment to the actor himself of the role of spectator; and eventually, as we know, the affirmed superiority (in the physiological register) of the brain over the diaphragm, or of the center over the periphery; or finally even (in the metaphysical order) the privilege accorded to the intelligible and to ideality, at the expense of the sensible and of sensibility—all of this is merely a consequence. The paradox itself bears upon the art of "imitating everything," the "equal aptitude for all sorts of characters and roles." In other words, the absence or suppression of any property [*propriété*].

Further on in his text, and at least twice, Diderot will attempt another formulation of the paradox. Each time the statement of the paradox will follow rigorously the same structure:

> Your fiery, extravagant, sensitive fellow, is forever on stage: he acts the play, but he gets nothing out of it. It is in him that the man of genius finds his model. Great poets, great actors [we are already familiar with this proposition], and, I may add, all great imitators of nature, whoever they might be, beings gifted with fine imagination, with broad judgment, a fine tact, a sure taste, are the least sensitive of all creatures. *They are equally apt at too many things* [emphasis added], too busy with observing, considering and imitating, to have their inmost hearts affected with any liveliness. ("Paradox," pp. 17–18)

Or:

> The man of sensibility is too much at the mercy of his diaphragm to be a great king, a great politician, a great magistrate, a just man, or a close observer, and, consequently, a sublime imitator of nature—*unless, indeed, he can forget himself, distract himself from himself* [emphasis added], and, with the aid of a strong imagination, make for himself certain shapes which serve him for models, and on which he keeps his attention fixed with the aid of a tenacious memory. Only then it is not his own self that is concerned; it is another's mind and will that master him. ("Paradox," p. 56)

The paradox lies, then, in the following: in order to do everything, to imitate everything—in order to (re)present or (re)produce everything, in the strongest sense of these terms—one must oneself be nothing, have nothing *proper* to oneself except an "equal aptitude" for all sorts of things, roles, characters, functions, and so on. The paradox states a *law of impropriety*, which is also the very law of mimesis: only the "man without qualities," the being without properties or specific-ity, the subjectless subject (absent from himself, distracted from himself, deprived of self) is able to present or produce in general. Plato, in his way, knew this very well: the mimeticians are the worst possible breed because they are no one, pure mask or pure hypocrisy, and as such unassignable, unidentifiable, impossible to place in a determined class or to fix in a function that would be proper to them and would find its place in a just distribution of tasks.

Except for an inversion of values, Diderot is saying exactly the same thing as Plato:

> *The Second:* According to you the great actor is everything and nothing.
> *The First:* Perhaps it is just because he is nothing that he is before all everything. His own particular form never interferes with the shapes he assumes. ("Paradox," p. 41)

Or again: "A great actor is neither a pianoforte nor a harp, nor a spinnet, nor a violon, nor a violoncello; *he has no pitch proper to him* [emphasis added]; he takes the pitch and the tone fit for his part of the score, and he can take up any. I put a high value on the talent of a great actor: he is a rare being—as rare as, and perhaps greater than, a poet" ("Paradox," p. 46).

Let us go back now and reconstruct the argument. "It is nature," Diderot said at the start, "that gives the qualities of the person"; it is art "that perfects the gift of nature." But what do we find at the conclusion? This: the *gift of nature* is the *gift of impropriety,* the *gift of being nothing,* even, we might say, *the gift of nothing.* I would add, to bring out what lies in this "nothing," the gift of *the thing itself.* By this I mean nature's gift of itself, not as something already there, or already present—"natured," as one would have said at the time—but more essentially, as pure and ungraspable poiesis (in withdrawal, and always withdrawn in its presence): a productive or formative force, energy in the strict sense, the perpetual movement of presentation.

The natural gift—the gift of nature—is consequently the *poietic gift.* Or, what is the same thing, *the gift of mimesis:* in effect, a gift of nothing (in any case, of nothing that is already present or already *given*). A gift of nothing, or of nothing other than the "aptitude" for presenting, that is, for substituting for nature itself; a gift for "doing" nature, in order to supplement its incapacity and carry out or effect, with the aid of its force and the power proper to it, what it cannot implement—that for which its energy alone cannot suffice.

Art is this gift. Diderot will call it "genius"—and the latter, as opposed to a gift that one "more or less" acquires, like taste, he will define as "belonging properly to nature." A pure gift in which nature gives itself up and offers itself in its most secret essence and intimacy, in the very source of its energy, as the nothing it is once this energy is spent and has passed into the given. Pure gift, in other words, because it is the gift of the thing or of Being, of the secret and of the withdrawn, of the unassignable and the unrecognizable as such, to which nothing from our end, not even gratitude, could respond: because it is nothing, the thing of no economy and no exchange.

This is why the artist, the subject of this gift (which is not the gift of any property or quality) is not truly a subject: he is a subject that is a nonsubject or subjectless, and also an infinitely multiplied, plural subject, since the gift of nothing is equally the gift of everything—the gift of impropriety is the gift for a general appropriation and presentation. For here, finally, is the paradox, that hyperbolical exchange between nothing and everything, between impropriety and appropriation, between the subject's absence and its multiplication and proliferation: the more the artist (the actor) *is* nothing, the more he can be everything. "An equal aptitude for all sorts of characters."

By consequence—and in a certain way, this is where I've been heading—the logic of the paradox, the hyperbologic, is nothing other than the very logic of mimesis. That is to say, if I may again be allowed the formulation, *mimetologic.*

This means simply that the logical matrix of the paradox is the very structure of mimesis. In general. It is not by chance that the law of mimesis should be enunciated, and should never be enunciated in anything but, the form of a paradox. But neither is it by chance, inversely, that the logic of paradox is always a logic of *semblance,* articulated around the division between appearance and reality, presence and absence, the same and the other, or identity and difference. This is the division that grounds (and that constantly unsteadies) mimesis. At whatever level one takes it—in the copy or the reproduction, the art of the actor, mimetism, disguise, dialogic writing—the rule is always the same: the more it resembles, the more it differs. The same, in its sameness, is the other itself, which in turn cannot be called "itself," and so on infinitely . . .

Hence the disquiet to which mimesis gives rise (and in Diderot first of all: I will come back to this point). One can escape from it through admiration or wonder, with the usual "It's so real!"—which simply covers over the alteration. Just as one is easily rid of the obscure discomfort provoked by the paradox by invariably saying that it is "brilliant." One can also condemn in a single gesture the whole crowd—people of the theater and dealers in paradox, artists and "sophists"—out of disquiet before this disquiet. But where is the disquiet itself born, if not from this demonic or daemonic marvel of the semblance (always dissimilar, and all the more semblant the more it is dissimilar), of semblance *and* truth, of *mimesis* and *aletheia*, of re-presentation *and* presentation: from the exchange, without end and without any possible halt, between same and other, withdrawal *and* giving, distancing *and* approximation?

*

I will leave this question for now. It would lead us too far afield if we were to develop it further, and moreover it does not belong to Diderot (although it certainly belongs to the tradition that Diderot paradoxically opened—in Germany).

What pertains to Diderot, on the other hand, and remains to be treated now, is the question of sensibility. Or the question of enthusiasm—in the "Paradox," the two terms are nearly equivalent. The problem, as we know, turns upon a contradiction: Why would Diderot reject what he previously appeared to defend, and which is nothing other—we are always told—than a theory of inspiration?

Here again it is necessary to read closely, because beneath the contradiction, there is perhaps a (paradoxical) retreat on the part of Diderot with regard to the very thesis of the paradox (and of the "Paradox").

First of all, one will notice that throughout the "Paradox" there is not a single description of the work of the actor that does not give a place, and a most rightful place, to inspiration. In other words, to a certain form of possession.

I will take the first example that presents itself:

> What acting was ever more perfect than Clairon's? Nevertheless follow her, study her, and you will find that at the sixth performance of a given part she has every detail of her acting by heart, just as much as every word of her part. Doubtless she has imagined a model, and to conform to this model has been her first thought; doubtless she has conceived the highest, the greatest, the most perfect model her imagination could compass. This model, however, which she has borrowed from history, or created as some vast spectre in her own mind, is not herself . . . When, by

dint of hard work, she has got as near as she can to this idea, the thing is done; to preserve the same nearness is a mere matter of memory and practice. If you were with her while she studied her part, how many times you would cry out: "That is right!" and how many times she would answer: "You are wrong!" Just so a friend of Le Quesnoy's once cried, catching him by the arm: "Stop! you will make it worse by bettering it— you will spoil the whole thing!" "What I have done," replied the artist, panting with exertion, "you have seen; what I have got hold of and what I mean to carry out to the very end you cannot see."

I have no doubt that Clairon goes through just the same struggles as Le Quesnoy in her first attempts at a part; but once the struggle is over, once she has reached the height she has given to her spectre, she has herself well in hand, she repeats her effort without emotion. As it will happen in dreams, her head touches the clouds, her hands stretch to grasp the horizon on both sides. ("Paradox," pp. 15–16)

This torment, this struggle, this panting, all this *work* to construct the phantom (and almost give birth to it), to elaborate outside oneself—as an other—this mannequin that one can then inhabit in perfect security and confidence, in perfect mastery: it all results from being possessed or from a visitation ("what I have got hold of . . . you cannot see"). The actor is not in a trance (where did Diderot ever make a *serious* apology for frenzy or confuse genius with manic delirium?); rather, it is a kind of dream, a sign, as we know from the *Salon* of 1767 as well as from the "Rêve de d'Alembert," of unconscious work (or the work of the unconscious):

The First: . . . It is not in the stress of the first burst that characteristic traits come out; it is in moments of stillness and self-command; in moments entirely unexpected. Who can tell whence these traits have their being? They are a sort of inspiration. They come when the man of genius is hovering between nature and his sketch of it, and keeping a watchful eye on both. The beauty of inspiration, the chance hits of which his work is full, and of which the sudden appearance startles him, have an importance, a success, a sureness very different from that belonging to the first fling. Cool reflection must bring the fury of enthusiasm to its bearings. ("Paradox," p. 17)

Thus, nothing in inspiration is rejected, except frenzied possession. Whereas everything that appears in the form of self-possession, coolness, and mastery presupposes precisely a splitting of the self, an alteration, a being-outside-oneself; in short, alienation. Doubtless, when it is a question of execution or the actor's performance, "the extravagant creature who loses his self-control has no hold on us" ("Paradox," p. 17). But in the preparatory and creative work, in the construction of the character, things are quite different. When Clairon constructs her phantom, it "is not herself"; later, "following her memory's dream," she is able "to hear herself, see herself, judge herself, and judge also the effects she will produce. In such a vision she is double: little Clairon and the great Agrippina" ("Paradox," p. 16).

Do we have, then, a new paradox? Certainly not. Rather, a consequence of the paradox itself, and above all an attempt to master it by definitively stopping the vertigo. This is even relatively easy to demonstrate.

Who, in fact, is the "man of sensibility" the "Paradox" so continually condemns?

The answer never varies: the man of sensibility is a being who is *moved* or *affected*. Consequently, an alienated being who is carried beyond himself, but in the mode of a *passivity* or *passion*. In the realm of art, the paradigm of passion is musical enthusiasm, such as that created by the Greek theater, as the "Lettre sur les sourds et muets" forcefully reminds us; or that incarnated by Rameau's nephew (though this is more of a counter-example)—that false mimetician or abortive genius who simply *mimes the mimetician*. In the "anthropological" order, passion is of course identified with femininity: one need only turn to the "Essai sur les femmes," which is an essay on possession, delirium, hysteria, and collective mania—passivity. Or listen again to the words of the First, where we hear repeated in summary one of the most ancient of all discourses: "Think of women, again. They are miles beyond us in sensibility; there is no sort of comparison between their passion and ours. But as much as we are below them in action, so much are they below us in imitation" ("Paradox," p. 18). This does not mean that women do not imitate or that they do not undergo an alienation, a splitting, or an alteration of self. But if they imitate, if they alienate themselves, split or alter themselves, it happens only in passion and passivity, in the state of being possessed or being inhabited. Consequently, only when they are *subject*.

For this is where the distinction is made—the *decision*. This is in fact where Diderot halts the paradox and closes, for himself, what for others (and for a long time) he opens up: fundamentally, the enigmatic possibility of thinking the identity without identity of contraries. Nothing, in effect, resembles mimesis more than enthusiasm and frenzy: we are back to Plato again, who placed them together—at least this is what was thought in the tradition—and condemned them both at once. But in fact, nothing differs more from mimesis than possession. For inasmuch as it implies a subject absent from itself, without properties or qualities, a subjectless subject, a pure *no one,* mimesis is by definition (so long as one is not frightened by it in advance) *active.* Possession, on the contrary, presupposes the supposit itself or the supporting medium, the matrix or malleable matter in which the imprint is stamped. When women have genius, says Diderot in the "Essai sur les femmes," "I believe they bear a more original stamp of it than we do."[12] Possession, in other words, presupposes a subject; it is the monstrous, dangerous form of a *passive mimesis,* uncontrolled and unmanageable.

It is bad theater. The theater of life, the "comedy of the world." Let us recall: "Men who are passionate, excessive, sensitive, are on stage; they give the play." This is the aberrant spectacle of an alteration without force or energy ("Sensibility . . . is . . . that disposition which accompanies organic weakness"—"Paradox," p. 43), the spectacle of a role taken on passively—in the worst of cases, under the effect of a contagion, a sort of "epidemic disease," as Diderot says, once again, in the "Essai sur les femmes."[13] The riot, in which the social bond comes undone, is the horrible and fascinating paradigm of this last form. It is the aberrant spectacle of madness: "In the great play, the play of the world to which I am constantly returning, the stage is held by the fiery souls and the pit is filled with men of genius. The actors are in other words madmen; the spectators, whose business it is to copy their madness, are sages" ("Paradox," p. 18).

*

All evidence indicates that quite a bit is at stake here, and that the stakes are moral. The real matter lying beneath the description of the threat of madness is an ethics: an ethics of wisdom. That is to say, of sovereignty. The impassive genius described by Bordeu in "Le Rêve de d'Alembert," in strictly identical terms, "will rule himself and all that surrounds him. He will not fear death."[14] In the "Paradox," the figure of the great courtier will incarnate this sovereign genius. A few years later, it will be the figure of Seneca.

12. "Essai sur les femmes," *Oeuvres,* p. 988.
13. Ibid., p. 984.
14. "Le Rêve de d'Alembert," *Oeuvres,* p. 955.

But there is also a politics involved: that is, the "social function" of the theater.

Against the Platonic tradition, against the Socratic (or, in this case, Rousseauistic) utopia of a social transparency founded on "subjective" or functional appropriation and economy (or, what is the same thing, on the rejection of mimesis as an uncontrolled alteration, an unmasterable disappropriation), Didero *plays* the theater: a second theater within the theater of the world, a re-theatricalization of the "comedy of the world." Diderot plays the strategy of mimesis—implying, as we know, that a *decision* would be possible in mimesis. The gesture is absolutely classical. The active, virile, formative, properly artistic or poietic mimesis (deliberate and voluntary alienation, originating from the gift of nature, and presupposing no preliminary subject according to the very logic of paradox) is played *against* passive mimesis: the role that is taken on involuntarily, dispossession (or possession)—an alienation all the more alienating in that it occurs constantly from the basis of the subject as a material support.

In other words, Diderot plays the strategy of the renunciation of the subject, and consequently the *catharsis* of passion. This passion, as would be easy to show, is nothing other than mimetic passivity itself: *pity* or sympathy, compassion, which Diderot, like Rousseau, takes for the first and most primitive moral and social aptitude (it is identification, "the aping of the organs"). Or it is *terror*, which is nothing but the reverse or obverse of the former, and which is born from the fright created by the mimetic epidemic or contagion, that is to say, the panic movement that is the dissolution of the social bond.

In summary, it is a question of *converting* mimesis. With regard to Aristotle—there is hardly any need to insist on this—one can see that there is still absolute fidelity.

The "Paradox" is probably a response to the "Lettre à d'Alembert sur les spectacles." Rousseau had repeated the old condemnation of mimesis, the old Platonic (then Christian) gesture of exorcism: "What is the actor's talent? The art of disguising oneself, of assuming a character other than one's own, of appearing different from what one is, of becoming deliberately impassioned, of saying something other than what one thinks as naturally as if one actually thought it, and of finally forgetting one's own place by taking that of the other." [15]

15. Jean-Jacques Rousseau, *Lettre à M. d'Alembert sur son article "Genève"* (Paris: Garnier-Flammarion, 1967), p. 163.

The "Paradox," then, is to be in praise of the actor. And this—*despite everything,* paradoxical—inasmuch as Diderot will seek in mimesis the remedy for mimesis: "It has been said that actors have no character, because in playing all characters they lose that which nature gave them, and they become false just as the doctor, the surgeon, and the butcher, become hardened. I fancy that here the cause is confounded with the effect and that they are fit to play all characters because they have none" ("Paradox," p. 48).

*

To have no character, to be no one—or everyone. Who can know this? And who, above all, can say it? Who, for example, could have written to one who was once an actor, "I too know how to alienate myself, a talent without which one can do nothing of value"? [16]

Who, consequently, will have enunciated the paradox?

I have no answer to that question, no more than anyone else. I do not believe, for example, that we can simply say: it is he, it is Diderot who states the paradox—even if we recognize his prodigious intelligence and his genius, his stylistic gifts, the liberality of his thought, the rigor of his judgments, but also his weaknesses, and his moving desire for wisdom. For something was compelling him too powerfully to renounce the subject.

But I would say that this subject that refuses or renounces itself—that risks, everything considered, this impossibility—has something to do with what we ourselves should give up calling the subject of thought, art, or literature. In the wake of the "Paradox," elsewhere, and later, this point will have begun to be understood.

16. Cited in Belaval, *L'esthétique,* p. 204.

6

Transcendence Ends in Politics

1. Against the background of work from which I propose to detach a frag-
ment, I shall here pose a question: Is any politics possible that could take into
account Heidegger's thought?

To refer in this way to Heidegger's "thought" is to recognize—in a man-
ner that is questioning, conflictual, by no means simple—the relevance of the
"question of metaphysics." But it is also, in consequence, to run the risk of
seeing invalidated (or strictly circumscribed), in each of its terms as in its
very possibility, the question of a "possible politics." In particular, nothing
guarantees that the very concept of politics *should retain any validity in this*
context whatsoever.

2. To test this question, and to have any chance of articulating it in some-
thing of a rigorous manner, it is first of all necessary to question what might
be called for the sake of economy "Heidegger's politics": What might Heideg-
ger's thought have implied politically—and in what mode (accidental or
otherwise, mediate or immediate), up to what point, with what degree of
rigor, in what political style, involving what relation with the philosophical,
etc.? What were, or were not, the political consequences of the delimitation of
metaphysics?

3. To carry out such a questioning presupposes that one take on directly—
the first stage of work that has been too carefully avoided up until now—the
question of Heidegger's political engagement in 1933. And it presupposes that
this question not be posed in an extrinsic fashion, from a "point of view" dis-
qualified in advance by the radical character of the questions posed by Hei-
degger (historical, sociological, ideological, or simply political), but rather
starting from Heidegger's thought itself. That is to say—no other vocabu-
lary is available here—that it be treated as a philosophical question. A ques-
tion itself double:

a. On what philosophical basis could the alignment in 1933 with the Nazis have been made? What was it in Heidegger's thought that made possible— or rather, did not forbid—the commitment, this political commitment?

(A first question, brought in indirectly, of general bearing: Under what conditions can the political sway the philosophical? Is there an unavoidable political overdetermination of the philosophical? And to what point is the political more powerful than the philosophical? These are perhaps among the weightiest questions in the legacy of "totalitarianism.")

b. What was, in 1933, the meaning of Heidegger's political commitment? What politics—and what concept of the political—were brought into play?

4. In this perspective, I shall attempt an analysis of the only political text that Heidegger did not disavow: the "Rectoral Address."[1] It goes without saying that this again is purely an economic measure: the "posthumous" recognition of the text lends it an incontestable privilege. But if time were not a factor, it would be appropriate to examine all of Heidegger's political proclamations (in 1933–34, but also later).

I shall attempt to show that the "Rectoral Address" stands in a direct line with the "destruction of the history of ontology"; that is to say, not within the enterprise of a de-limitation (or, even less, of deconstruction) of metaphysics, but within the project of its fundamental instauratio *or re-foundation. Heidegger's politics, in 1933, are a clear consequence of the "repetition" of the Kantian "foundation"—and thereby of the resumption of the (Greek) question of the sense of Being.*

What was it in Heidegger's thought that made possible—or more exactly, what was it in Heidegger's thought that did not forbid—the political engagement of 1933?

This, as best as I can formulate it, is the question I ask myself here, and for which I would like to be able to offer a preliminary answer or the sketch of an answer.

For it is, as everyone knows, an enormous question. In itself. And so enormous, moreover, literally now (bearing in mind in particular the norms, that is to say the interdictions, of our philosophical practice), that in spite of appearances (and a great deal of noise) it has almost never been posed. And in any case, at least to my knowledge, never worked out in these terms.[2]

1. *Die Selbstbehauptung der deutschen Universität* (Breslau: Korn, 1935), trans. Karsten Harries as "The Self-Assertion of the German University," *Review of Metaphysics* 38 (March 1985): 470–480. Hereafter cited in the text as "Self-Assertion."

2. In France, only François Fédier has posed the question; see "Trois attaques contre Heidegger," *Critique* 234 (November 1966): 883–904.

The first task, in consequence, is to elaborate the question rigorously. First of all, however, and to prevent all risk of misunderstanding, I want to point out two things.

1. My intention here—the more so because the question seems to me in every sense formidable—will be analytic, not prosecutory. But this absolutely does not mean some sort of "neutrality" on my part; nor does it mean some submission to the ideal (if it is one) of impartiality, of abstaining from or suspending judgment. Nor do I believe—in fact, I deny—that one can adopt with respect to this "affair" a serene "historian's" posture: the time has certainly not yet come to examine things with the "required distance," and it will probably never come. Just as the moment will never come when we will be able to think of the "wound of thought" (to use Blanchot's term) as healed.[3] There is such a thing as the absolutely irreparable; and there is also, however repugnant the idea may be, such a thing as the unpardonable. Beyond the inevitable taking of a political position (and I am not unaware that it is also, as such, the universal and unrenounceable legacy of "totalitarianism"), it is a matter of a necessary ethical condemnation—even if, like me, one is ignorant of what constitutes ethics and what makes it necessary. In saying this, I do not call into question only what is coyly referred to as "the episode of '33," even though to compromise, as little or as briefly as may be, with an explicitly racist and anti-Semitic regime and ideology is already a scandal. But in saying it, I likewise call into question (and perhaps above all) the absence of any repentance and the apparently obstinate silence on the most serious point: the Holocaust.

2. To some extent, by way of consequence: the question I thus pose, concerning Heidegger, is in no way a simple historical question, but precisely a "contemporary" question.

One will recognize the famous remark: "Whoever thinks greatly must err greatly."[4] Let the error, or rather the *fault*, of Heidegger be what it may; I persist in believing that it removes absolutely nothing from the "greatness" of his thought, that is to say, from its character—today, for us—as decisive. A thought can be less than infallible and remain, as we say, "impossible to avoid." Its very fallibility, furthermore, gives us to think. This is why I persist in believing that it is also this

---

3. Maurice Blanchot, "Notre campagne clandestine," in *Textes pour Emmanuel Levinas* (Paris: Place, 1980), pp. 79–87.

4. Heidegger, *Aus der Erfahrung des Denkens* (Pfullingen: Günther Neske, 1954), p. 17.

thought itself that poses to us, out of its weaknesses, as out of its most extreme advances, the question of politics.

What is the general problem of the political? What is the origin, what are the historico-philosophical underpinnings, what are the limits or the bounds of the concept(s) of the political that we manipulate? What does the political [*le politique*],[5] in its essence, consist of? (If you prefer: Does the concept suffice today to designate what we take ourselves to be designating by the word? Can we, and at what price, at what philosophical risk—or no longer philosophical: at what risk of "thought"—still base anything, innocently or almost innocently, on the word?) And inversely, which cannot be excluded if we push to the limit certain Heideggerian questions: What is at bottom the political overdetermination of the philosophical? Up to what point is it not the political, or something political, among other things, but especially, that makes us so uneasy and continually gets in the way of the delimitation of the philosophical? Up to what point is politics not what perpetually unaccomplishes [*inaccomplir*] the philosophical, with all the consequences of a domination whose end is not in sight?

It seems to me difficult, today, to avoid such questions; and difficult not to recognize that it is Heidegger alone who allows us to pose them. As such—that is, as "limit questions"—because that is where we are today and because it would be futile to hide it from ourselves. In other words, the question I would like to put to Heidegger is itself a Heideggerian question. It is a question *of* Heidegger—by which I wonder if we must not understand: it is *Heidegger's question;* that is to say, the question which in his way, more or less openly and more or less lucidly, Heidegger did not cease to ask himself after 1933.

That is why, from where we stand now, it can take this apparently naïve form (but it was such "naïveté," it seems to me, that led the way for Hannah Arendt and, in large part, for Georges Bataille): Is there a possible "politics" that would take account of the thought of Heidegger? And it is clear that "taking account," here and from where we now stand, which evidently excludes "criticism" (even self-announced "internal" criticism), does not for all that include the least subservience. It

---

5. Lacoue-Labarthe is drawing here upon a distinction between *le politique* and *la politique* ("the political" and "politics"), which he explains in his contribution to the seminar "Politique" in *Les fins de l'homme: A partir du travail de Jacques Derrida,* ed. Jean-Luc Nancy and Philippe Lacoue-Labarthe (Paris: Galilée, 1981), pp. 493–497, and which is further developed in the "Ouverture" (written with Jean-Luc Nancy) to *Rejouer le politique* (Paris: Galilée, 1981), pp. 11–28.—*Editor*

is not a question of thinking merely "with" Heidegger; not even, like Habermas—who thought it enough to borrow the formula from Heidegger himself—of thinking "*with* Heidegger *against* Heidegger."[6] But it is perhaps simply a matter—and this is very difficult—of attempting to enter into a free relationship (a relationship, that is to say, which is unstable, divided, neither internal nor external, with no status properly defined or prescribed in advance) with, if not a respected thinker, at least a recognized thought.

So much established, I return to my initial question, that is to say, the limited question of a beginning: What was it that authorized, what did not forbid, in Heidegger's thought, the political commitment of 1933?

To pose this question, within the framework I have set out, comes down to putting two texts in relation to each other and comparing them, if indeed it is a question of two texts: the philosophical text and the political text. I understand by the latter, in a very empirical fashion, the set of addresses and proclamations, pronounced and published, which Heidegger expressly placed under the sign of political intervention. (As I have indicated, it is for reasons of economy—and solely for reasons of economy—that I restrict myself here to the Rectoral Address. That this should be the only political text that Heidegger did not disavow[7] lends it a certain privilege. But this does not disqualify all the other texts that Heidegger has attributed to inevitable "compromises." The political text, if such a thing exists autonomously, is the totality of the declarations that have been documented and preserved.[8]

What does it amount to, however, to place these two texts in relation to each other and to compare them?

It should be obvious now, the results having been what they were, that we can no longer content ourselves with saying: Heidegger put the thought and the language of *Sein und Zeit* at the service of National Socialism. Or again: Heidegger translated *Sein und Zeit* into the vocabulary of the "conservative revolution," of "national bolshevism,"

6. Jürgen Habermas, *Profils philosophiques et politiques* (Paris: Gallimard, 1974), p. 99.

7. Martin Heidegger, *Réponses et questions sur l'histoire et la politique* (Paris: Mercure de France, 1977), p. 21. As is well known, this is the text of an interview granted by Heidegger to *Der Spiegel* in 1966 and published, as he requested, after his death. The translation cited here is by David Schendler, and appeared under the title "'Only a God Can Save Us Now': An Interview with Martin Heidegger," in *Graduate Faculty Philosophy Journal* 6 (Winter 1977): 5–27.

8. Guido Schneeberger, *Nachlese zu Heidegger* (Bern, 1962).

of *völkisch* literature, and so on. To proceed in this way is clearly to provide oneself in advance with the means of breaking through, of making
the leap from the philosophical to the political—which is precisely
what is to be called in question. I admit that it is not useless to know in
what politico-linguistic domain Heidegger's philosophical discourse
moves, or what the "ideological" overdetermination is of a certain vocabulary or certain themes at work in *Sein und Zeit*. But it is still necessary to be convinced of the autonomy, in relation to the philosophical,
of such a politico-linguistic domain or such an ideology. When we
have observed that such-and-such a word is particularly marked or
such-and-such an ideological element particularly striking, what have
we proved if it turns out that this word or ideological element could
equally well, for example, take us back to Nietzsche, to Hegel, or to
Fichte? What relationship is there exactly between the philosophical
lexicon and the political (or ideological) one? Which guides or marks
the other? Or again, the other way round: If a mutation affects Heidegger's philosophical vocabulary in 1933, how are we to decide that
this mutation is due simply to the borrowing (and under what conditions?) of a political language? Lexical decipherment—to which would
have to be added also the analysis of syntax and of tone (of "style"), the
critical examination of the "genres" utilized, of circumstances, of those
addressed, of supporting media, and so on—such a decipherment is
certainly necessary, on condition however that the transcription of
philosophic-political connotations does not go without saying and is
not authorized by some unspecified historico-sociological certitude. It
is necessary, but it does not touch the essential: that is, the question of
the *philosophical tenor* of the political discourse practiced by a philosopher *in his capacity as such*. In other words, the question still remains: Is
it his philosophy or his thought which engages Heidegger in politics
(in *this* politics), and allows him to state and justify his position?

If one takes as a point of reference Heidegger's own "posthumous"
declarations, the Rectoral Address inscribes itself in the wake of the
Inaugural Lecture of 1929, "What Is Metaphysics?"[9] Not only does
Heidegger indicate that he entered politics "by way of the University"
and limited his political engagement and his philosophical responsibility to university politics, but he avows at bottom that the political discourse of 1933 says nothing other than the philosophical discourse of

9. "What Is Metaphysics?" trans. Walter Kaufmann in *Existentialism: From Dos-
toevsky to Sartre*, ed. Walter Kaufmann (New York: New American Library, 1975).

1929—or even than the philosophical discourse that precedes 1929. It is a *philosophical* discourse. I excerpt these two passages:

> In those days [he is speaking of 1930], I was still wrapped up with the problems I deal with in *Sein und Zeit* (1927) and in the writings and lectures of the following years, basic questions of thought, which are indirectly relevant to national and social problems. [The "indirectly," here, is evidently not accidental.] As a university teacher I was directly concerned with the meaning of intellectual studies and therefore with the determination of the task of the university. This effort is expressed in the title of my Rectoral Address, "The Self-Assertion of the German University." [10]

> The reason I assumed the Rectorate at all was already indicated in my 1929 Freiburg professorial inaugural address, "What Is Metaphysics?" There I said: "The various sciences are far apart and their subjects are treated in fundamentally different ways. This uncoordinate diversity of disciplines today can be held together only through the technical organization of the universities and faculties and through the practical intent of their subject matters. The rooting of intellectual disciplines in the grounds of their being has died away." [11]

And in fact, the Rectoral Address retains essentially the same language (except for an invocation of a "will to essence," on which I shall have more to say) and organizes itself in very large measure around the same central motif: "If we want to grasp the essence of science, we must first face up to this decisive question: should there still *be* science for us in the future, or should we let it drift toward a quick end? That there should be science at all, is never unconditionally necessary. But if there is to be science, and if it is to be *for* us and *through* us, under what conditions can it then truly exist?" ("Self-Assertion," p. 471).

Of course the tone is modified and Heidegger attacks the matter from another direction. I will return to this in a moment. This does not prevent the gesture, in what it indicates or in what it aims to produce, from being the same here as there: it is a foundational gesture. In 1929 as in 1933, Heidegger's philosophic-political discourse is the very discourse of the *instauratio,* in the Latin sense of renewal or recommencement, of refoundation; [12] that is to say, in the sense in which in the same period Heidegger interprets the *Critique of Pure Reason* as a

10. "'Only a God Can Save Us Now,'" p. 8.
11. Ibid., p. 7.
12. A motif frequently invoked, in Heidegger's wake, by Hannah Arendt, and refined by Emmanuel Martineau in his introduction to Rudolf Boehm, *La métaphysique d'Aristote* (Paris: Gallimard, 1976), p. 63.

Grundlegung of metaphysics (an unveiling of its "internal possibility" or a "determination of its essence"), and in which, above all, he thinks his own enterprise as a "repetition" of the Kantian foundation, as an active and transforming bringing to light (or radicalization) of its "problematic" character.[13]

As it happens one is not entirely in error, even if one is not wholly correct, in connecting this foundational gesture with the speculative institutional projects for the University of Berlin: in both cases it was a question of reorganizing the University around, or rather of replanting the University in, the foundations of all science and all knowledge— metaphysics or philosophy, in the sense of primary philosophy. The difference, however, is that metaphysics is henceforth, for Heidegger, "metaphysics of metaphysics"[14]—and primary philosophy is fundamental ontology. And the question of essence or foundation is now none other than that of the *né-ant* or *Ab-grund* (of the abyss). Thus, if there is speculation, we must still ask of what nature: whether it is not closer to Schellingian than to Hegelian speculation and whether, despite the frequent appeals (explicit or not) to *On the Essence of Human Freedom*, Schellingian speculation is not itself already (before the lectures published in 1936) on a tight rein.[15]

I leave this question hanging: it would require a very detailed examination.

In 1929 as in 1933, then, the question of the University is the question of the essence of science, because the foundation or the refoundation of the University is not itself possible except on the basis of the rigorous determination of its essence. Between 1929 and 1933, however—but Heidegger is not very talkative on this point, the context having been totally modified and Heidegger's own position having changed—the sense of this same question had been radically overturned.

It is not that this new position as rector of the University of Freiburg suddenly gives to Heidegger the power to do or to undertake what in 1929, from the place he then occupied, he had to be content to

---

13. See the introduction and the beginning of the fourth section in Martin Heidegger, *Kant and the Problem of Metaphysics,* trans. James S. Churchill (Bloomington: Indiana University Press, 1962).

14. Ibid. See also Ernst Cassirer and Martin Heidegger, *Débat sur le Kantisme et la philosophie,* ed. Pierre Aubenque (Paris: Beauchesne, 1972), p. 21.

15. It should be shown here how "Vom Wesen des Grundes" still refers more or less to Schelling for an elaboration of a problematic of freedom, which will be explicitly abandoned in 1941; see Martin Heidegger, *Schelling's Treatise on the Essence of Human Freedom,* trans. Joan Stambaugh (Athens: Ohio University Press, 1985).

suggest. He assumes this position on request (and almost, if he is to be believed, against his will), and he assumes it in due order, on the outcome of a legal election; but he owes it, as he knows perfectly well, to the change of regime and to the brutal (and illegal) deposition of his Social Democratic predecessor. Not only, furthermore, does he know it, but up to a certain point he accepts it: the corps of professors has not turned to him simply because of his reputation and his intellectual authority, but with the knowledge of his political orientation, about which he probably did not make, and in any case will never afterward make, any great mystery. In the explanations that he will reserve for *Der Spiegel,* he will maintain that the salute rendered at the end of the Rectoral Address, four months after Hitler's accession to power, to the "grandeur" and the "magnificence" of this "departure" (or, in Granel's translation, "to the nobility and grandeur of this irruption") [16] then entirely reflected his "conviction"; he will speak also of his hope of capturing "whatever constructive forces were still alive [in order] to head off what was coming"; [17] and just as after his resignation he will still speak of the "internal truth" and the "grandeur" of National Socialism. So there is no reason to impute to tactical prudence or circumstantial rhetorical emphasis the constant reminder, in all the texts, of the "total overturning of German existence" provoked by the National Socialist revolution. [18]

In spite of this he is still clearly aware, at this time, of a danger or menace that looms over the University and augments that of the University's fragmentation into regional disciplines, of its subordination to extraneous ends (i.e., professional ones), and thus ultimately to that of the collapse of its foundations.

This menace is, if you will, the menace of "ideology." But the word is too weak. It is in reality the *totalitarian* menace itself, that is to say, the project of the "politicization" of the University and of science. In other words, in the vocabulary of the epoch, the *politische Wissenschaft* called for at the time, "within the Party and by the National Socialist students," Heidegger will say in 1966, and which, far from designating political science, was understood to mean that "science as such, its

---

16. Lacoue-Labarthe refers to the translation of the Rectoral Address proposed by Gérard Granel and published, with a facsimile of the original German edition, in *L'auto-affirmation de l'université allemande* (Paris: Trans-Europ-Repress, 1982).—*Editor*

17. "'Only a God Can Save Us Now,'" p. 5.

18. Martin Heidegger, *An Introduction to Metaphysics,* trans. Ralph Manheim (New Haven: Yale University Press, 1959), and the "political texts," passim.

meaning and value, was to be assessed according to its actual usefulness to the German people."[19]

This is why the Rectoral Address also follows, if not first of all, a *defensive* strategy. (The *Selbstbehauptung* of its title, moreover, "self-assertion" or "assertion of self," may also be immediately understood, in German, as "self-defense.") More exactly—looking more closely and taking account of the fact that, as regards the discursive strategy at least, one would have great difficulty in suspecting Heidegger of "naïveté"—the Rectoral Address follows a double strategy. At least double, moreover, because if self-defense is *also* a self-assertion, that is to say, a demand (as "affirmative" as it can be) for University autonomy and self-determination, this demand in its turn is made, can be made, only within the apparently acceptable limits—I mean on the basis of a concept, or bearing in mind an essence, of autonomy that accords with the exigencies and principles of the ongoing "revolution."

Now it is here, it seems to me, that philosophy and politics come to be articulated one with the other. It is where, if you prefer, the philosophical text and the political text communicate, or, more exactly, where the political text shows itself to be fundamentally (and almost exclusively) a philosophical text.

The question which, in effect, underlies this somewhat devious strategy is the question of hegemony, of *Führung*—of conducting or leadership, of guiding. It is a matter of knowing who (or what) is the *Führer* of whom; who (or what) leads whom, and toward what, that is to say, in the name of what. Where, in other words, the veritable and incontestable hegemony lies; and whence all hegemony, of whatever nature, draws its hegemonic power. In short, it is a question of knowing what is the hegemony of hegemony.

This, without the slightest oratorical precaution, is the opening motif of the Rectoral Address:

> The assumption of the rectorate is the commitment to the *spiritual* leadership [*Führung*] of this institution of higher learning. The following [to translate so the feudal (and corporatist) term *Gefolgschaft*] of teachers and students awakens and grows strong only from a true and joint rootedness in the essence of the German University. This essence, however, gains clarity, rank, and power only when first of all and at all times the leaders are themselves led [*die führer selbst Geführte sind*]—led

19. "'Only a God Can Save Us Now,'" p. 8.

by that unyielding spiritual mission that forces the fate of the German people to bear the stamp of its history. ("Self-Assertion," p. 470)

Which is nevertheless very clear: the leadership of the University (let us say, Heidegger's *Führung*) makes no sense, as spiritual leadership, unless the whole of the University body truly determines itself as being of the University, unless it grounds itself "veritably in the essence of the University"—and of the national University, the German University. (In comparison to 1929 this certainly represents a new departure, but I suspect that it does no more than make explicit philosophical propositions that are already present, in a very definite way, at an earlier period.) Now, in its turn the essence of the University is not such—that is to say, does not effectuate itself—unless it (including its leader) answers to what constitutes it integrally as spiritual and national (the essence, in the last analysis, is the German people as Spirit) or, not to be reductive in any way, unless it submits itself to the true hegemony, which is the "spiritual mission," from the point of view of destiny and history, of the German people.

The hegemony of hegemony, the *Führung* of the *Führung*, is the spiritual mission of Germany. And this goes, as one cannot help but understand in the *jederzeit* (in the "at all times"), this goes for every *Führung*, for every leadership and for every attempt at leadership: for the vocation for leadership and the (limited) *Führerschaft* that the Inaugural Lecture of 1929 already reserved to men of science precisely because of their submission to the thing, their being placed at the service (*Dienststellung*) of what is [*l'étant*], but also, if not above all, for political *Führung*.

Further, this is not simply said in passing, as a way into the subject, to "draw attention" to it. But it is insistently repeated, like a theme or leitmotiv. For example, toward the end: "All leading [*Führung*] must grant the body of followers [*Gefolgschaft*] its own strength. All following, however, bears resistance within itself. This essential opposition of leading and following must not be obscured, let alone eliminated" ("Self-Assertion," p. 479). And similarly this, a little earlier, which is perhaps clearer still: "What is decisive if one is to lead is not just that one walk ahead of others, but that one have the strength to be able to walk alone, not out of obstinacy and a craving for power, but empowered by the deepest vocation and broadest obligation" (p. 475).

This discourse is evidently and expressly—in its continual insistence—addressed to students, that is, to the future leaders of society (we would say "executives") and to those who are already leaders, that is, to professors and deans. It seems to be very limited and circumscribed. This, however, in no way prevents it from arrogating to itself the right to define leadership, *Führung,* in its essence; or from assigning and referring it to a *Führung* of an altogether different kind: major, or general, if you will, in contrast to minor and restricted. The University campus here in fact fills the whole of space; it extends its limits to the entire outside world, it breaks out of itself and breaks out of, exceeds (that is, transcends) every institution and every political domain. So the voice which arises from it—and which is itself that of a *Führer*—to announce the necessary submission to destiny and the compulsory acknowledgment of a leadership above all leadership, this voice sounds a solemn warning, and dictates its own conduct to every leadership. The University campus could almost be seen as the desert where prophecy takes place, and its rector, if I may be forgiven this redundancy, as the Tiresias of a political tragedy.

Absolute hegemony, a superior or general *Führung:* this, then, is the spiritual mission of the German people. What are we to understand by this?

Heidegger himself formulates the question like this: "Do we have the knowledge that goes with this spiritual mission?" And this question, in all its aspects, is the whole question of the Address.

"We," the *we* who articulate the question, certainly means: *we* in the University, *we* the University body taken together, which is such, effectively and properly, only as it relates itself to the essence of the German University. The question having been set forth in this way, it is not a matter of letting it be understood that only the University can respond to the question (to tell the truth, we already suspected this), but of asserting that only the (German) University can answer it if *as a minimum* this University is capable of grasping and instituting itself in and in accordance with its own essence. This provides in consequence a motive for the autonomy (the independence) of the University in relation to the political order, an autonomy that can alone guarantee to the University its political function. But "on condition," and an *internal* condition: namely, on condition of rooting the traditional "University autonomy" in an authentic conception of autonomy—in a *Selbstbesinnung,* in a self-reflection or self-meditation of the University, which must be the first task of the University; and of subordinating this *Selbstbesinnung* itself to a *Selbstbehauptung,* which must be thought (I borrow this definition from one of the many passages where Heidegger, after the fact, returns to this expression, and precisely from a text devoted to the clarification of the concept of the "will to power," which is undoubtedly one of the major concepts of the Address) as "the original assertion of self" or again as "the assertion of essence."[20]

The question was: "Do we have the knowledge that goes with this spiritual mission?" Here is the answer:

> The self-assertion of the German University is the primordial, shared will to its essence. We understand the German University as the "high" school that, grounded in science, by means of science educates and disciplines the leaders and guardians [*die Führer und Hüter:* a "guard" here doubles and "oversees" the *Führung,* unless the *Führung* should itself in reality be this guard] of the fate of the German people. The will to the essence of the German University is the will to science as will to the historical mission of the German people as a people that knows itself in its State. *Together,* science and German fate must come to power in this will to essence. ("Self-Assertion," p. 471)

The answer is thus very simple (I leave aside here the rhetoric of *Entscheidung* and *Entschlossenheit,* of decision and resolution, of the will to essence, where the will institutes its hold over the one who wills, and where the command submits itself to the order it gives, in such a way that the will goes beyond itself, and, going beyond itself, comes to power, dominates what is resolved, reveals itself as power in its essence, etc.)[21]—the answer is thus simple: The mission of the German people, its spiritual mission, is science. Or if you prefer: What determines the German people in its essence, what "forces the fate of the German people to bear the stamp of its history," what leads it, commands it, gives it its destiny (all of this is included in the *Auftrag* or "mission"), is science. And nothing else. In passing, it has been clearly stated that the new regime and the new State, the political *Führung,* give the German people "knowledge of self" or consciousness-of-self; they do not give it "power"—that is, Being. *Führung* in essence is spiritual because the destiny of Germany is science. The German people will realize itself, will answer to its destiny and will properly reach its essence—will essentially *find its identity* only if it commits, consecrates, and submits itself to the accomplishment of science. Only if it wills science.

Whence the double task (but it is in reality unique) that only the University is in a position to define and, if it has the will, to accom-

20. Martin Heidegger, *Nietzsche* (New York: Harper and Row, 1979), vol. 1 (trans. Krell), pp. 61ff.
21. Ibid., pp. 40ff.

plish—which gives it by right the leadership of all leadership: "to expose science to its innermost necessity [*Notwendigkeit*]" and to endure or sustain the German destiny "in its most extreme distress" [*Not*] ("Self-Assertion," p. 471).

Whence again—and in this respect, as Heidegger himself has had reason to recall and emphasize, the strategy of the Address is perfectly plain—the hierarchical ordering of the three "obligations" which must link the "student community" to the "people's community," to "the honor and the destiny of the nation among the other peoples," and finally to the spiritual mission itself of the German people. That is, to be straightforward about it, the subordination of "work service" and of "armed service" (of "defense service") to the "service of truth"—a subordination the more obvious because, although the three services are declared "equally necessary and of equal rank," work and defense are themselves considered forms of knowledge or at least as practices that are themselves "grounded in and illuminated by knowledge."[22]

Whence finally—but this is now self-evident—the need to "regain a new meaning" for the University,[23] to break up its "technical" organization and recenter it, in each of its "fundamental forms" (faculties and disciplines), or to bring it under the sole "spiritual legislation" of science, understood as the "formative power" (the power that shapes, *die gestaltende Macht*) of the German University.

It is therefore incumbent on the German people to realize science in its essence: "Science," says Heidegger, "must become the fundamental happening [*Grundgeschehnis*] of our spiritual being as part of a people [*unseres geistig-volklichen Daseins*]" ("Self-Assertion," p. 474).

What, then, is to be said of science in its essence?

The answer is immediate, and expected. Science in its essence is Knowledge—*das Wissen:* it is philosophy. "All science is philosophy, whether it knows and wills it—or not" ("Self-Assertion," p. 472). This is still the speculative—the "return of the speculative," if you will (but has it in truth ever ceased, has it ever departed?). The manner, at all events, is speculative. But the tenor? This needs a closer look.

Science, first of all, science in its essence, is determined by its having been initiated in Greece (I will come back later to the mode and the sense of this backward reference)—not a return—to the beginning, to an initial launching):

22. "'Only a God Can Save Us Now,'" p. 9.
23. Ibid., p. 8.

If there is to be science, and if it is to be *for* us and *through* us, under what conditions can it then truly exist? Only if we again place ourselves under the power of the *beginning* of our spiritual-historical being [*Dasein*]. This beginning is the setting out [*Aufbruch*] of Greek philosophy. Here, for the first time, Western man raises himself up from a popular base and, by virtue of his language, stands up to *the totality of what is,* which he questions and conceives [*begreift*] as the being that it is. ("Self-Assertion," pp. 471–472)

And a little further on:

Science is the questioning holding of one's ground in the midst of the ever self-concealing totality of what is. (p. 473)

Science, in other words, is existence (*Existenz*) itself, or *ek-sistence,* in the sense that attaches to this word in the fundamental ontology after *Sein und Zeit*—or, what amounts nearly to the same thing, in the sense of what the *Kantbuch* calls "the metaphysics of *Dasein,*" which is the locus of the founding or the refounding of metaphysics as such and the truth, in consequence, of what Kant called for under the name of "metaphysics of metaphysics."[24]

I will say nothing for the moment about this assignment to a people (and to a people as "language," as an essentially if not exclusively linguistic community), about the "irruption of knowledge," this breaking out, this fracturing emergence of Occidental man. (*Aufbruch* here is undeniably more violent than the *Einbruch* systematically used in the "philosophical" texts to designate the temporal-historial advent, the *Geschehen* of the existence of *Dasein*.) Even though the motif was not very insistent, the determination of *Dasein* by the people, by the "ontological" concept of the people (which strictly speaking ought to rule out its being a simple political category), had been on the program for a long time, in particular since Paragraph 74 of *Sein und Zeit*. I shall have occasion to speak of this again. What seems indispensable for the moment is to emphasize that science, finally, designates nothing other than the transcendence of *Dasein*—that is to say, metaphysics as such.

This is in perfect conformity with what Heidegger constantly affirmed, in particular in the texts and declarations that in 1929–1930 accompanied the publication of the *Kantbuch* and the assumption of the chair at Freiburg: that is, in all the "resumptions" of the fundamental project of *Sein und Zeit* in which Heidegger, anticipating the publica-

24. See Cassirer and Heidegger, *Débat*.

tion of the Second Part, is really trying to hold off a failure and make up for an already irreparable break, and sinks—literally—into the problematic of the foundation without managing to get to the point (the question of the essence of Being itself) from which, as his multiple rectifications and reiterated warnings, the cautions with which he accompanies the republication of all these texts, bear witness,[25] the possibility might emerge of a delimitation of metaphysics and as a result a kind of "escape" from metaphysics.

Everywhere, in fact, the transcendence of *Dasein, finite transcendence* itself—that is to say also, the understanding or the preunderstanding of Being—is assigned in its historial character to the effectivity of the "act of philosophizing,"[26] the irruption of knowledge, the advent of metaphysics, etc. I will limit myself to a few examples.

Thus, in "What Is Metaphysics?": "Man—one entity [*Seiendes*] among others—'pursues science' [*treibt Wissenschaft*]. In this 'pursuit' what is happening is nothing less than the irruption [*Einbruch*] of a particular entity called 'Man,' into the whole of what is, in such a way that in and through this irruption what is manifests itself *as* and *how* it is."[27] And further on in the same text, past the celebrated analysis of the experience of nothingness intended to illuminate the abyssal foundation, the bottomless depth of all knowledge of being:

> The simplicity and the intensity of scientific *Da-sein* consist in this: that it relates in a special manner to what is and to this alone . . . Scientific *Da-sein* is only possible when projected into the Nothing at the outset . . . Only because the Nothing is obvious can science turn what is into an object of investigation . . . Man's *Da-sein* can only relate itself to what is by projecting into the Nothing. Going beyond what is [the transcendence of what is] is of the essence of *Da-sein*. But this "going beyond" is metaphysics itself.[28]

Or again in the lecture (from the same period) "The Essence of Truth"— which we know, it is true, only through its publication in 1943:

> Ek-sistence . . . is ex-posure [*die Aus-setzung*] to the disclosedness of beings as such . . . The ek-sistence of historical man begins at that moment when the first thinker takes a questioning stand with regard to the un-

25. Or as the disavowal of "Vom Wesen des Grundes" in the course of 1955–56 on "the principle of reason" again attests.
26. Cassirer and Heidegger, *Débat,* p. 39.
27. "What Is Metaphysics?" p. 243.
28. Ibid., p. 256.

concealment of beings by asking: what are beings? . . . History begins only when beings themselves are expressly drawn up into their unconcealment and conserved in it, only when this conservation is conceived on the basis of questioning regarding beings as such. The primordial disclosure of being as a whole, the question concerning beings as such, and the beginning of Western history are the same.[29]

The Rectoral Address says, strictly speaking, nothing other than this. In its hardly more exoteric manner, it reaffirms the finite transcendence of a *Dasein* exposed to what is and questioning it, thrown into the midst of the "superpower" (*Übermacht*) of what is and yielded up to the problematicity, to the *Fragwürdigkeit* (to the at once doubtful and question-worthy character) of Being. It recalls, according to the Greek model or determination of knowledge, the fundamental submission of knowledge to necessity (*ananke, Notwendigkeit*) and its "creative impotence." It makes of the "passion" of knowledge—a term already used in 1929—or the "will to knowledge" the only thing that is adequate to grasp human existence in its totality, whether this existence be defined as a people or—the cases are not mutually exclusive—as a Western tradition ("the spiritual power of the West").

That in the first instance, at least, the *Dasein* in question should be the German people, that the sum of these propositions should amount to designating the German people (in terms that will be used a year or two later) as the "metaphysical people" par excellence,[30] might be enough to lead one to think that a certain political step has been taken beyond an already evident "Eurocentrism," and that at bottom this political repetition of fundamental ontology, far from being a simple clarification of its "mediated relation" with "national and social questions," signifies its complete diversion toward politics or its submission to the political. This could be the case; once again, all the indications are present. But it is also the opposite: for nothing allows us to exclude the possibility that this kind of transcription of fundamental ontology into a political key might have as its deliberate end the delimitation of the political—from the position, itself apparently limited, of knowledge—and its bringing into submission. A logic of hegemony still. And perhaps it is not by chance that there is a particular insistence on, a reiterated accentuation of the concept or motif of "world"; perhaps it is

29. "On the Essence of Truth," trans. John Sallis, in *Heidegger, Basic Writings*, ed. David Farrell Krell (New York: Harper and Row, 1977), pp. 113–141.

30. *An Introduction to Metaphysics*, p. 38.

not by chance that the will to science—the advent of knowledge—is interpreted as the creation of a world. For example: "*This* primordial concept of science obligates us . . . to make our questioning in the midst of the historical-spiritual world of the people simple and essential" ("Self-Assertion," p. 477). Or again:

> If we will the essence of science understood as the *questioning, unguarded holding of one's ground in the midst of the uncertainty of the totality of what is, this* will to essence will create for our people its world, a world of the innermost and most extreme danger, i.e., its truly *spiritual* world . . . Only a spiritual world gives the people the assurance of greatness. For it necessitates that the constant decision [*Entscheidung*] between the will to greatness and a letting things happen that means decline, will be the law presiding over the march that our people has begun into its future history. ("Self-Assertion," pp. 474–475)

Here we clearly find a heroic-revolutionary pathos, a warlike rhetoric (or simply a military one: the rhythmic step [*Schrittgesetz*]), at once brutality and inflation—and more, I have not quoted it all—which mask and unveil the philosophical propositions. At the same time, if one translates, it is clear: the world here is what it is in fundamental ontology, that is, what transcendence points to, what *Dasein* produces before itself as the sketch or project of its possibilities[31]—the condition of the general possibility of all relation to what is. The world in question here is, in other words, what "Vom Wesen des Grundes" designates as the "transcendental concept" of world.

Now the world so defined, as we know, is not only the possibility of the manifestation of what is as such but also, indissociably, the possibility of selfhood in general (of *Selbstheit* as the self-reference of *Dasein* to itself), which is, in its turn, in its very "neutrality" with respect to ontic determinations (including sexual ones), that on the basis of which alone the separation of "I" and "thou" can be established and *Dasein* can relate itself to the Other. The world is the condition of possibility of *relation* in general. To outline for *Dasein* its own possibilities (and these always take the dichotomous form, within the limits of finite freedom, of an ontological choice: grandeur or decline, authenticity or inauthenticity, etc.), to break into what is from the midst of what is in going beyond it, to come as oneself into one's power-to-be, is each time to open up the possibility of a community, of a being-together—

31. I take up again here the vocabulary of "Vom Wesen des Grundes," in *Wegmarken*, vol. 9 of Heidegger, *Gesamtausgabe* (Frankfurt: Klostermann, 1976), p. 157.

which is first of all, for Heidegger, and will always be, a community of language. In this way, moreover, is explained the fact that Paragraph 74 of *Sein und Zeit* can neatly equate being-in-the-world, *In-der-Welt-sein,* with the people:

> If Dasein, by anticipation, lets death become powerful in itself, then, as free for death, Dasein understands itself in its own *superior power,* the power of its finite freedom, so that in this freedom, which "is" only in its having chosen to make such a choice, it can take over the *powerlessness* [*Ohnmacht*] of abandonment to its having done so, and can thus come to have a clear vision for the accidents of the Situation that has been disclosed. But if fateful Dasein, as Being-in-the-world, exists essentially in Being-with-others, its historizing is a co-historizing [*ein Mitgeschehen*], and is determinative for it as *destiny* [*Geschick*]. This is how we designate the historizing of the community, of a people. Destiny is not something that puts itself together out of individual fates, any more than Being-with-one-another [*das Miteinandersein*] can be conceived as the occurring together of several Subjects. Our fates have already been guided in advance, in our Being with one another in the same world and in our resoluteness for definite possibilities. Only in communicating and in struggling does the power of destiny become free.[32]

The world, to summarize briefly, is the condition of the possibility of politics; and the essence of the political, that is to say, the fundamental political agency, is the community as people. If science in its essence—in other words, metaphysics—is the creation or the possibility of the creation of a world, if knowledge is transcendence itself, then it is the ensemble of the political that orders itself, ontologically, in relation to the philosophical. And this is exactly what the Rectoral Address *recalls:* in all senses the philosophical is the rationale or the foundation of the political.

But why, in spite of everything, should this privilege be accorded to the *German* people? Why this mission, confided to it, of completing science? Why does responsibility for the intellect and "spiritual power" of the entire Western world fall upon it? Or more strictly: Why is the access of science to "power" made to depend on the access of the German people itself to "power," and inversely?

In other words a question of Heidegger's "nationalism," of a delib-

---

32. *Being and Time,* trans. John Macquarrie and Edward Robinson (New York: Harper and Row, 1962), p. 436.

erate choice, of a deliberate *political* choice. Or if you will, but it is
really the least one can say, of an "ontic preference." Since it is absolutely necessary to do so, how can we approach this question? How
even articulate it? Is it a possible question?

One will always be able to say, in effect, that Heidegger's political
choice begins (at least) when Being-in-the-world and the Being-with
(or the advent-with) of *Dasein* is thought as a people. That is, also—
and on this point Heidegger will always remain consistent—as a belonging to a same destiny or as a sense in common of an identical
Geschick, of an identical "destiny" (but as is known, the word indicates
also skill and adroitness, aptitude and talent, in short, *savoir-faire:* in
Greek, *techne*—I shall return to this). One will always be able to say
this, but it will also always be necessary to say, in the same breath: this
political choice, this first political choice, is philosophical through and
through; it is not a *first* political choice, it is not even a *political* choice,
because the first choice, if it is a choice, is a *philosophical* choice. In fact,
the choice of philosophy itself (I leave the formula here to its own
equivocation).

And if one reiterates the same objection when this people, this historial co-belonging, will reveal itself, in its turn, to be paradigmatically
not simply German but—there are, however, only two genuine *examples*—either Greek or German, how will one be able to contend that
the privilege thus accorded to these two "peoples" (with everything it
implies and with which we are quite familiar—the Address itself
pauses over these points: a low estimation of Latinity, distrust of the
"christo-theological interpretation of the world," a strict demarcation,
for which Descartes is responsible, of the mathematico-technical
"thought of modernity") is not first of all philosophical, that is, is not
the (incommensurable) privilege of ontology, of metaphysics? And if
one should notice, between 1930 and 1933, between "Vom Wesen des
Grundes" (where, for example, a very particular fate is reserved for the
evangelical and Augustinian interpretation of world as an "anthropological concept")[33] and the Address, a hardening in the system of
(de)valorization, even this, if accurate, will not prove a great deal: at
the same time, in 1930, and in the same text (among others), Kant—
and Kant alone—was recognized straightforwardly as the first thinker
to have been able to reappropriate the positions and questions of the
great age of Greek philosophy.

33. "Vom Wesen des Grundes," sect. 2, pp. 135–160.

The circle, in reality, remains unbroken. Heidegger's nationalism is undeniable. It expresses itself, in 1933, in all its most suspect political consequences, and in the worst of rhetorics. I will not dwell on the polemic aroused by the use he made of the word *völkisch* or of barely altered forms of the watchwords of the German far right. Even if *völkisch* does not mean "racist" it is quite sufficient to speak, in connection with the people, of "the power that most deeply preserves [or safeguards: *Bewahrung*] . . . [its] strengths, which are tied to earth and blood" ("Self-Assertion," p. 475). Still, this nationalism is nothing but the consequence of a philosophical commitment (if not of philosophical commitment itself), and it aims at nothing other, politically, than submitting politics itself to the *sense* of this philosophical commitment.

This is why it is certainly possible to identify all the traits which seem to overdetermine Heidegger's philosophical message politically even before it declares itself as political. In this respect, moreover, the motif of the people is certainly not the only one, although it is probably the most important, since, bringing with it the motif of language (unless it proceeds from it), it determines among other things Heidegger's rhetorical and stylistic choices. In the same way one can and always will be able to, in the wake of all this, consider the declarations of 1933 as *the* declaration (the making explicit) of all that was essentially political in the earlier philosophical texts. But this will never get us out of the circle. The proposition "Heidegger's philosophy is political through and through" will always be reversible. One will always be able to bring the ontico-ontological difference into play, and nothing will be able to loosen the Heideggerian grip on the political. So long as the Heideggerian concept of politics remains more fundamental than the concepts of the political that one tries to oppose to it, there will not be the least chance of assigning the philosophical in Heidegger to the political. If you prefer: no concept of the political is powerful enough to broach the Heideggerian determination of the political in its essence. And the whole question hangs on this.

As a consequence, it is necessary to modify the angle of attack. And perhaps, here, to awaken an entirely different suspicion.

The possibility of this comes to light when one realizes that the inability to break into the circle it has seemed to me necessary to enclose us in, and to counter, at least up to a point, Heidegger's strategy, depends no doubt only on the Heideggerian determination of the philosophical. I say "at least up to a point" both because the episode of 1933 signifies the failure of this strategy and because Heidegger is perhaps,

in the end, the first victim of his relative underestimation of the political: the "hegemonic" dream will after all have been of short duration.
But in saying this I do not overlook, either, that the reverse (or defeat)
of 1934 will not in any way modify, in Heidegger, the relation of the
philosophical to the political, and that the same circle reestablishes itself ineluctably as soon as one examines, from this point of view, the
texts held to be subsequent to the *Kehre*.

What is to be understood here, however, by the "Heideggerian determination" of the philosophical? And why bring the whole question
down to this?

The Heideggerian determination of philosophy or the philosophical
means first of all (and these are terms I use only for convenience): the
unconditional valorization or, if you will, overvalorization of the philosophical. (In which terms the absolute weapon turns against the one
who wields it, as is perhaps, strategically speaking, always the case.)

The main symptom here, and one of the most constant themes, is
the fundamental reduction of existence to philosophizing: to the posing of the question "Why?"—to the interrogation of what is as such,
to the metaphysical, etc. That is to say, in the vocabulary of 1933, to
knowledge and to the spiritual mission. For that is undoubtedly (but I
admit that the word must be put in quotes) Heidegger's most radical
"political" gesture. In this first of all, that if it does not provoke the
political commitment of 1933 it gives it at least its sense, and moreover
makes it possible, retroactively, to decipher Heidegger's political "vocation" in the earlier philosophical writings. But in this equally, and
above all, that in referring all practice—and privileging here social and
political practice—to the activity of philosophizing (or in Greek all
praxis to *theoria*, in the strongest sense), it is inevitable that the philosophical or the "theoretical" should determine themselves in this very
movement as essentially political. There is not, in other words, an exte-
riority of the political in relation to the philosophical—doubtless not
even a true division between the philosophical and the political: every
philosophical determination of the essence of the political obeys a political determination of essence; and the latter inversely presupposes a
gesture that one can only characterize as political. This belonging-
together of the philosophical and the political is as old as philosophy
(and as old as what is still for us called politics). And this is what
Heidegger always submits to, even in his desire to subjugate the political, or at any rate to circumscribe it.

I quote again from the Rectoral Address:

What do the Greeks mean by *theoria*? One says: pure contemplation
[*Betrachtung*], which remains bound only to the thing [*Sache*] in question, and to all it is and demands. This contemplative behavior—and
here one appeals to the Greeks—is said to be pursued for its own sake.
But this appeal is mistaken. For one thing, "theory" is not pursued for its
own sake, but only in the passion to remain close to and hard pressed by
what is as such . . . They were not concerned to assimilate practice to
theory; quite the reverse: theory was to be understood as itself the
highest realization [*Verwirklichung*] of genuine practice. For the Greeks
science is not a "cultural good," but the innermost determining center
of all that binds human being to people and state. ("Self-Assertion,"
pp. 472–473)

In sum (and leaving aside for the moment Heidegger's operation
with respect to *Verwirklichung* and "putting into work"), this contem-
poraneity of the philosophical, or the theoretical, and the political is
the pure and simple consequence of finitude: here, of "the passion of
remaining near to what is as such and under its constraint." It is from
the midst of what is (*inmitten des Seiendes*), out of *Befindlichkeit* ("find-
ing-oneself" amid what is) that finite transcendence occurs. Opening
up the possibility of relationship in general, and in consequence also of
Being-in-community (of the political), it can effect this opening only
from the very interior of what it makes possible. By definition. Because
of finitude, to put it differently, transcending (philosophizing) is included in the space of the very thing it makes possible. And if, as "Vom
Wesen des Grundes" insists, transcendence (or freedom) is fundamental, we are compelled to suppose that the philosophical is pre-included
in the institution or the founding (*Grundung* or *Stiftung*) of the political. This does not mean that the *polis* is nothing but a social magma (or
not even social) prior to the philosophical gesture that founds it;
rather, it means that the *polis*, when something of the sort comes about,
when it posits and institutes itself, is a space or a locus that is philosophical through and through. There is no political foundation that is
not philosophical, because the philosophical is itself the foundation.
That is to say, politics [*la politique*]. In this connection furthermore,
and if it were necessary to overwhelm with proofs, there would be no
difficulty in showing the precise itinerary which for example leads
Heidegger from "Vom Wesen des Grundes" (from the analysis of finite
freedom as "freedom to found," *Freiheit zum Grunde*), by way of the
National Socialist commitment of 1933, up to the *Introduction to Meta-*

physics of 1935, where, among other things, the *polis* is thought as "the foundation and the locus" of *Dasein,* the very *Da* of *Dasein* [34] (and thereby as something *archi-political:* the "political" [*le "politique"*] is obviously not a Heideggerian concept).

This overvalorization of the "philosophical" (I keep the word, but all the same something quite different is involved) is thus the first mark of Heidegger's belonging to the philosophical (to the metaphysical), and the first political determination of his philosophy. And it is not by chance, as we now understand, that the latter is primitively dominated by a problematic of the (re)foundation of metaphysics; just as it is not by chance that Heidegger at the beginning continually claims for himself the Kantian definition of metaphysics as "a natural disposition of man." [35]

But to claim Kant for oneself, in the context of the thirties and against the neo-Kantian interpretations, is also to lay claim to Nietzsche—whose *Trieb, der philosophiert,* under the authority of which Heidegger once placed himself, [36] is moreover not unrelated to the "natural disposition" invoked by Kant. It is probably even to lay claim to Nietzsche above all. For Nietzsche is in reality the "hero" of Heidegger's political adventure. To such an extent that to call into question the "Heideggerian definition of philosophy" amounts to incriminating in its turn the Nietzschean overdetermination of such a definition.

"Hero," here, is to be understood in a strictly Heideggerian—which is to say, no doubt, a strictly Nietzschean—sense. That is, in the sense given to the term in *Sein und Zeit,* still in Paragraph 74, and only a few lines after the assignment of the *Mitgeschehen* as a people. [37] The hero appears at the precise place where it is necessary to bring in something in history (in the temporality of *Dasein*) to compensate for the fact that the origin of the possibilities on which Dasein projects itself are not made explicit. More exactly—because such a making explicit, says Heidegger, is not indispensable (and because in any case, in transcendence toward the world, there is no explicit grasp of the projected outline, of the *Entwurf*)—the hero appears at the place where it is revealed that in

34. Ibid., p. 162; *An Introduction to Metaphysics,* p. 152.

35. See, among others, *Kant,* p. 263, and "What Is Metaphysics?" p. 256.

36. Heidegger, *Die Kategorien und Bedeutungslehre des Duns Scotus,* vol. 1 of *Gesamtausgabe* (Frankfurt: Klostermann, 1978), pp. 195–196.

37. I am indebted to Christopher Fynsk [see Ch. 1 of *Heidegger: Thought and Historicity* (Ithaca: Cornell University Press, 1986)] for having drawn my attention to this motif. It must be emphasized that the "hero" appears very soon before the name of Nietzsche is invoked, for only the third time, in *Being and Time* (Paragraph 76).

history it is tradition (*Überlieferung,* heritage and transmission), that is to say, the repetition (*Wiederholung*) of "past possibilities of existence," that suffices to provoke an explicit grasp of possibilities:

> It is not necessary that in resoluteness one should *explicitly* know the origin of the possibilities upon which that resoluteness projects itself. It is rather in Dasein's temporality, and there only, that there lies any possibility that the existentiell possibility-for-Being upon which it projects itself can be gleaned *explicitly* from the way in which Dasein has been traditionally understood. The resoluteness which comes back to itself and hands itself down [which is for itself its own tradition], then becomes the *repetition* of a possibility of existence that has come down to us. *Repeating is handing down* [*Überlieferung*] *explicitly*—that is to say, going back into the possibilities of the Dasein that has-been-there. The authentic repetition of a possibility of existence that has been—the possibility that Dasein may choose its hero—is grounded existentially in anticipatory resoluteness; for it is in resoluteness that one first chooses the choice which makes one free for the struggle of loyally following in the footsteps of that which can be repeated.[38]

In short, and to put the matter in quite different words, the hero is a "model" or an "example" in the sense in which Nietzsche borrowed the concept from the tradition of the agonistic *paideia* (see, among others, the *Thoughts Out of Season* on history). He is, and I shall shortly come back to this, a pure and simple "means of identification." And in any case the decisionism and voluntarism that are an obligatory requirement of any theory of *imitatio* and rivalry (of *agon*), that is, of any mimetology, will have been recognized in passing.

But if in the immediate context it seems to me appropriate to make Nietzsche the "hero" of Heidegger's political adventure, this is not because he is the only philosopher, along with Plato, whose name occurs in the Rectoral Address.[39] It is really because his name is invoked in a decisive place, and to indicate—as it happens, to place under the sign of the death of God—the fundamental rupture and mutation that have intervened in Western history:

> And if, indeed, our ownmost being [*Dasein*] itself stands before a great transformation [*Wandlung*], if what that passionate seeker of God and the last German philosopher, Friedrich Nietzsche, said is true: "God is dead"—and if we have to face up to the forsakenness of modern man in

38. *Being and Time,* p. 437.

39. The two other proper names are those of a tragedian (Aeschylus) and a strategist (Clausewitz).

the midst of what is, what then is the situation of science? What was in the beginning the awed perseverance of the Greeks in the face of what is, transforms itself then into the completely unguarded exposure to the hidden and uncertain, i.e., the questionable. Questioning is then no longer a preliminary step, to give way to the answer and thus to knowledge, but questioning becomes itself the highest form of knowing. Questioning then unfolds its ownmost strength to unlock in all things what is essential. Questioning then forces our vision into the most simple focus on the inescapable.

Such questioning shatters the division of the sciences into rigidly separated specialties . . . ("Self-Assertion," p. 474)

Nietzsche is thus the "hero" of this (tragic) philosophic-political heroism which brings knowledge back—beyond the Greek *thaumazein*—to its bare root, which substitutes pure questioning for the vain proliferation of responses; which above all destines Germany (and its universities), from out of the experience of modern dereliction, to open, to endure, and to preserve the question as such, that is, the question of Being.

This of course is not without consequences, especially as it is not only in his capacity as "prophet of the death of God" that Nietzsche is invoked here, but because at a fundamental level it is Nietzsche's metaphysics itself—although within it, in fact, what comes above all from a certain interpretation of Kant—which overdetermines Heidegger's whole philosophic-political message. The citation of the name, the choice of such a "hero"—if these do not indicate a demagogic allegiance, they are at least the sign of an avowed (philosophical) recognition.

Long analyses are called for here. I will limit myself—let us say out of prudence—to identifying a few points of reference.

One in principle, by reason of the crucial role that it plays in the economy of the Address. I am referring here to the "energetic" reinterpretation of the concept of world, or, since it comes down to the same thing, of the concept of *schema*. It seems to me difficult to avoid recognizing that over and above the Husserlian and strictly phenomenological reference, the concept of world, at least in *Sein und Zeit* and the texts that immediately follow, is principally thought as the product of the transcendental imagination, itself interpreted in conformity with the analyses carried out in the *Kantbuch*, as an "ontological faculty." It is essentially for this reason that it is treated in terms of sketch or outline (*Entwurf*) and image (*Bild*), even "prototype" (*Vorbild*), and that *Dasein* itself, which "produces" the world before itself, is defined as world-forming (*Weltbildend*). For example (I refer again, for convenience, to "Vom Wesen des Grundes"): "'*Dasein* transcends' means that in the essence of its being it is *world-forming*, and indeed 'forming' [*bildend*] in the manifold sense that it lets world happen and through the world provides itself with an original view [*Anblick*] (form) [*Bild*] which does not grasp explicitly, yet serves as a model [*Vorbild*] for, all of manifest being, to which belongs each time *Dasein* itself."[40] This is the vocabulary of *Einbildungskraft*, or, as Nietzsche prefers to say, of the *bildende Kraft*, orienting the Kantian imagination in this way toward the plastic and the formative. That is to say, in a certain sense, toward the will to power.

Now an orientation of the same kind is clearly working in the Heideggerian text. "Vom Wesen des Grundes" already reinterprets in terms of "foundation" (*Gründen, Stiften*, etc.) what we have just heard expressed in terms of image and "formation"; but the Rectoral Address takes a further step—in the direction of Nietzsche. It does so by interpreting formation and foundation in their turn in terms of "creation" (*Schaffen*) and, above all, by referring this creation to the Greek *energeia*.

This, too, occurs in the passage—definitely the crucial passage in the Address—devoted to *theoria*, to knowledge in its Greek philosophic-political determination. Theory, said Heidegger, "does not come about in view of itself, but only in the passion to remain near what is as such and under its constraint." I interrupted my reading there and passed over in silence the following: "But, for another, the Greeks struggled precisely to conceive and to enact this contemplative questioning as one, indeed as the highest mode of *energeia*, of man's 'being-at-work' [*das Am-werk-sein*]" ("Self-Assertion," p. 472).

We must not rush to think that Aristotle suddenly comes to take over here from Nietzsche. Aristotle is involved of course—as always in Heidegger, and fundamentally—but he is "translated," and translated, as we will soon see confirmed, in Nietzschean terms. On the other hand, however, we should not rush to believe either, according to the most common version of Nietzsche, that art is what is designated here as "being at work"; art, in its turn, is undoubtedly involved, but it is not designated—and some time will have to elapse before it appears (not without some difficulty moreover). To be very precise, it will be necessary for the political adventure to first come to an end. What *energeia* designates, in reality, is knowledge itself. That is to say, in Greek still, and following Heidegger's reading of Greek, *techne*.

On this point, the Address is perfectly clear:

40. "Vom Wesen des Grundes," p. 157.

Here we want to regain for *our* being [*Dasein*] two distinguishing properties of the original Greek essence of science.

Among the Greeks an old story went around that Prometheus had
been the first philosopher. Aeschylus has this Prometheus utter a saying
that expresses the essence of knowing.

τέχνη δ'ἀνάγκης ἀσθενεστερα μακρῷ (Prom. 514, ed. Wil.)

"Knowing, however, is far weaker than necessity." This is to say: all
knowing about things has always already been delivered up to over-
powering fate and fails before it. Just because of this, knowing must develop its highest defiance; called forth by such defiance, all the power of
the hiddenness of what is must first arise for knowing really to fail. Just
in this way, what is opens itself in its unfathomable inalterability and
lends knowing its truth. Encountering this Greek saying about the creative impotence of knowing, one likes to find here all too readily the
prototype of a knowing based purely on itself, while in fact such knowing has forgotten its own essence; this knowing is interpreted for us as
the "theoretical" attitude. ("Self-Assertion," p. 472)

There then follows the passage on *theoria* (and thus *energeia*) that we
have already seen.

Techne means, then, "knowledge"; or rather, in order not to invert
the order of things here, "knowledge" means *techne*. Philosophizing as
such, the challenge by which knowledge aims to accede to the "veiled
being of what is" is in its very failure (by which, nevertheless, is produced the manifestation of what is) "technical." Or, what comes down
to the same thing: theory is energy, being-at-work, and effectuation,
wirken and *Verwirklichung*. Metaphysics, in other words, is the essence
of technique, which is understood as energy or creation and which is
the "combat" against the power of Being (and the superpower of destiny) that is to make possible the relation to what is in general and to
open the possibilities for the existence of historial Dasein. Being-in-
the-world, in this sense (finite transcendence), is technique. From this
perspective, we may perhaps better understand the equivocal *Geschick*
to which *Sein und Zeit* referred being-in-community; just as we may
certainly understand better the famous phrase from *An Introduction to
Metaphysics,* which summarizes fairly well, finally, the "message" of the
Address concerning the truth and inner greatness of Nazism: "namely
the encounter between global technology and modern man."[41]

But this is a properly Nietzschean determination of "technique" (of

41. *An Introduction to Metaphysics,* p. 199. *Techne* is here again defined as
"knowledge."

"metaphysics"). Not only because it presupposes that knowledge is thought in relation to will—the *Willen*, for example, that "Vom Wesen des Grundes" drew from the *Umwillen*, the "for-the-sake-of" [or "in view of": *en vue de*] that is constitutive of transcendence, and that is at the same time "in view of" the world and in view of *Selbstheit*, of the self or the subjectivity of what modern philosophy thinks as the subject. But it is a Nietzschean determination above all in that Being itself is thought as power, and because the articulation of will and power (it is the power of Being that wills the powerless and creative will to knowledge of *Dasein*) is finitude itself: the finite transcendence of *Dasein* as the finitude of Being, whose power is subject to the superpower of destiny.

For this reason, the doctrine of hegemony, that is, the doctrine of the "spiritual mission," leads back also in a profound sense to Nietzsche. Thus, for example: "The *third* bond of the student community binds it to the spiritual mission of the German people. This people shapes [or "works at": *wirkt*] its fate by placing its history into the openness of the overwhelming power of all the world-shaping powers of human being [*Dasein*], and by ever renewing the battle for its spiritual world" ("Self-Assertion," p. 476).

For this reason again (but from what source can we decipher it, if not from the long debate with Nietzsche, and also with Jünger,[42] which begins in effect with the "retreat" of 1934–1935?) it is the whole vocabulary of what I have called elsewhere ontotypology that comes to punctuate the Address throughout: *Prägung* or *Gepräge*, the stamp, the imprint, or the type; *Gestalt*, figure, or stature[43]—a motif, as we know, that Heidegger will end by crediting to the "plastic" metaphysics of Nietzsche (to the "philosophy of the hammer"), that is, to a particular interpretation of schematism, itself referred to the conception (as old as Platonism) of the "poetizing essence [*dichtende Wesen:* rendered *essence fictionnante* in the French] of reason." An adequate analysis of this

42. See *The Question of Being*, trans. William Kluback and Jean T. Wilde (New York: Twayne, 1958).

43. For example: "The faculty is a faculty only if, rooted in the essence of its science, it develops into a faculty for spiritual legislation, able to shape those powers of human being [*Dasein*] that press it hard into the one spiritual world of the people" ("Self-Assertion," p. 478). Or again: "The German University will only take shape and come to power when the three services—Labor Service, Armed Service, and Knowledge Service—primordially coalesce and become *one* formative force [*prägenden Kraft*]" (ibid., p. 478). Everywhere, as we might expect, the vocabulary of ontotypology is associated with that of the will to power.

motif would quickly show how lightly we are accustomed to assume without further precaution that the Heidegger of 1933 is based on Jünger: for the *Gestaltung,* in the Address, the figural conferring of sense, is never for a moment "work" but is "knowledge"—and knowledge as *techne.* In the same way the *Gestalt* is not the Worker but the Philosopher: Nietzsche, the modern double of Plato. And whose "hero," in a word, is named Prometheus.

I stop here: I would like, provisionally, to conclude.

And not simply to say (this is an account, I think, which is often circulated) that the political commitment of 1933 derives from the insufficiently radical posing of the question of Being as it "begins" to articulate itself in *Sein und Zeit.* Not, if you prefer, to say simply that Heidegger's "fascist" temptation is to be imputed to his starting point in a desire for the (re)foundation or *restoration* of metaphysics, and is hence to be seen as perfectly compatible with his declared hostility to the side of neo-Kantianism and of epistemology (of all imaginable forms of *Fachphilosophie*), but above all to the side of "philosophy of culture" and of attempts to "realize" metaphysics anthropologically. Heidegger's political commitment is undeniably "metaphysical," in the strictest and most powerful sense of the term: he repeats or means to repeat the initial gesture of Nietzsche (no doubt overlooked), that is to say, taking due account of an irreparable historial break, the founding gesture—for the West—of Plato.[44] And in this light it was no doubt one of the last possible grand philosophic-political gestures.

This version is probably "just." It is not, for all that, sufficient. And first because the other side of the coin seems to me more and more suspect on many grounds. The other side of the coin: namely, the symmetrical version, moreover given considerable credit by Heidegger himself, according to which, cured by the lesson of the Rectorate (or enlightened by the test of politics), the thought of Being would succeed in taking the step that incommensurably separates the question of the sense of Being from the question of the essence of Being, or the

44. To whom the Rectoral Address leaves the last word, through a "translation" whose ideologico-political overdetermination is only too evident: "But we fully understand the splendor and the greatness of this setting out only when we carry within ourselves that profound and far-reaching thoughtfulness that gave ancient Greek wisdom the word: . . . 'All that is great stands in the storm . . .' (Plato, *The Republic,* 497d9)" ("Self-Assertion," p. 480). (Jowett has "All great attempts are attended with risk"— *Translator*)

enterprise of the restoration of metaphysics from the attempt to "pass beyond" metaphysics.

With respect to this necessary corollary of the earlier version it is not, again, that one can say it is simply false. On the contrary, it corresponds in a totally unarguable way to the manner in which Heidegger followed, after 1934, his own itinerary—or to the "way of thought" that with some difficulty opened up to him after that time. And it is difficult to forget that the first "result" of the episode of 1933 is the pure and simple *collapse* of fundamental ontology. But apart from the fact that too many things from the earlier career subsist or maintain themselves *after* the too notorious *Kehre* and consequently resist the auto-deconstruction of Heideggerian *philosophy* (or, rather, the always self-justifying and thus ambiguous deconstruction of *Sein und Zeit*), there is—at least this is the hypothesis I find myself compelled to formulate from where I now stand—a formidable unanswered, or unformulated, question that continually haunts Heideggerian thought from *Sein und Zeit* to the last texts. And this unformulated question, again from where I now stand, seems to me not unrelated to the question of the political.

I want to speak here of Heidegger's constant refusal, as it seems to me, to take seriously the concept of *mimesis*. I say "refusal," of the concept as of the term (or, what amounts to the same thing, as I have tried to show: the pure and simple acceptance of its Platonic depreciation),[45] because on the other hand it seems to me more and more difficult not to see a fundamental *mimetology* at work in Heidegger's thought.

What, in fact—to stay within the confines of the territory I have marked out for myself—what is the *world* if not the product of what we should indeed agree to call an "original mimesis"? What is the world, if not an *original mimeme*? There would be no "real," says "Vom Wesen des Grundes," there would be no "nature" in the accepted sense—but also, it is repeated everywhere, *phusis* itself could not break out in (and from) its unfathomable retreat, there would be no "earth" of *The Origin of the Work of Art* or "forces of earth and blood" of the Address—if there were not, projected from the unpresentable "milieu of what is" (from the attunement, the initial and distanceless *Gestimmt-heit* of *Dasein* to the being that dominates, traverses, and impregnates it), an "image," itself moreover imperceptible (unpresentable), of a possible presentation of what is. If there were not, in other words, a "sche-

45. See "Typography."

matization" or, which is the same thing, a *techne*.[46] The structure of transcendence is the very structure of *mimesis,* of the relation between *phusis* and *techne,* taken over from Aristotle and Kant, and reinterpreted.

Now this would be of no consequence "politically speaking" (although we might wonder about that) if toward its conclusion *Sein und Zeit* did not open out onto the theme of tradition as repetition, that is, as *imitatio*—the motif, as we have seen, of the "hero," which is probably inseparable from what *An Introduction to Metaphysics* will define as the authentic thought of history: mythology.[47] Or if, in the same spirit, the Rectoral Address did not divide itself between (at least) three great agonistic scenes, there also of characteristically Nietzschean design.

The scene of "hegemony," of course.

But also that of the relation between master and pupil, in school or university. Thus, for example: "The teaching body's will to essence must awaken and strengthen and thus gain the simplicity and breadth necessary to knowledge about the essence of science. The student body's will to essence must force itself to rise to the highest clarity and discipline of knowing . . . The two wills must confront one another, ready for *battle*" ("Self-Assertion," pp. 478–479). Or again, a little further on, this paraphrase (for University purposes) of *polemos,* "father of all": "Battle alone keeps this opposition open and implants in the entire body of teachers and students that basic mood which lets selflimiting self-assertion empower resolute self-examination to genuine self-governance" ("Self-Assertion," p. 479).

And finally the major scene of the historial or historical agonistic, of the necessary repetition and the necessary radicalization of the "Greek beginning."

Science, as you will remember, could "find its true consistency" only on condition that the German University place itself anew "under the power of the beginning" of the spiritual-historial existence of Germany: "the irruption of Greek philosophy." To which Heidegger added shortly afterward the following, which hardly requires commentary:

> But doesn't this beginning by now lie two and a half millennia behind us? Hasn't human progress changed science as well? Certainly! . . . But this does not mean that the beginning has been overcome, let alone brought to nought. For if indeed this primordial Greek science is something great, then the *beginning* of this great thing remains what is *great-*

46. See Jean Beaufret, "*Physis et techne,*" *Aletheia* 1–2 (January 1964).
47. *An Introduction to Metaphysics,* p. 155.

est about it. . . . The beginning still *is*. It does not lie *behind us*, as something that was long ago, but stands *before* us. As what is greatest, the beginning has passed in advance beyond all that is to come and thus also beyond us. The beginning has invaded our future. There it awaits us, a distant command bidding us catch up with its greatness. ("Self-Assertion," p. 473)

I do not recall this text for the thought about time, or even exclusively for the thought about history that it contains, but for its political tenor. Because like every thesis about history, and it is a thesis about history, it takes a political stand. It seems to me even that it formulates very precisely, and in the terms that since Lessing and Winckelmann have been those of German historico-political thought, the matrix of the response that is properly the Heideggerian response to the German political problem par excellence: the problem of national identification. Which, like all problems of identification, is a problem of imitation— and inevitably at the same time of the refusal of imitation. The theory of the beginning, in other words, is the Heideggerian (that is to say, up to a point, still the Nietzschean) solution to the immense historical *double bind* in the grip of which Germany has struggled since the end of the Renaissance and the decline of French neoclassic imperialism, which is perhaps the decline of Latin domination (in relation to which revolutionary and postrevolutionary neoclassicism was unable to recover ground).[48] This solution, in principle at least and except for its radicality, is, as in Nietzsche, paradoxically of a Winckelmannian type: "We must imitate the Ancients . . . [to be understood: better than the others have] in order to make ourselves inimitable." That is, it is not the Schillerian-Hegelian solution (the dialectical solution, the *Aufhebung* of the Greek moment, rejected here under the name *Überwindung*), or (or at least not yet) the Hölderlinian solution, if it is a solution; not even, in spite of everything, the "linguistic" solution of the Fichte of the *Discourse to the German People*. The *Wiederholung* represents another model, the determination of another means of identification and another relation of imitation, in reality infinitely more powerful than all the others because it is the model of an identification with (or an imitation of) *what has taken place without taking place*, of a past that is not past but still to come, of a beginning so great that it dominates every future and remains still to be effected: in short, of an irruption that must be wrenched out of its oblivion or its more-than-millennial reserve through the most extreme violence of combat (*Kampf*

48. See Chapter 4, above. Also Philippe Lacoue-Labarthe and Jean-Luc Nancy, "Le mythe nazi," forthcoming.

or *polemos*). It might perhaps be appropriate to call this solution "polemical." It outlines in any case the sharp and somber contours of a task whose accomplishment Heidegger, at a certain period, believed incontestably to be incumbent on the German people (his own people, because he wished there to be one).

An unacknowledged mimetology seems to overdetermine the thought of Heidegger politically. This remains to be shown. It leaves us, today at any rate, with a question: Why would the problem of identification not be, in general, the essential problem of the political?[49]

49. I set this question against the background of work on Freud carried out in collaboration with Jean-Luc Nancy: "La panique politique," *Confrontations* 2 (1979): 33–57; and "Le peuple juif ne rêve pas," in A. Rassial and J. J. Rassial, *La psychanalyse est-elle une histoire juive?* (Paris: Seuil, 1981), pp. 57–92.

Memorial Note

Two years before his death in 1983, Eugenio Donato conceived the project of presenting the work of Philippe Lacoue-Labarthe in English. In collaboration with Lacoue-Labarthe, he made an initial selection of essays, and by 1983 he had seen and begun to edit "Typography," "Hölderlin and the Greeks," and what was then an incomplete version of "The Echo of the Subject." He had also found a translator for "Diderot: Paradox and Mimesis." Several weeks after his death, I discovered through a chance remark by one of his students that a number of the translations were nearly complete. I asked Lacoue-Labarthe's permission to continue the project as a memorial to Donato, and invited Christopher Fynsk to take over Donato's task of editing the translations.

With characteristic loyalty, Donato had drawn upon the project's potential benefit to his students, seeing to it that all who were capable of negotiating Lacoue-Labarthe's prose were given an essay to translate. I have attempted to maintain Donato's wish in this regard. With the exception of "Transcendence Ends in Politics" and "The Caesura of the Speculative," all of the essays have been translated by Donato's students and friends, including those Donato arranged for before his death and those I commissioned afterward.

In light of Donato's initiation of the project and its subsequent memorial tribute to him, I asked Donato's colleagues whether they wished to contribute to the preliminary work on the rough translations before they were sent to Fynsk. The response was immediate. From November 1983 to July 1984, when I sent the last translation to Fynsk, Donato's students and friends throughout America and Europe pitched in unhesitatingly; some took a single translation, others two, and one,

Barbara Harlow, translated a missing piece herself. Though the work of Donato's friends constitutes only the most preliminary effort toward the present volume, it indicates the number of people who came forward to pay homage to Donato and to his commitment to Lacoue-Labarthe's work.

Translation was, for Eugenio Donato, more than the necessary means of passage between the languages and cultures (Armenian, Egyptian, Italian, French, English, and American) in which he lived and worked. He took on the task of opening pathways between these cultural worlds almost as a mission, and would have translated, if he could, everything his generous and keen critical sense told him should be shared by the community to which he belonged and to which he dedicated himself. In the years before his death, he became especially devoted to the task of bringing Philippe Lacoue-Labarthe's work into English. His admiration for Lacoue-Labarthe's efforts to assume in his critical writings, to "translate," the heritage of the German philosophical tradition undoubtedly helped dictate this choice. But more particularly, there was a shared taste and sensibility between the two men, a love for painting, music, and poetry which both of them were committed to developing in analysis and thought.

In his article "Idioms of the Text," in which he discussed the problematic of translation and its treatment by Lacoue-Labarthe, Donato noted the varied but related definitions of *übersetzen* given in Grimm's *Deutsches Wörterbuch*. "Among its meanings," he wrote, "we find 'to transport from one place to another,' 'to transform,' 'to metamorphose,' 'to jump over or above something.' And incidentally, here Grimm significantly gives the example *den Abgrund übersetzen*, hence to jump over an abyss or groundless space." The continuation of Donato's project has assumed all these meanings of "translation." While it has involved numerous "transportings" of manuscripts, it has, more strikingly, reminded all those involved of the "transforming"—indeed, the "hyperbolic"—character of such a project. I know I speak for Donato in expressing thanks to those who were willing to make that leap: first to Philippe Lacoue-Labarthe himself, who gratefully agreed to let me renew this project after Donato's death and to dedicate it to his memory; to Barbara Harlow, who quickly, and under great pressure, filled in with a translation of "The Echo of the Subject"; to Homer Brown, Joel Black, Tom Conley, Jacques Derrida, Rodolphe Gasché, Josué Harari, Judd Hubert, Marie-Hélène Huet, Lindsay Waters, and Sam Weber for their help and guidance; to Wilda Anderson, Eduardo

Cadava, Alain Cohen, Richard Macksey, Kerry McKeever, Kishin and Angela Moorjani, Edward Said, and Ningkun Wu for their much-needed support, and last—because especially—to Christopher Fynsk for the splendid job he has done.

Had Eugenio lived, this would have been "his" project. It is still "his." Simply translated.

Linda Marie Brooks

A Note on Sources

"*Désistance*": Translated by Christopher Fynsk.

"*Typographie*": Originally published in the collection *Mimesis: Des articulations* (Paris: Flammarion, 1975), pp. 166–275, copyright © 1975 by Flammarion. A portion appeared in translation in *Diacritics* 8 (Spring 1978): 10–23, and this translation has been used here, with some modifications, with the permission of the Johns Hopkins University Press. Translated by Eduardo Cadava.

"*L'echo du sujet*": Originally published in *Le sujet de la philosophie: Typographies I* (Paris: Aubier-Flammarion, 1979), pp. 217–303, copyright © 1979 by Flammarion. Translated by Barbara Harlow.

"*La césure du spéculatif*": Originally published in Friedrich Hölderlin, *L'Antigone de Sophocle,* edited and translated by Philippe Lacoue-Labarthe (Paris: Christian Bourgois, 1978), pp. 183–223. Collected in *L'imitation des modernes: Typographies II* (Paris: Galilée, 1986), pp. 39–69, copyright © 1986 by Galilée. The translation presented here is based on the translation by Robert Eisenhauer in *Glyph 4* (Baltimore: Johns Hopkins University Press, 1974), pp. 57–84.

"*Hölderlin et les grecs*": Originally published in *Poétique* 40 (November 1979): 465–474. Collected in *L'imitation des modernes: Typographies II*, pp. 71–84, copyright © 1986 by Galilée. Translated by Judi Olson.

"*Diderot: Le paradoxe et la mimésis*": Originally published in *Poétique* 43 (September 1980): 267–281. Collected in *L'imitation des modernes: Typographies II*, pp. 13–36, copyright © 1986 by Galilée. Translated by Jane Popp.

"*La transcendance finie/t dans la politique*": Originally published in the collection *Rejouer le politique* (Paris: Galilée, 1981), pp. 171–214. Collected in *L'imitation des modernes: Typographies II*, pp. 133–173, copyright © 1986 by Galilée. An initial version of Peter Caws's translation appeared in *Social Research* 49 (Summer 1982): 405–440.

Index

M E R I D I A N

Crossing Aesthetics

Hans-Jost Frey, *Studies in Poetic Discourse: Mallarmé, Baudelaire, Rimbaud, Hölderlin*

Pierre Bourdieu, *The Rules of Art: Genesis and Structure of the Literary Field*

Nicolas Abraham, *Rhythms: On the Work, Translation, and Psychoanalysis*

Jacques Derrida, *On the Name*

David Wills, *Prosthesis*

Maurice Blanchot, *The Work of Fire*

Jacques Derrida, *Points . . . : Interviews, 1974–1994*

J. Hillis Miller, *Topographies*

Philippe Lacoue-Labarthe, *Musica Ficta (Figures of Wagner)*

Jacques Derrida, *Aporias*

Emmanuel Levinas, *Outside the Subject*

Jean-François Lyotard, *Lessons on the Analytic of the Sublime*

Peter Fenves, *"Chatter": Language and History in Kierkegaard*

Jean-Luc Nancy, *The Experience of Freedom*

Jean-Joseph Goux, *Oedipus, Philosopher*

Haun Saussy, *The Problem of a Chinese Aesthetic*

Jean-Luc Nancy, *The Birth to Presence*

Library of Congress Cataloging-in-Publication Data

Lacoue-Labarthe, Philippe.
[Essays. English. Selections]
Typography : mimesis, philosophy, politics / Philippe Lacoue-
Labarthe ; with an introduction by Jacques Derrida ; edited by
Christopher Fynsk ; Linda M. Brooks, editorial consultant.
    p.   cm. — (Meridian. Crossing aesthetics)
Originally published: Cambridge, Mass. :
Harvard University Press, 1989.
Includes bibliographical references and index.
ISBN 0-8047-3282-5 (pbk. : alk. paper)
1. Philosophy.   2. Literature—Philosophy.
3. Deconstruction.   4. Hölderlin, Friedrich, 1770–1842.
5. Diderot, Denis, 1713–1784.   I. Fynsk, Christopher, 1952– .
II. Title   III. Series: Meridian (Stanford, Calif.)
[B29.L264   1998]
194—dc21   97-41649
                                                      CIP

∞ This book printed on acid-free, recycled paper.

Original printing 1998
Last figure below indicates year of this printing:
07 06 05 04   03 02 01 00 99 98